Portrait of a Cold Warrior

Portrait of a Cold Warrior

by
Joseph Burkholder Smith

G. P. PUTNAM'S SONS
NEW YORK

SBN: 399-11788-1

Library of Congress Cataloging in Publication Data:

Smith, Joseph Burkholder.
  Portrait of a cold warrior.

  Includes index.
  1. United States. Central Intelligence Agency.
I. Title.
JK468.16S525   327'.12'06173   76-13567

PRINTED IN THE UNITED STATES OF AMERICA

To Jeanne

Contents

AUTHOR'S NOTE

I have had no access to classified documents since I retired in June, 1973. This book is based on my personal recollections supplemented by a careful reading of newspapers and periodicals covering the years and events described. The excellent files of the New York Public Library and Widener and Lamont libraries of Harvard University facilitated this effort.

I have not mentioned the complete true name of any CIA officers who have not already been publicly identified elsewhere. The non-Americans I have named I show were not agents whose services were bought by CIA, but people who thought that CIA might help their countries. I do not want to endanger any former colleagues who are still active or their operations, whatever they may be. Hence, I have altered the identities of several people.

Tequisquiapan, Qro., Mexico
February, 1976

FOREWORD

I quit. Hell, who wouldn't have? As of June, 1973, I had been for twenty-two years a covert action specialist in the Clandestine Services of the Central Intelligence Agency, and everything was going wrong. I had spent the last year destroying the part of the Agency's clandestine apparatus for which I was responsible in Latin America. I had just been passed over for promotion for the fourth time. The only bright spot in my life was that my current post was Mexico City. My wife and I liked the climate, the cost of living, and the Mexicans. Call me a disgruntled employee, if you like.

As a result of the defection of Philip Agee most of the operations of the Western Hemisphere Division, as the CIA's Clandestine Services Latin American division was known, were ordered canceled by Ted Shackley. Shackley took over the division in early 1972 when he returned from his tour as station chief in Vietnam. Previously he had been the hard-driving, no-nonsense boss of JMWAVE, the Miami station set up at President Kennedy's insis-

11

tence after the Bay of Pigs. Shackley had no desire to inherit operations Agee had revealed to his Cuban and Soviet intelligence friends in Havana in the fall of 1971. In addition and even worse, it had been learned that Agee was writing a book in which he would make public an astoundingly long list of names of officers and local agents that he had told the Cubans and Soviets about.

A defensive operation was started immediately and every activity, agent, and officer was scrutinized to determine if Agee had already blown them or if he would write about them in his book. A Shackley henchman was installed as chief of operations and a cryptonym, the Agency's badge of security significance, was assigned to the task of getting rid of the division's operations and much of its officer staff—the pre-Shackley staff, some people were quick to point out. They doubted whether so much destruction was necessary, especially since Shackley had a reputation for ruthlessness and for filling key jobs with his favorites.

Whether or not such a vast amount of house cleaning was really necessary, I could not decide. All I knew was that it was dismal work. As far as I was concerned, I was safe. There was no indication in any of the checking that Agee had mentioned me. There was also no mention of me in the copy of his manuscript that the Agency managed to steal from him in Paris. Agee had forgotten that our paths had crossed when he had come from Uruguay to Argentina in 1965 to assist me in giving lie-detector tests to two of my prize Argentine agents, an officer of the Argentine intelligence service and his wife.

Nevertheless, I was disturbed to have to dismiss so many loyal men and upset to have the defenses I kept putting up to try to salvage something of their old lives summarily dismissed by the Star Chamber conducting the purge in Washington. When Agee's book finally appeared, not one of the people I was ordered to fire was mentioned. This was not the only time in my career when my judgment was ignored by my superiors. I'm glad I decided it would be the last.

In the midst of this, I learned that the strongly worded recommendation by my immediate superior for my promotion had been turned down. Obviously, I would never reach the CIA equivalent of a general's rank. Although I had never received a fitness report less than superior, and most all of my ratings had been "outstanding," the highest evaluation given, and I had been commended in

12

writing twice (written commendations were held to a minimum, lest their recipients claim to have a right to be promoted), I had been passed over four times in a row. Once the comment had been recorded that I was an operator rather than an administrator. I suspected that this had something to do with the matter. Also, although I had gone to Harvard, it would have been better if I had gone to Princeton and been a member of the OSS. I was not a Catholic, nor an East European ethnic. I just did not fit into the ruling cliques in the Clandestine Services. Furthermore, I had always been in the minority of officers who sought to enlist the efforts of the non-Communist left. Perhaps my greatest shortcoming, I guessed, was that I could not treat people as unimportant spare parts to be used up and thrown away as administrators like Shackley could. I asked for early retirement, and I decided to stay in Mexico.

About a month after my retirement, I heard the last word on my career. The Mexico City station chief called me into the embassy and met me in the ground-floor reception area (I was no longer qualified to enter the station offices). He let me read a citation awarding me a medal for meritorious service. When I had read it, he took it back. At headquarters I had attended ceremonies for colleagues who had received similar medals. They had been presided over by a high administrative officer and were rather impressive affairs. Even though I did not share the honor of such a ceremony, these medal recipients and I had one thing in common. None of us got a medal to keep or even a copy of the citation. These were retained by the CIA for security reasons.

In the nearly two and a half years since my retirement there has been an almost constant barrage of revelations of nearly every dark secret about CIA's activities that I had been told should never see the light of day: the attempted assassinations of Fidel Castro; the many anti-Cuban paramilitary missions of the JMWAVE station in Miami; the "secret war" in Laos, MHCHAOS, the attempt to infiltrate and destroy political dissenters' groups in the United States; and dozens of other operations, including some I had thought my own special story, such as how some colleagues and I had made a porn picture about the amorous adventures of Sukarno.

Not satisfied with having destroyed the old agent network in Latin America, Agee continued to haunt his old colleagues. On October 4, 1974, when I picked up my copy of *Excelsior*, Mexico City's

13

leading morning daily, I read on the front page the startling headline "37 Agents of the CIA in Mexico: Richard Sampson Is the Chief, Agee Assures."

Agee's list, I quickly realized, was developed by his reading a copy of the embassy telephone book for the spring of 1974. I recognized this when I saw that he had correctly named the chief and deputy chief of station and a number of other officers, secretaries, and clerks, but had incorrectly included the names of at least four persons who had left the station on reassignment between June and August. Agee simply had noted the room numbers of people in the offices the CIA had occupied when he served in Mexico (and had occupied unchanged since the embassy was built, for that matter) and given these names to the reporter. Even worse, another paper, *El Universal,* gave the home addresses of everyone on the list, further proof to me of how he had gotten the information. It was a sickening stunt that could cost these people their lives—any and all would-be terrorists in Mexico now had a printed list of victims.

How this dreadful betrayal was possible three years after the Agency first knew of Agee's defection and after Shackley's year-long purge might seem unbelievable. Unfortunately, it's not at all hard to understand. Embassy telephone books are not classified. They could hardly be and still serve to facilitate communication between all employees. CIA stations don't like the fact that the embassy won't classify the books, because it makes feats like Agee's so simple to accomplish. But the State Department administrators don't run embassies for the benefit of the CIA, and will not budge on the subject. However, a token effort is made to limit the distribution and circulation of these books. Old phone books are collected when new ones are issued and persons leaving the embassy permanently must surrender their copies. Nevertheless, it is next to impossible to police the distribution and circulation of telephone books among, as is the case in Mexico City, nearly six hundred people. The alternative for CIA would be to try to give its stations better cover. For a number of reasons I will discuss later, this is not done. Understanding the Clandestine Services of the CIA requires more thought than most people are willing to give the subject and more information than has been disclosed or leaked.

After the Agee incidents, I was more determined than ever to examine the events of my life and my participation in the cold war as

14

carefully as I could. I wanted to be sure that I comprehended them. I wanted to write an account that would explain these things to others—to my children, to my friends and acquaintances, to everyone else who had not personally taken part in my covert life.

This determination was reinforced by an incident that took place at the Alcott School, the school my son attends in Mexico City. Alcott is an experimental school, an alternate school. As part of the alternate program, I was invited to tell the students what the U.S. Foreign Service actually does (until this writing I have simply said to people that I am a retired Foreign Service Officer—living cover is second nature) and what so many people could possibly be doing at the American Embassy.

I had barely concluded my bland account of the visa section, other consular duties, economic reporting, and so forth, when all the students at once seemed to want to know only about the CIA. Was the Agee story in the October, 1974, press true? What were so many spies doing? On whom were they spying? Why? Why had the CIA killed Allende? Why did the CIA always support reactionary governments? Was it really true that the CIA had killed John F. Kennedy?

I decided to try to answer these questions "as best a knowledgeable Foreign Service Officer could." This gave me the opportunity to speak as much truth as I cared and fudge up what I wanted, exactly the manner of answering questions that had become second nature after twenty-two plus years. One question I could not swallow—the one about the CIA's killing President Kennedy—probably because it was part of a romantic myth in American politics I deplored. Even though I had been an ardent Kennedy supporter when the nation faced the awful alternative of choosing John F. Kennedy or Richard Nixon as President, I knew that Kennedy was a confirmed cold warrior, determined to destroy Castro's Communist enclave in the Western Hemisphere.

I told the students that Kennedy had definitely not been killed by the CIA, and that actually, after recovering from the shock of the Bay of Pigs disaster, he had been a staunch friend and admirer of the Agency. I told of a remark a friend of mine had heard Kennedy make at a White House meeting when the President declared, "There are more brains in one square foot in that building in Langley than in all the rest of Washington bureaucracy." I said that I knew he was encouraging the Agency to work for the overthrow of

15

Castro at the time he was killed. I told them I knew that among the last people he had seen in his office at the White House the night before he flew to Texas were CIA Western Hemisphere officers who brought him details on the mysterious arms cache found on the shores of Venezuela that was later blown up into the reason for the OAS hemisphere-wide economic boycott of Castro, declared in 1964. He had told them, "Great work. Be sure to have complete information for me when I get back from my trip. I think maybe we've got him now."

"Stop," cried a girl who had been one of the most eager questioners, "it's like telling us that Mr. Greenjeans is a CIA agent."

I know that Mr. Greenjeans in not a CIA agent, but, more important, I think I know who is. I think I can explain who I am and who many of my former colleagues are. I think this is something I should do, but not something that I could accomplish in a hour at the Alcott School.

If there are in Russia today people well intentioned toward peace, we see no prospect of their influence prevailing.

—Henry Steele Commager, "Five Great Problems of the Next Half-Century," *New York Times Magazine,* January 1, 1950

Constitutional scrutiny of Intelligence Services is largely an illusory concept. If they're good, they fool the outsiders—and if they're bad they fool themselves.

—John le Carré, Introduction to *The Philby Conspiracy,* by Bruce Page, David Leitch, and Philip Knightley

1

A Point In Time

I was born in Harrisburg, Pennsylvania, June 16, 1921. This was because of the chance occurrence, rare in the 1890s, that my grandfather moved from Baltimore to Harrisburg to head the Highspire Distillery. In Baltimore he had been one of the founders of the street railway company. But Grandfather was restive after the war ended in 1865. First, he returned to Ohio and thought about reopening his law practive, but the business venture in Baltimore beckoned. Then, the Harrisburg project seemed better. My grandfather's main business skill was tracking down new ventures. He backed the inventor of the telephone, and he backed the inventor of the air brake. Unfortunately, the inventor of the telephone Grandfather backed was not named Bell, and the genius whose air brake he sunk a large sum into was not named Westinghouse.

As a consequence, my father, the last of his five children, born when Grandfather was fifty years old, was unable to follow his father to Miami University of Ohio. He signed up for what was then the training school for merchant marine officers, and sailed away on the school ship *Saratoga* in 1903. This was a square-rigger and Dad learned how to be a real sailor. Two years later he was graduated and got his mate's papers and began a career that promised someday, he hoped, command of a major passenger liner.

Then, home on leave back in Harrisburg, he met my mother. Their romance prospered but Dad's career as a merchant marine officer did not. My mother did not want to marry a captain and perhaps be only part of his paradise. Besides, it would have been convenient and sensible to move to New York, the port from which he sailed. Mother would never leave Harrisburg. So Dad gave up the sea and began working in the freight tariff department of the Pennsylvania Railroad. He was brought into the company by a rising executive, who promised to take Dad along with him up the rungs of the corporate bureaucracy. Unfortunately, after too few years, this man died prematurely of a heart attack. Another took his place in the PRR pecking order. My father's advice to me was never to work for a large bureaucratic organization. What kind of son takes his father's advice?

I was named for my grandfather—Joseph Cannan Smith. Between the time my mother registered my birth information at the hospital and my baptism, some friends of hers convinced her that naming my brother Robert Craighead Smith, Junior, for my father, and me for my paternal grandfather, was servile submission to male chauvinism. They suggested she give me her family name as a token of independence. Hence my Pennsylvania state birth certificate listed me as Joseph Cannan Smith and my baptismal certificate as Joseph Burkholder Smith. No one realized at the time how appropriate it was that the future spy should start life with two different identity documents.

So I grew up in Harrisburg in a middle middle-class neighborhood, with the prejudices and world view this implies. My grandfather had been a leading light in the local GAR. The Major (he always liked to be called by his proud Union cavalry rank) once served, in fact, as chairman of the Harrisburg Board of Trade, thanks, I'm sure, to his GAR not his business connections. Of course he was a Republican, and that's how he raised his son and how my father raised me. My mother's uncle was a life-long local politician in the Grand Old Party, serving several terms on the city council. Thus my political background was solidly Republican on both sides of the family. As for religion, all my progenitors had

20

been Scotch Presbyterians since before they came to America in 1748, but my father was a professional church choirmaster, so I was born a Lutheran, the church that employed his services.

Politics was always in the air in Harrisburg, since it's the state capital, and politics always interested me—Republican politics, of course. A Democrat had never been elected mayor since the Civil War and only one Democrat had ever been elected governor since then, until George Earle made it in 1934. I still remember the shock in our family when that happened. I remember, too, how ardently I campaigned for Alf M. Landon. I had the small talent of being able to draw rather good copies from photographs, and I had Alf drawings all over the house. I enthusiastically pushed Landon and Knox sunflower buttons all over the neighborhood and onto my junior high schoolmates. My chagrin at the results on November 3, 1936, was almost fathomless. I read the *Literary Digest* regularly, as did all my family, and I simply could not believe its polls that showed a Landon landslide in the making could have been so wrong since they reflected with complete accuracy the voting preferences of everyone in my world. My favorite history teacher tried to console me with words that expressed what we all felt. "Never mind," he said, "seventeen million better-thinking Americans voted for Landon."

When I was twelve years old, I experienced my greatest trauma, one that changed me more than anything else that ever happened to me, I have always thought. I was playing baseball in the yard of my best friend, who lived next door, on a hot July afternoon in 1933, when a car drove up quickly and the sister of my brother's college roommate jumped out and ran to my father, who was dozing over the Sunday paper on the front porch. She was screaming as she ran, "Mr. Smith, Mr. Smith, Bob's in the river and we can't find him." My father bolted from his chair and both of them ran to the car and drove off.

I went on playing for a short time, not comprehending the girl's indirect wording. Soon I heard my mother scream, and my aunt came to the door and ordered me in the house. My nineteen-year-old brother had drowned in the Susquehanna River, the mile-wide stream that is Harrisburg's only distinguishing feature. There followed three harrowing days. His body could not be found.

All this time I was in a daze of fear and loneliness. My father spent most of the time at the river. My mother was in a state of collapse. Finally, my brother's body floated to the surface, and we buried him. My mother did not cease to grieve for a year and didn't seem aware of my existence. My father had to bear his grief and hers and try to pay what attention he could to me. I became obsessed with the idea that Dad, my only link to what had once been my family, would walk out of the house to work one day, just as my brother had gone off to swim, and not return. If he were five minutes late in coming home from the office, I would rush out of the house and run to the bus stop to wait for him.

The really important impact of my brother's death, however, was not this personal state of shock or the effect of my mother's unending mourning and despair. My brother had been considered by all the family to be someone special. He had been a frail child, but a very bright one. He could read at three. Because of his many illnesses, my mother kept him out of school until he was past eight years old. After one day, he was promoted to the fifth grade. He was valedictorian of his class in high school at sixteen. He was fluent in German and Spanish and read Greek and Latin poets for amusement.

I was a stocky kid whose main interests were baseball and football. My mother permitted me to delay entering school too, until I was more than seven, because I begged her to let me stay home and play with my friend next door, who was one year younger than I. When I went to school three months after my seventh birthday, nobody thought of skipping me ahead four grades or even up to my age group.

My wounded psyche gradually evolved the idea that I would have to replace my brother. I can't recall ever thinking this overtly, but I began to try to read his books and to try to excel at school. Soon I was more interested in American history than in football.

As I went on in school, I became interested in dramatics and in the school newspaper, as my brother had been. Like him, I became editor of my junior and my senior high school papers. I played leads in every school play, and even received some general acclaim for my performances, as Ko Ko in *The Mikado*, and Grandpa Vanderhof in *You Can't Take It With You*. As a result of these triumphs, I was asked to join the Provincetown Players as a summer apprentice. I considered an acting career, but my father was vehemently opposed. He said if I went into the theater I would meet up with a lot of loose women and be surrounded by people of no moral character.

I was only salutatorian of my class, but I was class president, something my brother had never been. These accomplishments helped me win a scholarship to Harvard, which I entered in September, 1940.

One of the first discoveries I made in the Harvard Yard was that the most stimulating professors and the most interesting fellow students were New Dealers. I was especially shocked to find that classmates from the elitist prep schools were for FDR. I was for Wendell Willkie. The traditional small-town Republican dogma on which I was raised had it that all respectable people were Republicans and only drunken Irishmen, radical Jews, and others of the foreign element were Democrats. The fact that the past two presidential elections had shown that the majority of millions of Americans were such riff-raff, I had never examined too closely before. My education had at last begun.

The convictions of a life-long liberal Democrat were not all that I acquired at Harvard. I learned a lot about history and politics, the things that interested me most. I think I also learned what a critical mind should be, and that my education would never be finished.

My years at Harvard were cut short, as were the college years of all my generation, by what happened on December 7, 1941, at Pearl Harbor. I followed my newspaper-editing interests in college, so I was with my fellow editors at the *Harvard Crimson* that Sunday night. We shouted "scrap iron," "scrap iron" at the AP news ticker that kept pouring out grimmer and grimmer news, to show our disapproval of the Japanese and our government's policy of supplying this important war material to them—something we had been attacking editorially for the past year. This collegiate bravado also helped conceal what we really felt, which was, of course, that we would now be leaving Cambridge soon and that some of us would not come back.

A decision that I made at once was somehow to try to get my degree before I entered military service. I did not know what the war would bring for me personally, but I knew my father's health and financial resources were probably too slim to enable me to continue my studies, even with a scholarship, after who knew how many years of war. So I began an accelerated studies program and,

23

thanks to the fact that as an honors student I could count my honors thesis in lieu of course credits, I was able to complete all degree requirements, except one half-course credit, in two and a half years.

Actually, the most important consideration was a girl with whom I had begun a love affair when I was in high school. She followed me from William Penn High to Cambridge, entering Radcliffe a member of the class of 1946. We got married on a snowy Saturday in December, 1942, and although we may no longer be as romantic as we were when we eloped, we never have been any less in love.

My myopia (which I would like to think was caused by my switching from the life of sports to which I had been dedicated at the age of twelve to a life of study, but which is really congenital) barred me from the glamorous Navy V programs that many of my classmates entered. I staved off entering the service until I could complete my comprehensive examinations for my degree in February, 1943, by signing up in the College Enlisted Reserve. I entered the Army with the Harvard Enlisted Reserve contingent at Ft. Devens on March 11, 1943.

One reason Jeanne and I eloped when we did was that our families, while not disapproving of the marriage in principle, thought we should wait until I got my commission. If we had listened to them we never would have gotten married, because I never got one. When I was urged to take a commission and go to Japan in February, 1946, as a Japanese-language officer, the war was over, Jeanne was nine months pregnant, and I could be discharged on length of service.

I spent the war as a Japanese-language specialist in the enlisted ranks, first at Yale as a member of the Army Specialized Training Corps (ASTP) and then as an Army Military Intelligence Japanese Language Specialist Fifth Class. While at Yale I was able to arrange for Harvard to count my Japanese-language training as one half-course. I could not have done it without the help of Whitney Griswold, the future president of Yale, who was the university's liaison officer with the Army training program at that time. He remarked rather wryly when he told me the good news that he was taking note of the fact that Harvard was giving me one half-course credit for nine months' Japanese-language study at Yale, but he congratulated me nonetheless. I didn't realize then that receiving a

Harvard degree based on work done at Yale was a harbinger that I would live more than twenty years of my life on false credentials.

The day after I got home to Harrisburg from the Army, in February, 1946, Jeanne gave birth to our first daughter, Ruthven. I had been accepted for Harvard Law School in September. As we wrung the diapers through the wringer washer in the months following our daughter's birth, we thought harder and harder about our economic circumstances and whether, even if we could swing it, we wanted to try to raise her in a Quonset hut, which we heard from friends in Cambridge would be the only quarters we could likely afford. An alternative occurred to us.

Perhaps I could commute to Dickinson Law School, only nineteen miles away in Carlisle, and help out in the college as a teaching assistant while we continued to live in the quarters Jeanne's grandmother was renting us for a modest sum. My father knew a Dickinson College trustee, and I got a letter of introduction from him to the acting president of the college.

My interview at Dickinson was a surprise. The head of the history department was Herbert Wing, of the Cape Cod whaling family, Harvard '09. He liked my background immediately. He quickly said he could use me as a full-time instructor, but he was adamantly opposed to my teaching and going to law school at the same time. He gave me one week to think it over. I could join the faculty of Dickinson College as a history instructor or go to law school if I wished, but not both.

Jeanne and I discussed the offer. The salary of $2,900 a year was so much more than the $20 a week I had drawn from the ex-servicemen's benefit scheme (the 52/20 Club, which gave ex-service personnel $20 a week for one year while they readjusted to civilian life) or the job I had held as a reporter for the local newspaper that we decided good current work was better than a future law degree. I could always change my mind since the faculty appointment, of course, was not a permanent, tenured one.

I began teaching at Dickinson in August, 1946, in the second half of the summer session. Dickinson had reputedly been founded in 1773 by the efforts of the Philadelphia philanthropist Benjamin Rush to try to "civilize" the unruly settlers of what was then the wild frontier of the foothills of the Alleghenies. Actually, what was founded in 1773 was a small grammar school, but the college liked

25

to indulge in the common public-relations practice of making the most of itself at the expense of the facts. As anything like a real college, Dickinson dated from the mid-1830s when the Methodist church took the struggling institution in its charge. Most of Dickinson's presidents were Methodist clergymen. In 1946, when I joined the faculty, a Methodist minister, who had just retired as a Navy chaplain, assumed the presidency. He was the great promoter of the "colonial college, founded in 1773" legend. His approach to selling Dickinson, in fact, was based on standards that the Clandestine Services would have applauded as smart operating. He had one brochure prepared for general public distribution stressing the colonial-college line, with no mention of the college's Methodist connection. For distribution in Methodist church circles, he prepared another brochure that dropped the colonial-college line and plugged a historic church-related school message.

In 1946 the college had expanded, thanks to the GI Bill of Rights, from its prewar student population of 300 to 1,200 enrollees. In addition to helping in the general introductory course as a section man, I taught my own courses in American history, Far Eastern history, and a course in international relations, for the fledgling political science department.

I was at Dickinson during all the early skirmishes of the cold war. These events had to compete for my attention with the dramas of raising a firstborn infant and getting settled in a new profession, and they came out a poor second.

For example, Jeanne had just brought the baby home from the hospital when Winston Churchill established the rhetorical foundations for our side of the struggle when he declared at Fulton, Missouri, on March 5, 1946, "From Stettin in the Baltic to Trieste in the Adriatic, an iron curtain has descended across the continent." I didn't pay too much attention to the speech. I was too much involved in preparations for my part in my first Dickinson commencement to pay much attention, either, to the speech that Secretary of State George C. Marshall made in Cambridge at the Harvard commencement exercises on June 5, 1947—the speech that launched the European recovery program that was to bear his name and the success of which institutionalized economic assistance as a fixture of U.S. cold war foreign policy.

2

The Last Half of the Twentieth Century Begins

I did not change from a college instructor into a cold warrior by instant conversion. I saw no sign in the sky. A number of things contributed to the transformation. In a way, it resembled how I ended up teaching when I started out to be a law student. I think the process began on New Year's Eve, 1950.

By the end of 1949, to all appearances, I was firmly embarked on an academic career. I had been engaged in graduate studies since 1947 in pursuit of the American college teaching license—a PhD. First, I thought I would go into the international relations field. I signed up at the Walter Hines Page School of International Relations of the Johns Hopkins University in Baltimore—only seventy-odd miles from Carlisle. The Page School's director was Owen Lattimore, the well-known China expert, and I was interested in the Far East.

Johns Hopkins, however, did not have a flexible enough schedule for a part-time PhD candidate, and after a year of international relations, I also found that I still thought my reason at Harvard for concentrating in history rather than any of the social studies was valid. Historical data is tangible—it lies in old books, old letters, documents, newspapers, in maps and charts and monuments and buildings. The social sciences are desperately trying to decide what their data really is and pretending that human affairs somehow can be studied by the methods of the physical sciences. By the time I went to the annual meeting of the American Historical Society in Boston, Christmas week of 1949, and then on to New York to celebrate New Year's Eve, I had already earned a master's degree in American history at the University of Pennsylvania, commuting weekly from Carlisle to Philadelphia, and was well under way on my PhD program. I had also been promoted to assistant professor.

At 6:45 on the evening of December 31, 1949, William O'Dwyer was sworn in for a second term as mayor of New York. Jeanne and I and Nancy and Bill Taft, our closest friends in Carlisle, were totally oblivious to this event. We were hurrying through our cocktails. We had dinner, the theater, and a party in Greenwich Village on our agenda for the evening.

This New Year's Eve visit to New York was something we and the Tafts had been planning for two years. Planning a trip to New York was the way we passed the dreary winters in central Pennsylvania, Bill Taft liked to say. Bill was Carlisle's best and busiest doctor and a trip like this wasn't something he could very easily take time for. We couldn't spare the cash. Dickinson, however, gave a small stipend to faculty members who attended their professional society's annual meetings. With the help of this, a free car ride with a colleague, and the chance to stay with Jeanne's relatives in Cambridge, we were able to attend the American Historical Society's get-together in Boston and to budget a stopover in New York en route home. The Tafts decided it was time to abandon Bill's patients for a few days, and the long-heralded New York trip finally came to pass.

The high point, we all agreed, would be the New Year's Eve party, because it was being given by one of our favorite Dickinson faculty members, Eric Josephson, and promised to bring together our small crowd from the provinces and Eric's New York friends, plus the sociologist Eric had replaced at Dickinson and his wife, who had also been close friends of ours and the Tafts, and some former and current Dickinson students, possibly the Saypol twins, whose father, Irving Saypol, U.S. Attorney for New York, was gaining

28

fame as the prosecutor of Alger Hiss, the high-ranking State Department officer accused of spying for the Russians.

What the four of us looked forward to most was the mixture of people of different backgrounds and points of view. Our need for this kind of stimulation was what brought us and the Tafts together. It was impossible to say whether the townspeople of Carlisle or the staff of Dickinson College were the more stultifying. Both believed that tradition and strict adherence to custom were the criteria for the good life. The best example of how the town felt on this subject was the obituary of the oldest trustee of the college, who died in 1948 at the age of ninety-three. The obituary began with the words "Although not a native of Carlisle, Mr. Wray moved here with his parents when he was nine months old." The most memorable faculty meeting at Dickinson for me was the occasion on which one professor declared, "If we don't have enough traditions, we must make them up!"

The Tafts were stuck with the townspeople and we were stuck with the faculty, because, of course, town and gown were kept apart by even hoarier tradition. So we had bound together to form our own nonconformist circle, all the principal members of which we expected to find at Eric's party trading thoughts with his friends from *The New Republic,* Columbia University, and the New School for Social Research. The more divergent the people turned out to be the more we would enjoy it. We not only respected individual differences, we thought they were what life was all about.

On this basis we lived what we thought was the best existence we could eke out in Carlisle. Bill was an uncannily skillful diagnostician, but his view of society and his politics were archconservative. I was a New Deal Democrat, elated with the triumph of Harry Truman in 1948. Nancy spent more on clothes in one month than Jeanne had been able to afford since we were married. But we resolved our differences by reading plays aloud together, discussing books, music, and antique furniture instead of politics or family budgets. We enjoyed the fact that people couldn't understand our being such good friends.

The party took place in the apartment of Eric's parents, the writers Hannah and Matthew Josephson. Eric was a little sensitive about standing in the shadow of his father's best-sellers. Actually by the late 1940s the shadow of *The Robber Barons* and Matthew Josephson's other once well-known exposés of the ruthless practices

29

of late-nineteenth-century American business was no longer very long, except among the academic company that Eric kept. These people, of course, were wont to mumble about the elder Josephson's journalistic approach, which made matters even more awkward. Although I had been an ardent reader of Eric's father's books, I made a point of never mentioning this to him. I respected Eric's desire to be his own man and establish his own reputation in his field. I was certain he would succeed.

Eric had been a sociology student of Robert K. Merton at Columbia. On the basis of my one course in sociology with Talcott Parsons, I liked to argue points of his profession with him. About politics, we agreed in general, although Eric usually took positions a little to the left of mine. During the 1948 presidential campaign he had been pretty consistently sympathetic toward Henry Wallace, who had run on a platform of peaceful coexistence with the Russians. The veteran Socialist Norman Thomas called this "preaching peace by blind appeasement." United Auto Workers president Walter Reuther declared that Wallace was "a lost soul used by the Communists." I thought that this was overstating the case, but I could not agree with Eric that there was something a bit sinister about Harry Truman's firmness toward the Soviets. I just did not see Truman as the tool of some sort of conspiracy of bankers and international lawyers with business interests in Germany—an idea to which Eric was inclined to give credence. Eric thought that Truman was a phony liberal—a label he also applied to the New York *Times*. Eric preferred to read the *Herald Tribune*, which he called "an honest Republican paper."

I didn't talk much with Eric at the party that night, as one never does with a host. People drifted in and out as they usually do at such affairs, leaving a memory of nothing more than a sea of faces. However, I remember more than that. I recall that I became caught up in a discussion of the cold war and found myself defending Truman's policies against attacks that made Eric's position seem almost pro-administration.

My first antagonist was a girl who was a political science PhD candidate at Columbia. After she fixed me in her mind linguistically as having a Philadelphia accent because, she said, I pronounced the word "attitude" as "adeetude," she asked me if I didn't agree that the North Atlantic Treaty Organization Council meeting scheduled to begin in Washington on January 6 wasn't proof that Truman intended to back up his economic imperialism with the atom bomb. I replied that I didn't agree. This established my political position, as far as she was concerned, as "an hysterical interventionist," and the fight started.

Soon she was joined by some others and we were engaged in a general review of all the confrontations between the United States and the Soviet Union that had marked the past four years, and that I had never paid so much attention to before. I also found myself alone in taking the side of the United States. I began to look around for the Saypol boys, hoping either for some help or for some other objects upon which my opponents could focus their attack. The Saypol boys never showed up.

We went all the way back to the Soviet refusal to withdraw its troops from Iran in the spring of 1946. My antagonists insisted that the United States had no business demanding that the Soviets withdraw their troops from an area adjacent to their country from which reactionary elements could threaten Soviet security. The Soviet occupation of all the countries of Eastern Europe was also explained to me as a logical security measure. This led to a discussion of the 1948 coup d'etat in Czechoslovakia.

"Do you mean to tell me that the Communist government in Czechoslovakia, which the Soviet military has to support so the people won't rise up and restore a democratically elected government, is not interventionist?" I cried. "If you can't agree that the people of Poland and all the other countries in Eastern Europe shouldn't have the right to choose the governments they want, you guys are the phony liberals," I said.

They brushed this off too and continued their argument that the Marshall Plan and the Berlin airlift crisis, in particular, were examples of a carefully planned policy for achieving U.S. economic domination of Europe being carried out under cover of confrontation with the Soviets.

"Anyone who can defend Truman's provocations the way you do must believe in the American Century," my original female foe declared.

"Given a choice between a Soviet Century and an American Century, there's no other position I can take," I replied.

"Cold war rhetoric. You're no better than a professional cold war propagandist."

"The next thing you'll be telling us is that you believe the court

31

was right in finding that the American Communist Party is 'a conspiracy to overthrow the government by force and violence,' as the court said, and that Russia was able to build an atom bomb last fall only because spies gave her the information."

They had me now. I really needed the Saypols, because I thought that the subversion theme, which had been saturating the country for the past three years, was difficult to believe and to accept.

"What kind of justice do we have in America when courts base their decisions on the testimony of Louis Budenz, who sits smugly up at Fordham and has made $70,000 betraying his friends?"

This question from the group that included my good friend Guido, who had been Eric's predecessor at Dickinson and was now back in New York finishing his degree, had certain merit, I thought.

My grandfather had spent much of the Civil War leading his cavalry unit in a chase across Tennessee trying to find General Nathan Bedford Forrest, the great Confederate irregular warfare expert and later first wizard of the Ku Klux Klan, whose guerrilla tactics drove the Union army wild. Forrest staged surprise raids, intercepted Union orders, and sent false messages to Union troops over captured telegraph lines in a manner of fighting that my grandfather considered unspeakable. My father had taught me that Grandfather would never stoop to retaliation in kind and never would use an informer to try to get a lead on his foe. He would rather never surprise Forrest (which as far as I know, he never did) than deal with despicable degenerates who sold or otherwise provided purloined information—the practice ex-Communists like Budenz and Elizabeth Bentley et al. had made popular in recent years.

I had been raised, in short, on the old-fashioned belief that confidences and friends were not to be betrayed and that "gentlemen did not read each other's mail." I wasn't too sure that modern warfare could afford the luxury of these beliefs, but I had a well-conditioned distrust of the type of inquisition that seemed to be going on in the past several years. On the other hand, the Saypol boys were open and fair-minded young men, and so I presumed was their father, who I thought must therefore be attempting to ascertain the truth in the Alger Hiss case, for example. My training in historical

32

research made me aware that the truth cannot be found by over-looking or discarding relevant information because of a nicety of feeling concerning its sources.

Although I was unable to make up my mind on the subversion question, I began that night to think much harder about it and about the cold war. I was frankly disturbed to find people whom I thought intelligent arguing these matters in such a dogmatic way. They all claimed academic credentials, yet they wanted to discuss the cold war in black and white terms and force me into their mold. It wasn't enough for me to be willing to concede the Soviets a claim to a measure of security in their part of the world, I had to accept the attacks the Soviet delegation in the United Nations made on U.S. policy too as fair and objective political analysis. I began to wonder about these people and the source of their ideas. Was there really a Communist conspiracy abroad in the land? Did it reach even into Eric's parents' apartment?

I broke off the discussion. Dissonance and not diversion was all we and the Tafts found that night in Greenwich Village. Nancy and Bill, in fact, had a fight, something that happened too often between them but wasn't supposed to that evening. Jeanne accepted Guido's suggestion to go out for some fresh air and discovered that what he really wanted was to take her to bed. Was betraying friends wrong only when applied to conspiratorial politics in Guido's mind, I wondered.

Despite my hangover and otherwise glum mood, I bought a New York *Times* for the tedious train trip to Harrisburg and the bus ride to Carlisle.

Those who had the responsibility of finding something to make the New Year's Day edition interesting, as well as people like me with an overdeveloped sense of history, were aware that January 1, 1950, marked the midpoint of the twentieth century. Thus, the magazine section that Sunday morning carried an article by the historian Henry Steele Commager on "The Five Great Problems of the Next Half-Century."

Commager considered the five great problems of the next half-century to be: securing world peace, the use and control of atomic energy, the effective and beneficial management of our physical environment, the establishment of justice, tranquility, and the other goals of the Preamble of our Constitution, for ourselves and the rest of the world, and the reconciliation of liberty with order. I considered this pretty obvious stuff and the part about the beneficent management of the physical environment a lot of eyewash.

Commager wrote, "The compelling consideration is that the twentieth century population is increasing and the basic resources are decreasing faster than ever before. . . . Our soil is blowing or washing away, our water levels sinking, our streams are polluted, our forests shrinking, our familiar resources of bird and animal life, of oil, coal, gas, and minerals being exhausted. . . . We have the skills and the knowledge; it remains to be seen whether we have the moral qualities requisite to saving the resources of earth for posterity." This seemed to me to be a matter of filling up the space allotted for the article.

The part of the piece that got my attention was something very much related to my debate of the previous evening.

"It is clear," Commager commented, "that the responsibility for the solution of the most urgent problems that confront the world rests largely with the United States. Both the peoples of the old world and the new acknowledge that America must direct, if she does not indeed control, the course of world history in the second half of the twentieth century. Outside Russia and her satellite countries few look upon this situation with misgivings. It is inevitable that Americans will be sobered by this heavy responsibility. Only the future will reveal whether they have the intelligence, the persistence, the courage, the vision and the magnanimity to fulfill this responsibility."

This was the doctrine of the American Century in the most straightforward language—adherence to which the girl at the party had accused me of last night. It was something I had to think about.

I remembered my freshman roommate and I discussing the editorial Henry Luce wrote in *Life* magazine in which the phrase and doctrine had been coined. In February, 1941, when Luce's editorial appeared, the Nazis had all but won World War II, the German army having swept over Europe in less than a year. Hitler's panzer divisions were poised on the beaches of northern France, Belgium, and Holland, apparently about to launch a final attack on Great Britain, the only remaining one of the powers that had united to stop Germany's achieving control of Europe in the First World War that was not already under Nazi domination.

The winter of 1941 was an age away from the winter of 1950. In

1941 a significant number of Americans still clung to our ancient isolationist tradition. Henry Luce wanted to rally the nation to a different view of ourselves and the world. He urged Americans "to accept wholeheartedly our duty and our opportunity as the most powerful and vital nation . . . to exert upon the world the full impact of our influence for such purposes as we see fit and by such means as we see fit." Were these brave or merely arrogant words?

The discussion my roommate and I had about them concluded that it didn't really matter, because they reflected a political reality that would inevitably come to pass whether we approved or not. Bob, although certainly not a Nazi sympathizer, was a Germanophile, and he couldn't for the moment help being pleased at the prowess of the German military machine. His feelings were the same as those of one of my Chinese agents in Singapore many years later. Although an ardent supporter of Chiang Kai-shek, this man couldn't help being proud, he explained to me, during the Geneva Conference in 1954 that ended the French phase of the Vietnam War.

"Do you realize," my agent asked, "that Chou En-lai was the first representative of China the great powers ever invited to an international conference and had to pay attention to?"

Thus, Bob was almost wistful when we contemplated what we thought the ultimate outcome of the war was going to be. We agreed Germany's moment of glory would be short-lived. Bob said, "Look, we'll end up in this war and we'll win it. Germany can never match our strength when we get fully mobilized. After that we will go on to dominate the world simply because we have the power to do it and we will go wherever that power takes us." Borrowing a term from Hitler's Thousand Year Reich, he added, "Who knows, maybe one day, since you're fascinated by politics, you may be an American *gauleiter*, giving orders to people in some small Asian country."

I recalled this conversation so clearly not because I ever wanted or expected to be a *gauleiter* of the American Reich, but because I could see that what Bob had said had come to pass. American worldwide interests had grown enormously since the war ended and promised to continue to do so. The war had left a power vacuum that only we could fill. If we didn't want to, the Russians had been demonstrating since 1946 that they were most willing to do the job.

After my argument of the night before, I frankly was glad we were accepting the role. If the Soviets' world view was as well represented among American intelligentsia as last night had shown, we had better be about the business of seeing to it that our position was made clear everywhere abroad. If this made me a follower of Henry Luce, whom my liberal prejudices inclined me to scorn, such would simply have to be the case, I thought.

Three and a half weeks after returning from New York, I read the news that Irving Saypol had won his case against Alger Hiss. Hiss, who had been one of Roosevelt's top State Department advisers at the Yalta Conference, was found guilty of perjury in denying his contact with Whittaker Chambers, the ex-Communist agent, and was sentenced to five years in jail. Sixteen days later, the freshman Senator from Wisconsin, Joseph McCarthy, declared that he had a list of eighty-one persons with Communist leanings who were working in the State Department. The subversion-of-America theme was to reach a crescendo in the next couple of months. Although I thought McCarthy more a master of innuendo than a serious political figure, he soon touched someone I knew, and I could not ignore his charges.

On March 25, Senator McCarthy named Owen Lattimore, the director of the Walter Hines Page School of International Relations at Johns Hopkins, as "the top U.S.S.R. spy" in the United States. He also called Lattimore "Hiss' boss in the State Department ring" and the man responsible for "our loss of China." He had been promising to name this sinister individual for weeks, but when he came up with Lattimore as the man, I was stunned. I had studied under him for a year in 1947 and could not believe what I read in the papers—except for one thing, the memory of the New Year's Eve argument with what I had thought also to be reasonable people.

Lattimore immediately denounced the charges as absurd and accused McCarthy of being in the pay of the China lobby. According to Lattimore, the head of this group was Alfred Kohlberg, a New York export-import merchant, and director of the American China Policy Association, that Lattimore claimed was financed by the Chinese Nationalists as a lobbying group in the United States.

One of the charges that McCarthy brought against Lattimore was his possible link to one of the earliest spy investigations of the postwar period, the so-called *Amerasia* case. *Amerasia* was a magazine

36

financed by Frederick Vanderbilt Field, heir to the Chicago department store fortune who spent most of his money supporting causes of the U.S. Communist Party—a fact that had been well established by numerous ex-Communists by the time Field became a principal financial supporter of Henry Wallace's presidential campaign in 1948. Field was also a supporter of the Institute of Pacific Relations, whose journal, *Pacific Affairs*, Lattimore had edited in the late 1930s, about the same time *Amerasia* was a flourishing publication known principally for its strong and consistent anti-Chiang Kai-shek position in an era when Chiang appeared to be the secure heir of Sun Yat Sen and president of China. Since December, 1949, Chiang had been isolated on Formosa, an island we had just liberated from the Japanese and returned to the Chinese, from whom Japan had taken it in 1895.

The *Amerasia* case was a murky affair. In 1945, two raids were made on its offices, one an illegal entry in March by the OSS, the predecessor organization to the CIA, which like its successor felt that burglary was national security business, and the other done by the FBI in June with a legal search warrant. The OSS had found that an *Amerasia* article that appeared in the January, 1945, issue concerning American-British rivalry in Thailand had been based largely on a secret OSS report. Both the OSS and the FBI allegedly found a great many classified documents in the office. Lattimore had briefed OSS men going to China and on this thin thread and his tie with Field an attempt was made by McCarthy to make this one of the proofs of his spectacular claim about Lattimore.

I could not believe such flimsy charges. I had never heard anything I would call Communist propaganda in Lattimore's seminar. He never talked like the people at Eric's party. He did not try to hide his conviction that Mao had won a fair fight in China and was now its rightful ruler. I found no fault with this. I used the State Department White Paper on China, published in 1949, in my Far Eastern course. It seemed to me to be a well-documented factual account of what had happened in China. I wasn't impressed by the exponents of the "we lost China" argument because I didn't think the country had ever been ours to lose. However, I didn't consider that I knew enough about the subject to make a definitive judgment. I was eager to learn all I could about the matter.

I decided to take a look at Dickinson library's files of *Pacific Affairs* when Lattimore had been its editor. This might shed more light on both China and Lattimore, I thought. I found nothing that added to what had been said about Lattimore's supposedly incriminating support of the thesis that Mao's Communists were agrarian reformers, but I came across something else that did disturb me considerably.

I found that *Pacific Affairs* in June, 1938, began to run an exchange of letters about the Moscow purge trials that seemed out of place in a magazine devoted to matters concerning the Far East. In that same issue, Lattimore reviewed a new Soviet World Atlas with lavish praise. He said the work "reflects a vigorous, growing, experimental society, alive to new discoveries, inventive and creative."

The first letter in the exchange was written by Mary Van Kleeck, who was very active in the late 1940s trying to win support for the outlawing of nuclear weapons on the basis of Soviet, not U.S., proposals. Her letter declared "the recent release of transcripts of the three trials by the Soviet government, and especially the last one, showed that the Soviet Union had actually stopped the plans of Hitler for treasonable alliance between internal disloyal elements and external Nazism."

This letter was replied to in the September issue by William Henry Chamberlain, who had been Moscow correspondent of the *Christian Science Monitor* and was a well-known anti-Communist. He said the things that everyone, except Stalinist apologists, had always said about these trials—that they were a prime example of the man's paranoid power urge and that the confessions were a staged performance of a police state. This provoked an editorial comment from Lattimore which seemed to be the reason the letter was printed—the letter provided the opportunity to declaim about democracy in the Soviet Union.

"In reading the verbatim reports of the trials," Lattimore's comment said, "I naturally went over most closely the testimony and confessions of the only two accused whom I had met personally, they were Radek and Rokovsky. There was nothing out of character in the testimony of either man."

Lattimore went on to say, "The real point for those who live in democratic countries is whether the discovery of the conspiracies was a triumph for democracy or not." He concluded that it definitely was, arguing that since the trials "Moscow correspondents all emphasize that a great many abuses have been discovered and *rectified*." (Emphasis, Lattimore's.)

"A lot depends," Lattimore ended his comment, "on whether you emphasize the discovery of abuse or the rectification of it, but habitual rectification can hardly do anything but give the ordinary citizen more courage to protest loudly whenever in the future he finds himself being victimized by 'someone in the Party' or 'someone in the government.' That sounds like democracy to me."

I thought that it might sound like democracy to Lattimore but it sounded like propaganda to me. Good government had not been what the trials were about. Mary Van Kleeck had taken the line that the Soviets used to justify the trials. The concensus of all experts I had read was that the trials were rigged and the accused brainwashed. Lattimore skirted this issue. He used Chamberlain's letter to launch the propaganda point about democratic development in the Soviet Union. It sounded like the kind of spurious incantations I had heard in New York about the cold war. I now had some doubts.

Just as these doubts had begun to assail me, I read that F. O. Matthiessen, whose American literature course had been one of my memorable experiences at Harvard, had committed suicide. He died in a plunge from the twelfth floor of the Manger Hotel in Boston early Saturday morning, April 1. The paper, in addition to pointing out he was one of the nation's leading literary scholars, quoted his suicide note: "I am depressed over world conditions. I am a Christian and a Socialist and I am against any order that interferes with that objective."

I remembered Matty's meticulously organized lectures, gentle wit, and kind, round face, made rounder by his bald head, with much affection. He had made me conscious and proud of America's intellectual history. As I recalled him, either lecturing to his American Lit course, or at lunch at the Signet Society, I could only think of him as a model of completely self-controlled scholarship.

I remembered now that he had been involved in organizing the world peace conference at the Waldorf Astoria almost exactly a year before. The Arts, Sciences and Professions Committee, a prominent group on the Attorney General's Subversive List, had been in charge of the affair. Harlow Shapley, the Harvard astronomer frequently involved in many leftist activities, opened the meeting and Matthiessen had been one of the speakers, I recalled.

The Sunday New York *Times*, April 2, ran a story about his death that disturbed me still more. Howard Fast, the Communist writer who had joined the Party in 1943 and written a book that tried to show Thomas Paine as a Communist precursor and who had told the Waldorf conference he feared the repressive government of the United States was about to jail him for his beliefs, claimed in this story that Matthiessen was a victim of the cold war. "We cannot accept the designation of his death as suicide any more than we could accept the death of Harry D. White." Harry Dexter White was a U.S. Treasury Department official who had died of a heart attack after being interrogated by the House Un-American Affairs Committee concerning charges made against him by Elizabeth Bentley based on her work as a Soviet intelligence source.

Howard Fast gave his press statement as chairman of the publishing and writing division of the New York State Council of the Arts, Sciences and Professions Committee. The *Times* added the comment that spokesmen for the Fast group said they had "no special crime information" upon which Fast's remark could have been based.

The story went on with further information about Matty's political activities. He had been a member of the National Executive Committee of the Progressive Citizens of America, trustee of the Samuel Adams School of Social Studies, which the paper pointed out was on the Attorney General's Subversive List. He had been a delegate-at-large from Massachusetts to the Progressive Party convention that had nominated Wallace for President, and Joseph B. Matthews, former research director of the House Un-American Affairs Committee, had charged in 1949, at a hearing of the Massachusetts legislature about Communist activities in the state, that Matty was a supporter of Communist organizations. The phrase about being a Christian and a Socialist that had appeared in the suicide note had been used by Matthiessen in answering Matthews's charges, the article added.

I had no friends at Harvard at the time to give me information on Matty's suicide. The press did contain some material that tended to counter the Fast statement, however. For one thing, Matty had spent the evening before his death with his friend Harvard dean Kenneth Murdock. Murdock reported that he had been depressed about many things, among them his work on Theodore Dreiser he had taken a year's leave to try to finish. Murdock released the full text of Matthiessen's suicide note.

"I am exhausted," the note began, "I have been subject to so many severe depressions during the past few years that I can no longer believe that I can continue to be of use to my profession and my friends. I hope that my friends will be able to believe that I still love them in spite of this desperate act. How much the state of the world has to do with my state of mind I do not know." Then followed the statement of his principles, that had first been reported in the press and that the Communists had chosen to use to prove he was a victim of the cold war.

Another piece of interesting information was Matthiessen's will. A story on the will appeared a week after his death because his sister was contesting it. The will showed that Matty had cancelled two bequests that had been in an earlier will—one to the International Labor Defense of New York and the other to the Samuel Adams School of Social Studies.

The same day that the story of Matty's will appeared, April 7, the feature news item was the testimony of Owen Lattimore to the Senate investigating committee. Lattimore denied under oath that he was a Communist, something that those questioned by the various investigating committees usually conspicuously refused to do. He also showed that he had no connection with *Amerasia* after 1941, four years before the OSS and FBI broke into its offices. He further named William J. Goodwin, a registered Chinese Nationalist agent receiving $36,000 a year plus expenses for his lobbying activities, as the associate of Kohlberg who had provided information on him to McCarthy. Two days later, when receiving an American Legion Award in Passaic, New Jersey, Senator McCarthy scrupulously avoided calling Lattimore a Communist in his otherwise rousing anti-Communist speech.

I was greatly shaken by the realization that obviously there was a vast struggle going on, one that was largely hidden and that the cold war confrontation headlines only partially reflected. Dickinson, my teaching job, and my tiresome graduate studies seemed more banal than ever before.

Between commencement, which was always held the first Sunday in June at Dickinson in those days, and the opening of summer session, the United States went to war in Korea. On June 25, the army of Communist North Korea invaded South Korea. The next day at the UN the United States charged North Korea with aggression.

41

One day later the Security Council gave approval to the United States' request that UN members help defend South Korea. On June 28 President Truman ordered air and sea support by U.S. forces, and by July 1 ground forces were ordered into action.

It seemed to me that the attack by the North Koreans was indeed an act of aggression. The Soviets' fulminations about the UN action only seemed proof to me of their guilt by association, as well as, of course, pique at their own precipitous walkout from the Security Council in January over the issue of the admission of Communist China that left them unable to veto the Council's vote in June. Argument about the Wallace view concerning the right of the Soviets to a security belt of friendly states on their borders was over as far as I was concerned. It was time to take a firm, realistic view of the situation.

The most lucid account I had ever read of how the world found itself at war again just twenty years after concluding the "war to make the world safe for democracy" in 1919 was E. H. Carr's *The Twenty Years' Crisis.* Carr found the reason peace could not be kept was the unresolved conflict between the approaches to international relations of what he called the utopians and the realists. He quoted Albert Sorel to nail down his point. "It is the eternal dispute," Sorel wrote, "between those who imagine the world to suit their policy, and those who arrange their policy to suit the realities of the world."*

I considered myself a realist and my reading of Carr was that the utopians, with their mistaken faith in a harmony of interests that did not in fact exist, had brought about the Second World War. The Treaty of Versailles satisfied the Allied Powers and they assumed that the peace it imposed was in everybody's best interest. Germany was not satisfied and the Treaty of Versailles was not in Germany's best interest.

It seemed to me that the past five years had shown that Soviet interests and ours were as out of harmony as those of the Allied Powers and the Germans from 1919 to 1939. It was certainly not in our interest to have a Soviet satellite power overrun Korea, the dagger that the Japanese had always thought to be pointed at their heart. By the terms of the occupation of Japan and the peace treaty that

*E. H. Carr, *The Twenty Years' Crisis, 1919–1939,* 2nd ed. (New York: Macmillan, 1946), p. 11.

was shaping up, Japan's defense was now our responsibility. We were the ones who now were facing the dagger. We must meet this Soviet–North Korean aggression now, as England and France should have met Hitler in the Rhineland in 1936, to prevent a third world war.

The beginning of the Korean War was the final piece that put my personal puzzle together. I decided that I could not sit on the sidelines, teaching history, when the opportunity of some kind of direct involvement in the history that was being made was now so greatly expanded. Surely the war would mean that there must be some job for me in Washington that would make me feel part of the action.

I began to scout possibilities. I soon made the discovery that not only were there job opportunities, but a glance at the Civil Service salary schedules for Defense and State Department positions indicated that almost anything for which I might be eligible would pay me more than my boss, Dr. Wing, was making after thirty years of devoted service to Dickinson. While I might succeed in moving on from Dickinson, where I obviously did not feel I had a rewarding job nor, despite our friendship with Bill and Nancy, Eric, and a few others, the quality of life I wanted, I recalled that V. O. Key, one of the most widely recognized scholars of American government, who headed the political science department at Johns Hopkins when I talked over my graduate study plans in 1947, told me I was taking the vow of poverty in entering an academic career. I decided to go on a job hunt to Washington in the summer of 1950.

I was not immediately successful. My background, I believed, qualified me for a job as a political intelligence analyst, which I thought would be interesting and important work. Instead of analyzing why Andy Jackson decided to break Mr. Biddle's United States Bank, I could try to figure out what Russia's next move in Asia might be. I considered it logical to try the Defense Department first.

Both Naval and Air Force Intelligence were interested in me as a commissioned officer, but I ran up against the same problem I had in World War II. I didn't meet their vision requirements. I tried the State Department. It was suggested that I take the Foreign Service exam, but I had no stomach for that. I had always heard that it was terribly tough and that the orals were stacked against anyone the examiners' whim decided was not a likely member of the club. Anyway, I thought a diplomatic career pretty stuffy business. I did not try the CIA on my initial Washington visit because I couldn't find out anything about it. It was too secret.

After convolutions that amazed me, the CIA was where I wound up more than a year later, having a strange job interview that I could not imagine happening to me.

3
Brief Encounter

It's not easy to find a place to park near the Lincoln Memorial. It is one of the principal tourist attractions in Washington. Space is available for tourist buses, and there are wide areas reserved for persons on foot to cross the street and approach the monument with some dignity. There are, however, few places for cars.

After circling three times, hugging the lane closest to the monument in order not to be swept away in the tides of traffic turning into Ohio Drive and Rock Creek Parkway, I was able to fit my red 1947 Jeepster into a spot marked NO PARKING AFTER 4 P.M. I had a one-thirty appointment, on this March 27, 1951, in Temporary Building "L."

"L" Building was one of four two-floor wooden temporary buildings put up during World War I on the south side of the Lincoln Memorial Reflecting Pool. The Reflecting Pool forms the central attraction of a park area, reached by descending a broad flight of steps across the street directly in front of the Lincoln Memorial.

The park runs from in front of the Memorial to 17th Street. The four temporary buildings ran the length of the pool, parallel to it almost all the way.

In 1951 these buildings were thirty-five years old. Although they were only partially occupied on a part-time basis from 1919 until 1933, somehow no one got around to tearing them down. Then the New Deal expanded the government to try to swallow up the depression, and the buildings had tenants again. World War II assured continued tenancy, and after it ended, again, no one had gotten around to tearing them down.

"L" was the building nearest the Memorial, and I noticed that it and the building after it in line were surrounded by eight-foot-high steel-mesh fences. I also noticed that, while there were a number of possible entrances, only one was not enclosed by a gate of similar construction. This entrance obviously was where visitors went in.

Inside the two swinging doors was a rather shabby vestibule with a brown linoleum floor. The doors and the walls, inside and out, were painted gray. The vestibule was level with the ground. There were a couple of steps up to the main hallway. At the head of the steps, barring further entrance, were a desk and a guard dressed in policeman's blue, but some years older and inches grander around the waist than most policemen. He asked to see my pass. I showed him the letter I had brought with me, and he asked me to go into a small waiting room reached by a door behind his desk. He said he would make a phone call and someone would come for me shortly.

The waiting room had a rug. Otherwise it reminded me of a World War II sick-call receiving room. It was furnished with uncomfortable wooden chairs designed originally to discourage soldiers from goofing off by coming to sick call. After forty-five minutes in one again, for the first time since 1945, I began to wonder whether the CIA was using them to produce the same reaction in job applicants. At that point, however, something happened that never did when I was in the Army. A girl came into the room and called my name.

"Clip this badge on the upper pocket of your jacket," she said, "and you can follow me." She opened the door and indicated, with a nod, our direction.

"Is this your first visit?" the girl asked, with a smile.

"Yes," I replied, assuming that she meant to "L" Building, and not to Washington.

46

"How do you like it?"

"Well, fine."

"Where are you staying?"

"With some friends in Alexandria," I answered honestly.

We kept walking along the corridor, alone, just the two of us. We passed a number of doors. All closed. All with the upper glassed portions opaqued with paint. No one went in or out as we passed by.

Finally, she opened one of these doors and motioned me to go in.

We were now in another waiting room as nearly identical to the first as I could imagine it possibly could be.

"Please just wait here a few minutes," she said, and left, closing the door.

As I sat down, with only a preliminary glance at my surroundings, I did not immediately begin to brood about their solitary sterility. But my mood soon changed.

Again, there was a rug on the floor, a beige carpeting that added no color to the room. There were four chairs along one wall and four along the opposite wall. At the end of the room, opposite the entrance, was a table with a chair at either end. There were no furnishings at all on the side of the room where I had come through the door. It was an interior room so there were no windows. Two overhead fluorescent lights, rectangular banks of three light tubes each, lit the place more than adequately. The walls were freshly painted a shade of gray that was just beginning to replace the tan that had been the favorite of apartment landlords and custodians of public buildings for the past several generations. This was the only decorative flair. No pictures or other objects adorned the walls.

I sat down on one of the four chairs along the side of the room farthest from the door. It was an instinctive move, I guess, governed by the desire to make room for other people to come in and fill up the place. However, I soon began to be very acutely aware that I was all alone.

Thinking about the matter, I realized that I had been all alone in the other waiting before the girl came in. It dawned on me that, except for the guard and girl, I had seen no other human being since I had entered the building.

I glanced at my watch and discovered that I had been inside "L" Building for more than an hour. My appointment, according to the letter I took out of my pocket to look at again, was for one-thirty. Because I knew job applicants were supposed to be prompt, I had allowed myself plenty of time to get to the building, and even with circling the monument, I had made it to the door at one-twenty-five. It was now a quarter to three. I was not only lonely. I was nervous.

This was not what I had pictured my interview to be. As I had rehearsed it to myself while driving from Alexandria to the District, I had seen myself confronting a senior academic colleague, puffing on a pipe, and being impressed by my quietly, but steadily, affirmed intellectual credentials. He would make some attempts to ruffle my calm, but I would respond with just the right combination of wit and wisdom to thwart his efforts.

Also, my wife had coached me before I took off for the appointment to watch my tendency to say too much. So far this afternoon neither her coaching nor my imaginary practicing had served any useful purpose. I could only rehearse some more and wonder what kind of situation I had gotten myself into. To be challenged by a guard when I came to an office where I had an appointment, then to be abandoned for nearly an hour, then escorted to another room and abandoned again was not what I had bargained for.

When I had applied ten months earlier for a job as an intelligence analyst, I had been assured by the friend who suggested I apply that the CIA has a "serious research atmosphere." I had sought out this friend's counsel and assistance in Washington the previous summer, on my second job-hunting expedition.

My friend had been my favorite college professor. He had left Cambridge during the early days of World War II, in 1942, to become involved in intelligence research. Having left the halls of academe almost ten year earlier, never to return, he agreed with me when I explained my views to him and called several colleagues.

I had two interesting talks in different offices at the Pentagon with these people. I remembered now, as I sat staring at the empty room, their offices piled with documents, papers, and maps. They had been surrounded by people, reading, writing, telephoning. Theirs was an atmosphere of serious research, I thought. They told me that there were no openings under their jurisdiction, however, and sent me back to my friend.

"Don't worry," he said, "we'll try CIA. They're always doing a lot of hiring over there."

With that, he picked up the phone and called someone. He discovered that his contact was out of town and asked to talk to the man's deputy. He explained who I was, and, very kindly, embellished my record quite handsomely.

"Okay, fine," he said, putting down the phone, "I'll send him right over."

"Look," he explained, "my friend Stan is out of town but his deputy says that they are building up their Far Eastern research division and you sound good to him. Unfortunately, he can't see you today or tomorrow, but he says not to worry, you should pick up an application at 2430 'E' Street, fill it out, and you'll hear from them in a couple of weeks.

"These guys run the research show over there," he concluded, "so I know you'll get attention."

We shook hands, I thanking him for all his help, and he assuring me that he'd see me when I settled into Washington in a couple of months.

I went to 2430 "E" Street, which turned out to be not one but a group of buildings of neo-colonial design replete with Corinthian columns and cornices. After several inquiries, I was directed to the office where job applications were handed out. The girl gave me a booklet of papers entitled "Personal History Statement." A quick glance showed me that I would have to wrack my brain to answer the questions it contained. For one thing, I had to list, in order, from most recent to earliest, the addresses of all the places I had lived the past fifteen years. To answer the questions about my parents and relatives, I would have to consult the family Bible. I asked if I could take the Personal History Statement home with me and mail it back when I was able to fill it out properly. I was assured I could.

Before leaving Washington, I went to the Civil Service Commission and got a copy of the job description listing qualifications and duties of an intelligence analyst as a general guide to help me with the personal job interview I hoped the future would bring.

I managed to fill out the Personal History Statement in two weeks and mailed it back. The first week in August I received a form letter thanking me for my interest and saying that "as prompt action as possible will be taken to process your application." The letter also said I would hear further "in the near future."

That was the last I heard about the matter for the rest of the year. Meanwhile, I practically memorized the job description of an intelligence analyst. He "organized, collated and corroborated information." Such information was primarily "political, economic and geographical." The paper went on like that in general terms, and I was convinced, if I were ever to get a chance at a job interview, I could handle myself all right. My educational qualifications were certainly within the fields and at the level indicated, and the work seemed to me to be so similar to the kind of academic research and investigation I had done that I could certainly adapt myself quickly.

When January came and I still had heard nothing, I decided I had better forget the whole thing, and I threw the intelligence analyst's job description away. I was completely surprised when I received a letter in late February asking that I select a date, within the next four weeks, when I could be available in Washington for an interview. The CIA would confirm the date and time of interview when I let them know my choice.

Dickinson College always gave its students and faculty a long Easter vacation extending into the week following Easter Sunday, and I selected Tuesday, March 27. Then, I wrote to some friends who lived in Alexandria who had given me a standing invitation to stay with them whenever I would be job-hunting in Washington. They telephoned when they got my letter and insisted that I bring Jeanne and Ruthven along for a reunion.

We piled into the Jeepster the day before the interview and managed to make the entire ninety-mile trip to Alexandria without Ruthven's getting carsick once. My wife and I decided that this was such a miracle it must be a good omen for my interview. Now I was not so sure, as I sat in solitary confinement in an inside office in "L" Building.

At this point, the door of the dismal waiting room opened. Another young woman appeared.

"Oh," she said in a startled voice. "I'm sorry. I made a mistake." And she was gone.

I was left alone again as suddenly as I had been granted a brief moment of human contact. As the time went by I wondered grimly what she meant by a mistake. I simply could not understand how or why it was that there seemed to be no others in my same state. In a way, as I thought about it, the strange treatment I was now undergoing was really not any more unusual than the way I had been

50

treated from the moment I had first been in touch with the CIA. I reminded myself I had received confirmation that my application "was under consideration" two weeks after applying for a job and then not one single word more. By the time I got the letter suggesting this appointment, I had never expected to hear anything further. Now I wasn't certain I had really heard anything after all.

The way things had been going in Korea made me think that the CIA must be hiring. The months that had passed had witnessed a swing from an exhilarating high, when MacArthur had landed the Marines behind the entire North Korean army at Inchon in September, to a frustrating low, when the Chinese had entered the war in November and driven our army back across the 38th parallel. As I sat that afternoon contemplating the general situation, I did not feel at all reassured about what was happening in Korea. The morning newspaper had reported that "fierce fighting between UN and Chinese troops is continuing."

Clock watching is universally recognized as a totally unrewarding enterprise. Nevertheless, I think it was at about the twentieth time that I looked at my watch when the door opened again and a tall, dark, and very young man entered the room.

"Hello," he said with a broad smile, "my name's Dave." I got up and we shook hands. He motioned for me to take one of the two chairs at the table and he took the other. He had a folder of papers in his hand. I thought I saw a corner of my Personal History Statement among them and this somewhat reassured me.

"I'm sorry to be so late," he said, "but it's terribly hard to keep a schedule running smoothly around here. I hope you don't mind."

"Of course not," I lied, trying to get back into the confident, capable, affable applicant routine I had been trying to perfect on my way over from Alexandria.

"You have an okay drive over here from Alexandria?"

"Oh yes."

I was struck by his question since I had not said anything to him about my staying in Alexandria. I then recalled that I had told this to the girl. She apparently performed a number of functions around the place.

"Well," Dave said, partly swallowing his words as he opened the folder and began leafing through its papers, "we want to talk to you about some things." He had finished the social part of the conversation.

51

In a few seconds, he drew out of the folder a copy of a magazine, *The Korean Review,* that I recognized very well. It was the issue in which had appeared an article I had written a year before based on research I had done for Lattimore's seminar at Johns Hopkins. The article had been rather pretentiously entitled "The Koreans and Their Living Space," and I was a bit uneasy now about whether I had said anything in the article that remotely lived up to this promise of geopolitical insight. I was taken aback by his producing a copy of the magazine. I remembered I had mentioned the article in answer to the "Publications" question on the Personal History Statement, but I hadn't sent along my copy of the magazine, and it wasn't a publication found on newsstands around the country. I also wondered whether he were going to ask me about my relationship with Owen Lattimore.

"Interesting article," he commented. "How do you think the war's going these days?"

"I don't feel as good as I did last September," I managed in reply.

"How would you like to go to Korea?"

When he saw that this question had produced what must have been the slackening of my jaw he apparently anticipated, he continued.

"It's a little difficult for me to explain in detail in this interview the kinds of things we might have for you to do around here. The fact is that you have a good, interesting background.

"Do you smoke?" he asked, offering his pack.

"Yes, thanks," I replied, "but I'll have one of my own."

"We might say that we have two types of activity around here that you might like to try." Dave seemed more sure of himself now. We were both enjoying our cigarettes.

"One type of activity we might call action organizing. It involves a lot of personal responsibility, including responsibility for people and other things." He paused, "The idea of going to Korea doesn't appeal to you too much, does it?"

"No, it doesn't," I answered honestly. "I thought I was applying for a job in Washington as an intelligence analyst. I have a wife and very young child and I don't particularly want to leave them on their own at this time."

This was the truth, and, I thought to myself, I really could not understand what Dave was talking about. If I had wanted to join the Army again I would not be here. I had been a Japanese-lan-

52

guage specialist during the war and not a combat soldier, which I was sure he had seen in my record. My Japanese was now very rusty, as I had truthfully indicated in my Personal History Statement, and since Japan no longer occupied Korea, I just could not imagine what it was in my background that made him think that there was anything useful I could possibly do in Korea. I guessed that maybe the interview was over. I was neither right nor wrong.

"Well now," Dave said, "the other type of activity we have involves planning and making important executive decisions here in Washington. Would you be interested in this?"

I thought he must be kidding. Surely he could see that for someone like me, there was no question which I would choose. I could not understand his game, but I decided to play.

"I'd prefer the second type of activity, yes."

"Good," said Dave, "I'm glad to hear it. I'm sorry we haven't had much time to talk, but we have been reading your file carefully. Now there's someone else I want you to see." Dave smiled and rose. "I'll have him along in just a few minutes. Nice talking to you."

He gathered up all the papers and *The Korean Review* and put them back in the folder as he was speaking. He extended his hand and we shook.

"I'll be seeing you," Dave said as he went out the door, which he closed carefully behind him.

I was alone again, but at least I had been able to talk to someone more or less about the business I had come for.

What sense did the truncated interview make? I was unable to answer that question.

I had been spending the entire afternoon, it seemed to me, cooling my heels. What kind of a gag was all this? Asking someone if he really wouldn't prefer a job making important executive decisions to a job in Korea? Was this some kind of a trap? How many ploys are they using around this place? What had any of this to do with being an intelligence analyst? Dave had shown interest in my article in *The Korean Review,* but had immediately dropped the subject never asking me a single question about it. But then, in about another twenty minutes, the door opened again. There stood a short, bespectacled Japanese. He reminded me of one of my Nisei colleagues during the war. The age-old, expressionless Japanese stare was modified by just the suggestion of a smile that seemed to come from the corners of his eyes. During my days in Nisei compa-

53

ny I called this the San Francisco look—a sort of cultural transplant on the face of ancient Japan.

"Hello," he said, "my name's John."

We shook hands solemnly and somewhat weakly. I think we both knew that we should really have bowed.

"Will you please come with me?" he asked and held open the door.

Outside in the corridor again all was quiet. Still no one was in sight. When we had passed three wings down the long empty corridor we came to a stairway. John indicated we were to go upstairs.

Once upstairs the scene changed. Several men and women were working in the room we entered. None of them looked at me or spoke.

"Please come in here." John invited me to enter an adjacent office. At a larger desk than those in the other room sat a woman, who smiled at once when I entered and, without rising from her chair, extended her hand to me.

"Hello, my name's Kay. I see John got you here all right."

She was a small woman, with good regular features and some gray in her brown hair. She was dressed in a tailored suit and wore glasses on a string around her neck.

"John and I are glad to meet you," she continued. "How are your wife and daughter?"

"Fine, thank you," I answered. These people were obviously the ones Dave had indicated he wanted me to see. The word had again been passed along about the previous conversation.

"Well, we understand you are good at planning activities," she went on. "What experience have you had?"

I was not sure exactly how to answer this question. Among other things, I didn't recall claiming I was particularly good at planning activities, whatever they might be. I certainly had no idea what kind of activities these people might want me to plan.

"I've had some experience on faculty committees, planning programs and curriculum changes," I answered. "I've never worked in government before, so I'm not quite sure what it is you plan."

"Oh, that's all right," said Kay, with a little laugh. "We're not ready to talk to you yet about our program in any detail. We'd just like to get a preliminary idea and to become personally acquainted with you. How's your Japanese?"

"Very rusty, I'm afraid."

"That's all right, so is mine," said John.

"Well, I guess we must give you some idea about what it is that we do." Kay seemed to change her mind. "We have a lot of material here to study and to sort out to try to decide what's the best use to make of it. You've had a lot of academic research experience, haven't you?"

"Yes."

"Well, that's good."

"Say, John"—she turned to the young Nisei who was seated beside her while I sat in a chair at the side of the desk in front of both of them—"why don't you ask him some questions?"

"Okay," said John. "Have you been following developments in Japan recently?"

"Not very closely."

"Do you know there is a movement to encourage the Japanese to become active in a business way in Southeast Asia again?"

"No, I didn't know that."

"Well, how does the idea strike you?" John asked. "Do you think it's a good idea or a bad idea?"

"I think it's a very good idea," I said. "I think that we and the Japanese are confirmed capitalists and excellent businessmen. They'd make good partners of ours against the influence of the Chinese Communists in Southeast Asia."

John had unknowingly touched on a sensitive point with me. Two years before, I had written an article on the subject of the need for what I called a rebirth of the Anglo-Japanese alliance, stressing the fact that this alliance had kept peace in Asia very well for nearly three decades and that we had now replaced the British as the number one occidental power in that area. I sent it to an old college chum on the staff of a major journal of opinion. After keeping it for three months, he sent me a four-page rejection letter, the gist of which was that my idea was too controversial.

It did not seem too controversial in my present company.

"What is the lowest salary that you'll accept?" asked Kay.

"Six thousand dollars a year." I tried to remember what exactly I had said in answer to that question on my Personal History Statement.

"Unfortunately, we have to follow salaries for the grades in the

Civil Service System," was her reply to me, "and that salary is above the enter-on-duty salary at the nearest grade you qualify for. Would you accept four hundred dollars a year less?"

"Yes, I think so." I quickly calculated that this would be a salary six hundred dollars a year greater than Dr. Wing's.

"Good." She smiled. "Now the problem is that we can't tell you anything definite today. But we'll be in touch."

I'm sure my face fell. After sitting around all afternoon, being made to feel like a person in quarantine, after a conversation that included an agreement on salary, I was now exactly where I had been ten months ago, I felt, when my friend had assured me that I'd hear something positive in a couple of weeks.

John seemed to react to my feelings. He jumped to his feet.

"Here, let me see you out of this place."

"Very nice to talk to you," said Kay, extending her hand again.

John and I left quickly and went back down the same stairs.

"We'll have to check you out through the guard and give him back your temporary badge," John said as we descended the steps. "And I'll have to hand in this slip with the sign-out time on it."

We were back on the first floor and turned left up the corridor in the direction of the sole passable entrance.

"It must seem kind of strange to you the way we do things," John said, and his face, Oriental mask and all, showed me that he meant to be consoling, "but we have to be that way. You see, you have to have a security clearance to work here. They take a long time."

"Yes, I do feel rather strange," I admitted.

We had come to the guard by this time and I was relieved of my temporary badge. John looked at his watch and wrote the time and his initials on the slip and gave it to the guard. I was too preoccupied with my own feelings to notice what he put on the paper.

"Look," he said, holding out his hand, "you'll really hear from us, in time. Don't worry."

I went out into the gathering dusk and walked slowly back along the sidewalk beside the Reflecting Pool. I was trying to sort out my experience and my feelings and what I would tell my wife and friends when I got home. I climbed the steps up to the level of Memorial Drive and walked toward where I had left my car.

I was deep in my own thoughts still, although I was also beginning to try to pick out my car in the gloom of early night. The traffic in Memorial Drive, and in the streets feeding into it on all sides of the Memorial, was ten times greater than it had been when I had arrived for my appointment. It was four lanes deep and nearly bumper to bumper in front of the area where I had parked my car.

My car. I looked again. It had disappeared. I could not believe it. What in God's name had happened? How could my car disappear? How could it be stolen in broad daylight in Washington, D.C., in front of park policemen guarding the Lincoln Memorial?

Was this some kind of stunt of my mysterious friends who had no last names? Something they had arranged while they kept me cooling my heels to see what my reaction would be? They wouldn't tell me what kind of work they did or what kind of work it really was they wanted me to do. I had heard about some of the things OSS did to new recruits during the war to gauge their reaction to stress. Was I in the hands of the same kind of people?

And then, as I glanced around me in growing dismay, I began to realize that it was now far from daylight. I looked at my watch for the first time since I had met John in the waiting room and begun my last strange interview. It was now five-fifteen. I looked up and the sign in the area where I had parked my car caught my eye. NO PARKING AFTER 4 P.M.

Now I knew. My car had been towed away by the police. Where did they take it? How could I find out? I must find a cop.

I walked along but saw no policeman. I began to run, and to circle the Lincoln Memorial, the circumference of which is considerable. Suddenly, on the sidewalk, by the steps to the Lincoln statue, I saw a red Jeepster. I made my way somehow across the street through the stream of cars. Sure enough, the Jeepster had a Pennsylvania license plate. It was my car.

I jumped in and turned on the ignition. Halfway around the monument I could see Memorial Bridge spreading over the Potomac toward Virginia. I drove along the sidewalk until I came even with the approach to the bridge. With a quick glance to make certain no car was within a length of me, I accelerated, bounced off the sidewalk, and made my escape.

But who had put the car on the sidewalk? Had it been placed there on the orders of some hold-over psychologist from OSS who was now working for the CIA and still up to his old tricks for testing potential employees?

4

"You Have Just Joined the Cold War Arm of the U.S. Government"

On Tuesday, September 4, 1951, President Truman opened the Japanese Peace Treaty Conference in San Francisco. His speech inaugurated transcontinental television. The remainder of the conference, which lasted through Saturday, was also covered live across the nation. The conference thus became the first event of the international political arena to take place in the American living room. Eventually, most of the television sets on which Americans would watch future such happenings would be either entirely or in part products of the Japan that grew out of that treaty.

I did not watch the conference. Although television now spanned the continent, it didn't reach into the Cumberland Valley very well. The few people who had sets complained they saw almost nothing but snow. Even if I had owned a set, I probably still would not have looked at the conference because the CIA had called two weeks before asking that I report for duty on September 10. By the time the Japanese Peace Treaty Conference opened, our household was in the throes of the first of the many frenzied short-notice moves of my Clandestine Services career.

The person who had called requested me to report to Central Building at 2430 "E" Street at 9 A.M. on September 10, and ask for the medical staff office. The guard at the door accepted the request for the medical office as an adequate password, and pointed out the appropriate door to me and let me pass without the badge routine I had been through in March. Again, of course, I found myself in a waiting room, but this one was recognizable. A nurse sat behind a desk in the center of the room, and there were a number of reasonably comfortable-looking easy chairs and several out-of-date magazines were on the coffee table. This was a doctor's waiting room.

The nurse handed me a multipage medical history questionnaire which she requested be filled out and a tag with a number on it which she said would be called when the doctor was ready to see me.

Most of the chairs were already taken and their occupants were either filling out questionnaires or glancing at magazines, but I was able to find a seat and begin to look over the paper I had to fill out. The information required included not only dozens of obscure ailments I was supposed to remember whether I had ever suffered from, but also I was supposed to be able to provide similar information about my parents. After a few minutes' effort dedicated to trying honestly to accomplish these feats of memory, I decided that the way to handle the matter was simply to answer "no" to all the questions.

A group of eight of us were called from the waiting room at about the same time. We went through a side door and were told to strip to our shorts and were given a folder stapled shut. At every station in the exam, the medic would take the measurements or tests required, note the results on the chart inside the folder, and then staple the folder shut again. All the information being accumulated on the patient, in other words, was carefully concealed from him. Finally the doctor himself completed the exam with the usual thumping, and probing, and "cough please." He wrote his observations on the paper, stapled it again, and said, "That's all." No bedside manner here, the examination was too secret for that. Obviously in CIA even your body is top secret, I thought.

The nurse in the reception room handed me a visitor's badge

when I emerged from the examining rooms and told me to go to Room 212 for further processing.

In Room 212 I was given a thick booklet of top secret papers to read and sign. These explained how secret everything was, in case the reader hadn't become aware of this, and ended with an agreement for the reader to sign which pledged him not to tell anyone what he had read.

The processing of a new employee took considerable time. I was involved in a series of procedures for three more days. I didn't find out where I would be working until Friday morning. I read more long papers, I was photographed for a badge, and I was subjected to more examinations. One of these was a psychological assessment test that was popular in those days. William H. Whyte, Jr., told how to cheat on these tests in his book *The Organization Man*. This wasn't hard to figure out for yourself, actually, since all the questions were loaded. The trouble was you had to know what your prospective employer wanted to offer you so you could make the test show your personality profile to be the one that he had in mind for the job. It seemed particularly unfair for CIA to use this test on me since, although I had applied for a job as an intelligence analyst, my job interview had left me completely confused as to whatever position it might be that I was being considered for. The only thing that seemed reasonably certain was that it was nothing like the intelligence analyst job the Civil Service Commission's published job description indicated.

With my March interview in mind, it was fairly easy for me to handle the question "Do you enjoy reading books as much as having company in?" It seemed to me that my new employers would like to have extroverted people-oriented personnel in their employ, so, although I preferred books, I answered that I preferred having company in. The question "Do you sometimes feel self-conscious?" was almost too self-answering.

"Do you prefer serious motion pictures about famous historical personalities to musical comedies?" That was a pretty tough one. The extrovert answer was clear, but, even though I wasn't sure what my employers had in mind for me, CIA, I presumed, was supposed to be an intelligence organization, concerned with political and military problems. That should mean that a preference for famous historical personalities was the indicated answer. Since this

61

was such a dilemma, I opted for my own real preference for the historical films.

I decided that I would try to rescue the woman in the window of the burning building with the infant in her arms. During my afternoon in "L "building, I had made it quite clear that I did not want to be shipped to Korea in the near future, so now I thought a little boldness could not do me any harm.

The most notable experience of the four days' processing occurred on Thursday morning. I was told to go to Building 13. Here I was ushered into a small but well-appointed office. A large, serious-faced man motioned for me to sit down in an overstuffed leather armchair. He then began a speech that seemed rehearsed.

He explained that the CIA had been asked to cooperate in an experiment that could prove to be important in case the world situation suddenly deteriorated to the point we found ourselves in World War III. He recalled that I surely was aware that there had been a long delay between my filling out a job application and my job interview and between my interview and my being told to report for duty. Obviously, I was aware at this stage of the processing that in order to work for CIA, a person's background had to be scrupulously examined since the work involved was highly sensitive, secret, and important. The delays had not been due to anything in my record or I would not be with him this morning, he wished to assure me. They were due to the cumbersome method of conducting the investigation involving a number of investigators in various places I had lived, the checking of my university and service records, etc. If it would become necessary for a large number of people to be hired quickly in wartime, a faster method would have to be found. And so, the Agency was trying to find out whether this checking could be done by means of one simple test. "The test you are going to take today, therefore, is just another contribution to our survey. It is purely voluntary but now that I have explained what we are after, would you like to help us by taking the test?"

As I have said, this speech seemed rehearsed but I wasn't too put off by this. I had encountered the same thing before from researchers I had cooperated with in anthropology and psychology departments. They all seemed to memorize their pitches to subjects of voluntary experiments. So I said yes.

62

Immediately he pulled a piece of paper out of a folder on his desk and offered me a pen. The paper was a statement saying I was taking the test voluntarily. I signed.

He then took an apparatus out of the desk drawer. He said that it was a polygraph and explained in detail how it functioned. The machine recorded on graph paper variations in blood pressure from the cuff he would attach to my arm, changes in breathing from a rubber tube that he would fasten around my chest, and variations in the moisture on the palms of my hands that electrodes secured to my palms by springs would reveal.

Next he said he would go over with me a series of questions and, if they were all clear to me, then he would connect the machine and we would go over the same questions, recording the results. I was to answer the questions "yes" or "no" only. If I wanted to discuss any of the questions for any reason, we would do so before the test, and he would modify any of them I had doubts about so that these would all be resolved before I took the test.

"As I said before," the examiner continued insisting, "this is an experiment in which you are participating voluntarily so you have nothing to be concerned about. The purpose of the test, if it is ever used in security processing, would be, of course, to see whether or not the subject is answering all questions truthfully. If he is not, then this machine will reveal that by the variations in his blood pressure, breathing, and the moisture on his palms."

We went over a short series of questions. Some were simple statements about my name, place and date of birth, etc., which, he explained, were asked to determine what my normal readings on the machine would be since presumably I would not be trying to be deceptive in answering them. He then asked if I had ever been a member of the Communist Party, if I ever knowingly associated with Communists, and if I had ever had a homosexual experience. These were the important questions. After we had gone over all of them, he connected the machine and asked them again.

"Good, good," he muttered as the circulation came back into my arm when he deflated the cuff. "Anything bothering you?"

"No."

"Well, let's try it once more."

We went through the test again, and, after we covered all the questions I was familiar with, he asked, "Do you consider yourself a competent Far Eastern scholar?" I was startled and I didn't know what to reply. What's competent? I took a deep breath and said, "Yes."

He released the cuff and smiled broadly. "I'm sorry I broke my word and asked you a question you weren't prepared for. I did it to see how much I could make you react, so I could cross-check the other results." He thanked me. He said I had been a good subject. Then he asked me not to mention having taken the test to anyone under any circumstances. He said nothing more specific about the results of the test and I felt I shouldn't ask.

When the last procedures of the processing were completed I was given a telephone extension to call and told to report on Friday morning at 8:30 at "L" Building and ask the guard to let me call that number.

The next day, when I made the call, a woman's voice said, "Someone will pick you up in a few minutes." She was right.

In a few minutes, I was happy to see John appearing down the hall.

"Welcome aboard," John said. "Kay's very anxious to see you. We thought you'd never get here. The whole hiring procedure is so ridiculously long and drawn out."

When we arrived at the office where I had been interviewed by John and Kay, everyone had smiles and cheerful greetings for the new boy in contrast to their stony detachment last March.

"Welcome aboard"—Kay extended her hand—"you've just joined the cold war arm of the U.S. government. Come on into my office for a chat with John and me and then I'll introduce you formally to everyone."

"I told Joe that we were sweating out the whole business with him," said John when we were settled in Kay's office. "It's almost as hard on us as it is on you, Joe. You were wondering when you would ever know if you had a job or not and we were wondering when we could expect you. We pestered Personnel as much as we could to speed things up, but they always go on their merry way. Then, of course, we've known you were here all week, but they wouldn't let us contact you until they were through with all their procedures. How did you like Building 13?"

I was glad that I didn't have to break my vow in order to have a chance to talk about this strange episode.

"Well, it certainly was an interesting experience. I don't know

64

why I was picked to volunteer. He didn't tell me. He also didn't tell me what the results were. I guess they were all right."

"They were all right, or you wouldn't be sitting here," John replied a bit grimly. "Did he really use that line about volunteering for a special experiment? That's terrible. A lie-detector test is standard procedure for all of us. I don't know why they think they must trick people into signing a statement that the test is voluntary."

I had lost my innocence. I would learn that the deception by the deception-tester was not an exception to the manner in which the Clandestine Services regularly dealt with their employees. In time I would come to realize that it was more nearly standard operating procedure. Telling an employee that his performance is not what is expected, or that he cannot get the promotion he wants, are difficult to do, and many persons in many organizations resort to a little fudging. In the same way I was tricked into signing a statement that I took the lie-detector test voluntarily, but changes in assignments, scheduling of duties, requests to perform overtime work were usually handled by telling the employee a cover story and not the truth. The tradecraft of the espionage profession, as I came to know it, was always more assiduously practiced inside the office than on the streets of foreign capitals.

Since John had been so frank with me, I thought I'd tell him and Kay about what happened to my Jeepster last March. They listened carefully to my story. I finished by saying that the incident had been bothering me ever since. After taking the personality assessment test and the lie-detector test I said, "Now I'm wondering about it more than ever. Was this some sort of test of how I was going to react? Or did the police do it? Putting a lightweight car on the sidewalk isn't too hard to do to get it out of the way of rush-hour traffic."

They exchanged glances. After a long moment's hesitation John said, "I think it was the police. They don't like to tow away cars of out-of-town tourists. Gee, I'm sorry we seemed so weird. We'll try now to tell you what kind of an outfit this is and what your job will be."

"First of all," said Kay, "let me explain what I meant by saying you've just joined the cold war arm of the U.S. government. We're not in the intelligence business in this office. We're an executive action arm of the White House that's trying to counter the Sino-Soviet bloc by using the same covert tactics they do, because the top level of government has decided that this is essential if the cold war isn't going to turn hot. The Communists have already shown in Korea that they are prepared to turn it into a hot war wherever they think there's a spot weak enough to try."

Kay went on to explain that in April, 1950, the National Security Council in a document known as NSC 68 had determined that the Soviets were bent on world domination and that the United States must develop all possible means of preventing this. She told me that I was joining what was known as the Office of Policy Coordination, OPC, which was a cover title that disguised the fact the real missions of the office were covert psychological warfare, covert political action, and covert paramilitary action—including sabotage, countersabotage, and support to anti-Communist guerrilla groups.

"Some people call us the 'dirty tricks' department, but that's too superficial a thing to say. What we are doing is carrying out the covert foreign policy of the United States government. Obviously, we can't let the Soviets or Chinese or anybody else know this is the case, but everything we do is authorized by the President's own National Security Council and, organizationally speaking, our chain of command is through the NSC directly to the President. We're put under CIA because CIA's intelligence collection and preparation activities afford the necessary amount of secrecy to protect our work. Defense and State are too loose security-wise and they're too open to public scrutiny to provide us the protection we need. In other words, we give the President the opportunity to carry out programs that he doesn't want his diplomats or his generals to talk about."

John produced a chart that showed me where OPC fitted into CIA. The CIA was divided into two parts, the chart revealed. One was under the command of an official known as the Deputy Director for Intelligence and consisted of an Office of National Intelligence Estimates, an Office of Current Intelligence, an Office of Strategic Intelligence, an Office of Economic Intelligence, and an Office of Basic and Geographical Research. Other special groups also belonged to DDI, such as the Foreign Broadcast Information Service, an Intelligence Requirements Service, and a Secretariat for the United States Intelligence Board. Kay and John dismissed the DDI rather quickly, pointing out that these were the overt func-

66

tions and overt employees of the Agency. They turned to the other major division, headed by the Deputy Director for Plans (DDP).

"You see," said John, "we are under the DDP, and you notice that his title, like OPC, is a cover. He's not in charge of plans. He directs all the covert operations of the CIA, the really secret part, the action part. DDP is divided into OPC and OSO—that's the Office of Special Operations. They're involved in espionage and counterespionage."

"We won't bother you with any more about OSO just now," Kay put in. "But all of us in DDP, as you recall from your processing, can't tell anybody we work for CIA. You must make up some story to tell people who ask you where you work."

I didn't bother to point out that no one had told me that when I was ordered to report for duty in the CIA on September 10. Jeanne and I had hurried down to Alexandria when I got the news. With the help of our friends there, we had leased the only apartment we could find, in a World War II duplex development, called Fairlington, and I had listed CIA as my place of employment.

The DDP, they continued, was Frank Wisner. He had replaced Allen Dulles in that job when General Bedell Smith became Director of Central Intelligence and Dulles had moved up to become Deputy Director. Wisner, like Dulles, had been a key officer in OSS during World War II.

The OPC and the OSO were each headed by an official with the title of Assistant Director of CIA. They were known as "Adpic" and "Adso" for short. "Adpic" was Colonel Johnson, son of the iconoclastic first director of the NRA in early New Deal days. Colonel Johnson had under his command a staff for paramilitary operations, staffs dealing with various aspects of psychological warfare, and the staffs of the area divisions: Western Europe, the Soviet Union, Eastern Europe, the Middle East and Africa, the Western Hemisphere, and the Far East. Each area division was organized along roughly the same pattern. Each division had a division chief's office with a Plans Staff, an Operations Staff, and an Administrative and Logistics Staff, and was broken down into branches that gave support to field stations in the various countries under the division's jurisdiction.

Kay and John told me that I was to be working in the Plans Staff of the division chief's office of the Far East Division. FE/Plans was

67

headed by a lieutenant colonel who had served in the China-Burma-India theater during the war. Kay was his deputy. She had been in G-2's Asian affairs office in the Pentagon. I soon discovered she was the only woman in as high a position in all of OPC and that she deserved this unique place in a man's world. Kay knew who all the key players were and how they played the game.

FE/Plans was responsible for seeing that a psychological warfare plan and a political warfare plan were drawn up for every country in the Far East so that Communist efforts to take over any Asian nation by subversion or guerilla warfare could be thwarted. Our office had two military men working on contingency planning for counterguerrilla action, support to resistance movements, and escape and evasion routes for downed airmen and other friendly elements caught behind enemy lines in case the cold war turned hot. Two senior officers were working on economic warfare planning—plans for developing effective boycotts, preemptive buying of key goods, and similar ways for unsettling the economies of any countries that might fall into Communist hands. The colonel paid all his attention to the paramilitary planners, and Kay supervised the psychological and political warfare activities and the economic warfare planning.

"I know you applied for a job as an intelligence analyst," said Kay, "but right now OPC has top priority for hiring people in CIA. NSC 68 is based on the assumption that the United States must act fast to build up all possible capabilities, and I've been told, although I haven't seen it, there's a national intelligence estimate that says Russia may be planning to launch World War III. Anyway, OPC can look at files on all applicants to CIA. We saw yours and thought that you were what we were looking for. What do you think of what we've told you so far?"

Thanks to their general briefing, I now knew considerably more than I had before, but it was difficult to answer Kay's question. I had burned my bridges and resigned my job at Dickinson to become an intelligence analyst for CIA. Now I knew my work was going to be far different. Before I could reply, Kay added, "Being an intelligence analyst is nowhere as interesting, I can assure you. I was one for four years. You impressed John and me as someone who liked challenging work. There is no more challenging work in the U.S. government today, believe me."

You're right, I thought. I suddenly remembered a conversation I had in June, 1950, with Dickinson's one Korean student. He was a kind of academic ward of mine. His English was rudimentary, and since I still knew some Japanese, he asked if he could take his history exams in that language. The college administration, proud of the claim to an international student constituency his presence gave, approved. We became good friends. He told me that he was not surprised at the outbreak of war because the Communists had been sabotaging crops, infiltrating political groups, and infiltrating the government bureaucracy. I told him I thought that two could play at the game, and that I hoped the United States and its friends would use the same tactics. I said this kind of secret warfare, nasty as it might be, was to be preferred to open armed conflict that could lead to nuclear disaster. I saw no reason why we couldn't win this far less dangerous alternative struggle, if we really tried.

I doubted we would try, however. I told him the government and the American people have a deep-seated aversion to being prepared or taking preventive action to deal with impending danger. Popeye is the person the American people prefer to be—never taking initiative toward enemies, always being surprised by them, nearly being overwhelmed by the foe before finally eating the spinach and getting up off the floor to beat the bullies.

It was wonderful to know now that I had been wrong. We were not waiting until we could barely get the spinach to our lips this time.

"I agree with you, Kay," I said, "this sounds like the most interesting job I can imagine. But specifically what will my work be?"

"As I told you, I concentrate on psychological warfare, political action, and economic warfare planning. I want you to be our psychological warfare specialist for Southeast Asia. John, here, is my assistant for north Asia, that is, Korea and Japan. He's just finished his PhD at Georgetown specializing in Japanese politics. I want you to be my assistant for Southeast Asia."

"When you said challenging, Kay, you really meant it. I'm afraid I don't know anything about Southeast Asia or psychological warfare."

"Don't worry. We picked you because we thought you had potential. There are no experts on any country in Southeast Asia in this division, except maybe the Philippines and Burma," Kay reassured me. "We have more material here on the area than any university library, and I'm sure you will be able to read into the situation quickly.

"As far as psychological warfare is concerned, it's a brand-new field. We are all learning. You remember, it was one of Hitler's strongest weapons. The Communists depend on it a lot too. We figure that if we analyze what they're doing and study the countries in our area closely, we can beat them at their own game.

"Oh yes, another thing," she added. "We won't be able to spare you for any clandestine tradecraft training. That would take another three months. We need you now. You'll have to learn the business on the job, I'm afraid.

"Well," she added as an afterthought, "we will be able to help you on psychwar. Paul Linebarger, our consultant, is one of the few real experts and he gives evening seminars for us. We'll try to get you into one of them after you've settled in."

My job, she told me, would consist of two parts—helping to draw up the political and psychological plans for each of the six Southeast Asian countries, and assisting the officers of each country desk in preparing suggestions for propaganda themes and psychwar campaigns for their field stations. FE-3/OPC was the branch responsible for Southeast Asia. It handled Indochina, Thailand, Malaya and Singapore, Burma, Indonesia, and the Philippines. I had to learn all I could about the situations in each country, and I had to get to know the key officers I would be working with. All my effort at mastering my unfamiliar subjects would have to take place in the office, Kay warned. I was not to let anyone, even my wife, know the nature of my assignment. I couldn't even give a hint by reading books on Southeast Asia at home.

When I got home that Friday night, Jeanne was anxious to hear the news. She knew that I had been growing increasingly impatient with the endless processing and not knowing what it was that I was being processed for. I had told her when I left for work that morning that at last I was going to find out what my job was.

"How is the new job?" she asked.

"Oh, it's very interesting, very challenging," I answered, more weakly than my words implied.

"Well, what do you mean? What is your new job?"

"I can't tell you, I'm sorry," I replied. "But it really is interesting."

"It certainly sounds like it."

70

5
Instant Southeast Asian Psychwar Expert

I was glad that I couldn't tell Jeanne what I was doing. I didn't want her to know I had uprooted us to be a specialist in a field I knew nothing about. Five years in academe had made me sensitive about specialists' pedigrees. I was reassured, however, that my new employers found me qualified for the job, and I enjoyed the newness and strangeness of everything about it—the myriad security measures, the people, and the need to become an instant Southeast Asian psychwar expert.

It took some time to get used to wearing a badge with my picture on it on a chain around my neck and to having my working habits dominated by a three-way combination safe. Everything had to be locked securely in the safe at night, even typewriter ribbons, and three different people in turn checked the offices and safes each evening to see that all was secure. Those guilty of violating these security rules were punished by receiving an extra week's security check duty. It was rumored that three violations meant dismissal.

I thought the security practices that controlled my life were often odd and sometimes even funny. For example, in addition to the high fences and guards at the entries that protected the physical security of the buildings by the Reflecting Pool, the security was further enhanced, I was told, by their not bearing any signs that showed they were CIA offices. No one seemed concerned that they were the only office buildings in Washington that were not identified.

Personal security measures were as contradictory as the physical security precautions. Employees were instructed never to reveal the fact that they worked for the Clandestine Services nor even admit they worked for CIA. Yet no one bothered to give new employees a cover story. Where a new member of the Clandestine Services told his neighbors he worked was left to the ingenuity of the employee. In the essential matter of a credit reference for landlords and opening bank and shopping accounts, every employee was given the same name to use—Viola Pitts, 2430 "E" Street, N.W.

Although we were warned never to let anyone see our passes, which gained us admission in the mornings, until we were safely inside, no one seemed concerned about the security problem the parking situation caused. Every day a parade of people tramped from their cars to the buildings. The line of march was so conspicuous that no other identification was needed to indicate whose employees we all were. Any Soviet spies so inclined could savor the sight of hundreds of people trekking down Ohio Drive every weekday morning to the unidentified buildings by the Reflecting Pool.

Office hours in "L" and "K" buildings began at eight-thirty, but the parking problem made it necessary for most people to begin arriving in the area long before that time. The early arrivals congregated in the cafeteria for coffee. I was always in that number.

On these mornings I had a chance to take a good look at my colleagues. The change from the Dickinson faculty could not have been more marked. The majority here were young. The exceptions were men about ten years older than the rest, who always entered the cafeteria wearing hats. Hats had disappeared from the dress of younger men. Not only did these older men wear hats, but they nearly all wore them the same way, tucked low over their brows.

I couldn't help commenting on the hat wearers to my new friend John. He explained, "You'll find out all about it when you get to Clandestine Services training, but since this may take a while, I

72

won't keep you in suspense. First of all, these guys are either former FBI men or former officers in the Army Counter Intelligence Corps. They were taught that it is essential for a secret agent to wear a hat."

"How's that again?"

"You gotta wear a hat. It's the best way to be anonymous," John replied.

According to the FBI training manual, John said, a hat makes it difficult for an onlooker, a passer-by, and, most important of all, the secret agent's enemies, to identify the person wearing it. Ergo, wear a hat and be difficult to spot.

Since the FBI had acquired a reputation for high professional competence, thanks to the unfailing talent of J. Edgar Hoover for public relations, the Bureau's methods were taken as the best possible model for the Army Counter Intelligence Corps to follow, and in these early days, the Clandestine Services trainers in CIA followed suit. The power of a prevailing myth is so great that it took ten years for the Clandestine Services to realize that the quiet man on the corner in the hat was the most conspicuous person on the block, not the least.

In addition to my Nisei friend, John, there were other Asians who, of course, stood out from the crowd, the only nonwhites. Black officers did not appear until a decade later when Africa became a target of attention and someone thought they might fit in over there. In the fifties, blacks worked on the night office cleaning crew, and some drove the CIA buses that shuttled employees around to other agency buildings.

There were several other tables whose occupants were distinct. They wore suits with trousers that were belled from top to bottom and jackets that never covered the seats of their pants, looking as if they were tailored to a packing box rather than a man's torso. They haunted me at first, until I realized where I had seen people like this before—in the newspaper photos of the men reviewing the May Day parade in Moscow from on top of Lenin's tomb. These people in the cafeteria, I learned, were our specialists in Soviet and Eastern European affairs.

One difference between employees was not as readily discernible as racial origins or clothes, but anyone who worked in these offices recognized it. It also helped determine who drank coffee with whom. Some people belonged to the Office of Special Operations, known as OSO, and others belonged to the Office of Policy Coordination, known as OPC. These two offices divided the work of the Clandestine Services between them, but shared as little else as possible. In the Far East Division, where I went to work in September, 1951, OPC and OSO personnel, though located on opposite sides of the hall, did not cross each other's thresholds.

OSO had been established shortly after the Central Intelligence Agency was organized in 1947. Its tasks were counterintelligence— to protect the United States, its installations and organizations from Communist and other hostile penetrations; and foreign intelligence operations—to collect information on Communist activities and other intelligence requirements determined by higher authority.

OPC was born of the worsening world situation. Its first recruits began organizing the office in early 1949. OPC's missions were so secret that they were deliberately hidden behind the misleading title Office of Policy Coordination.

In the fall of 1951, it was rumored that OSO and OPC were going to merge. The stories had it that all OSO personnel were to be fired or that all OPC personnel were to meet that fate, depending on which group was doing the talking. "Adso" and "Adpic" were reported to be making a world tour to decide just how the assets of the two outfits could best be merged in the field. All sorts of stories about the trip were circulating. The best one was that Colonel Johnson, "Adpic," had insisted all personnel, including secret Japanese agents, be lined up for inspection at the Air Force base at Atzugi, Japan, our field station's headquarters, when he alighted from the aircraft.

Kay told me to ignore the talk and concentrate on absorbing all the information available about the six Southeast Asian countries I was to be working on and getting to know all the people involved.

All of Southeast Asia, I soon learned, had been lumped together in the minds of Western geopolitical thinkers for their own convenience. Each country had a distinct history and a distinct culture. In 1951 each also had more than a rice bowl full of distinct problems.

In Indochina the outstanding Communist anti-Japanese resistance leader during World War II—the former Anamese mess boy in the French merchant marine who called himself "Enlightened Persistence," Ho Chi Minh—had been fighting the return of the French since 1946. How enlightened and persistent this man was to prove to be no one in FE/OPC imagined in 1951, but when I began reading into the situation, even the legendary Foreign Legion was bogged down by Ho's Viet Minh guerrillas.

Next door in Thailand, whose pliant people had instantly become loyal subjects of Japan in 1942, the picture looked brighter. "If you can't beat 'em, join 'em" is not an old Siamese saying, but the Thais in 1951 were offering fullest cooperation to us in fighting Communist expansion in Southeast Asia. FE/OPC had established a large unit under the loose cover of a civilian reconstruction organization called the SEA Supply Company. As I began to read into operations, I found SEA Supply engaged in trying to set up an invasion of Communist China in cooperation with our station on Taiwan and Chinat army remants in Burma.

In Malaya, the British were fighting a Communist guerrilla group whose leadership, as in the case of Indochina, had gained its expertise by harassing the Japanese occupation army.

The newly independent nation of Burma was led by a mystical scholar, U Nu, who claimed to be developing a socialist democracy, but no one, including U Nu himself, seemed able to explain exactly what this meant.

Offshore, Sukarno and Mohammad Hatta, Indonesia's leading nationalists, had proclaimed the islands' independence on August 17, 1945, just three days after Japan agreed to accept unconditional surrender. For the next four years periods of negotiation were interspersed with periods of fighting with the Dutch. The most interesting thing about the Indonesian struggle for independence, I thought, was that the United States consistently through these years insisted on the negotiation of a settlement that would satisfy the Indonesians. By 1951, the Indonesians seemed to have forgotten this completely.

In the other island republic in the area, the Philippines, the United States also played the role of anti-colonialist. We had granted independence before World War II to go into effect at the war's end. But this new nation, too, was plagued with problems. First of all, the fighting in the final days of the war had taken a terrible toll. The Japanese appeared to want to leave nothing behind when they departed and, thus, to the usual destruction caused by heavy fighting was added deliberate devastation. The city of Manila was left a shell. In addition, the Filipinos shared with the other newly formed governments of the area all the many difficulties of administering affairs for themselves for the first time. None of the governments of the six countries was very good at these tasks.

Their difficulties were succinctly summed up by a British businessman I happened to land in Rangoon Airport with one night in 1955. When it seemed that none of us would ever clear immigration and customs in a normal lifetime, he declared, "The chaps who are running these countries these days used to be the messenger boys. They knew the offices to take the papers to, but they didn't know what anyone did with them."

The common fate all these governments shared which concerned us most was that they were all experiencing guerrilla warfare challenges, all of Communist inspiration, according to the files I read.

In February, 1948, the Soviet Union sponsored a meeting in Calcutta of all Asian Communist parties plus the Communist Party of Australia. The meeting was publicized in Communist media. CIA had intelligence reports on it as well. The meeting resolved that "anti-Imperialist forces unite to oppose oppression of Imperialism and reactionaries within each country." All the trouble that followed in Burma, Malaya, the Philippines, and Indonesia stemmed from this conference, according to these reports. Ho Chi Minh had already been at work for two years in Indochina. Between March and September, 1948, guerrilla wars or Communist coup attempts developed in all the other countries. In sum, the panorama presented by these six small countries I had been assigned to deal with was not promising. The metaphor of indigent infants with terribly high mortality risks seemed to fit them all. And, like such infants, they were not receiving the best of care and attention.

I found out as I got to know what the FE Division was doing that I was stuck with the stepchildren. FE/3, the Southeast Asia branch, didn't get the attention from the division chief and his deputy that they lavished on Branch 1, Japan and Korea, or Branch 2, China. Manpower and time were concentrated on these areas. They were where the big operations were. Of course, these countries were where the great drama of war and revolution was being enacted, and the leaders of the division were determined to make an impact on Korea and China.

The chief of FE/OPC was Colonel Richard Stillwell, rumored to be the youngest full colonel in the U.S. Army, whose talent for organizing and commanding unceasingly loyal effort was transcendent. His deputy was scarcely less impressive. Desmond Fitzgerald, a man of classically handsome Celtic features, was as driving and driven as Stillwell. Des would one day become Deputy Director of Plans.

In Korea the big task was to get counterguerrilla operations going. We were trying to put hundreds of paramilitary personnel behind enemy lines in North Korea. The range of activities under way with the Chinese Nationalists on Taiwan was rather spectacular, I thought, considering the Chinats had set up shop on the island only in the closing months of 1949.

Having listened to the critics of the Truman administration hammer ceaselessly on the theme that Truman had abandoned Chiang Kai-shek, it was a major revelation to me to learn that this was far from the truth. Perhaps, more than anything else, our large-scale efforts with the Chinats shaped my appreciation for what I was learning a covert adjunct of foreign policy was evidently meant to be. President Truman silently took all the criticism of his overt policy, which indeed did appear to be rather lukewarm toward Chiang, particularly before the Chinese Communists entered the Korean War, and never mentioned that he had authorized massive support to the Chinat plan to retake mainland China. If the Chinats were successful, he undoubtedly planned to look very surprised. Of all the acts of this gutsy little President, I have always remembered that never once did he blurt out his secret, no matter what his tormentors said or how seriously he and his party got into trouble.

FE/OPC had more than six hundred persons on Taiwan providing guerrilla training, logistical support, overflight capabilities, facilities for propaganda coverage of the mainland by radio and leaflet balloon, and doing other tasks. They were covered by a fictitious commercial company called Western Enterprises. Western Enterprises and its sister cover facility, SEA Supply Company in Thailand, were cooperating in support of the Chinat General Li Mi and his audacious scheme to invade Yunnan Province from Burma.

The Li Mi adventure nearly wrecked relations with Burma completely and continued to be an issue between our two countries until January, 1961, when the Chinat troops were finally driven out. The Li Mi operation was a pet project of Des Fitzgerald. Li Mi was a Chinat intelligence officer who commanded twelve thousand troops who had escaped from the Yunnan army in the last days of the Chinese civil war and camped themselves in northern Burma. Liaison with Li Mi was linked up in Thailand, where the police chief, General Pao, was very cooperative with the SEA Supply Company. Pao also had a personal interest in the opium trade in the area of northeastern Burma where the Chinese troops controlled the countryside. Somehow, the invasion of China never seemed to come off, but Li Mi's troops would not give up their Burmese poppy fields.

Despite the heavy concentration on the Korean War's ancillary guerrilla support effort and the help given Chiang Kai-shek to realize his dream of returning to the mainland, the little countries of Southeast Asia were not neglected. Kay was right, however, when she said no one was an area expert. The branch was headed by a tough regular Army colonel who was a veteran of the death march on Bataan. This was as close as any of the officers came to personal area experience. What they and I lacked in the way of such knowledge we all tried to make up by studying the situations and trying to use the social science backgrounds we had on the data we were learning. This kind of background we had in abundance, all of us having degrees, including advanced ones, in the social sciences.

OPC stations had been established in each of the countries. The station chiefs were, in most cases, men with OSS backgrounds. Thailand was the biggest station and, as already noted, deeply involved in what was known as "third country" paramilitary and psychological warfare operations against the Chinese Communists. The other stations were only one- or two-man affairs.

What I was supposed to do was to help the desk officers of each country develop useful propaganda themes and new ideas for operations for the six stations. Every day I poured over the Foreign Broadcast Information Service résumés of Communist programs beamed to Southeast Asia to learn what the enemy was saying and tried to think of how to refute them. I read stacks of intelligence reports and country studies to discover the psychological vulnerabilities of the people. I attempted to discover what character traits they had which would make them scorn Communist appeals. I had so much to do at once I had a difficult time deciding what my priorities should be. When I found that an old college friend of mine had been in CIA since its beginning, I was sure he was the person to help me. I looked him up and asked him to have lunch.

Bob Komer, I discovered, when we got together, was a member

of the National Estimates Staff. This was the brain trust of the Deputy Director for Intelligence. Their job was to write estimates for the President of the probable course of development of the most critical issues, areas, or topics he was interested in. They functioned by gathering opinions from the State Department, the three armed services, and Defense Department experts, but the final product, in all but very special cases, was theirs. The estimates were meant to be enlightened and objective summaries that would help the President choose the country's course of action.

I thought this kind of a job just right for Bob, who had concentrated in European history with emphasis on military affairs, and who never failed to give us his own incisive interpretations of every move Hitler made while we sat around Cambridge waiting for our draft boards to involve us more directly in the war. It might be said that Bob was a born estimater of situations. I said I hoped he could give me a good estimate of my present one, after explaining what my job was.

"Joe, you must become an expert on one country," Bob told me. "The big trouble around here is that there is simply not enough solid, genuine expertise. Once you've established a reputation as such an expert, you'll be on your way to the top. All sorts of people will find you indispensable. Now, did you say you're working on Southeast Asia?"

"Yes."

"Well, then, pick Indochina. There's no one in the U.S. government who is a real expert on Indochina, and it will soon be terribly important that there be one."

I valued Bob's advice, and I tried to put it to practice. I began to spend all my spare time studying the background of the Vietnamese as well as keeping up with the unfolding events there and paying particular attention to the extensive monitoring reports of the Viet Minh radio broadcasts that we received daily.

Every day I spent more time visiting Southeast Asian country desk officers than I did at my own desk. During the year 1952 I began to spend the most time with my colleagues handling Indochina. We became very good friends and exchanged a lot of ideas. I also found out more about the activities of the man we had in Saigon and the man we had in Hanoi than I did about those in any other country. They were both untiring workers who had developed good contacts with some Catholic priests and lay leaders since some of them controlled small newspapers and other press outlets. Because I was spending so much time absorbing Viet Minh propaganda broadcasts, I was soon sending Saigon a series of items I wrote to counter the Communists' victory claims, ridicule their land-reform programs, and show their arbitrary use of power in organizing the workers under their control. Sometimes I wrote what I thought were catchy slogans. Other times I made up what appeared to be news items.

Because I had become convinced of the importance of the eclectic religiosity of the Viets, which enabled many of them to worship their ancestors, Buddha, and the Virgin Mary, in limited numbers, at the same time, I put together some examples demonstrating that Communism didn't tolerate such variations from orthodoxy. I was particularly fascinated by the Cao Dai and the Hoa Hao, the two twentieth-century versions of Vietnamese eclectic religions. Hoa Hao were Buddhist reformists. Cao Dai had grown out of spiritualism. According to its doctrine, Li Tai Pe, a Chinese scholar of the Tang dynasty who had reestablished Chinese literature after a book burning, was said to have reappeared as a messenger from the Lord of the Universe to found a new universal religion. The Lord of the Universe now wished to be known as Cao Dai and the religion was to bear his name.

I wrote some material I thought should stimulate local pride in Vietnam's being the seat of the center of a new universal faith. I inserted a large number of insinuations about the Viet Minh's subservience to a foreign materialist faith that pretended to a false universality. When I took this to my friends on the Indochina desk they told me their officers in the field would not be able to use it. The reasons they gave me I have always thought were a clue to the miserable failure the United States made of all its efforts in Vietnam.

The material was unsuitable, I was told, because our agents and all their contacts were Catholics and considered the Cao Dai an irresponsible rival to the true faith. Hence, they wouldn't talk to the Cao Dai. They also couldn't talk to the Cao Dai since neither of our people spoke Vietnamese, only French. Catholic converts in Vietnam spoke French because they had been converted by priests who were natives of that hated colonial power.

I pointed out to my friends that the French-speaking Catholic minority in Vietnam represented only some million and a half persons out of a total population of twenty million. They acknowledged this was the generally accepted statistic.

"Well, maybe we need to add to the staff out there a couple of officers who are not Catholics and who are trained to speak Vietnamese," I said. "If you wanted to do convincing psychological warfare in Italy and all you had to work with were a couple of Buddhists, don't you think it would be wise to try to find some additional personnel?"

My friends agreed I had a point.

In addition to helping the country desks of each Southeast Asian nation for which Branch 3 was responsible, I also helped prepare the so-called country plan. The planning function of our section, FE/Plans, was, in fact, something that intrigued me very much. Most interesting was the idea that we could sit in Washington and plan in advance the future development of these societies struggling to take shape in Asia, and that we were not neglecting any contingency. One important contingency to consider in case a situation worsened rapidly and a take-over by the Communist guerrilla armies appeared imminent was the operational effectiveness of assassination of the leaders of these groups.

For example, in Indochina, would the Viet Minh fall apart if Ho Chi Minh were assassinated? He appeared to be the soul of the movement. The evidence indicated that he was the one man nearly all Vietnamese respected and his efforts had provided the decisive cohesion that held the Communist cause together. If he were removed, wouldn't this one death perhaps save the lives of many?

This was the key point on which discussions of assassination turned, the same kind of reasoning that led to the dropping of the first atomic bomb. An assassination meant the death of one person. If the situation is one of armed combat, killing is an accepted activity. Maximum accomplishment via minimum violence became a prime consideration.

Thus, assassination was always a contingency action to be included in the plans, though approval would have to come from the National Security Council before any assassination was attempted. Another practical problem was where to find the assassins. The reading of case studies of the successful assassinations by Soviet secret service counterparts, such as the killing of Trotsky, wasn't much help because the Soviet service exercised a control over its agents we could not impose, certainly not on Asians. That left only criminals and cranks to be considered for recruitment to perform this service.

Looking back from my office in "L" Building on the events that had happened in the world since 1946, when I had been discharged from the Army expecting to find a brave new world, it seemed to me that my new job was terribly interesting and important. I found myself giving very little thought to a number of questions about what I was doing that I once would have expected any of my bright students to ask.

Around FE Division we heard much about the importance of the area as a whole in support of the thesis that its fall to Communist control would be a grave matter. It was thought that Communist control of the area would block the sea lanes between the Indian Ocean and the South China Sea and prevent what had for centuries been normal commercial routes between Europe and Asia. The area produced 90 percent of the world's natural rubber and 60 percent of the tin. Malaya was supplying the new Japan, since the end of World War II, with all the iron Japan needed to rebuild its steel industry. Oil, wood, and fibers were abundant and important products and, finally, the region was the rice bowl of Asia, capable of helping the giants India and China sustain their overpopulated countries.

This area-wide approach to the question of Southeast Asia's importance was reinforced by the longer historical record and the more immediate past. Historically, every great Chinese dynasty that developed sufficient military capabilities took a turn at trying to conquer mainland Southeast Asia. Most had succeeded to greater or lesser degrees. The number one goal of Japan's pro-war party of the 1930s had been the conquest of Southeast Asia. The area was considered the cornerstone of the foundation of a new era to be known as Japan's "Asian Co-prosperity Sphere." Taking these past trends into consideration made it seem inevitable that the newly emerged power in Asia, Red China, having proved its military prowess in Korea, would want to make history repeat itself.

No one lingered long over asking what a particular country meant to our strategic interests, however. This kind of question was assumed to have been answered by looking at the big picture one more time.

On January 12, 1950, Dean Acheson announced our defensive perimeter in the Pacific and all of mainland Asia was excluded from it. Acheson said, "This defensive perimeter runs along the Aleutians to Japan and then goes to the Ryukyus. . . . (It) runs from the Ryukyus to the Philippine Islands."* Six months later we were beyond that perimeter fighting in Korea. By the end of the decade we would have assumed responsibility for the fate of Vietnam and pledged ourselves by treaty to defend the rest of the area if required.

It was considered by critics of the Truman administration, and popularly believed by many, that Acheson's announcement invited the challenge in Korea. This was a rather persuasive point. American troops had been withdrawn from Korea. If there was any truth at all to the fundamental premise of the cold war that the Soviets were bent on expansion, they naturally would try to see if we meant what we said about the outer limits of our military commitment in Asia. Whatever the merits of this case, it had considerable bearing on other questions I ignored.

I did not ask myself why the United States needed a covert as well as an overt foreign policy. It did not bother me that we had an overt "hands off" policy on the Chinese Communist–Chinese Nationalist confrontation and a covert policy of helping Chiang Kaishek get back on the mainland. Why we rejected the overt proposal of General MacArthur to cross the Yalu River in hot pursuit of Chinese Communist troops, while we spent vast sums to infiltrate guerrillas into the territory held by the North Koreans and their Chinese allies, I never asked.

If I asked myself these questions now I would be inclined to answer that Truman's covert China policy was intended to pick up the pieces of the mistake he thought he had made in handling the Chinese civil war. In light of the political grief his failure to give all-out aid to Chiang had caused him, I believe Truman had second thoughts.

His Korean policy reveals another facet of the usefulness of covert operations. By not sending troops across the Yalu River, yet covertly infiltrating guerrillas into North Korean territory, Truman was trying to do what his Missouri neighbors would have called having your cake and eating it too.

I might also have asked myself whether we were not becoming

*Dean Acheson, *Present at the Creation* (New York: W. W. Norton, 1969), p. 357.

involved in every country in Southeast Asia in case Chiang did not make it back to the mainland. Having a two-sided foreign policy meant that responsibility for the four cardinal points of diplomacy was split between the State Department and CIA. The State Department took care of the first two points while we took care of three and four. State emphasized the positive and expanded on the obvious while we tried to stay in with the outs and not get caught between dog and lamppost.

Somehow, such questioning just did not seem to fit in with the way of life that was being lived in the temporary buildings beside the Reflecting Pool.

6

At the Foot of the Master

As the Christmas season approached that first year, attention around the Clandestine Services office began to center more on the impending merger of OSO and OPC and less on the fate of Asia. The merger was evidently a serious decision. The closed doors across the halls from one another that sheltered OSO and OPC personnel from mutual contact began to be opened cautiously. People actually introduced themselves to one another.

These cautious self-introductory sessions in the Far East Division had several purposes. On one level, they indicated a healthy curiosity about the people who were soon to be colleagues. On another, they represented a calculated sizing up of a person to estimate the chances he might replace you rather than your replacing him if the merger really turned out to mean the outfit would shrink. The ostensible reason, however, was to discuss the joint Christmas party being planned for December 24.

The party was not only supposed to mark the beginnings of the merger, it was going to celebrate another equally momentous event. The last two temporary buildings along the Reflecting Pool, in addition to "L" and "K," were going to disgorge their Veterans Administration personnel. The buildings were going to become the property of the Clandestine Services. Everyone took this as a good sign. Obviously, whatever happened, the Clandestine Services were not going to get any smaller. The merger might mean changes but we wouldn't be adding two new buildings if it meant that anyone was really going to lose his job.

The heralded Christmas party turned out to be not much of an event. I thought one incident was significant. Dick Stillwell turned up in a Confederate forage cap and gave a couple of rebel yells. Lloyd George, OSO division chief, knocked Dick's hat off. All this took place in a friendly boozy way, but I thought I saw who was going to be the chief of the newly merged division.

Except for the personal merger arrangements some officers made with some secretaries at the Christmas party, there were no further developments in the merger of OSO and OPC for nearly a year. Throughout 1952 the process of consolidation gradually went on until at last intelligence collection was married to covert action. In time both functions came to be performed by the same people. It was a momentous move. The new style of operating may not have led straight to the Bay of Pigs, but it helped speed us on our way. Some of the same Cuban agents who helped in the landing also gave us the information that the Cuban people would rise up against Castro immediately when our battalion hit the beach.

All this was far in the future and far less important to me in the early winter of 1952 than the fact that I got the chance to attend Paul Linebarger's seminar in psychological warfare. Linebarger had served as an Army psychological warfare officer in Chungking during the war. He had written a textbook on the subject in 1948. In 1951 he was serving as the Far East Division's chief consultant. He also served the Defense Department in the same capacity, giving advice on U.S. psychwar operations in Korea, and he was professor of Asian politics at the School for Advanced International Studies of the Johns Hopkins University. His book by this time had gone through three American editions, two Argentine editions, and a Japanese edition.

He was far from a textbook warrior, however. He best described himself when he wrote in the introduction to his book, "Psychological warfare involves exciting wit-sharpening work. It tends to attract quick-minded people—men full of ideas." His wits scarcely needed sharpening, and he was never at a loss for an idea.

The seminars were held for eight weeks, every Friday night at his home. Going to Paul Linebarger's house on Friday evenings was not only an educational experience for those who attended the seminar, it was also an exercise in clandestinity. Learning covert operational conduct was considered part of the course. Each seminar was limited to no more than eight students. They were told to pose as students from the School of Advanced International Studies, to go to Paul's via different routes, and to say they were attending a seminar in Asian politics. Senator McCarthy had alerted everyone to the possibility that Communist operators might be expected to turn up at almost any place in Washington. The School of Advanced International Studies had its campus in Washington, but over in Baltimore at the main campus of the Johns Hopkins University, Owen Lattimore, the expert on Asian geography, held sway. McCarthy had called Lattimore the principal agent of Communist China in the United States. Although no one called Paul Linebarger the principal agent of Chiang Kai-shek, his father had been Sun Yat Sen's legal adviser and Paul never hid his full devotion to the Chinat cause. The feeling of the clash of mysterious powers was abroad in the cold winter nights in northwest Washington around Paul's house. It could just be possible that some Communist surveillant might follow one of the students up Rock Creek Park to 29th Street. They might even be operating from the Shoreham hotel, a few blocks away. We had been thoroughly indoctrinated in the fear of Communist subversion. *The Front Is Everywhere,* by Lt. Colonel William R. Kintner, a star in the senior staff of OPC who in 1973 would be Nixon's ambassador to Thailand, was a book we were all expected to read. Kintner taught us not only that Communist conspirators were all around us but that "Stalin's book *Leninism* is the equivalent of Hitler's *Mein Kampf.*"*

It would be difficult to say whether it was the political atmosphere in general, the office routine of the day just closed, or the drawn drapes in Linebarger's living room, but students at the seminar met in an appropriately conspiratorial mood that raised the level of their appreciation of their subject.

The mood was fitting if not essential to an understanding of the material. The first point that Linebarger made was that the purpose of all psychological warfare is the manipulation of people so

*William R. Kintner, *The Front Is Everywhere* (Norman, Okla.: University of Oklahoma Press, 1950), p. 8.

that they are not able to detect they are being manipulated. Wartime psychwar had been a matter of undermining the enemy civilian and military will to continue to fight. The audience, in brief, was very clearly defined. Determining just who it was they wanted to manipulate and for what ends was also pretty clear to the OPC personnel. Their targets were the Communists and their allies. Having this firmly in mind, any methods of manipulation could be used, especially "black propaganda."

Black propaganda operations, by definition, are operations in which the source of the propaganda is disguised or misrepresented in one way or another so as not to be attributable to the people who really put it out. This distinguishes black from white propaganda, such as news bulletins and similar statements issued by one side in a conflict extolling its successes, of course, or other material just as clearly designed to serve the purposes of its identifiable authors.

During World War II black propaganda operators had a field day. German black operations against the French consisted of such enterprises as sending French soldiers letters from their hometowns telling them their wives were committing adultery, or were infected with venereal diseases, giving away mourning dresses to women who would wear them on the streets of Paris, or intercepting telephone communications in the field and giving confusing or contradictory orders.

Paul Linebarger's was a seminar in black propaganda only. One reason for this was that the United States already had an overt propaganda agency as part of the cold war apparatus. In those days this was run directly by the State Department, but in 1953 it would become formalized into the United States Information Agency and become the independent government agency responsible for worldwide United States propaganda operations. Furthermore, the view of the state of affairs in the world that was the fundamental assumption of all OPC activities was that the United States was faced everywhere with an enemy that was using an untold array of black psychwar operations to undermine the nations of the world in order to present us with a fait accompli one fine morning when we would wake up to find all these countries under Communist control. Hence, it was vital to understand all about such operations from a defensive standpoint if nothing else. There was, however, something else. This was an attitude produced by the mixture of the ancient wisdom that a good offense is the best defense, and the spirit of the times that made the existence of conspiracy seem so real. It was good to feel that we were learning how to beat the Communists at their own game.

Paul Linebarger loved black propaganda operations probably because they involved the wit-sharpening he liked to talk about. Also, he was so good at them that his was one of the inventive minds that refined the entire black operations field into shades of blackness. Linebarger and his disciples decided that propaganda that was merely not attributed to the United States was not really black, only gray. To be called black it had to be something more. Furthermore, they divided gray propaganda into shades of gray. So-called light gray was defined as propaganda that was not attributed to the United States government, but instead, for example, to a group that was known to be friendly to the United States, or that might be thought to be a friendly source. Medium gray or "gray gray" was the term Linebarger used for propaganda that was attributed to a neutral source or, in any case, to one that was not suspected to be about to say anything friendly concerning the United States or its national or international policies. Dark gray was the term for propaganda attributed to a source usually hostile to the United States. This left the term black propaganda for a very special kind of propaganda activity. Black propaganda operations were operations done to look like, and carefully labeled to be, acts of the Communist enemy.

Not only was the attribution given the source of the propaganda activity used as a criterion for defining what kind of propaganda it was, but equally important was the kind of message used. Gray activity involved statements or actions that supported U.S. policies. Black propaganda operations, being attributed to the enemy, naturally did not. In fact, black propaganda, to be believable, supported the enemy's positions and openly opposed those of the United States.

Gray propaganda was considered to be useful because it added strength to our side by putting praise of the United States or, at least, a reasonably stated understanding of U.S. positions, in the mouths of those whom the world at large would not identify as U.S. spokesmen giving out the official line. In one sense, gray propaganda is a close cousin of the endorsement in a commercial advertising campaign. Where the Clandestine Services came in was in the role of sponsor—but a sponsor that was not supposed to be known to anyone who heard or read the endorsement of the U.S. government's policy product.

Although the term "credibility gap" had not been invented, it was a key problem with which gray propaganda was designed to deal. We used to play around in the seminar, for example, with ways in which we could manufacture statements denouncing the Chinese brainwashing of U.S. prisoners in Korea and attribute them to leaders of the Congress Party of India. India's neutrality and lofty humaneness would add great weight to the U.S. complaint about brainwashing among all the countries of the world who were inclined to think we were complaining merely out of a sense of frustration since we had decided it was too risky to drop an atom bomb on China. If disinterested India didn't like brainwashing, it must be bad.

Mostly, however, we followed our mentor through a series of actions that were to be attributed to various of our Communist enemies—either the Soviets, the Chinese, the followers of Ho Chi Minh, or one of the other Communist parties and groups at work in Asia. The reasoning was that we would strike the most effective blows if we could do or say things that would divide these groups among themselves or alienate the general population from them in the countries concerned. In the first type of action the objective was obvious—weaken the Communists' ability to achieve further success because they would have to devote their time to straightening out their own affairs and have no time to meddle in the affairs of others. In the second instance, the idea was that it would be more effective to do or say something that was considered wrong or even abhorrent, by the peoples of the countries we were addressing, and do it in the name of the local Communist Party than to spend our time saying that the Communist Party did evil things. Saying that the Communists were evil was merely talk. Doing something evil, disguised as Communists, would have real credibility.

Linebarger was always careful to point out that to have any chance of success, these black operations must be based on good solid information about how the Communist Party we proposed to imitate actually conducted its business. He also stressed we needed an equally solid basis of knowledge about the target audience and what it would really find offensive and objectionable if the Communists were to say or do it. This, he liked to emphasize, was why such operations belonged in an intelligence organization where suffi-

90

cient expertise and specific knowledge of the kind required was most likely to be found. Intelligence information, especially the kind that is clandestinely collected, should serve more than as bits and pieces of the jigsaw puzzle known as enemy intentions. It should be used directly against the enemy while it is fresh. Otherwise, the distinction between intelligence reporting and historical writing tends to blur.

In order to copy the Communists, in other words, we had to know what they were saying, how they were saying it, and in what media. If we were to disrupt them, we had to have some idea in a fairly precise way of the kinds of issues they were concerned about. The most effective and credible thing we could do was to forge their messages.

If we simply said, in a newspaper story or column that William Pomeroy, a renegade American leader among the Communist Huks in the Philippines, was planning to massacre all the women and children in the next village that the Huks attacked, it would anger the Filipinos who were anti-Huk, alarm a lot of people who were fence-sitters, but be denounced as just another piece of anti-Huk propaganda by sophisticates who were tired of the fighting. If we produced a copy of an order to massacre and mailed it to the Manila Times, ostensibly from a disillusioned Huk, we would gain a lot more credibility. The editor of the paper could take the message to the authorities, presumably, but they would be convinced of its authenticity if the job was well done, and the paper could then run a photo of the message along with the story of its grisly threat. We assumed that this would shut up the skeptics unless they were prepared to yell "fake," which they might not be inclined to do since this would label them as more than skeptics. Most people would then consider them to be out-and-out Huk sympathizers and sympathetic to the cause of a band of butchers.

It may seem curious, but it did not bother anyone at the seminar to be blithely engaged in planning a forgery, although no one there had ever been arrested for any serious crime. Otherwise they would not have been there. They would not have been granted the necessary security clearance to have gained employment by the Clandestine Services. The finer points about forgery, however, were actually the most fascinating to this group: how to obtain authentic paper, how to be sure to use the same kind of typewriter that Huk orders were usually written on, and of course, how to be

91

certain to use the proper language that would make our work indistinguishable from the real thing. These were the topics examined with the most minute care.

Linebarger undertook a kind of group therapy approach to try to show us that tricking someone into believing that black is white comes naturally to everybody and is something that is practiced from childhood.

"Look," he began, "can't you remember how you fooled your brothers and sisters and your father and mother? Try to remember how old you were when you first tricked one of them."

This got the class confessional under way. Soon people began recalling how they had stolen their brother's and sister's favorite toys and hid them to play with secretly while helping in their siblings' frantic search for the lost love objects. They remembered telling their mothers how they drank their bedtime glasses of milk while actually pouring the contents down the toilet and presenting the empty glass the next morning as proof of their good behavior.

Our girl executive recalled how she and her girlfriend managed to get out of school to listen to "Teatime Tunes" when they were in sixth grade. This operation showed good teamwork as well as deception. The girlfriend would claim to be suffering from a terrible toothache. Our seminar companion would plead with the teacher to be allowed to take her home to put oil of cloves on the aching molar. Upon winning approval, they would go to the sufferer's house and turn on the radio for an hour's enjoyment of their favorite radio program. Fortunately for the girls the house was near the school, but the teacher didn't seem to realize this. When the program ended, they went back to school.

"The whole thing actually hinged on the fact that we were both thought to be such nice little girls," she explained in a satisfied voice.

"You have got the idea," Paul commented.

As the stories progressed from grade school to high school and college capers, the tales of manipulation of parents and peers grew darker, if not black to the point of Linebarger's definition of black operations. Everyone had either forged the time of return when coming back to a dormitory after hours or forged parents' signatures to bad report cards, or used false credentials to buy a drink when under age.

We found these exchanges so interesting that we decided to open each evening's session with twenty minutes of confessions. They undoubtedly helped us to study the art of falsifying Communist documents with the high enthusiasm we all developed.

After listening to these recitals for a couple of weeks, Linebarger asked, "Haven't any of you done anything more exciting than figure out ways to have your drinking and sexual adventures? I know none of you was in a psychwar outfit during the war, but has anyone done anything more nearly operational?"

To everyone's surprise Boston Blackie, our group antihero and skeptic, was the one who replied.

"It was the fall of 1942, just before I left college for the Navy," he began in his deliberate fashion, "and there was a referendum in Massachusetts on the question of birth control information. Massachusetts law, as you may know, prohibits public dissemination of this kind of information. The Church, of course, wanted the law upheld, and some friends and I helped some priests put on a visitation campaign in South Boston to get out a big vote against changing the law.

"The visits weren't producing a great deal of interest," he went on, "and we were pretty concerned about this. Then one of the priests got an idea. He suggested that we explain to the parishioners that if the voters approved the change of the law and permitted birth control information to be legally disseminated, this would mean that they would have to get a written permit from the government if they wanted to have a baby.

"This may sound a little strong," he continued, beginning to smile faintly, "but these people had great faith in their priests' word. I know, because I went along on some visits when this line was used. For good measure, of course, we threw in reminders of how the New Deal forced farmers to plow under their crops and stuff like that. Anyway, it must have helped. The change in the law was defeated and there were only a handful of votes in favor of changing the law from all the precincts in South Boston."

Linebarger thought this was an excellent story. He beamed. "I wish we had access to Church records for the past thousand years, we'd have so many case histories that we would be sure to find something to fit all our needs in Asia right now. The Catholic Church didn't last this long as an unalterable institution without giving God's will some assistance.

"I want you all to go out and get a copy of David Maurer's classic on the confidence man. It's called *The Big Con,* and it's available now in a paperback edition," Paul continued. "That little book will teach you more about the art of covert operations than anything else I know.

"Your job and the confidence man's are almost identical. The point of our little confessionals has been to show you what I mean by that statement. I'm happy to say I think you've been getting it. The girls' escapade in school was a wonderful example. As Betty said, it worked because they had the teacher's complete confidence. The priest's clever con of his parishioners is further excellent proof of my point.

"Of course, your motives and those of the confidence man are different. He wants to fleece his mark out of his money. You want to convince a Chinese, Filipino, an Indonesian, a Malay, a Burmese, a Thai, that what you want him to believe or do for the good of the U.S. government is what he thinks he himself really believes and wants to do.

"Maurer's book will give you a lot of ideas on how to recruit agents, how to handle them and how to get rid of them peacefully when they're no use to you any longer. Believe me, that last one is the toughest job of all."

We were all soon avidly reading *The Big Con.* The tales it told did, indeed, contain a lot of hints on how to do our jobs. For me one sentence seemed to sum it all up beautifully, "The big-time confidence games," wrote Maurer, "are in reality only carefully rehearsed plays in which every member of the cast *except the mark* knows his part perfectly."*

Besides this course reading, exchanges of experiences, development of model situations, study of Communist propaganda, especially its style and content with an eye to copying them, Paul taught by the oldest method, precept. His injunction was to follow the example of proven successful practitioners.

He had two leading operational heroes whose activities formed the basis for lessons he wished us to learn and whose examples he thought we should follow. One was Lt. Col. Edward G. Lansdale, the OPC station chief in Manila, and the other was E. Howard Hunt, the OPC station chief in Mexico City. Both of them had what

*David W. Maurer, *The Big Con* (New York: Pocket Books, 1949), p. 102.

he called "black minds," and the daring to defy bureaucratic restraints in thinking up and executing operations. He had a number of stories to tell about the exploits of both. He was particularly fond of Lansdale, whom he claimed had "invented" the Philippine Secretary of Defense, Ramón Magsaysay, around whom he built a plan of action that was slowly but surely bringing the Huk uprising to an end. His esteem for Hunt lay in his admiration for what he considered Hunt's great ability to invent a clever way to thwart the Communists in their efforts to achieve success in the everyday affairs of life. He had a favorite Lansdale story and a favorite Hunt story to illustrate what he admired in each and to demonstrate two widely different kinds of black operations. Lansdale's was somewhat complex and required the support of a number of people and pieces of equipment. Hunt's was disarmingly simple.

Lansdale ordered a careful study of the superstitions of the Filipino peasants, their lore, their witch doctors, their taboos and myths. He then got hold of a small aircraft and some air-to-ground communications gear. He would fly the aircraft over areas where Huks were known to be hiding and broadcast in the Tagalog language mysterious curses on any villagers who deigned to give the Huks food and shelter. He actually succeeded in starving some Huk units into surrender by these means. The only drawback was that Lansdale could use the operation only in the rainy season when the cloud cover hid the airplane from its audience on the ground.

Linebarger's Howard Hunt story was much less heavy. It also fitted better Linebarger's definition of a black operation. No one had quite the heart to ask him whether the Filipino spirits to whom the curses were attributed were Communists, as his definition of black propaganda would require, and, if so, why were they cursing their own team, the Huks.

Linebarger liked to stress that his Hunt story was a good example of how to cause the Communists a lot of grief on a low budget. Hunt learned that a Communist front in Mexico was planning a reception to honor some Soviet visitors. Drinks, refreshments, and a lunch were planned for the event. Hunt got hold of an invitation. He then went to work with a friendly printer and printed up three thousand extra invitations, which he had widely distributed.

On the day of the reception Hunt obtained the desired results. Before the reception was a quarter under way, the Communists

95

had run out of food and drink. Those who crowded into the hall where the event was taking place began to complain about the lack of refreshments. At the same time, the Communists had to shut the doors on the crowd of invitees that swarmed outside. So much commotion ensued that the event had to be brought to a premature close. Rather than promoting friendship with the Soviet Union, the sponsors suffered the ire of both the Russians and the Mexicans. The cause of Soviet-Mexican friendship was definitely damaged, at least for a while.

A note of caution that Linebarger added to these discussions of black operations sounds like a bell down the years. He would explain, after someone had come up with an especially clever plan for getting the Communists completely incriminated in an exceedingly offensive act, that there should be limits to black activities.

"I hate to think what would ever happen," he once said with a prophet's voice, "if any of you ever got out of this business and got involved in U.S. politics. These kinds of dirty tricks must never be used in internal U.S. politics. The whole system would come apart."

I recall that there was a nodding of heads when Linebarger delivered this admonition. I do not recall that anyone agreed in a loud, firm voice. Perhaps the remark was thought to be really rather irrelevant. We had more serious business to attend to.

We would say good night to Paul in the vestibule of his house, and slip, one by one, out into the night to our cars parked at discreetly different distances from his home. We had just completed another session in the art of confounding our enemies. We had learned some more of the tradecraft of deception. We were inspired to go back to work the following week and look for fresh opportunities to devise new operations against the Communists.

Linebarger's seminar inspired me to encourage the Indonesian desk to try a black operation when the preliminary announcement was made that the Soviets and Indonesians were about to open formal diplomatic relations. The components of the operation were as simple as Howard Hunt's Mexican operation and it was at least equally, if not more, successful. Exchange of formal diplomatic missions was held up for six months as a result. Conservative Moslem elements, without any contact with us, saw to it that the Indonesian government examined carefully the matter of how many Russians would be coming to Djakarta before agreeing to let any into the country at all. The operation, in fact, was written up some time later by the senior psychological warfare staff and circulated around the Clandestine Services to encourage better black operations.

I remembered that the Soviets had a big embassy in Bangkok. I also remembered that OPC had Bob North, a psychwar expert of OSS days, in Bangkok under cover as a film producer and that Bob had a large psychwar workshop that should be able to assist. I found out from my friends on the Indonesian desk that there was a severe housing shortage in Djakarta. This was one of the things that made it difficult to attract officers to serve there. Housing of the type our people or any European diplomats or other official personnel thought adequate was almost impossible to come by.

I suggested we have the Bangkok station arrange to send a cable, ostensibly from the administrative officer of the Soviet Embassy in Bangkok, to the Indonesian Foreign Office official in charge of helping make arrangements for the housekeeping of foreign missions in Djakarta. The cable would be a query concerning the availability of housing for a large number of Soviets. The Indonesian desk fortunately knew the name of this Indonesian Foreign Office official. All we needed to get was the name of the proper Soviet official in Bangkok. I found out from the Thai desk that we also knew who this man was.

A cable was drawn up for Bangkok station explaining the idea. We suggested their fake Soviet cable inquire whether two hundred houses might be available. We knew that this was a very large number, but we also knew the Indonesians were accustomed to Americans, at least, asking to see more than one house. Hence, although the number was frighteningly large, which we wanted it to be, we didn't think it would be considered beyond the realm of the Indonesian authorities' belief. We also insisted that the message say no more, because we thought the briefer it was the more plausible it would be. The recent public announcement of the plan to establish a Soviet Embassy in Djakarta made it unnecessary to say any more. Finally, the Soviet Embassy in Bangkok was the largest in Southeast Asia at that time; hence we reasoned the Indonesians would think it logical that a request for information about an administrative matter of this kind might come from Bangkok rather than Moscow. They would think that Bangkok had been delegated

97

responsibility for such details because of its proximity to Indonesia and because it obviously had the staff to provide support in such a matter.

We guessed correctly. The Indonesian official was terribly upset when he got the cable. He showed the message to a number of colleagues and to other Indonesian government functionaries, including the conservative Moslems already mentioned. They immediately demanded an investigation into the number of Soviets to be included in the coming mission, and they suggested that the number be held to as small a group as possible.

It took several days for the Soviets to react. Meanwhile the matter became public knowledge and our press assets had the chance to add the extra touch of speculating whether the Soviets were planning to send a large number of spies under embassy cover to Djakarta. We had counted on this Soviet delay in making our calculations. It usually took the tightly controlled Soviet bureaucracy some time to react to anything in those days. Thus, by the time the Soviets got around to saying the cable was not an official message, few people in Indonesia believed them. They had heard so much of this piece of disturbing news about the size of the new Soviet Embassy they could only ask what else the Soviets would say in such an embarrassing situation.

Paul Linebarger and I became good friends as well as professional associates. He could think of more useful ways to apply behavioral science findings to our work than anyone else I ever met. He introduced me to the ideas of Harry Stack Sullivan about interpersonal relationships. He also tried to give me some sound advice about a Clandestine Services career.

"Joe, you won't be happy with a lifetime career in an organization like this," Paul said. "Right now it's exciting. The outfit has a great sense of mission. It needs and welcomes ideas, but this won't last. Gradually it will become just another Washington bureaucracy, mainly concerned with covering up its mistakes like all the rest. I see the types around everywhere who will make sure of that. Men whom ideas make very nervous. Dick Stillwell will surely lose out to Lloyd George.

"What you ought to do," he continued, "is to come up with a proposal that benefits your country, helps the Agency meet some of its important goals, but that enables you to establish an independent career. When you've done all you can for the outfit, you can say

98

goodbye and continue your own career. They'll be happy and you'll be happy. Perhaps you will be able to help them again someday when it's again mutually beneficial."

Paul even found the project for me. Johns Hopkins School for Advanced International Studies, where he taught, was almost to a man a Clandestine Services adjunct. Dean Phillip Thayer and all the top staff, such as Paul, were consultants, and they regularly fed their best students into CIA operations jobs. Thayer liked the Far East and had developed the idea of establishing a branch study center in the area. He wanted to set up a school in Rangoon and had convinced the Burmese officials that this was what they needed. Paul suggested that I jump at this opportunity.

"I think you have enough academic credentials to head an infant institute of this kind," Paul said. "Agency support in the form of paying your salary and expenses is about all the financial help needed in addition to what's already available. You could spot and develop likely recruits from among the students and you could write a lot of useful stuff, and find students who could do the same thing. So you'd be serving the Agency well and at the same time establish an international reputation as an Asian expert."

The scheme got as far as my being investigated by security to determine whether I was known as CIA. They found that the Fairlington rental office had me listed as an employee. This was my mistake, as I have mentioned. No one told me I was a Clandestine Services employee until after I entered on duty. The fact that every place I had used the name Viola Pitts as a credit reference also had me listed as a CIA employee was not my fault.

Anyway, I thought, a career in the Clandestine Services may not prove as bad as Paul thinks. There were so many things going on as the year 1953 began, I was sure there would be lots for me to do.

7
We Make a President

The United States' fateful entanglement in Vietnam began in Manila in the early 1950s, not in Saigon in the early sixties. The CIA's operation that made Ramón Magsaysay president of the Philippines in 1953 established a pattern of paramilitary, psychological, and political action mistakenly imagined to be workable anywhere, anytime. The same Americans and Filipinos who created the Magsaysay administration in Manila created the Diem government in Saigon—Ed Lansdale and his team.

Why we should elect Magsaysay president and precisely when the idea developed are difficult to determine. Something that conditioned the decision was the new atmosphere that swept the offices of the Clandestine Services in the wake of Dwight D. Eisenhower's victory in November, 1952. Eisenhower campaigned on a platform that read like the country plans I wrote in FE/OPC. As he proposed to wind down the unpopular shooting war in Korea, he also called for expanded psychological warfare against Communism everywhere. Liberation, not containment, was the theme of the new administration.

In the Clandestine Services we were ready. On the morning after the election of Eisenhower one of the senior paramilitary officers home from the SEA Supply Company in Thailand ran through the offices shouting, "Now we'll finish off the goddamned Commie bastards. We'll get rid of the fucking pinkos in the State Department and around this place too. They'll all be as dead as that little bald-headed son-of-a-bitch who said he thought he was going to cry last night when he had to concede to Ike."

I thought Adlai Stevenson had run the loftiest campaign American politics had ever seen, but I had to admit the future seemed to hold enormous possibilities for exciting work. John Foster Dulles, who would obviously become Secretary of State, had shown explicit faith during the campaign in the effectiveness of my new profession. Dulles had declared that by means of a "psychological and political offensive the United States should make it publicly known that it wants and expects liberation to occur. The mere statement of that wish and expectation would change, in an electrifying way, the mood of the captive peoples. It would probably put heavy new burdens on the jailers and create new opportunities for liberation."

Everyone sensed we would play a key role in the new administration's plans. Paul Linebarger had been active in the Eisenhower election effort and he assured me reliance on greater covert psychological warfare activities was certain, hinting he himself expected to assume some important new responsibilities. We all agreed that with foreign affairs being managed by John Foster Dulles, his brother Allen's outfit should become more important. We didn't realize in the early winter months of 1953 as the new administration took shape just how cozy the Dulles brothers' arrangement for handling all American business abroad would be. It came to mean very quickly that when a situation would not yield to normal diplomatic pressure, Allen's boys were expected to step in and take care of the matter. The situation in the Philippines was one of these.

The problem plaguing the Philippines even more than self-government was the Communist insurgent guerrilla band—the Hukbalahaps. The Huks had been founded in 1942 in a hideout near Mt. Arayat in central Luzon as a "people's army" to fight the Japanese. They would not surrender their arms as other guerrilla movements had done in 1946 and 1947.

On April 6, 1948, Manuel Roxas, the first president of the new republic, died of a heart attack. When Roxas died, the Huks were already launched on a wider war in response to the Calcutta directive. They continued to take advantage of the confusion caused by the president's death. They engaged in terrorist spectaculars, such as ambushing the family of the late independence hero, Quezon. They made gains throughout central Luzon, controlling most of the territory just outside the limits of Clark Field and even part of the city of Manila.

A clause of the "bases" agreement signed in 1947 provided for American advisers to help the Philippines train its newly independent army. Lt. Col. Edward G. Lansdale arrived as one of these advisers. He was in reality the chief of OPC operations in the Philippines. Military cover was the expedient that best served the Clandestine Services where, in cases like the Philippines, large U.S. military establishments were a major part of the postwar scene. Operations against the Soviets and their satellites depended heavily on this cover in Germany, where occupation forces were overwhelming not only in size but authority. The situation was not quite the same in the Philippines, but in many ways even more favorable. The U.S. uniform was not a sign of the conqueror, but the badge of liberation.

The task of defeating the Huks was a common objective. How best to do it was the problem which beset both the Filipinos and their advisers. On August 31, 1950, Congressman Ramón Magsaysay was named Secretary of Defense by President Quirino, the man who had succeeded Roxas. The Lansdale-Magsaysay saga began. As the Lansdale program developed, changes took place back in Washington which made it an increasingly pointed and notorious affair.

The Far East Divisions were merged during the course of 1952. Dick Stillwell was gone. Lloyd George, the OSO division chief, took command and Des Fitzgerald remained as deputy. The two men could not have been more different. Lloyd George could come into a room and not be noticed. Des Fitzgerald's presence could be felt before he entered. Perhaps my keen awareness of their contrasts was affected at the time by my reading Harold Lasswell. I was studying Lasswell at Linebarger's suggestion to gain an understanding of political personality. Lasswell, in *Power and Personality*, seemed to me to describe both men. Lloyd George was obviously

103

what he labeled a "compulsive character" and Fitzgerald was a "dramatizing character." Lasswell, with impressive insight, observed that in a bureaucracy these two types were often teamed, as were Lloyd and Des. He explained that the compulsive type realizes that his narrow approach to every decision may mean he will miss some opportunity which an expansive view of the problem might provide, so he likes a dramatizer as his deputy. The dramatizer will prefer a compulsive for his deputy in order to have someone grab his arm as he is about to take some foolish risk. As I looked around the division, I was certain I saw this pattern emerging in all the branches and desks as OSO and OPC joined forces.

Another product of the merger, which, after all, meant the bruising of many egos at the upper levels of the Clandestine Services, was the creation of the job of "senior representative" overseas. This officer was to supervise both chiefs of the former OSO and OPC stations. This kind of bureaucratic jockeying brought about the creation of a large command structure in the field for FE Division, and Lloyd George went off to become the deputy to a retired admiral who was chief of the "North Asia Command." The North Asia Command was supposed to provide a sort of wartime theater commander's supervision of operations in Korea, Japan, Taiwan, Okinawa, Hong Kong, a base at Subic Bay in the Philippines, and Saipan, where the division trained Asian agents who were brought out of their countries on "black," i.e., untraceable, flights and returned the same way.

George Aurell took over as chief. He had been raised in Japan, where his father had long been in business before World War II. Physically he was quite the opposite of Lloyd George. For one thing, he was six feet three instead of five feet three. Des remained as deputy. George hesitated to make the smallest decision. Des suggested three ways to do the same thing—all at the same time. Theirs was the command that directed the election of Magsaysay. The chain of command and enthusiasm led always from the dramatizer in the field, Ed Lansdale, to Des, and George tagged along.

Lansdale's and Magsaysay's personalities meshed almost as well as did Lansdale's and Des's. Long before the presidential election of 1953 in the Philippines they launched a program that would make Magsaysay a national hero and Lansdale an authority on combating insurgency. Thus, Lansdale would be the man the United States would send to Saigon to create a country when the French collapsed in 1954, as well as take on the task of getting rid of Castro by any means, including assassination, after the failure of the Bay of Pigs operation.

The program that was developed for fighting the Huks was a multiphased activity. To the basic military operations of searching out and destroying Huk concentrations, Lansdale added a number of additional tasks for the new Philippine army.

A large psychological warfare unit was developed and trained. Almost everything a psychological warfare outfit could possibly be expected to do was incorporated into the program of the Philippine army's psychological warfare unit. History and traditions in all the Huk areas were studied for clues to the appropriate appeals to make to wean the populace from supporting the Huks. Paul Linebarger made a number of trips to the Philippines to advise Lansdale on operations.

It was in connection with Linebarger's involvement in Philippine operations that I had one of my few direct contacts with the events that transpired there. In the fall of 1952, I was given the assignment of picking up one of the Lansdale team, Napoleon Valeriano, at the Philippine Embassy and taking him to Linebarger's house for a training session. Valeriano was not only one of the key members of the team, but he was one whom Lansdale counted on in future operations. When Valeriano was in Vietnam helping Lansdale in the early days of the Diem regime, he carried off to Saigon the wife of a wealthy Filipino businessman. The injured husband immediately put out a contract on Valeriano, and he was never able to set foot in Manila again. It would have meant instant death. Subsequently, Valeriano worked in the Pentagon, trained the Cuban brigade preparing for the Bay of Pigs invasion, and was involved in post-Bay of Pigs activities with which Lansdale was concerned.

Valeriano and I arrived at Linebarger's at five o'clock one afternoon and stayed four hours. Paul concentrated on his con-man line concerning how to use a subject's own hopes and longings to achieve the results desired in a psychwar operation.

"You'll never get the Huks to surrender because the Philippine government wants them to," Paul stressed. "They'll give up only if they think they're going to get something they want which is even more important to them than the satisfaction they get from defying authority by fighting in the hills."

Valeriano explained that the program his outfit was following was already based on that concept. We went over a number of specific items about which he wanted to question Linebarger. I learned how the central core of the Magsaysay program functioned. The key ingredient was the resettlement deal that was offered the Huks. It was not just a psychwar effort, but a major economic rehabilitation endeavor. Being a country boy from Iba, the impoverished capital of the poor province of Zambales, Magsaysay already understood the minds of rural Filipinos before Lansdale or Linebarger ever met him. EDCOR, the Economic Development Corps, which evolved from the combination of his native understanding of his people and the urgings of his advisers, gave a tract of land, a carabao, tools, seeds, and a small amount of cash for basic provisions to each Huk who surrendered. The deal was a five-year loan to be worked off by the newly established independent peasant freeholder.

"If a farmer owns his own piece of property," said Magsaysay, "he will resist anyone who tries to take it away from him."

The resettlement program for Huks and Huk sympathizers, thus, was established not only to give these people something they wanted more than a fight with the Philippine army, but had its own built-in defense against unreconstructed comrades who might try to attack the new settlements.

Supporting this basic program were propaganda efforts—films, special radio programs, and so forth. George Aurell, the new division chief, never felt comfortable about any of this. He used to come over to our Plans office and unburden himself to Kay. "What in hell is an intelligence agency doing running a rural resettlement program?" he used to ask. "I'm glad to help fight the Huks, but is it our job to rebuild a nation?" Ed Lansdale and his team in the Philippines, and later elsewhere, were convinced it was. Des Fitzgerald had no trouble tolerating this sort of diversity.

In 1953 we heard that the Quirino government was corrupt beyond belief or salvation. The president's brother Tony, it was said, had part of the action in every government transaction. The United States Economic Survey Mission, appointed at the request of the Philippine government in 1950, had reported a degree of inefficiency, injustice, economic backwardness, and official corruption that jeopardized the success of the effort to defeat the Huks.

This was the crux of the Magsaysay election operation's rationale. The campaign against the Huks was in jeopardy, it was said, from the failure of the government to implement further reforms and support the resettlement program. Outside the Philippine department of defense such support was almost nonexistent. If the Philippines were to have four more years of Quirino it might not survive as a free nation. Magsaysay was a proven leader, a man of the people who understood them, and he was honest. He and his team offered the chance to change the whole pattern of Philippine politics to make the country a model of democracy in action that would be a banner around which all the threatened new nations of Southeast Asia could rally.

Actually Des Fitzgerald had recruited a New York lawyer and politician, Gabriel Kaplan, whose sensitivity for political nuances he admired, to go to Manila to help Lansdale elect Magsaysay president two years before the election was to take place. Gabe Kaplan was a Jacob Javits-style Republican, but New York apparently had appetite for only a limited number of this type or any type of Republican when Gabe Kaplan ran for Congress. Gabe used to say of his unsuccessful campaign, "Fortunately, I'm Jewish. But even that wasn't enough. I needed just a bit of Italian blood besides." His understanding of the significance of a hybrid background stood him in good stead in the Philippines.

The Filipinos had absorbed a great deal of guile from many Chinese incursions into the native Malay bloodline. The traditions of extended family of both Malay and Chinese cultures meant that the habit of helping out a vast array of relatives was a well-established cultural trait long before the Spanish conquered the country and gave it their religion. The Filipinos quickly took to the practice of supplying godfathers for infants facing the baptismal font. *Compadres* bound by life-long ties of respect and mutual support represented just a further extension of a system of interdependent rewards they already understood. Then came the American ward heeler with his techniques for keeping his flock happy and getting them to vote right at the polls. Taken altogether these created a political life-style which made the task of changing the politics of the Philippines into the model of democratic society for Southeast Asia too much for even Lansdale's Magsaysay team. Gabe Kaplan at least knew how to make it work.

Gabe had a gift for dealing with organizations like Chambers of Commerce, Rotary Clubs, and veterans, and he found Filipinos with similar talents. Together they worked these groups into a na-

107

tionwide umbrella to deal with the need for educating the public to the importance of free and honest elections and showing them practical steps that could be taken to assure the desired results by individuals and groups, associated or not with the current governing structure. This nationwide organization was the National Movement for Free Elections, NAMFREL, which Gabe organized and tried out for the first time in the congressional elections of 1951 in preparation for the presidential contest.

NAMFREL, ostensibly sponsored by these various civic groups, was actually run by Gabe and funded by the station. NAMFREL chapters sprang up all around the country. They preached the virtues of ensuring there would be no tricks at the polls and showed the practical ways to prevent them. They taught people how to make proper thumbprints on ballots—the system used to verify registration certificates. One method of throwing out ballots was for government-appointed polling supervisors or protesting-party poll watchers, who feared ballots were being cast for their opponents, to claim thumbprints were illegible and declare the ballots invalid. Many times these same officials did a little ballot smudging themselves in order to accomplish their mission. People were alerted to look out for this.

Other people were taught photography and instructed to take pictures of all persons entering polling places in order to identify for prosecution the squads of multivoters that corrupt politicians used around town. A second team of photographers were instructed to go along and take pictures of any strong-arm types who might try to prevent the first group from photographing the people entering the polls.

Another large organization that was created was the Magsaysay for President Movement, MPM. This group stressed the idea that the election of Magsaysay was not a partisan choice but a national one. The tactics that had been used to take the Republican nomination away from "Mr. Republican," Senator Robert Taft, in 1952, were repeated to insure that the old Nationalist Party machine would not be the ultimate victor. Magsaysay would have a nonpartisan base.

All was not sweetness and light, however. A number of the maneuvers of old-school politics had to be undertaken by the station and the Magsaysay team of reformers in order to get their man nominated and then elected. First, Magsaysay and his group, all members of the pro-American Liberal Party which had elected Roxas but was now stuck with the corrupt vice-president who succeeded him, had to break with the Liberal Party and somehow get the old-guard leadership of the Nationalists to accept the idea that Magsaysay should be their candidate. The two principal figures of the Nationalist leadership in 1953 were José Laurel and Claro M. Recto. Laurel and Recto had both participated in writing the Philippine constitution upon the basis of which the Philippines were promised independence in 1935 by President Roosevelt and the U.S. Congress. Both had been key figures in the puppet government the Japanese had established after 1942—Laurel as president and Recto as his foreign affairs expert. In the postwar Philippines, these men and the dashing anti-Japanese guerrilla leaders who made up the Magsaysay band were the oddest of political bedfellows.

Laurel and Recto proved deceptively easy to handle. Linebarger should have been in the Philippines for these negotiations to point out that conning one another is the second favorite activity of con men. Laurel and Recto, assessing the situation shrewdly, saw the opportunity to lay to rest their Japanese collaborator ghosts by joining forces with Ed Lansdale's American team. They supported Magsaysay in the same spirit Daniel Webster supported William Henry Harrison—certain they would control the stupid soldier. Years later Recto told me, "I thought it amusing to arrange a deal with the American military who spent most of their time unjustly defaming me. As for Ramón, he was so dumb I knew I could handle him."

I learned about another maneuver of the Magsaysay men by accident—the way they split the Liberal Party. The day I moved into my house in Manila in 1958, my landlady appeared with a distinguished-looking man. She introduced him as Senator Fernando Lopez, former president of the senate. I, of course, knew something about his political career. He had been vice-president under Quirino and had joined the Magsaysay team in the 1953 elections, and then later followed Recto in breaking with the Magsaysay administration. I mentioned my meeting him to my Magsaysay-follower contact. He grinned.

"Your landlady has been Lopez's mistress for years. When you meet some of her children, after you've seen more of Lopez, you'll understand," he said. "Actually, it's hardly a secret anymore. As

109

you found out, they go all sorts of places together quite openly. It wasn't always like that, though, but we knew about it and took advantage of it once when we wanted to be able to lean on him a bit.

"When he was vice-president and secretary of agriculture at the same time, I was working in the agriculture department and I found out he had a side room, next to his office, where the two of them spent a lot of afternoons. So I got some equipment from the station and bugged the room. In fact, we discovered there was a bed in the room, so we bugged that too. Boy, we got some interesting recordings."

Vice-president Lopez broke with Quirino and agreed to run as vice-presidential candidate with Carlos P. Romulo, whose only claim to fame was having his picture taken wading ashore behind MacArthur when the general kept his promise to return. But this ticket split the Liberal Party. As one of the Philippines' sugar barons from the southern island of Iloilo, Lopez not only controlled his home state but added a note of substance and money to the Romulo ticket. I didn't want to ask whether this move by Lopez was related to the recordings, but I did.

My friend grinned even more broadly. "I'm going to plead the Fifth Amendment," he replied.

The Romulo-Lopez ticket was approved by the acclamation of one thousand delegates to the Progressive/Democratic Party convention (first, they said they would be known as the Progressive Party, but almost immediately changed their minds and said they were the Democratic Party). Their campaign was brief but it did have an effect on the Liberals. Between those who followed Magsaysay into the Nationalist Party, and those who went with Romulo and Lopez, the Liberal Party leadership suffered important losses.

There began to be talk, almost at once, of some sort of merger between the Democrats and the Nationalists, involving endorsement of mutually determined candidates for the senate and congress. Somehow, strangely, this never came about, but it made the point that important leaders were deserting from the Liberals stronger than ever, as names of possible candidates were bandied about.

On August 21, Romulo announced he was quitting the presidential race, and that he was going to support Magsaysay. "Fighting alone, the Democratic Party cannot hope to compete with the heavily financed, strongly entrenched power of the Administration

110

party's machinery," Romulo declared. "The reasons which motivated this decision are of the most critical importance," he added, "namely, the imperative need for a change in the national leadership."

Romulo was named campaign manager of the "coalition campaign," a title that emphasized the idea that a shift in political forces was taking place and coalescing behind the leadership of Magsaysay. Senator Rodriguez, a Nationalist stalwart of many years, announced he was willing to withdraw as senior senatorial candidate and that, in any case, he would support his new colleague, Fernando Lopez, for senate president after the Nationalists had won the elections.

From this point on, the campaign ran a fairly smooth course. Magsaysay was a wonderful candidate. At forty-six, he was the youngest man to campaign for the Philippine presidency, seventeen years younger than his opponent, Elpidio Quirino, and fourteen years younger than Roxas had been when he had been elected. He not only had youth, he had charisma. This term was not a household word in 1953, except to social scientists. We had enough social science background in FE and at the Manila station to understand the implications of the expression and how to exploit the qualities it represented. Identifying this candidate with the common man was not difficult. "Magsaysay's My Guy" buttons were proudly pinned on campesino chests.

Ramón Magsaysay was a big man for a Filipino, a generous six feet tall and built like a defensive tackle. He smiled easily. Most important of all, he was a son of a rural schoolteacher and knew the Filipino farmer both because he had lived alongside him and because his slightly superior station in life provided him sufficient intellectual background to know what to make of this experience. He knew how to go campaigning in the rural barrios. He could hurtle irrigation ditches in paddy fields to shake the calloused hand that guided the carabao. And he knew when to do it, and when to look serious as a proper political candidate should.

His intellectual powers beyond that point were subject to differences of opinion. His detractors, like Recto in later years, were fond of picturing him as a man of very limited talents beyond his almost instinctive understanding of what humble Filipino people wanted from him as a candidate and as a president. Magsaysay stories illustrating this point were spread by the opposition during the

111

campaign and later when he was president. His followers liked to tell them too, in later years. One story of the presidential years was that one day Magsaysay was discussing the economy with his secretary of finance, who remarked, in the course of the conversation, that administration plans for spreading a more abundant life were blocked by the law of supply and demand. "Let's repeal the damned law!" Magsaysay roared.

The point of this story, for his followers, was to admit that their leader might not have been as well prepared for his job as some, but that this scarcely mattered. What counted was his determination and drive and his ability to get things done, move obstacles, achieve solutions to problems. These were very unusual qualities for one of their countrymen to have, they thought, and for this and his dedication to fighting the rural poverty that gave rise to the Huks, and for his fanatical devotion to honesty they would have followed him anywhere.

As the campaign wore on, a frightened Quirino claimed the U.S. Army had a secret plan to supervise the polls. U.S. supervision of the election, however, didn't occur. It wasn't necessary. On the ground, NAMFREL and the MPM did an effective job of thwarting corruption. From the United States did come, though, a large number of reporters. They came from Asian countries too. This operation was "orchestrated" (a favorite word of Frank Wisner whenever he referred to the propaganda operations of the Clandestine Services) by the Manila station and FE Division. The purpose was to scare Quirino out of trying any last-minute tricks under the eyes of so many trained observers who would have liked nothing better than a good story or two about Philippine corruption, which they had been hearing about for months. Many of their editors back home had long been echoing our station's themes. Some of these echoes were the result of direct contact. Others apparently were picked out of the air. The New York *Times*, for example, in an editorial about the election on September 17, not only took the station's line but, without so identifying it, praised nearly the entire CIA election effort. The *Times* wrote:

> The major interest of friends of the Philippines in this campaign and this election is not primarily its outcome. It is rather the manner in which it is conducted. . . . This is a vital matter because of the fact that the Philippines is the

showcase of democracy in Asia. The Filipinos have the opportunity to be the outstanding leaders in the cause of human liberties in their part of the world.

It is a good thing to know, therefore, that there are important elements and groups in the Philippines that are working industriously to make this election the same sort of model as was that of 1951. At that time there was organized the National Movement for Free Elections and it is still functioning. In addition, there is the newer Committee for Good Government which is doing an important job in political instruction at the village level. There are civic groups, likewise, in the Philippines that have an alert attitude and a sensitive conscience. High in this list must rank the Junior Chambers of Commerce with about 40 chapters and more than 2,000 members. They are doing a good job both in their country and in international relations.

Magsaysay's election was a landslide. He received 1,688,172 votes to Quirino's 708,398. The triumph was received with acclaim in the Philippines and the United States. Rodrigo Perez, a pro-Magsaysay minority member of the National Election Commission, declared it was one of the cleanest elections in Philippine history. President Eisenhower commented to the press, "This is the way we like to see an election carried out." Since Eisenhower had approved the election operation and had sent his congratulations to the station via appropriate channels, we liked to think he meant his remarks as a kind of public tribute.

Senate majority leader, William F. Knowland of California, declared in a speech to the Executive Club of Chicago that Ramón Magsaysay should call a conference in Manila of representatives from Korea, the Chinese Nationalist government, Thailand, Vietnam, Laos, and Cambodia and that these nations together with the Philippines should form a military, political, and economic coalition against Communism in Asia. He said that Magsaysay's leadership in this matter would "remove the charge of colonialism from the propaganda arsenal of the Communists." He warned that the world should not accept the words of Jawaharlal Nehru as the voice of Asia.

The administration in Washington, it was clear, was extremely pleased with the results of the operation. They were looking ahead to the role that the newly elected chief executive of the Philippines could play in their liberation scheme for Asia. John Foster Dulles had already found that "unleashing Chiang Kai-shek" was not a feasible project. It might turn out like Des Fitzgerald's Li Mi operation. Evidently he was going to "unleash" Ramón Magsaysay instead. If we couldn't liberate the Soviet Union or China just yet, at least we had found something else to do.

8

Allen Dulles Had a Farm

While the Republic of the Philippines was being arranged as the showcase of democracy in Asia, I was taking CIA's operations course, twelve weeks' intensive training in the tradecraft of a spy. I began the course at the beginning of September and by the time I was graduated at the end of November, Magsaysay had been successfully elected. Before I describe the course, let me explain how I happened to have the chance to take it two years after I joined the Agency.

In addition to the developments of great importance in the larger world of which I was part as a Clandestine Services officer, there were significant changes in my own career in 1953. I was transferred to the Indonesia/Malaya/Australia Branch as the replacement for an unfortunate officer who had been the branch psychological and political (PP) chief, and had unsuccessfully attempted suicide. In the merged FE Division, affairs in Southeast Asia were handled by three branches instead of one as they had been in FE/OPC. FE/4 handled Indochina, Thailand, and Burma; FE/5 Indonesia, Malaya, and liaison with the Australian intelligence services; and the Philippines was a branch in its own right.

The reasons for my predecessor's suicide attempt had been personal and tragic, as these cases usually are, but the principal project he was trying to support in Indonesia was a Rube Goldberg creation that might well have stimulated suicidal thoughts. The project was supposed to provide both "cover for status" and "cover for action" (two terms I learned to appreciate in the operations course) for PP activities throughout all the islands of the Indonesian archipelago. The mechanism chosen to accomplish this was a chain of bookstores that were to be set up in Indonesia with a phony book and school supplies company established in New York City as a backstop. The idea evidently had been the product of the mind of someone who had taken some of the doctrine of the operations course too literally, and who also had read too many stories about how spies use bookstores for meeting places, locations where they can leave messages, and assorted other intrigues. "Cover for status" is a tradecraft term meaning some occupation or activity that gives a person a viable ostensible reason for being in a country when his real reason for being there is his espionage or other illegal clandestine activity. "Cover for action" means an activity that explains by some believable story, other than the truth, why a spy sees the people he does, is surrounded by the accoutrements he possesses, lives the way he does, and so forth. Young Americans running around Indonesia as representatives of a New York firm (status cover) setting up bookstores (action cover) was a great idea theoretically, only no businessman in his right mind would have attempted to do this in that country in 1953.

Indonesia, like all new countries, had a preferential tariff structure to encourage local enterprise. The rates were astonishingly high for nearly every product produced by man, books and school supplies included. Besides the tariff, an importer had to pay additional penalties for his unpatriotic behavior. There were also taxes just for making any kind of business transaction. The result was that, although the project had been running more than two years when I inherited the mess, only one bookstore had been established and one officer sent to Indonesia. He spent all his time trying to clear book shipments through the Indonesian bureaucracy and performed no operational tasks whatsoever. The project was not even accomplishing what had been considered its minimal activity,

116

channeling good anti-Communist books to Indonesia. A few had been sent, but the officer in Djakarta could never get them out of customs, all political books being suspect. He begged us and New York just to keep sending textbooks lest he be interrogated and thrown out of the country. In tradecraft terms, he was "continuing to build his cover." This made the higher echelons nervous when they reviewed the project each fiscal year and were told this was all that was going on.

To make matters worse, the project was subject to the scrutiny of the Commercial Division. This division had been established to oversee proprietary projects. Such projects were business enterprises, incorporated with a board of persons who lent their names, but whose capital was CIA money and whose assets were actually owned by CIA. The Commercial Division was down on the project because it cost $100,000 a year and had a completely red balance sheet and almost no cash flow. One reason for the costs was the Madison Avenue address of the New York company (status cover) whose president, a brother of a well-known media personality, required it for the occasional meetings with the nominal board that included one important name in publishing.

When he wasn't arguing with customs or some bureaucrat in the treasury department, our poor man in Indonesia was trying to answer the lengthy questions on the bookstore's balance sheet I transmitted to him from the Commercial Division as well as trying to give me ammunition to satisfy the senior PP staff that the project was really just about to get off the ground, and if it was not turning Indonesia into another showplace of democracy, at least it was flooding the country with the kind of propaganda the staff wanted to see distributed throughout the world.

The dilemma was heightened by the disclaimers of both the senior PP staff and the Commercial Division of any responsibility for, or even interest in, each other's realms. The PP staff would say they didn't care how bad the balance sheet was if I could assure them that the project would produce operational results within the next six months. The Commercial Division said they did not want to interfere in operations in any way, but they could not approve the project's continuation much longer if the business did not improve. It was not only spending too much money, it would never stand any outside scrutiny, if banks and creditors got curious. Spinning between these two alternatives was not a pleasant way to spend the day, but that was my lot as the pressure of the end of the fiscal year, June 30, drew nearer.

After a number of lengthy conferences, always inconclusive, we arrived at a compromise. Des Fitzgerald asked me to give him my frankest opinion, following one of these sessions, and I told him that I simply did not know enough about what was really going on in Indonesia to make any definite recommendation. He told me to write up an amendment to the project to provide the funds for the president of the New York company and me to go to Indonesia to look the situation over. He said that he would accompany me to the Project Review Committee, a top-level group that passed on all projects costing $100,000 or more, and we would base the project renewal on the fact that this trip would result in a reorganization of activities that would put the bookstore on its feet. He told me to do my homework especially well for the Project Review Committee meeting. Allen Dulles himself might be there, Des said.

I read every piece of paper we had in the files that was in any way related to the project: the need for unofficial cover positions in Indonesia, the potential operational leads for press and political recruitments our bookstore personnel might develop, the way these could be exploited not only for psychological warfare purposes but also to meet intelligence reporting requirements. We met the committee after waiting to be called for three-quarters of an hour, their having been delayed by the details involved in another case they were considering. Mr. Dulles was not there. The meeting was chaired by a Special Assistant, Richard Helms. Our session was very brief. Des presented our proposal. Helms said, "Well, I don't think we can give you a year's renewal, but we can approve $10,000 for the trip and we'll give you three months to write a recommendation." The meeting was over. I wasn't asked to say a word.

Thus I found myself in Djakarta in the summer of 1953. I was documented with cards saying I was a representative of the New York company. I had traveled by KLM via Amsterdam so that I didn't look like a government employee who, of course, was allowed to fly only on American-owned airlines. The president of the New York company met me in Djakarta. He came via Tokyo, Taipei, Saigon, Bangkok, Hong Kong, and Singapore, and made the journey into a trip around the world, returning via Europe. He claimed this was good for his cover and the operation's. The more stops he made, he insisted, made him appear to be the head of a large company with various interests and hid the fact that he was just supplying one small bookstore in Indonesia.

Djakarta in 1953 was distinguished mainly by the fact that nothing worked; the lights failed, telephone calls could not be completed, food spoiled in broken refrigerators, ceiling fans stuck, toilets didn't flush, and even the mosquito netting around the beds had holes in it. Life centered around the *kali*, a canal that ran through the center of town. At one time or another during the day, most of the city's population could be found in the *kali*, which they used for drawing drinking water, washing clothes, taking baths, and as a public latrine.

When I had grown accustomed to the cultural shock and daily diarrhea, I could cope with my assignment. After three weeks in the company of the president of the New York outfit and a first-hand look at the bookstore, I knew that one improvement in the project would be to eliminate the New York overhead costs. More important, I got some understanding of what Indonesians were like from the political writer who was the Indonesian partner in the bookstore and people he introduced me to as well as from the experience of living in Djakarta. It might have been a vain thought, but as I padded down the hotel terrace in zoris and bathrobe to shower in the one men's bathroom, I felt that Americans could never communicate their values to these people and probably shouldn't try. They didn't mind taking a shower by soaping themselves and then pouring cold water over their bodies from a stagnant pool in the corner of the bathroom. Poverty was a way of life their ancestors had learned to live and they had taught the art to succeeding generations. As I winced with each dipper of cold water, I could hear gamelons—the Indonesian version of a xylophone—and singing coming from somewhere in the evening dark. They really didn't have time for reading anti-Communist books. Would we be doing these people a favor by bringing them our plumbing? Perhaps they would find their own solution to keeping foreign ideologies like Communism out of the country.

My six weeks in Djakarta had two other results. For one thing, I decided that I didn't want a tour of duty there; for another, my gastrointestinal system was never the same again.

Back in Washington, we rewrote the project, eliminating the expensive New York office. The bookstore survived, but it never developed to be of any operational use. Happily, USIS subsequently launched a large book subsidy program in all of Asia which solved the bookstore's financial problems. We dropped the project, but the young officer gained enough experience that he was able to get a legitimate job in publishing back in the United States.

When I returned I found that the branch was searching for someone to go to Singapore to replace the man who had been the OPC chief. My recent experience convinced me to apply for the job before anyone got the idea that my temporary duty in Djakarta might indicate an assignment there was a logical overseas post for me. It was agreed I would go to Singapore, but that first I must take the operations course.

Before that, the matter of cover had to be worked out. The USIS slot that the former OPC chief held was considered an ideal solution, but it had to be renegotiated for a new man because USIS had just become an independent agency instead of an appendage of the State Department. One of the requirements for a USIS appointment, according to its new charter, was a security clearance by the FBI. I, of course, had an equivalent clearance, but the investigation on me had been done by the CIA Office of Security. We thought that it was ridiculous to have the FBI duplicate this work, which would take four months. We proposed that our clearance be accepted. It was decided that the legal staffs of CIA and of USIS would work out the matter. The result was that the clearance was not arranged in four months. It required six. There was ample time to take the operations course.

Training was an obvious requirement for overseas duty and, given the great amount of specialized experience necessary to handle the activities of the Clandestine Services, ought to have been the first priority for every new employee. In time it would be, with incoming personnel designated Junior Officer Trainees, later Career Trainees (when it was thought that the "Junior" label was too condescending), and receiving a total of an academic year of course work before going to their first assignments. In the 1950s, most supervisors thought that there was too much work to be done to allow people to be away from their desks long enough to be trained how to do it. Training was considered a sort of frill, and no substitute for common sense and skill at learning by doing at a desk. Fortunately, the authorities did demand that officers receive training before going overseas, and although there were groans when a warm body had to be given up for twelve weeks, candidates for overseas assignments were shipped off to ISOLATION.

Giving the training site this cryptonym added a touch of mystery to the training experience. It was also necessary to keep the location secret for the same reason the temporary buildings were not marked "CIA." Clandestine Services personnel could not be identified. For years it was the pride of the Office of Training that no unauthorized person knew the location of the training site. No one ever had the heart to tell the training staff that the students of William and Mary College in nearby Williamsburg, Virginia, were aware of who the people at Camp Peary were. When not called ISOLATION, the training base was always called the Farm.

Camp Peary had been a SEABEE training camp during World War II, and in 1953 was a collection of wooden barracks and administrative buildings and some Quonset huts. Before becoming a military reservation, the area had contained a small Virginia village, and there were remnants of this ghost town that were used in some of the training exercises. The base was located in the same narrow neck of land between the James and the York rivers where the first English settlers struggled to survive in 1607, fighting malaria and other infirmities contracted in the brackish swamps. Camp Peary, which lies on the York River side, was nicknamed Camp Swampy by the staff that lived and worked there. By the early 1950s DDT had been added to man's arsenal for coping with the diseases that had killed Captain John Smith's men; otherwise, physically, not too much had changed. The camp looked like one of the less promising posts I had been on during the war. When I returned, more than ten years later, ISOLATION looked like an English "red brick" university. By then training had not only been better institutionalized in content, it had the physical plant that its higher status demanded.

Our class arrived on a bright September morning and we were immediately "processed" in proper military fashion. We were issued military fatigue uniforms, school supplies, quarters assignments, and given cards and name tags with false identities. We were told that we were to use our false identities at all times on the base. This precaution, we were told, was taken because some people in the class were going on highly sensitive missions. Since we would have seminar sessions on the areas to which we were being

121

assigned in addition to our general subjects, we would soon find out where we all were being posted overseas. If this important information had to be thus compromised, at least we wouldn't know each other's true names. We could not go off the base, except on weekends, when those who wished and had transportation could go home to their families provided they returned no later than seven P.M. Sunday.

The security briefing was, in fact, the main topic of the first morning. Our cover story was to be that we were special trainees of the Department of Defense. The post housekeeping chores were conducted by a small Army detachment, whose commanding officer was the only person we could mention in any situation where we might find ourselves off the base and required to identify our training unit. We could not talk to the Army personnel or the Marine guards that had camp security duty. As in the case of the Washington cafeteria, we were warned that the mess hall personnel were "cleared but unwitting." The same was true of the bartender in the officers' club, where we could assemble only between the end of afternoon classes at five o'clock and the renewal of our studies at six and again after evening classes from ten until eleven. Dinner, of course, had to be eaten during the five to six P.M. break in our studies.

Work was the theme of the orientation lecture. A tough full-day's schedule, it was explained, would keep us under pressure. Learning how to function under pressure was considered one of the main parts of the curriculum. "We're not trying to make any of you crack," said the chief instructor, "but if anyone can't take it, now's the time to find out, not when you're in the field. If you're going to survive in this business, you have to learn to live with tension and to think fast under pressure, and we're going to make you do it."

The chief instructor called himself Stan Archer. He and the other instructors, like us, used false names. He was as high-strung and tense as he declared he would make the class. A former Counter Intelligence Corps (CIC) officer, he was one soldier who always went by the book. His assistants were a varied group. In time we learned that only one of them had actually served at a CIA station. The rest, like the chief instructor, had military intelligence backgrounds of one sort or another and had been hired as training officers on the strength of these qualifications. While the divisions were reluctant to give up their employees to be trained, they simply refused to let one of their able and experienced officers be assigned as an instructor. The result was that the operations course was tilted toward the practices and perspectives of military policemen and counterintelligence agents. The instructional methods were also highly military.

Stan Archer's lectures were based on the U.S. Army's principles of pedagogy: if a concept cannot be oversimplified, it cannot be explained; if a cliché cannot be found to express an idea, the idea cannot be mentioned. The rest of the staff followed his lead. This is a satisfactory way to teach a recruit how to strip and reassemble an M-1 rifle, but frequently inadequate for anything that is not mechanical. The operations course's major focus, Archer explained, was to be "activity at the agent level" with the implication that this meant the rock bottom of the spy business.

So spy school started with a Basic Tradecraft Manual that had been developed to train local agents. Terms were defined and explained. We were told it was important to learn to use the vocabulary of espionage. While it seemed to me quite understandable that we know exactly what some terms meant, other words in the special language were obviously jargon.

An "agent" was a person used to obtain information or do other tasks because he had access to the information desired and could do the things required of him for some plausible reason other than that he was working for American intelligence. A "double agent" was a person who had been discovered to be working for an opposition intelligence service and who was allowed to continue to do so only under the control of the service that he had been spying against. "Espionage" was the collection of positive secret information that a government or organization did not want any outsider to know. "Counterintelligence" was the discovery and control of the intelligence and other clandestine activities directed against the nation or organization the counterintelligence service served. "Cutouts" were people or devices used to separate and thus hide the fact that contact existed between an agent and an intelligence officer. A "courier" was recruited to carry messages for such a purpose. A "live drop" was a person used without his knowledge to transmit messages between intelligence officers and agents. A "dead drop" was a place or an object where messages between these two could be passed without direct contact between them taking place. These were significant definitions. Why an activity that was compromised was said to be "blown" or an agent whose services were no longer needed was said to be "terminated" seemed to be using the language as sociologists did, to provide a means of communicating with one another that only they could understand.

At the same time this vocabulary was taught, we were warned never to use it except among ourselves and with agents under secure circumstances, because its use would identify us as spies. Obviously, learning the language of espionage was partly a familiarization with the tools of the trade and partly an initiation rite.

The operations course taught the doctrine that the person in charge of agents who collected intelligence and performed other clandestine tasks, the case officer, was the key figure in the activities of the Clandestine Services. We were all case officers, and upon our shoulders rested the success or failure of the missions of the service. The doctrine was not meant as a morale booster, but rested on some basic realities of the business. The case officer is the ultimate link between the giant bureaucracy in Washington and the information it wants to collect, and the actions it wants to see taken. In accomplishing the desires of Washington, the case officer acts alone and in secret through the services of a foreign agent who operates in a hidden and hostile world that neither the American officer nor his superiors can enter directly to obtain what they want. If it would be possible for an American official to learn the Communist Party's plan or advise the prime minister what he should do to make sure his government is not harmed, by simply walking into the Communist Party's headquarters and talking to the chairman or calling up the prime minister to chat about the matter, there would be no need for the secret agent. Once clandestine activity is actually undertaken, everything depends upon the clarity and honesty of communications between the case officer and his agent and, then, upon the way the case officer communicates with his station and home office.

Major portions of the course, therefore, centered on clandestine communications and agents and the need for prompt, accurate, and full reporting of activities.

How to find suitable agents, induce them to work for us, be assured that they were doing a good job, keep them at work as long as they were needed, and get rid of them without their causing trouble in the future by possibly revealing to the wrong persons what their services for us had been, were topics with which military pedagogy could not cope as facilely as it could with tradecraft terminology or clandestine communications devices.

Agent assessment, agent recruitment, agent handling, and agent termination were matters of human relations that did not lend themselves to Army basic training manual analysis, but Stan Archer and his crew did their best to reduce human nature to the simplest possible terms. No time was wasted in reading psychology; we dove into case studies. Some of these were simulations and some actual past operations of the CIC or the FBI. In examining these cases, the instructors, while paying lip service to the reality that varieties of human reactions are vast, tried to fit motivation into just three categories. Agents were motivated by financial considerations, ideological convictions, or coercion.

Assessing a potential agent, then, was a matter of looking for one of these three ways that could be used to lead up to the recruitment pitch. The man who could be bought was an easy case, but considered tricky. If one intelligence service could buy him, two or more could probably purchase his services. A person who was willing to work because of his conviction either that he hated Communists so much or admired the United States so greatly that he gladly joined the team was also considered to be a mixed blessing. For one thing, his cover for really sensitive missions, where his true feelings had to be absolutely unsuspected, was bad. A violently anti-Communist individual could not possibly penetrate a Communist front or party, and a person who was known to be sympathetic to the United States was unsuitable for a large number of political intelligence collection or action missions. Then, too, the manipulation of a person's ideological convictions posed problems of understanding the mind that our instructors preferred to stay away from. They liked coercion as the solution of the method of motivating an agent.

By coercion, they meant a number of things. One was blackmail. They liked to point out how successfully the Soviets used this technique, and we read a number of stories of how the Soviets lured diplomats in Moscow into love nests in KGB-controlled apartments for appropriate picture-taking sessions. We went through a couple of rooms in the old houses on the post that were equipped with various types of two-way mirrors so we could see how easily this kind of thing could be done. We saw training films showing how Soviets seduced secretaries.

Another coercive technique that the instructors liked was ex-

125

ploiting links with illegal activities or criminal conduct. Embezzlement, black market operations, misuse of company or government funds, counterfeiting, and similar offenses were favorites. Their choice as useful coercive devices reflected the experience of the instructors in the postwar occupation of Germany or their past FBI backgrounds. To these men most of the world was remembered as a happy land of strong policemen who could be counted on to cooperate with a friendly intelligence service. In that kind of world potential agents were confronted with proof of their past misdeeds and promised immunity from prosecution in exchange for their espionage services. It did indeed seem to be the easiest and safest way to get results. The use of liaison with police and security services around the world was the foundation of most Clandestine Services activities, accounting for more than 70 percent of all intelligence collection at the height of the cold war. Whether this was because of the teaching in these early training courses or because it was such an obviously simple and efficient way to work, is impossible to say.

Unfortunately, although a lot of the world is governed by police states, not all of them are friendly toward the CIA. In particular, this is the case of the number one priority target, the Soviet Union, and also the case of Communist China. To learn to operate against these, and other so-called hard targets, requires more experience and understanding of human relations than was taught at ISOLATION.

Simplification of human motivation was not the only sin committed by our instructors when they guided us through case studies. They sometimes cheated a bit also in making their teaching points on other matters of operational decision.

The lecturer on target analysis for counterintelligence operations was a prime offender. This man had been an FBI agent and, during World War II, he had been assigned to an important case involving Nazi espionage activities in the United States targeted at defense plants on the East Coast. He based his lecture on target analysis on the experience gained in that operation.

First of all, he explained the situation. The Nazis were trying to obtain information on defense production in a number of factories making ammunition and arms in several states. According to him, the FBI had discovered the operation by careful surveillance of several of these installations, observing strangers loitering in the vicinity of the plants, and even following what appeared to be agents having meetings with their case officers.

"We found out that the Nazis had landed a couple of case officers by submarine on a remote beach on Long Island," he said, "and the chief of the operation, we discovered, was a German illegal who apparently had been born in Wisconsin, only his papers had been faked. He wasn't a German American, but another Nazi intelligence officer who also had been planted in the U.S. by a black landing."

It seemed that this chief of operations worked out of Washington, and our instructor had been a member of the FBI surveillance squad who covered him. The squad had a most unproductive time. They were never able to pick up their target in any kind of compromising situation upon which a case could have been made for his arrest and interrogation.

"Other operations we had going against this bunch, though, showed us that their activities were spread out from New England to the Carolinas. Most important of all, we found out that they evidently had a radio operator on Long Island who was transmitting their reports to Germany."

The instructor's question to us was what should the FBI do to break up the operation? What target should they select for possible recruitment from among the large number of members of this spy network about whom they were compiling information? Who would be the one member of the network, if compromised and forced to work for us, who could not only enable the Bureau to plug up the leaks in national security but perhaps mislead the Germans into thinking that the operation was still not compromised? Who could most logically feed the Germans phony, but important-appearing information so that they would continue sending further intelligence collection requirements enabling the FBI to get a still better idea of what the Germans needed to know? Knowing what the Germans needed to know about U.S. defense production would help intelligence analysts determine what Germany's military problems were, what Germany was afraid we were going to be able to bring to bear against their armies. In other words, what recruitment would best enable the FBI to run not merely a police operation to wrap up a spy net but also an aggressive counterintelligence operation that would continue to produce useful information?

The class speculated about the possibility of picking up the principal agent whom our instructor had been following in Washington. He was the man in charge, so if he were compromised and recruited, we would control the entire operation, argued a large number of the class.

"Not a chance," said the instructor. "You guys are shooting too high. This man was a real old pro. As I told you, we could never pin anything on him."

We asked about the major installations that the net was reporting on and the information regarding its agents in these places. If one or two major installations could be controlled, couldn't we hope to obtain the results we wanted?

The instructor fed us some of this information and we debated the possibilities for a short time. Then he scored his point.

"Look, you are missing the main idea. Don't we tell you that the key to operations is communications? Don't we try to teach you that full and reliable communications from the case officers in the field is what the whole thing is about? Who controlled the Nazis' communications? Who was it that we could recruit, who could control all the communications, and still have the net continue to function exactly as before, working on its requirements, giving Germany the information it wanted? Who, thanks to our recruitment, could enable us to alter this stuff so they would just get junk that would keep them sending new requirements but wouldn't damage our national security? The radio operator. We recruited the radio operator."

We had to admit that we had not grasped the key points sufficiently. We had not made the obviously correct target analysis that the FBI had made. Someone in the class raised his hand. The instructor acknowledged him. "How did you ever manage to recruit the radio operator?" the student asked.

There was a pause, and then the instructor said quietly, "He walked in."

The shrewd analysis and the stunningly correct and successful recruitment had been the product of chance and not of the careful evaluation of choices our instructor was trying to teach us was the way business was done. Most of us would soon learn that the Clandestine Services depended on walk-ins for their best results. The walk-in, the person who volunteered to help, made up a significant number of the corps of our clandestine agents, we would subsequently discover.

More interesting than these cases with their sometimes distorted presentations and conclusions were the guest lecturers from TSS.

TSS, the Technical Services Staff, supplied the operators in the field with the support needed for communicating with agents in situations where personal meetings between case officers and agents were impossible or highly dangerous, as well as a range of other services, including installing bugging equipment. When the full-scale Junior Officer Trainee program was in effect, the JOTs would be trained in some of these specialties as part of their operations course. The JOTs would also be taught the techniques of guerrilla warfare. We just heard lectures and were shown films of TSS products and of the art of insurgent forces' violence. Anyone requiring more knowledge and specific skills was required to take courses from TSS or the paramilitary staff.

As these were the years when agents were being dispatched into the Soviet Union and satellite countries and when Hans Tofte was supposedly sending them into North Korea, the TSS men took a lot of time describing radio transmitters with which these agents were supplied and the process of documenting them with the necessary papers.

TSS was especially proud of being able to supply agents going into the Soviet Union with all the necessary papers, in perfect copies, they modestly assured us. Their ability to do this was due to a lucky find a TSS staff member had made while he was in the Army. When his unit was taking command of the small Alpine village of Oberstdorf near the Austrian border, he had discovered a number of metal boxes in a warehouse. Because of his background as an intelligence sergeant in OSS, he realized the significance of their contents. The boxes were stuffed with thousands of Russian identity documents and documents from other East European nationals as well. They had been stripped from prisoners and dead soldiers serving in the Russian army or looted from the archives of cities as the German Wehrmacht marched across Russia.

Included in the documents were the green passports, which every Soviet citizen aged sixteen and over must carry always; the red draft booklets every Russian boy over eighteen must have; the gray-covered work booklets that record employment status and all changes that all employed adults have to hold; Communist Party and Communist youth, *komsomol*, membership cards, and many other civilian and military personal papers. What he had found were files of German intelligence used for the same purpose that TSS was to use them later, fabricating Soviet documents to enable agents to live and move around within the enormously detailed system of personal controls by means of which the Soviet government keeps an eye on its people and tries to prevent exactly what the Germans and we were doing.

The TSS lecturer was proudest of all of the fact that TSS had solved a major problem the Germans encountered when they had been forging the Soviet documents. German thoroughness and passion for perfection caused the Germans to make fatal mistakes which resulted in the discovery of all the agents they sent into the Soviet Union with these documents. One error was made in binding the passports, small cloth-covered booklets held together by two wire staples. German copying of the paper stock and its waffle-design watermark, and the stamped cachets was perfect, and so were the staples. As in the United States, German staple wire for many years had been coated to prevent rusting so that pages bound by them would not be spoiled by dampness or long storage. In Russia such a luxury did not exist. Every Russian passport had large rust marks in the middle, sometimes on every page.

German phony Soviet passports were too good in one other respect, as well. The Germans used German cloth to duplicate the Russian passports' covers. The Germans had been meticulous weavers for years, an art the Russians couldn't claim. Russian passport cloth was made of coarse irregular cotton that no one in Germany or the United States would consider buying even as bargain seconds. All the Russian counterintelligence needed to do was to handle a German fake and the difference was immediately apparent. The German passport was too slick and well made.

TSS profited by this and was careful to use nonrustproof wire for its staples. The lecturer pointed out it was harder to find any craftsman in America who would agree to weave the equivalent of the shoddy Russian cloth. They did, however, and the lecturer passed around the class examples of a real Russian passport, a German copy, and a TSS copy. Our boys had done a superior job of forgery.

For secure agent communications, in addition to the agent radios, TSS could provide a number of secret writing systems. The lecturer demonstrated a number of the less sophisticated ones. These were of two kinds, known as wet and dry. The wet systems involved using chemicals sometimes disguised as pills to enable the

130

agent to store them innocently in his medicine cabinet or carry them with him undetected. When dissolved in water the pills formed an ink. The agent was to write with this ink, using a wooden pick whose tip he had sharpened with a razor blade, on bond paper that he had previously prepared by rubbing with a soft cloth on both sides in all four directions to create an even texture. After writing the message, and allowing it to dry, he would rub the paper again in all four directions to conceal the message within the paper's fibers. After that, he would steam the paper and press it in a thick book. Finally, he would write an innocent cover letter on the surface. The cover letter might contain key words to signal that a secret message was contained on the page. Generally, it was thought advisable to avoid signals since poor imagination in their use could lead to the letter's being suspect.

The dry system was a variation of simple carbon paper. Bond stock was impregnated with chemicals. The agent would insert this piece of paper between one on which he wrote his message and a blank page. The invisible carbon would transfer the message to the blank page. The agent would then burn his message, and prepare a cover letter on top of the paper to which his message had been chemically transferred. A special developer disguised as a household item, as in the case of the pills, could be safely stored, and applying it with a swab, the agent could read the secret messages he would receive by this system.

We were given only a very superficial treatment of the more sophisticated microdot system, which, in those days, was in its infancy. This involved a special camera that could photograph a letter-sized page in an area of film equal to the dot of an "i" on a page. The dots would be glued to the "i's" or periods in the cover letter.

Special cameras for all kinds of uses were another stock item of TSS. The most important were the miniature cameras that were a new product and which could be concealed in various ordinary items an agent might normally carry so that he could securely copy documents or take other photographs required by his assignment without being detected.

Concealment devices were still another feature of the line of secure communications devices that TSS displayed. False-bottomed suitcases, briefcases, typewriter carrying cases, handbags, books, almost any item a traveler might logically and innocuously carry with him, TSS experimented with as a means of concealing agent communications, reports, films, stolen documents, whatever he might be trying to pass along to his case officer.

These presentations made us all feel that we were really being introduced into the secret world of clandestine operations. They were not the principal part of agent communications training, however. That training focused on arranging, conducting, and reporting agent meetings. We were introduced to the theory of the security-efficiency equation. Obviously, the most secure contact with an agent, a situation in which the case officer and agent relationship would be least likely to be compromised, was to have no personal meeting at all. The various TSS devices had been developed for cases when security considerations so outweighed efficiency of communication that their use was clearly indicated. To communicate efficiently, however, two people normally must see and talk to each other. The agent meeting was indispensable when explanation and discussion of actions were required. It was also needed when problems developed in the relationship of agent and case officer. To the task of holding such meetings, the training staff brought to bear its anemic psychological resources and its enormous faith in following memorized procedure.

Security was stressed as the most essential ingredient of personal meetings with agents. This, of course, was quite sensible, since an agent meeting, by definition, was the least secure communication system an intelligence operation could use. The past experience of the staff, however, caused them to give it an extra amount of emphasis. Operational security is one of the many worries that plague a counterintelligence officer, as our trainers mostly all were or had been.

Counterintelligence is paranoia made systematic by a card index. To a counterintelligence officer everyone and everything is suspect. All dossiers are assumed to contain derogatory information. If there is no derogatory information in a file, it is because it has not been reported yet. This was certainly the point of view of the man who gave us a presentation on aspects of the general situation we would confront at our overseas posts. Sometimes called the "operational climate," that is, the overall conditions under which we would be arranging meetings, he chose to consider it as a confrontation between the CIA case officer and what he labeled "the active opposition."

This term enabled him to point out that we had to take into consideration, in making our agent meeting plans, not only the Communist enemy, but also the local intelligence services of the countries where we would be stationed, the staffs of embassies of other countries to be found at our posts, the intelligence officers of these embassies, in particular, the national police of these countries, the local police, local security guards, bank guards, hotel policemen, private detectives, and even night watchmen. All of these, or one, or several of them, could take delight in uncovering our clandestine meetings for a great variety of reasons. Even though the country we were in might be friendly toward the United States, and even though we might be carrying on joint operations with the local intelligence or police against the Communists, one fine day these relationships might sour or the local counterparts might simply get curious about exactly what we might be up to in addition to agreed-upon operations against the Communists. They might even want to check on how we were handling an agent they had helped us recruit.

Other embassies, even friendly ones, might on occasion want to get something incriminating on the United States, or they might be about to make some move on the international political chessboard that would cause them to want to know something about our clandestine activities. Local security guards, bank police, private detectives, hotel cops, or night watchmen might be motivated by simple curiosity upon seeing something that their trained eyes would spot as unusual behavior. Also, any of them at any given moment might be recruited by the Communists or a local police or intelligence service to perform a surveillance job against us.

Special attention was paid to surveillance. According to our instructors, the basic surveillance unit was a team of three. They worked by covering the subject alternately, changing positions as required and signaling each other who "had" the subject and when he was about to turn the subject over to a partner because he was afraid that he was too close to the subject or that further coverage by him would require some awkward or revealing move that would cause the subject to "make" his surveillance.

Countersurveillance could involve a number of measures. The simplest one would remain part of my window-shopping pattern I could never shake. Almost all store windows can be used as mirrors to view what is going on across the street behind you and on either

133

side, if you use them correctly. After taking training, I was never again able merely to look at the objects on display in a store window. I always tested the mirror effect of the glass.

The threats to a successful meeting do not stop with checking for surveillance that might be being run by any of the myriad forces of the "active opposition." The meeting place itself has to be selected with great care and checked for any audio devices that might be hidden to record the conversations for the benefit of opposition elements. Preferably, the route to and from the meeting and the meeting site should be checked by a countersurveillance team belonging to our side. They should be watching the meeting from some appropriate spot where neither the agent nor opposition can spot them. In case of any sign of trouble, their job is to signal the case officer, who will break off the meeting immediately.

The discussion of signals was a highlight of the liturgy of definitions the staff followed. At every step of the operational meeting procedure—approaching the meeting place, checking surveillance, checking the meeting place before the meeting takes place, countersurveillance of the meeting, during the course of the meeting itself, and following the meeting—signals need to be employed to indicate any signs of trouble or need to change plans or cancel the meeting. The instructors could not decide whether these signals were best considered safety signals or danger signals.

They said that, if, for example, meetings took place in a safe apartment, that is, an apartment controlled by the station, maintained by someone who lived there, and to whom a visit from agent and case officer could be explained, the safe apartment keeper might put a flower pot in one window, or have a shade pulled down to a certain level to indicate no sign of trouble. If trouble were feared, he would remove the flower pot or alter the height of the window shade. The absence of the safety signal would be the danger signal. They insisted that the important thing was to keep the pattern of activities around the safe meeting place as regular as possible. If a pot were put into the window to indicate danger only on the one day a week that meetings took place, for example, the opposition might spot it. If they had been surveilling the place for some time and had grown accustomed to the pot, they might not miss it right away, or they might think its absence was only accidental. A great debate raged over the proper use of the pot, until someone suggested that signals not so directly associated with the apartment would be a better solution. But the point stuck that a danger signal was the absence of a safety signal.

This sort of thinking also led to the prescription of a format for an operational meeting. Presumably if this format were followed all would go well, or at least, would appear to, besides giving the officer a sense of having acted correctly.

The first item of business was to ask the agent if he had had any security problems since the last meeting or encountered anything untoward en route to the meeting. This out of the way, he should be carefully questioned about any item that required checking. Next, any financial transactions that were necessary were to be taken care of. Receipts should be obtained. Then new assignments should be given and more information sought about the report that was handed in at the present meeting, if called for. A time and place should be set for the next meeting plus an alternate schedule, in case any of the safety signals should turn into danger signals at any point in the process of complying with the plan for the next get-together.

Some instructors insisted that right after checking the agent for any bad news concerning security, the first item on the agenda, the next meeting plan and alternate should be arranged, in case the meeting in progress had to be broken off before covering all the topics.

In any case, most of the students thought the plan to be a little stark, since the personal meeting was being held presumably because the use of an impersonal communications device had been ruled out. Stan Archer reluctantly agreed that some time should probably be spent on "a little bit of rapport."

We tried to act out personal meetings. The results were usually as stilted as the staff's meeting format. We came a bit closer to reality and had more fun carrying out "live" surveillance and counter-surveillance problems and making meetings in the largest nearby city, Norfolk, Virginia. Norfolk, being a port town and the site of a naval base, had plenty of "active opposition" plainclothesmen as well as a good-sized police force that we had to try to keep unaware of our activities.

It was amazing how easily we could lose a familiar instructor who was trying to act as the subject of our amateur surveillance efforts. In order to make things a bit more difficult, as well as to provide a broader base for critiquing the problems, we were asked to prepare surveillance and countersurveillance plans and meeting arrangements which the instructors collected and handed out to other members of the class before these exercises. No one was allowed to use his own plan. Postmortems were indeed quite lively as a consequence, since everyone felt, at heart, had he used his own plan he would not have made so many silly mistakes.

Everyone found the live problems the highlight of the course, and these unanimous approvals in time resulted in the Office of Training's developing a week-long live problem in New York for the JOTs. Meanwhile, down on the Farm we learned something and the Norfolk police were provided a lot of free entertainment.

The human relations content of the agent operations course, superficial as it was on recruitment and agent handling, was weakest of all in the termination phase of agent relations. Once beyond the safety of a coercive police situation, where terminating an agent's service, without fear of his talking, could be assured either by his gratitude at being forgiven sentencing for his overt criminal acts or by locking him up for them if necessary, the instructors were out of their water. The "active opposition" came down upon them in full force. One reason they saw such a large opposition contingent just around every street corner was that, although reluctant to admit it to themselves, they realized that they were training us to engage in illegal activity. When they could think of themselves as adjuncts of the local law-and-order forces, working against the Russian foe and his subservient local Communist subversives, they were comfortable in the espionage business. Although they might talk about our missions to collect positive intelligence and do political action operations, in their minds they were always safe, honest counterintelligence officers.

When they looked at our collecting secret political information or covertly aiding a political faction in a foreign country, they were face to face with the reality that we were committing crimes before the laws of the countries where we did these things. If a case officer attempted to silence a talkative agent in these cases with the threat of revealing the agent's treason, the agent could threaten to reveal the case officer as a foreign spy. So when we discussed the case officer's using the threat of revelation as a means of coercing an uncooperative agent into silence, it was weakly suggested that possibly we could get the case officer out of town on the next plane after the

136

threatened revelation had been made. The agent would have to stay and pay the price.

The tough-minded insisted that we could always make our tradecraft language meaningful by literally terminating the agent. This brought the same shudders as discussions of assassination contingency planning, and some of the same practical problems. Who would hit the victim? As in assassination contingency planning, hiring a criminal seemed advisable. Arranged by cut-outs that would separate the case officer from any direct involvement, this seemed better than any other method. But the great majority of the class felt it was a very drastic way to solve the problem.

The lame solution that was generally agreed upon was to pay the agent a large separation bonus. How to dismiss an agent whose services were no longer required simply was too uncomfortable a reminder that the particular tasks that were ours to perform in President Eisenhower's and John Foster Dulles's anti-Communist crusade were outside the law, and no one cared to think too long about this.

Training at the Farm in the early fifties had the effect of hiding the reality of our work at the same time it taught us the trade. This was accomplished, in part, by the pressure that resulted from an overcrowded schedule that left little time for reflection. Most of all it resulted from the dominance that the counterintelligence perspective gave to everything. The world out there was a hostile place, full of so many Communist agents and deceitful fellow travelers that the job of thwarting their snares and delusions that were threatening everyone was enormous and one that demanded the use of any possible means. Besides this, tradecraft was intriguing. The case officer's work combined two essential elements of job satisfaction, responsibility and authority, far better than almost any other position in the bureaucratic structures of American government or corporations. Although the instructors tried to reduce everything to a military manual's checklist of dos and don'ts, obviously the variety of situations, problems, and decisions that concerned a case officer was as diverse as the human beings upon whom successful operations ultimately depended. No one but the case officer could decide whether or not the look on the agent's face belied or reinforced the information in the report he handed in. Only the case officer could hazard an educated guess whether or not this man could really accomplish what was expected of him. The decisions that the case officer had to make on the spot about these matters could not, in most cases, ever be unmade. The agent, once the decision had been made, was launched on a course from which it was too dangerous and compromising to retreat.

Stan Archer said, "There's no substitute for fast thinking on your feet."

If by that he meant to stress the need to be adaptable, I was to agree heartily from the moment I arrived in Singapore. Nothing about my cover, my job, and not too much about the world in general resembled what I had been taught at the Farm.

9
Is This Really It?

The Stoomvaart Mij. *Oranje* finally eased into Empire Dock in Keppel Harbour at noon on Thursday, April 1, 1954. More than an hour had been consumed in the operation before the pride of the prewar Dutch merchant marine came to rest. This gave Mike Campbell, our tablemate and friendliest feature of our nineteen-day voyage from Southampton, time to describe to me the first sights of Singapore that came into view. Mike was returning from home leave to his post as headmaster of the second largest boy's school in Singapore. He had come out east in 1939 as a member of His Majesty's Colonial Service's education staff and was on hand three years later for the unseemingly swift surrender to the Japanese which earned him four years in jungle prison camps and experience in bridge building over a river called the Kwai. It had also left him with a nervous laugh, with which he punctuated his remarks.

"The two important features, ones that will seem familiar to you, Joe, since they're our best effort to duplicate your ruddy skyscrapers, are the Asia Insurance Building over on the left there, ha, ha"—Mike pointed—"and your good friends the Red Chinese with their new Bank of China Building way over on the right, ha, ha. Now I must look for my trusty houseboy. Good old Ah Lok always meets me and has some sturdy Malay bloke bring my car."

I had no idea who was going to meet me and was uneasy with my cover story that I was a United States Information Service liaison officer with the British. I had mentioned once to Mike that I was to be the American contact with the propagandists on the staff of Malcolm MacDonald, British Commissioner for Southeast Asia, John Rainer, and his deputy, Dennis Ambler.

"Oh, you're going to work with old Ambler, eh?" Mike said with a notable rise in his heavy black Scot's eyebrows. I realized at once that Mike knew something more than I had expected. Ambler was a British MI-6 officer with a supposedly innocuous British Information Office cover much like my own with USIS. I was blown. My mentors at the Farm would have been sorely disappointed in me. I tried not to talk any more about my work with Mike after that.

So with the ship finishing its docking, I decided to leave him looking for his Ah Lok and go down to the cabin, hoping we could all get off somehow without my possibly blowing someone from the station since, for all I knew, someone from the station rather than from my cover office might meet us. I had Mike's phone number and promised to let him know where we would be staying when we got settled.

"It's good of you to show up now that I've got all the work done," Jeanne commented. Actually she wasn't as irritated as she sounded because she never appreciated my uncoordinated efforts to assist with her superior talents at organizing the children and the baggage.

There was by now considerable activity in the passageway outside our cabin. Sounds of baggage being moved, the scurrying of the Indonesian cabin boys, and the movement and voices of passengers and people who had come to meet them. We sat on the edge of our bunks. Julie was playing with some beads. Ruthven was restless.

"When are we going to go out, Daddy?"

"I don't know. I think someone will come for us soon."

"How soon? How soon?"

"I really don't know, dear. Soon I hope."

Fortunately this dialogue was not prolonged. A quick knock at

140

the door, followed immediately by its opening, ended our wait. In the doorway was a large woman with a broad smile and a take-charge air. Wilma was a tall, buxom blonde. She had just passed her thirty-second birthday. Subsequently I had a number of other secretaries who had just passed that birthday and I came to appreciate why it is called the desperate age for women. Wilma was compulsively efficient. She also talked too much about company business, I soon discovered. In her defense I must say this was a common failing in the Clandestine Services. Agee was able to tell the Cubans so much about activities in which he wasn't personally involved because CIA secretaries and most officers could never stop gossiping.

"You're the Smiths, and I'm Wilma," she said. "Welcome to Singapore. Do you have all your things? If so, we'll take right off. Mohammed," she called out into the corridor. "Mohammed is the USIS station wagon driver, so he'll take charge of your baggage and everything."

A skinny, rather tall, and very black-faced figure appeared. "Morning, mem; morning, tuan," he said to us. "I'm Mohammed, your driver." Mohammed's most distinguishing feature was his unmatched different-colored eyes, one brown, the other milky gray. Obviously, we were to enjoy our first drive in Singapore chauffeured by a one-eyed man.

By the time we and our belongings were assembled off ship and we were all being bundled into the USIS station wagon, the full impact of the noonday tropical heat was upon us all.

"My god, it's hot," my wife remarked.

"Oh, this is just a normal day. You'll get used to it," Wilma said. "I thought we'd drive over to the Raffles and get you and the children a cool drink and then I'll tell you about our arrangements for you.

"Bob Boylan should have come down to meet you, but he had a lunch with some newsmen and begged off. Typical. You'll see. He's not going to be a cover boss you'll have too much interference from, but on the other hand, he won't be of any particular help.

"Can you imagine, he even suggested that the chief of station should meet you in his car?"

We drove slowly out of the harbor area, past warehouses and customs sheds. Because of the station wagon's diplomatic tags, we were waved on and didn't have to show any of our documents. This was fortunate because in addition to the heat, and the brackish harbor water smells, the odor of Asia, that pungent mixture of the spices of food vendors' wares and lord knows what decaying in the monsoon drains that lined the road, was becoming more apparent by the minute.

Evidently it was also fortunate that Mohammed's bad eye was his left one. This enabled him to ignore completely the pedicabs, water carriers, peddlers, and others who occupied the side of the street along which we rapidly sped following the British custom of left-handed traffic circulation. They simply had to get out of Mohammed's way the best they could and he moved steadily on to his destination, the Raffles Hotel.

"Singapore would not be Singapore without the World Famous Raffles Hotel" was the legend of the hotel's ad in the *Straits Times* in 1954. It was impossible to enter the long corridor running the length of the public rooms, walk past the potted palms, feel the ceiling fans slowing turning the air far above you, and not agree. Sprawled in the oversized wicker chairs beside glass-topped wicker tables, English gentlemen and their ladies were dawdling tardily over their elevenses when we entered the lobby at about a quarter to one. As we settled around a table, we heard a linen-suited occupant of the table next to ours call out, "Boy, whiskey!" A white-clad Chinese waiter quickly got the message and dashed for the bar.

At any moment I expected to see Somerset Maugham come into the room and join the chap who had ordered the whiskey.

Wilma explained that the station's decision was to put us in temporary quarters at a family hotel, The Chequers, away from the center of town because they thought this would be pleasanter for the children. The Raffles would have been fine, I thought, especially since the USIS office was just one block down Beach Road from the hotel. But, Wilma said, the station chief didn't want us to be ostentatious. She went on with her briefing on relationships at the post while we ordered gin and tonics for ourselves and fruit squash for the children.

"It's important that you get off on the right foot with Boylan," Wilma began. "His wife's the niece of Senator Kerr, and Boylan is pretty much in the shadow of his important in-laws. I believe they're the only reason he's USIS chief here. Anyway, I think I've piled up enough points with Boylan to help us both.

"As you know, I've been here a year, working as the secretary for

142

your predecessor. Because there has been such a long delay in your getting here, I've actually done more work for USIS than I should, although our chief has me help with the station finances.

"Another problem is that, frankly, USIS is more than a little bit jealous of your position, or, at least, they were of your predecessor's manner of doing business. Since you're in contact with the Commissioner's Office and they're just putting out propaganda in the local press and printing their Chinese newspaper, they will want to try to boss you around. But you can't permit that, and the chief of station, of course, doesn't want anything like that. He wants to make sure that you understand you're working for him, and the hell with USIS."

This was a lot to digest within the first hour of my arrival. It was also hardly comprehensible to my wife, and certainly of no interest to the children. By this time, in fact, Julie would simply not sit still. And most of her drink was running down the edge of the table.

Wilma kept on.

"Now, we'll have to get the Boylans to set you up to make your courtesy calls. We'll also have to get you some transportation. You're authorized a car. We'll have to buy you one and we'll have to get you a driver. You should have a driver for prestige and the COS insists on drivers for taking care of station cars." She laughed.

"He had a real fight with the auditors the last time they were here. They didn't want to pay for his driver's salary from station funds. He told them it wasn't safe to leave a car parked on Singapore streets without someone to guard it. So if they wouldn't pay for this protection, he'd refuse to sign a property responsibility statement for the car, and if the car was damaged or stolen, the auditors could take the responsibility. He won."

I suggested that we had better move on to The Chequers. The Farm had not prepared me for a secretary that would have so much company business to discuss in front of my wife. I could also see that the children were not going to be able to take much more of this monologue either, without getting disturbingly restless.

"Well, there's a lot more to discuss," Wilma insisted, "but you know what you feel like doing."

"We can talk later. Please let's go."

Back into the station wagon we piled, our clothes rumpled from the noonday heat, our little girl asking about lunch, and our baby whimpering. Our Wilma, however, undaunted, continued to list

143

the things she thought it important for me to hear. I stopped listening and concentrated on Mohammed's miraculous maneuvering that consistently succeeded in just missing colliding with each pedicab we passed.

The Chequers Hotel was very definitely located away from the center of town, far up Thompson Road. As we drove up to the sprawling place, however, it did appear to have a large green lawn that perhaps the children would indeed enjoy.

Inside, in addition to the Chinese room clerk, we met the proprietress, who evidently wanted to get a first-hand look at her American guests. Her graying hair was drawn back severely and secured in a tight bun. Her dress was equally conservative and severe. When she spoke, it seemed that her previous experience might have been as warden in a women's prison.

"Now we hope you'll follow the mealtime schedule here, and be sure to remember that from two-thirty to four-thirty is quiet hour. The children should be napping. We do not provide any kind of services during that time."

The hotel had just two floors. Our rooms, one for my wife and me, and a communicating one for the children, were on the second floor. They smelled as though they had not been opened for several years, and the boy who brought the luggage upstairs hurried to open the wooden shutters that had been closed. The windows had no glass or screens, and stretching from the ceiling to nearly the floor, they seemed to provide a fine opportunity for our baby girl to crawl up their sills and fall out.

In addition to their musty odor, the rooms contained some other occupants. A trail of red ants led from the bathroom door across the children's room, disappearing behind the crib that had been provided for our baby. Several scouts had already started up one leg of the crib.

Wilma and I both saw the look on Jeanne's face. "Boy, use the spray," Wilma commanded of the room attendant. Soon Flit was added to the other smells. I looked around again at our surroundings. The squeaking ceiling fan slowly billowing the yellow mosquito netting, the Flit, and other smells made me think I was back in Djakarta. Except for the private bathroom, The Chequers wasn't much of an improvement over my quarters last summer, I thought. My wife and I exchanged glances, but the first order of business was obviously to try to get the baby a bottle of milk and into bed.

Wilma ordered the room boy to get milk and he disappeared. She seemed to sense our feelings, so she then said she would leave us and we were to call her at four-thirty and she would be glad to help us get anything we needed, using her Morris Minor rather than Mohammed for any transportation. We thanked her and she left.

"Do you think we'll ever get that milk?" my wife asked.

"I'll go downstairs and see what I can stir up," I replied. "Back soon."

In practically no time I was back with all sorts of good news.

"The dining room's closed till six. The baby will have to be fed in her room, no children under five are allowed in the dining room. There is no one to babysit while we eat, so I guess we'll eat in shifts. Here is her milk—it's canned but maybe she won't notice the difference."

We stared at one another. Then Jeanne, fighting back the tears, dug into her catch-all bag.

"We still have some crackers and cookies left over from the ship, so I guess that's going to be lunch for all of us."

After the girls had both been bedded down for naps, she looked at me and said, "Welcome to the mysterious east. It looks like the beginning of a real fun tour."

"Now, darling, you know this is April Fool's day. That probably explains all these things."

"Ha."

As the events of the next months of my first tour of overseas duty unfolded, I often thought that April Fool's day presaged more than my feeble joke intended.

It was the practice in 1954 to prepare a letter of instructions for an officer going on an assignment such as the one in Singapore. Singapore, however, presented a set of special circumstances, because it was not just another piece of the Far East Division's real estate, as headquarters people proprietarily referred to the countries within the division's area of responsibility. It was the site of the headquarters of all British defense forces east of Suez—army, navy and air—as well as the location of the office of the High Commissioner for Southeast Asia, to which were attached an office of MI-5, Britain's intelligence service charged with the "security of the realm," MI-6, the British secret service for foreign intelligence operations, an office for collating intelligence from all British and Commonwealth intelligence-collection organizations in the Far East, and the Information Research Department, IRD, Britain's cold war propaganda and psychological warfare service. The CIA Singapore station, hence, was located in the center of British intelligence and cold war activities involving all of Asia. Moreover, there was an agreement between CIA and the British services that they would not run operations in each other's territories. This, of course, meant the United States and Britain. Did it also mean Singapore and Malaya, where self-government had been promised and where there were obvious links between the Chinese Communists and the Malayan Communist Party, which was fighting a guerrilla war against the British?

To assume that the agreement precluded our running our own operations in Singapore and Malaya ran directly counter to the firmly established headquarters doctrine that the Clandestine Services should have a plan of operations for every country. Since it was our responsibility to roll back Communist imperialism everywhere, we had to be capable of developing the most effective means of doing so, and this certainly could not be the case if we were to accept arbitrary limitations on our freedom of action such as the agreement with the British.

How to deal with this matter posed a problem for the instruction letter writers that they solved by a careful selection of murky words.

My letter of instructions went something like this. First, it emphasized the prime responsibilities of maintaining liaison with IRD and MI-6 concerning propaganda and psychological warfare activities as shall be jointly determined and agreed upon by CIA and MI-6, especially as regards activities and programs of international organizations and the programs of the Asia Foundation, and exchanging information on developments in all the countries in the area. Then, at the same time, the letter ordered a series of other accomplishments, such as developing means of conducting propaganda and psychological warfare activities against the Malayan and Chinese Communists and creating capabilities of using Singapore as a base for third-country black propaganda operations in support of Agency activities in those countries. In other words, the gestation period of these developments and creations was left vague enough that if interrupted at any stage for any reason, such as their

146

being discovered by an irate MI-6 colleague, it could be claimed that the activity was purely exploratory and had not amounted to anything serious. As soon as the activity reached any important stage in creation and development, we could explain we had planned to tell them so that it could become one of the mutual interests jointly determined and agreed upon about which we were in liaison.

For that matter, however, activities of mutual interest with the British were not defined with any greater clarity or honesty. Southeast Asia was a mess in 1954. The French were obviously losing the war in Indochina, along with the will to do anything more about it. Sukarno, in Indonesia, had completely reversed his strong anti-Communist stance of 1949 when he had practically wiped out the Communist PKI after its feeble coup attempt against him. He seemed especially susceptible to the overtures of the Chinese Communists, and, every month, shiploads of Indonesian students passed through Singapore en route to high school and university training in Mao's institutions of learning. U Nu, the mystic socialist, was doing something in Burma, but no one, except he, could figure out what it was.

The United States was trying to base its strength in Southeast Asia on Magsaysay's government in the Philippines, and on support for the tough police chief General Pao, in Thailand, with backup throughout the area from Chinese Nationalist operators, who scurried about on myriad missions paid for by the six-hundred-man-plus CIA station in Taipei. With the Korean War over, our main strong point in Asia lay in the north, particularly in Japan.

The British, of course, held Hong Kong, as well as Singapore and Malaya. They also felt they had a special relationship with Burma. They were happy enough with the fact that "our guy" was in power in the Philippines, and they kind of conceded us Indonesia, since we had sided with Sukarno against the Dutch, and were glad they didn't have to try too hard to figure out what was going to happen there. They were happy too that we had plenty of hardware and clout in Japan. They were, however, somewhat dubious about what we were up to in Thailand, where they felt the country had been traditionally their friendly buffer against further French expansion in the area. Perhaps it would be more accurate to say they were hurt that General Pao preferred dealing with us just because we had so much money and they were rather short of funds. But it

147

was our Hong Kong station, with its guy lines trailing across the Straits of Formosa, that really set their teeth on edge. Hong Kong existed on the sufferance of the Chinese Communists. No more than a handful of saboteurs would be required to demolish the reservoir and parch the place out of existence, to name just one possibility, should the Chinese Communists ever become too annoyed by some operational prank of our Chinat agents.

We did agree on Indochina, but primarily to the premise that the French were through and that neither of us had a plan ready as to what we should do next.

Finally, they had their embassy in Peking, some China trade, and enough leftover assets in south China that they were willing to pass us a bag full of intelligence reports every month in Singapore. They insisted on exchanging these reports with us in Singapore for two reasons. First, the reports could be put through their large intelligence mill at the Southeast Asia Commissioner's offices in Phoenix Park to extract their most valuable contents before being handed over, and second, this procedure kept our Hong Kong station at arm's length from their people on the ground in that sensitive spot.

In regard to propaganda and psychological warfare operations against the Communists throughout the area, the British were extremely wary of the fact that we had such considerable sums to spend. In particular they were worried about the spreading into the area of the international anti-Communist front organizations we were supporting in Europe, like the World Assembly of Youth (WAY), the International Student Conference (COSEC), the International Confederation of Free Trade Unions, and the Congress for Cultural Freedom. The Asia Foundation, perhaps because it was already on the ground with representatives and offices in all the major Asia capitals, worried them most of all.

I had not learned anything about these concerns and disquietudes at the Farm, where I thought I was supposed to acquire all the professional skills of an operations officer. I received some indication of them in a series of conflicting briefings in the weeks between the end of my formal training and my departure for Singapore.

There were two schools of thought about liaison with the British. One was that it was a rare and beautiful thing to be nurtured with every care, because the British were the most sagacious spies in the business, with a long and remarkable tradition of success. The other was that it was a waste of time, the British officers were a bunch of supercilious snobs toward whom we should show an equivalent disdain. In time, the unmasking of Kim Philby, impeccable MI-6er and the most useful agent the Soviets ran during the cold war, may have brought the weight of the argument down on the second side, but in 1954 the first side had the upperhand. Allen Dulles enjoyed mulling over the exploits of Sir Francis Walsingham, the spymaster of Elizabeth I, whose hand, Dulles liked to point out, lay behind most of the major undertakings of Elizabeth's reign, such as manipulating the plotters around Mary Queen of Scots to the point where Elizabeth finally had the pretext to execute her cousin. Frank Wisner enjoyed the opportunity of going over operational details with such an astute intelligence officer as Kim Philby.

As a result of being briefed by representatives of both schools of thought, however, I arrived at my post with a formula for guiding my conduct that went something like this: our liaison with the British is one of our greatest assets; don't tell the bastards anything important. I would learn how things really worked from Bob Jantzen, the chief of station, Singapore, who belonged to a school all his own. Perhaps he could fashion his way through the maze because he had not been successfully indoctrinated at an Eastern prep school, as had many of the pro-British school, nor by poor Irish nuns at a parochial school, who hated even English muffins, as I suspected was the case of many of the anti-British school. In any case, he made British liaison work for CIA and for the good of his own career with impressive results.

"We'll get you out of The Chequers over the weekend and into your own house," Wilma affirmed, as soon as I had gotten settled in our office on Friday morning. She had heard out our complaints the night before when she came by after we phoned her at four-thirty, as we had agreed.

"It's actually a house far above your rank but there is no one higher to claim it now, so Jantzen just told the admin officer you were to have it. After all, they've got someone in our other house, which is brand-new. As you know, Bob insisted that the agency build two houses as part of our contribution to making sure there's adequate government housing at this post since rents are just impossible.

"And we won't worry about what Boylan thinks or anyone else in

USIS. After you get moved in, since it's in a very quiet neighborhood, Bob and Jane will come over to see you and you can arrange how you're going to get to work for the station. How much furniture did you bring?"

I explained that we had brought very little, that we had been told in Washington that we would get the second Agency house and that it was completely furnished, which naturally had influenced our packing and planning.

"Well, Bob didn't think it would be right for you to have the second house because it's right next door to his and this would be terrible for your cover."

Number 25 Rideout Road was what people at the turn of the century thought a comfortable townhouse in Singapore should be like. Plenty of room for air to circulate, and plenty of space to entertain your planter friends from up-country who happened to be in town. It was situated somewhat below the level of the street, and in addition to an ample front lawn, there was a sunken garden at the rear that was about half the size of a soccer field. The rooms were as oversized as the garden. Impressive dimensions, however, do not make a house a home. Rideout Road was fifty years past its prime.

The sunken garden, for one thing, had been neglected for some time before we moved in, and the stagnant water in its fountain bred the only mosquitoes in Singapore. City authorities requested that all residents clear their drains and report any signs of mosquitoes or larvae immediately. As soon as these reports were made, the sanitation department sent a truck and a crew to pour oil on the larvae and spray the area with DDT. With great pride, it was claimed that there were no mosquitoes in Singapore. And except for the failings of the lazy caretaker staff at 25 Rideout Road, the statement was correct.

As for the accommodations themselves, the rooms were huge, but a real estate promoter would have had to list it as a house with only a living room–dining room combination, kitchen, hall, two bedrooms, and two baths. There were only two bedrooms because the English shipped children home to England when they turned eight years old. They claimed that the climate was unhealthy for youngsters beyond that age, although, somehow, the climate was not harmful for infants or very young children. When pressed on this point by me one time, Mike Campbell admitted that it did not make sense to claim that the tropics couldn't harm infants but were bad for children over eight. He said that the real reason, actually, was that people were afraid that children who were exposed to natives after the age of eight might grow up speaking English the way they did and "become sort of half-breeds."

The furnishings were as limited as Wilma had indicated they would be. The two bedrooms contained nothing but beds and two straight-backed chairs. Our master bedroom, for some reason, also boasted a metal office desk. The living room–dining area, approximately forty feet by twenty, had no furniture besides the dining table, which extended to seat fourteen, and two rattan easy chairs and one small end table. There were no table lamps in the house. My wife thought the lights recessed along the walls made the living room look like a funeral parlor. Altogether, the house did not make us feel that our living arrangements had improved much over those at The Chequers.

A Buick pulled into the gravel driveway at about four o'clock Sunday afternoon. A man roughly six feet one got quickly out of the car. His large shoulders and head crowned with flaming red hair made him look at least six-six. He helped out a slight woman, blue-eyed, with very blond hair, probably bleached by hours on the golf course.

Bob bounced through the door, sweeping his wife Jane into the house with him.

"Joey and Jeannie," he greeted us with the inflection of a long-time friend that we came to learn he reserved for everyone he ever met. "How *are* you? *Great* to have you here."

Although we had only two chairs in the living room there were a few reasonably comfortable wicker ones on the porch, so Jeanne hastily summoned the houseboy to ask him to bring two of them inside and to take orders for drinks. We settled into a discussion of our situation.

Jane quickly assured Jeanne that we would love Singapore as soon as we became active socially. It was important to get out and meet people right away, she stressed, adding how fortunate we were to have such a large house for giving parties. My wife tried to explain she didn't see how we were going to be able to do much entertaining until something was done about the condition of the place, adding that she was more concerned at the moment that our baby girl did not fall down the fourteen feet of open stairway.

151

"Janie, why don't you and Jeannie go over the house together, and decide what it needs to fix it up, and we boys will get in a little shoptalk," Bob suggested. The wives took the suggestion and left the room.

"Well, Joey, what's the good word from Washington?" Bob asked.

"I was told, Bob, that I was to help you to find out just what the British think can be done to strengthen anti-Communist groups in all the countries in the area, try to get an idea of the kinds of themes they are using in their propaganda and why, and see what we might do jointly with them, if anything.

"On the other hand, Bob, I was told to be very careful not to give them any idea of the groups we are supporting, and to be very careful not to give away any of our programs. Frankly, this is a bit confusing to me. I mean, I don't see how I can expect to get them to open up to me while I'm not opening up to them. I was told you were the expert, and you'd tell me how it's done."

"Play it by ear, Joey, you gotta play it by ear."

"Well, could you tell me what you think I should stress? I mean, what do I do about the Asia Foundation liaison, for example, that the British seem so worried about?"

"Yeah, well, boy, I'm glad you're here to handle that one"—Bob was emphatic—"I've been telling them that you're the expert on that one, because, you know, we've just got a new Foundation rep in town and he doesn't want to tell them a damn thing. I have some ideas, of course, of what we should do, but what did they tell you in Washington?"

"Well, they said I was to work with you and figure out a way in which we could have meetings between you and me and the Asia Foundation man and the British and develop some kind of an agenda that we could talk about."

"That's what I've always said"—Bob nodded his head—"we gotta have some regular meetings and an agenda. Only, I want you to handle all of this, after the first meeting, okay?"

"Now, Bob, the other thing I'd like to talk about is that my letter of instructions says I'm to develop independent unilateral capabilities in addition to my liaison duties. I'd like to know what you think about that one?"

"Well, Joey, I don't know. I mean, we mustn't do anything to jeopardize liaison."

152

"You don't agree with headquarters, then, that we should develop our own capabilities for unilateral operations? Some people think, Bob, that we aren't getting enough information, for example, on what is really happening here in Malaya and Singapore, and we may be missing the boat on getting people into China from among this big bunch of Chinese. In other words, they told me in the branch that they wanted not only some independent propaganda ops but some independent intelligence ops."

"Who told you that?"

"The branch chief. He said it was a conclusion he'd drawn from his last field trip out here."

"That bastard." Bob dropped his Rotary Club composure. "You know how he spends his time on his so-called inspection trips? Inspecting Chinese cunt. Really, he comes by the office for about twenty minutes when he gets here, and I don't see him again until he's ready to leave three days later. The rest of the time he cats around town with Chinese broads."

"Well, he seems to have passed the word up to the senior staffs and they briefed me that they were serious about the need for unilateral operations here. They said that even though British liaison is very valuable, especially the China reports, they don't want us to be caught short of information and action capabilities in Singapore and Malaya. They said they frankly thought the British were holding out on us about the situation here because it's more serious than they'd like us to know."

"Of course, that's what I've always said," Bob agreed. "Look, I know some guys think I'm opposed to operations and I'm just a liaison man and like to take things easy. That's not true. I've always said we should have a unilateral operations here. Listen, it's all right, as long as you do it professionally."

The women were coming down the stairs, and Bob said, "Gee, Joey, we've covered a lot of important points. Look, I want you to get Boylan to bring you over to the consulate tomorrow morning to introduce you to the acting consul general. He should also introduce you to the other officers. Tell him to leave my office for last. Then after he's brought you there, we'll tell him to leave and I can show you the station and we'll continue this.

"Well, girls, what have you decided?" he asked.

"Bob, this place needs furniture badly," Jane said. "What can we do?"

"Oh, we'll take care of it, don't worry. Joey and I can talk to the admin man tomorrow. You know it takes some time to get things all worked out when you are first settling in. But don't you worry, Jeannie, we'll take good care of you."

"We've really got to go, Bob," Jane interrupted. "You know we're due at the Fultons for drinks."

"Hey, that's right," said Bob. "And that reminds me that we've got it set up for you to meet the Amblers tomorrow night. Dick and Molly will pick you up at seven-thirty and take you to the Amblers for dinner. You'll meet Dick tomorrow, Joey. I've had him hand-hold Ambler in addition to his other work until you got here."

"Well, so long for now, you guys," Bob said as they went out the door. "We've had a great visit with you and I think we got you all set up here. See you tomorrow, Joey, see you soon, Jeannie."

When they had gone Jeanne said to me, "You know, Jane said when she was upstairs that she didn't think any government furniture was available that could possibly fill this house. She suggested that maybe we would want to buy some things of our own, you know, things we can take back to the States with us. Where in the world would we put them in a U.S.-sized house? Where are we going to get the money to buy them? Weren't we told we'd have a furnished house?"

"Yeah," I said. "Things aren't exactly what we were told they would be. And I really can't say Bob gave me any answers to the questions I had for him."

Bob Boylan took me on my rounds of introductory courtesy calls on Monday morning. Boylan was a tall, lean Midwesterner, with an easygoing, relaxed manner. He explained that he would be glad to introduce me to anyone he knew that I thought might be useful to me, but that he really hadn't been briefed on what I was supposed to do either by USIS, Washington, or by Jantzen, so, he added, he felt not only pretty much in the dark but a little bit awkward.

I didn't know what to say to him. He certainly didn't seem to be the uncooperative fellow that Wilma had described or a person of whom I should be suspicious. However, at headquarters I had been told not to discuss my work in any way with my cover boss. So all I could say was that I felt as awkward as he did.

He said since he was going to be leaving in two months, he

guessed it really didn't matter. Meanwhile, we agreed we'd try to overcome our mutual awkwardness as best we could.

He put on a good performance at the consulate by saying to the economic officer, who was the last person we talked to before we went into Jantzen's office, that now he was going to introduce his new staffer to the "special people" across the hall. His words and his tone of voice were just right because they confirmed my legitimacy with the economic officer by including me in on the consulate-wide custom of always referring to Jantzen and his office as the "special people" with a knowing inflection.

The consulate occupied an entire floor above the National City Bank's office on Collier Quay. There were a number of offices, some of them communicating. Jantzen's office was across the hall from all of them. It was indeed special. To enter you pressed a buzzer on the locked door, which was then opened by a secretary who asked if you had an appointment. Once your bona fides had been established, the secretary let you in. Following this standard procedure, Boylan and I entered my first CIA station.

Except for the fact that it was smaller than most, the distinctive features of the station, its location and its "special" status and procedures, were not much different from any other station I was ever to enter in any country in Asia, Europe, or Latin America. There were certain standards dictated by the security required for the communications equipment, the classified material, and the language of cryptonyms and pseudonyms in the correspondence that the secretaries were working with that made it impossible for a station office to look like a normal office in a diplomatic mission.

Added to these physical differences from all the other offices in any consulate or embassy were certain other impediments that the CIA station in Singapore and all other stations were burdened with. The State Department never permitted CIA officers to be integrated into the Foreign Service as Foreign Service Officers (FSO). All CIA officers were given titles as Foreign Service Reserve Officers (FSR) or, if not of sufficiently high rank, as Foreign Service Staff (FSS) employees. The State Department establishment during the fifties gradually eliminated the use of FSRs in its own staff, and, of course, FSS personnel were limited to clerical and related activities. Thus, in every embassy there were these peculiar people, occupying offices very distinct from the offices of all the rest of the staff,

155

and with position designations distinct from the rest of the personnel who were performing top-level tasks of the embassy. In every country abroad there existed the anomaly of embassy personnel dealing with high-ranking local officials and moving in significant circles of local society who did not have the official designations that could explain such activity. On top of this, the State Department was reluctant to give appropriate diplomatic titles to CIA officers and, whenever possible, tried to deny them diplomatic passports.

The formal hierarchy of diplomatic titles dates from the Treaty of Westphalia of 1648, that ended the Thirty Years' War. They are about as relevant to anything today as their antiquity implies. Yet to a diplomat they mean everything. Whether an officer is a Counselor of Embassy, a First, Second, or Third Secretary, or a lowly Attaché determines his position on the Diplomatic List. This, in turn, determines whether or not he should be invited to important functions of the host government where he is serving. The State Department bureaucracy steadfastly fought to make sure that even the Chief of Station should not be given a diplomatic title superior to Attaché, if at all possible.

Because of the need for secure quarters in which to work, and because they were denied the normal perquisites of office, CIA stations and staff around the world throughout the cold war were units of United States missions abroad as noticeable as acne on a teenage face. Only local employees of embassies and consulates who happened to be blind or else were totally indifferent to their surroundings could fail to identify CIA stations and CIA personnel to any curious intelligence service, Russian, Chinese, or Hottentot, that cared to ask them for such information. For anyone who traveled in diplomatic services, however, it wasn't necessary to ask local employees who the CIA people in the American Embassy were. A favorite pastime of Foreign Service Officers and their wives was to point them out whenever the opportunity arose.

How we could function at all under these circumstances struck me immediately as a question I found almost impossible to answer. I decided that if I asked Bob Jantzen he would probably reply, "That's what I've always said," or, "Play it by ear." I also decided that these were as effective answers as I would ever get.

That morning I met my colleagues: Dick, Bob's assistant; Flo, the woman in charge of the counterintelligence files; Mary and Alice, the two secretaries; and Bill, the commo man. They were pretty

156

cramped for space, since the station consisted of just three small offices plus the commo room, which was sealed off from the rest of the area by a steel vault door. Most of the area was taken up by safes. Bob and Dick each had a small private office. The woman and eight safes, a duplicating machine, typewriter tables, adding machines, and other miscellaneous office equipment were jammed together in one room that also served as a reception area for those visitors that were allowed past the sole door that opened onto the corridor.

After Boylan left, and Bob called Dick into the office, I thought we were going to settle down to a more thorough discussion of business than Sunday's conversation. The phone rang, and Bob answered: "Loke, you old devil, I've been waiting all morning for you to call. Don't tell me you're working, you never worked a day in your life. What's that? You didn't want to interrupt me? You know I never have anything to do more important than talking with you, quit kidding."

There followed a twenty-five-minute conversation about golf, a cocktail party Loke had given the previous Friday night, plans for a possible fishing trip, and when Loke was going to go to Cameron Highlands for a holiday on which he invited Bob and Jane to accompany him. Bob finally hung up and said, "That worthless bastard is always calling me up when I have something important to do. I don't know why I bother with him. He's a Chinese businessman, and gives good parties, but he isn't any use to us at all. I'm really sorry, Joey, but I'm late for Phoenix Park now, so why don't you and Dick make your plans for tonight and I'll see you later."

Thus ended the first of many such business meetings I had with Bob over the next two years.

The only thing that stood out in my mind from Dick's briefing in preparation for my first meeting with my principal British liaison contact was that my wife and I were supposed to dress for dinner, meaning, of course, I must wear my dinner jacket. I couldn't decide how I felt about this, except that I was going to be uncomfortably hot. I finally remembered I had read somewhere that dressing for dinner is what enabled the British to keep their sanity in the tropics. I concluded this was probably the best way for me to look at the situation.

Dennis and Patricia Ambler lived in a moderately sized house in the Bukit Timah section of Singapore, in what I was later to learn was a kind of compound for the staff of the Commissioner for Southeast Asia. We were a bit startled to see a horse tethered in the not very large garden outside the front door, but we soon discovered the Amblers lived surrounded by a variety of animals. When our host and hostess greeted us they were accompanied by two big pye dogs. I saw several cats scurrying out of the living room behind them. Their favorite, however, who spent most of the evening with us, was their pet otter.

The Amblers were as relaxed and interesting as their life-style indicated they would be. Dennis was a jovial, round-faced chap going to fat. Patricia was an athletic type with the strong regular features of an old girl from an English girls' school that it was obviously proper to be an old girl from. The horse in the garden was hers.

Besides we four Americans, the Amblers had another guest who was introduced as Major Burke, "from the garrison at Johore Baru."

Our cocktail conversation consisted of the usual getting-acquainted talk. Dennis kept feeding the otter hors d'oeuvres at appropriate intervals, thus supplying the opportunity strangers need for a safely neutral topic upon which to comment. The Amblers, it turned out, had met and married in Malaya before the war and had returned to Singapore among the first British official families back in town after the Japanese surrender. They obviously felt very much a part of the place. Much later Mike Campbell would give me the full story of how the Amblers met and why they had reason to feel so much a part of Malaya.

We did not get involved in any discussion of our forthcoming working relationship. Patricia made the only allusion to our professional association, actually. When Jeanne asked about a painting that was rather prominently displayed, Patricia explained it was one of her special favorites of those she had done. It was a black figure standing on what appeared to be a windswept plain with a spotlight of sunshine on him. His disproportionately large and elongated head rested on a reversed torso and he had only one enormous foot.

"He's a rather startling figure," Jeanne commented.

"He's Kaki Kaki, the Indonesian god who punishes liars," Patricia replied. "I think he's rather nice to have about in view of your husband and mine's profession, don't you?"

158

Major Burke gave us his idea of the Emergency, as the British called the guerrilla war that had been being waged by the Malayan Communist Party since 1948. His thesis was that the war would never be won until the last Chinese in the country was either killed, in prison camp, or "shipped back to his bloody red country."

What incensed Burke, mostly, was the assassination by ambush of Sir Henry Gurney. The major had evidently arrived at the Amblers fortified for the evening with Americans, whom he obviously found only slightly less annoying than the Chinese. Nevertheless, he asked for a third scotch before dinner, and began recalling the details of Gurney's death vividly. In the course of his ramblings he also revealed that he and Dennis, Dick and I were all members of the fraternity of intelligence officers. What he told us of the Gurney case had never been made public and obviously Burke knew because he was an officer of Special Branch, the British police security intelligence service in Malaya.

"The bloody bastards, thirty or more of them," Burke explained, "had been waiting in ambush for at least twenty-four hours. But the thing is they really knew just when to expect Sir Henry because his bloody Chinese houseboy had told them when he would leave King's House."

"Oh, come on with that houseboy nonsense," Dennis interrupted, "it's a silly story."

"Now, Dennis, let's help your American friend get things straight," Burke went on. "I'll bet he's already hired himself a bloody Chinese, himself. Haven't you?"

I admitted I had.

"Well, look, you can't be too careful. You see, some stupid bloke who didn't want to scare the ladies, I guess, or maybe Americans like you, made us invent a lot of nonsense to cover up the fact that Sir Henry was really killed by the bloody informer right in his own house."

Burke gave a slight laugh which he swallowed with a grunt.

"We showed the reporters a diary the bastards were supposed to have kept and that was supposed to show they weren't really out for Sir Henry. The log showed them noting the passage of trucks, army vehicles, and like that on Friday. This was supposed to prove that it was just by chance they happened to hit Sir Henry. But we got the bloody Chinese servant and that's a fact.

"I hope to hell you've had your boy checked out recently, Dennis," Burke added. "He's probably listening behind the kitchen door to everything I'm saying."

"Don't fret, Patrick," said Dennis. And somehow at that moment the houseboy appeared to announce dinner.

When the men were having cigars and brandy, Burke began to show his feelings about Americans in earnest. He began by eliciting that this was the first time that either Dick or I had served in the Far East. This set him off about the general inexperience of Americans in world affairs. Not only were Americans inexperienced, he observed, but they had no history and no understanding of history.

"Look at the stupid things your wretched Wilson tried to do in Europe," he cried. "Tried to remake a map he couldn't even read. I had no time for the Hitler bastard, but really, your Mr. Wilson was just as much to blame for our having to fight the Huns all over again, you know.

"And now you're back all over Europe again. You and the Russians. A likely lot, I say. And you young blokes are out east here, trying to deal with bastards like the Chinese.

"Oh, you've got the power. Yes, you and the Russians have the power. But it takes more than power. It takes brains. You've got to have the brains, boys. And you've got to have a plan. That's the thing, you know, you've got to have a plan. The ruddy Russians have a plan, their damned Communist plan. Tell me, what's yours? You have more power than they do, but do you have a plan? Now that you'll be ruling the goddamned world, do you have a plan?"

I had had enough of Major Burke.

"Yes," I said, "we have a plan, but it's top secret and I'm not authorized to tell you what it is."

This worked. But honors for the evening went to the otter. In his unsteady and now somewhat nonplussed state, the well-lubricated major reached down to pet the otter, who was sitting quietly at Dennis's side. The otter bit the major on the thumb. A complete success.

10
Singapore—Crossroads and Crosscurrents

The next day at my first official business meeting at Phoenix Park, the British made it clear they wanted to get immediately to work on four items. These were that we develop a full exchange of information and plans both our services had for dealing with the World Assembly of Youth meeting that would bring representatives from nearly everywhere to Singapore in August. Second, they were most anxious to make some formal arrangement whereby they could be briefed regularly on the activities of the Asia Foundation. They were quite concerned about the fact that the Foundation had established an office in Singapore. London and Washington had agreed on this, but the MI-6 and IRD people on the ground evidently had been overruled when this agreement was reached. Furthermore, they wanted us to give them Asia Foundation briefings on activities in the other countries in Southeast Asia where the Asian Foundation was working. A third project was to interest us in a joint anti-Communist film program that would somehow result in the distribution of good anti-Communist short-subject films in movie theaters throughout the area. One problem that we would have to solve was finding an ostensible backer for the project, since the hand of neither MI-6 nor CIA was supposed to show. Since almost all the theaters in the area were owned by either the Shaw brothers, operating out of Hong Kong and Singapore, or Loke Wan Tho, presumably some arrangement would have to be made with them. Finally, they wanted to exchange themes that we were both using throughout the area in our press and other media outlets on some sort of basis that would prevent undue duplication and yet, to the greatest extent possible, provide mutual reinforcement.

These were not easy matters to address. Not only was the entire question of British liaison a subject on which opinion at headquarters was divided, these particular topics ran athwart another fissure in the structure of the Clandestine Services. The first two items were matters of principal concern to the International Organizations Division, responsible for covert action operation against worldwide Communist fronts, such as the International Union of Students, the World Federation of Democratic Youth, the World Peace Council, the World Federation of Trade Unions, and similar organizations. IO Division undertook to meet this responsibility by establishing organizations in the free world that would have greater appeal to the target audience the Communists were trying to influence than the Soviet-supported organizations had.

The other two items were of concern mainly to the Far East Division, which was responsible for running propaganda and political operations in the geographical area in its jurisdiction. To negotiate these matters to the satisfaction of the British was difficult for the American negotiator, who was receiving conflicting advice.

The reason for this divergence was that IO Division's operations were considered by FE Division officers to be rather vague and unprofessional. IO's activities were directed by Cord Meyer, a person whom many of the old-pro types distrusted and even disliked. Cord had won the Alpheus Henry Snow Award at Yale for the class of 1942 as "the senior adjudged to have done the most for Yale by inspiring his classmates." He accelerated his course work so that he could complete his degree requirements in December, 1941, and join the Marines. He still graduated summa cum laude. After the war, in which he was wounded and lost the sight of one eye, he helped organize the World Federalists and became its president.

162

To the former OSS and FBI officers in the Clandestine Services all this wasn't especially impressive. He had no past intelligence experience.

But he had had a great deal of experience in organizational activities of the kind he was now directing. Moreover, he had seen how the Communists operated in infiltrating and attempting to take control over special-interest groups of an idealistic bent, such as the World Federalists and the American Veterans Committee, in which he had also been active immediately after the war. He and his IO officers, many of whom had similar if not so distinguished backgrounds as he, were convinced that the main challenge the Communists presented to the free world was their ability to manipulate great masses of opinion against U.S. policies through their ability to capture these loosely structured worldwide organizations that they could then use as pressure groups and propaganda sources. By this means the Communists could influence not only world opinion to oppose the moves the free world was taking under U.S. leadership, but, more important, the governments in some countries and the United Nations.

IO's method of operation was to copy the Communists' technique. Organizations like the International Union of Students, for example, had been captured by the Communists by manipulating a few well-selected people into key executive positions. Executive groups of such organizations make the policy decisions, direct the group's propaganda and pressure tactics, and the rank and file is generally content to enjoy merely being members of an impressive-sounding organization with whose general aims they agree, as well as having the fun of attending occasional big conventions. What makes such groups particularly useful to the dedicated minority who wins control is that the membership at large is *not* under the kind of strict control intelligence professionals like to dream of having in all their operations. The importance of these groups in the forums of world opinion, or parliaments, or the United Nations General Assembly, is that they appear to be genuinely heterogeneous groups, representatives of all important factions of "youth" or "labor" or "women," etc., who have come to an agreement on a specific issue and, hence, deserve to be heard and paid attention to. The World Peace Council had been used very effectively against the United States in this manner during the Korean War.

Hence IO was very interested in trying to get people who were

163

friendly to our side in control of the WAY meeting that would bring representatives of Europe, Asia, and Africa to Singapore. Under our influence WAY could then be a worldwide spokesman for "youth" that would speak with a friendly voice on points of important world policy, such as whatever it was we would decide to do when the French pulled out of Vietnam, for example.

The Asia Foundation was a somewhat more amorphous animal. It had been founded originally in the first flower of OPC operations that gave life to the Committee for a Free Europe and Radio Free Europe, and, in fact, was first called the Committee for a Free Asia. As in the case of the Free Europe Committee, a number of prominent people had been induced to take an interest and, in the case of the Committee for a Free Asia, even actively participate. This complicated the situation as they did not wish to respond to daily directives from the buildings beside the Reflecting Pool. However, they did wish to have a bureaucracy, and field offices in all Asian countries, if possible. So IO Division was given the job of handling the funds for such large enterprises and trying to control them as best they could. Chief FE, who had China, the winding down of a war in Korea, and the mess in Southeast Asia to worry about, did not want this additional cross to bear. On the other hand, he and, especially, his station chiefs did not want a bunch of people poaching on their real estate. A sort of treaty was worked out between the Committee for a Free Asia (that some subtler minds in IO convinced to change its name to Asia Foundation, in order that it might have some chance of looking less frighteningly ours to a neutralist Burmese or Indonesian), IO Division, and FE Division. By this arrangement, the Foundation's proposed operational plan and budget for each country were reviewed by FE in addition to IO, and the Foundation's representatives were required to keep the FE stations informed of their general progress as well as to give the stations the names of all people they proposed to use, or deal with in any way, for checking in station and headquarters counterintelligence files.

On top of all this, now, was piled the British insistence on a role similar to FE Division's in the Foundation's work in Singapore, and as much of a monitoring role in its operations all over the area as they could get us to concede them. The Asia Foundation people quite naturally thought that this was a bit much. IO agreed with them, since they saw the matter as increasing the already too frequent headaches they had with the San Francisco home office of the Foundation. FE tended to look at the matter primarily as something negotiable depending on what the British might be willing to give us in return for yielding on the matter.

As for the WAY meeting, IO had a certain amount of liaison already going with the British in London, on all its operations in the world front field, and WAY in particular. But at the same time, they didn't want to disclose to the British who the people they were working with were. They wanted, however, to have British assistance in steering the meeting toward their ultimate objective of WAY's becoming a free world front group. On top of this, IO wanted the Singapore station, in particular me, to be the contact with the IO agent they were going to send to Singapore to direct operations with the student leaders they were trying to manipulate at the meeting. FE Division didn't particularly care what happened at the WAY meeting, but didn't want me to do anything that might embarrass my overall relations with the British because of what I did concerning the WAY meeting.

In regard to the film project, FE Division thought that this was a nice thing to string along in our liaison conversations—always to have something to bring up when the contradictions in instructions concerning the first two topics became too overwhelming. The British, on the other hand, were convinced that their film program in Malaya was really helping with the number one problem of that war—convincing the Chinese peasants not to continue providing food, funds, and informant services to the guerrillas. Hence they thought it would be a great idea to use films everywhere in Asia, and since we seemed to have unlimited funds, it was a matter of combining their brains and our money in a huge cold war psychwar success.

FE Division was adamant in not wanting to give them any clue as to what our propaganda assets were anywhere. Therefore, the exchange-of-themes subject was just about as bad to live with as the confusion concerning the matters of major concern to IO Division.

Jantzen took me to Phoenix Park for my first visit. He introduced me to the MI-5 officers with whom he exchanged intelligence reports, and then to James Fulton, the MI-6 chief of Far Eastern Operations. Fulton explained that he was trying the experiment of having headquarters in the saddle. He said that he wanted to see whether they could get better results if he made his base in Singapore and then traveled as frequently as needed to each of their stations to deal personally and immediately with major problems.

Bob explained to me, as we left Fulton to go to meet John Rainer, the IRD chief, and Ambler, "Don't let James fool you. The real reason he set this up for himself is that he has a broad in Bangkok. And you can be sure that every place he goes, he goes via Bangkok."

On the way to Phoenix Park, Bob had also given me an interesting account of the other officers and the general setup, as he had been able to figure it out.

"Look, Joey, I can understand how you feel," he began. "I came here to open the station in 1949. Jeez, that's five years ago now. Well, nobody told me anything. So don't be discouraged. I just gave these guys the laughing boy manner, and found out things as I went along."

The first thing that Bob had tried to sort out was what MI-5 and MI-6 were both doing together in British territory. MI-5, theoretically, has exclusive jurisdiction in intelligence collection and counterintelligence in British territory. The answer, Bob found, was that MI-6 claimed to be working from a Singapore base, which was a center for directing operations in other countries. They claimed they were not operating in Singapore or Malaya.

"Old James's deputy, Maurice Oldfield, used to be in charge here, but now he's back in London, handling the administrative problems, according to Fulton," Bob said. "Maurice is one hell of a nice guy, and he actually helped me get things straight better than anyone. The thing is, these guys are really nuts about security and won't even tell each other what they're doing, much less us. I mean MI-5 is just not talking to MI-6 and vice versa."

"Like in the old OSO-OPC days."

"A thousand times worse, if you can imagine. Take Rainer, for example. Now, you'll soon see he's quite a character. As far as I can make out, he's here only because he's a good friend of Malcolm MacDonald, the High Commissioner himself. They served together during the war, I hear. Anyway, no one talks much to Rainer. They say he's not a member of either service. So James has already made it clear to me he wants you to talk mostly to Ambler.

"Finally, Joey, speaking of MacDonald. He's the one. Boy, he's the one. I've spent a lot of time working on him. You know, he's old

166

Prime Minister Ramsay MacDonald's son, and they say he's a real lightweight. But I don't know.

"Anyway, I've entertained him and entertained him. And we play golf and we're pretty close. I don't know what he tells the boys, of course, but I try always to give them the impression that I've got his ear. I think it helps. I think it's good to work on the top guy. Then the others can't be sure whether you might be able to give them a hard time if they give you one.

"He drives 'em crazy. You know, he's the first guy to go into the Tanglin Club at night in a bush jacket? More than that, one night, he brought two Chinese babes in with him. That's his real weakness, by the way. In fact, his wife packed up and went home to Canada. But the thing is, no Chinese was *ever* allowed inside the Tanglin Club. That's the most exclusive British club in the Far East. But what could they do? He's the High Commissioner for Southeast Asia!" Bob laughed.

We had arrived at John Rainer's office. Rainer and Dennis Ambler were waiting for us. It was easy to see why Bob called Rainer a character.

Rainer was dressed in a bush jacket and a pair of old white walking shorts that looked as though he had worn them for the past week. He had a sharp, thin face, and a clipped Oxbridge accent, the kind most Americans find mimicking irresistible. The walls of his office were covered with clippings of old headlines. All were examples of editorial slips that produced double entendres, like "KING FLYS BACK TO FRONT" and dozens and dozens more.

Both Rainer and Ambler gave us very friendly greetings. After we were all seated, Rainer slowly undid the strings of a black hardcover file. It contained notes and papers for our meeting. I noticed as he arranged the papers that they, as well as the folder, were stamped "Most Secret." He saw what I was looking at.

"Oh yes"—he gave a slight, wise smile—"you see, our chats with you chaps are most secret certainly. But is it the language that you really find curious? Let me ask you something. I just don't know what you people are trying to say when you say something is top secret. What are you talking about, some place you think it belongs? Up not down, perhaps? After all, things are either secret, or more secret, or most secret, aren't they really?

"There's no doubt about it, we don't use the language very well in America," I said, and I added, "And you've just explained why you've collected your headlines."

The meeting covered the four points of main concern. We all agreed that the first thing we would tackle was making an arrangement to handle discussions of the Asia Foundation. Bob and I promised to talk to the Foundation representative, who had already paid a courtesy call on them, and work out a proposal that we would discuss the following Wednesday.

Pat Judge, the Asia Foundation representative, who had arrived in Singapore just three weeks before I did, was an amiable, volatile, and mercurial Irishman. He had red hair, thinner and sandier than Bob Jantzen's. His face too had a ruddy glow at all times. Sometimes I was to see it much brighter than his hair. He was a large man, carrying possibly twenty to thirty pounds more than his best fighting weight.

Over a two-day period we worked out our position. Bob and I had our communications from Washington and Pat had his from San Francisco. Fortunately, at this important moment when we were at last going to propose something fairly specific, headquarters' disparate points of view converged on at least a few matters.

The position that San Francisco had finally been forced to agree to was that Pat was to tell the British the general areas of his program and give them the names of people he proposed to use or give scholarships or other financial assistance. He also was to agree to entertain specific questions they might have about operations in other countries. The station was to relay these questions via our channels for answers that, in due course, he would be authorized to transmit to them.

Pat and I met with John and Dennis as scheduled and it was agreed that we would have monthly meetings at which Pat would give them a general rundown on his program, names of people to check, and receive their questions. It was further decided that if Pat needed a quick check on someone he could send the name at any time with Bob or me and they'd service his request on a priority basis. We settled into this nice bureaucratic routine, which functioned well until the lid blew off Singapore the following spring. A lot of other things had become unstuck all over Southeast Asia by that time.

On May 7, 1954, the French garrison surrendered at Dienbienphu. The day after the surrender, the Geneva meeting to discuss the settlement of the Vietnam war got under way. France, Great Britain, the USSR, Communist China, and the three Indochina states, Vietnam, Laos, and Cambodia, with the United States present only as an "observer," sat down to decide the fate of that land we were even then calling unhappy, little knowing how terribly tragic it would one day become. James Fulton took off to see his man in Saigon (by way of Bangkok). Bob also took off for Bangkok, where he planned to meet with our station chief from Saigon, who was coming over to discuss the situation with our people in Thailand. He then planned to go on to Hong Kong. Dick was left to exchange the weekly bag of reports and I was left to my own devices.

The moot point concerning our developing our own independent capabilities in Singapore for covert press placement and other activities was not really as moot as I may have indicated thus far.

My predecessor, who had been the one-man OPC station chief and had quit in disgust when Jantzen, not he, was named chief of the merged station, had already, in fact, developed two newsmen to the point where we were paying them monthly salaries. They had been put on ice during the long period in which I was involved in training and briefings and negotiations with USIS about my cover. I decided it was now time to de-ice them.

The shock of finding my job in no way like the role of the clandestine operator I had been so diligently trained for but rather a repetition of some of the tedious interagency coordination I had sometimes been engaged in back in Washington was one thing. The fact that nothing I had been told about living arrangements or my cover was true also made me restless. Finally I received a cable the day Bob left town which was a copy of a message addressed for action to a number of Southeast Asian stations, including Singapore, urging an all-out effort "including black operations" to bolster the French side in the negotiations at Geneva by showing China to be deeply involved in supporting the Viet Minh Communists. I considered this an order to get to work at something other than Asia Foundation liaison arrangements. Besides, I thought I had a good idea for an operation that would also serve as a "Test of agent's bona fides and capabilities," as Stan Archer used to say at the Farm.

One of the two newsmen my predecessor had recruited was a reporter for the *Nanyang Sin Pao,* the largest-circulation Chinese-language newspaper in all of Southeast Asia. The other was the local assistant of the bureau chief of a wire service. I decided that I would activate the latter, because my plan was to get the most mileage possible with a one-shot news story. If we could make the story good enough, the wire service might find it worth sending from the Singapore point of origin all around the world on its relay system.

A contact plan had been arranged by which the agent would respond to a coded call from Wilma that would have him drop by her apartment at an hour and day the code would indicate. Both agents had been given such plans for reactivation. They had both been introduced to Wilma. Wilma had also been given an idea by them of their most likely free times. The man I wanted was usually free after two o'clock in the afternoon until he checked in to read his evening wire at seven o'clock. So we decided on three P.M. on the day Wilma regularly gave her maid the entire afternoon off, and Wilma selected the appropriate code words for that day and hour and phoned him from a pay phone at seven-thirty on the day I decided to act.

Wilma suggested that I have lunch with her the day of the meeting as the best of various possible ways to avoid the agent and my seeming to arrive at approximately the same time. I thought this seemed a logical plan and agreed. I found out, as a result, another side of Wilma's nature.

We arrived at the apartment at a little after one o'clock. Wilma said I would agree with her, when I saw them, that the Orange Grove Flats was not a good place for meetings except in the afternoon. She also added that if we started early enough it was not only good tradecraft, but we could have a couple of drinks and a leisurely lunch that would have worn off before I met Li Huan Li.

The Orange Grove Flats was a three-story building surrounding a central parking area and green. Every apartment's living room faced out on this central area, and all had windows opening across their entire fronts. Singapore's health department had not encountered the slothful servants of 25 Rideout Road in the area of these apartments, and flies and mosquitoes had been eliminated. None of the windows had screens. The windows had shutters that could be closed at night and the first-floor apartments had some grillwork for protection. The result was that the occupants had as much air as possible, but anyone who cared to look could see whatever was going on in any of the living rooms.

At three o'clock in the afternoon most people partly closed their shutters to ward off the rays of the intense afternoon sun that drenched the open-faced living rooms with extremely hot air.

"You see what I mean?" Wilma commented. "When Li gets here we can have the shutters drawn like everyone else and people won't see him coming into the living room. Of course, you'll be able to have your meeting in the air-conditioned second bedroom in complete privacy. As you can imagine, everyone opens up as the sun goes down, and leaves the windows wide open in the evening. Wouldn't it be absurd to have a night meeting in one of these apartments?"

"As Bob would say, Wilma, I agree with you one hundred percent. It certainly would not be doing it professionally."

Wilma had had the maid make preparations for a very good lunch to which she need give only the finishing touches. While she went about them, she suggested I make martinis.

"Your reputation as a martini maker has preceded you," she said.

The remark, of course, had a pleasant effect on me.

We talked about the great things that could be done in Singapore if we could get going on a lot of independent operations. Wilma told me, in her opinion, I had made a shrewd choice in deciding to activate Li, especially at a time when, if we placed a good story, it would be bound to be well appreciated by headquarters.

The conversation went on like this during drinks and lunch. Wilma kept saying a lot of things that sounded good to me, about how she could tell I was going to have a great tour, how I was exactly the kind of man she liked to work for, and so forth. After lunch she suggested we look at the room where we would have the meeting. Like most rooms in Singapore it was large, designed for the maximum circulation of air possible in the days before air-conditioning. The station had provided a one-and-a-half-ton air-conditioner, however. The room had several chairs and a table that would do well for our meeting. It also had a double bed. Coming into the room from the hot living room was very pleasant. The cool air stimulated circulation.

Wilma gave me a long look. Then she sat down on the bed. This signal had not been included in meeting-signals training at the Farm.

"I'm sorry, Wilma, but I have to be in good shape to meet Li," I said.

171

Right on the appointed moment, Li Huan Li knocked at the door.

Li was an even-featured Straits Chinese, and although only thirty-eight years old, according to the biographical data we had on him, he was graying at the temples. He spoke perfect English, as did all Straits Chinese who had graduated from Raffles Boys School, which prided itself on the number of sufficiently affluent alumni it sent each year to Oxford and Cambridge.

Wilma quickly suggested we take advantage of the air-conditioned bedroom, and got us out of the shuttered but more exposed living room area.

I told Li that we wanted to use his services again, because the situation in Southeast Asia was obviously going to become more tense and difficult after the Geneva meeting on Indochina than it had been, and we were going to need to do a lot more work than ever before. I asked if he would be willing to help.

He said he would be happy to do whatever he could. Next, I asked him whether he could put stories on the wire that I would give him from time to time. I said these stories would be designed generally to show the Russian and Chinese Communist threat to the area. He responded with a detailed explanation of just how the service worked in Singapore, his relationship with his boss, and the possibilities and limitations of the kinds of things he thought he could do for me. I was impressed with his professional qualifications and the fact that he had obviously come well prepared for what I was going to ask him. I learned in time that we had in our employ the best journalist in Singapore. When the events of the coming year made Singapore a center of attention and the city filled up with big-name foreign correspondents from top U.S. media, their judgment of Li's qualifications was quickly demonstrated. They relied on him for all their scoops and legwork. Li dug up most of the news that left Singapore during the crises of 1955. This, of course, made him increasingly valuable to us.

I explained I wanted to put out a story that would indicate the Chinese were giving full armed support to the Viet Minh. The purpose was to strengthen the non-Communist side at the Geneva talks who would be trying to get the best deal possible for the anti-Communist Vietnamese. I said we didn't want to see them continue to be stuck with the colonialist-lackey label while the Viet Minh con-

172

tinued successfully to represent itself as a purely indigenous Vietnamese group of national patriots. We must identify them with the world Communist movement. The overall theme we want to get across worldwide, I explained, is that there is a new imperialism, that is the threat today in Southeast Asia. Li said he understood completely.

I then told him the general lines of the story I wanted him to plant. These were that convoys were regularly seen in the Tonkin Gulf bringing Chinese arms and ammunition to the Viet Minh. If possible, the story might hint strongly that Chinese troops were also being convoyed. We discussed how best to make this into a plausibly realistic news item.

We decided that we would try to be as specific as possible and make the sourcing appear to be British defense officials. Li said he thought he knew the best way to do this.

He explained that Malcolm MacDonald held bi-weekly press conferences. By luck, one would take place tomorrow morning. He said he always attended and he usually was one of the regular questioners. So he would first make up our story and ask MacDonald if he had any comment. MacDonald, of course, would say no. Then Li would put into the story a line something like this: "Malcolm MacDonald, British High Commissioner for Southeast Asia, would not elaborate when asked about this report at his press conference this morning."

We worked out this item.

MORE CHINESE SUPPLIES AND TROOPS SPOTTED EN ROUTE TO HAIPHONG

At the press conference of the British High Commissioner for Southeast Asia today, reports of the sightings of Chinese naval vessels and supply ships in the Tonkin Gulf en route from Hainan to Haiphong were again mentioned.

According to these reports, the most recent of many similar sightings occurred one week ago when a convoy of ten ships was spotted. Among them were two armed Chinese naval vessels indicating that the convoy consisted of troops as well as arms and supplies.

High Commissioner Malcolm MacDonald would not elaborate further about these reports.

Li said that if he were later asked by MacDonald about the story, which he doubted he would be, he'd say that he had heard this around Phoenix Park. "MacDonald respects the freedom of the press," he added, "and he will not ask me to name my source."

We agreed upon an open-code telephone message he would call in to me indicating he had sent the story and whether the story had been sent around the world by the wire service. He explained he would send the story tomorrow morning and he could tell whether the story had gone worldwide or not if it came back to Singapore on the European relay to Asia tomorrow evening. If it did not, this would indicate the story had been dropped at one of the relay points. He would not be able to tell which one.

I told Li I was very pleased with his responsiveness and suggested he meet me at Rideout Road at five o'clock Saturday afternoon, using the cover he had heard from USIS local employees I was looking for furniture and he had some for sale. We'd then make arrangements for salary and continuing secure contact.

"I hope you had a good meeting that wasn't too strenuous," Wilma said sharply when Li had gone.

"I certainly did, Wilma."

We drove back to the office in silence. As soon as we arrived, I prepared a cable telling headquarters what I had done in response to their request for action, saying that I would confirm tomorrow night the extent of use of the story by the wire service. It was not just my sense of satisfaction that prompted my sending the cable. Headquarters had told me before I left for Singapore that if I successfully reactivated this agent, I should give them lead time when planting a story on his wire service so they could instruct other stations to have their press assets ready to pick it up and make sure the story was used in as many newspapers as possible.

Li made his call the following night and the news was good. The story had been relayed back to Singapore.

By the time Jantzen returned the following week, headquarters had sent a well-done-Singapore message to the station about the story. Bob made a point of calling me in to tell me he was pleased with what I had done.

"Joey, you know I agree one hundred percent with your doing

these independent operations. I've always said we should do more of them as long as we do them professionally," he told me.

In Geneva talks concerning the fate of Vietnam dragged on through May and June and into July. In Singapore the British and I continued to spar about the forthcoming WAY convention. They kept bringing up specific people and suggestions for action they thought should be taken. I continued to receive instructions not to give the British any idea of who the people were that we were interested in, even when, as happened frequently, they were some of the same people the British were telling me about. This seemed to me to be making our liaison a silly waste of time not to mention the fact that we were obviously losing the chance to achieve our objectives by combined efforts.

To top things off, the IO contact, an official of the Institute of International Student Affairs in New York, arrived in Singapore to handle the operation. I had to put my tradecraft training to work devising means of concealing from the British my contacts with him for passing messages and funds which the station was authorized to provide him.

Over four hundred delegates from fifty-four countries at last arrived in August, and the Second World Assembly of Youth finally ended with the delegates being more influenced by the platitudes of the pontifical speech made to them by Madame Vijaya Lakshmi Pandit than by anything either we or the British were able to do. Madame Pandit had a gift for making clichés sound profound to idealists that was surpassed only by that of her brother, Jawaharlal Nehru.

On the larger stage of world affairs, the Geneva meeting had ended on July 21. The influence of its decisions were truly important. Vietnam was divided at the 17th parallel, both contending armies were ordered to begin with withdrawing immediately into their appropriate zones, neither side was to introduce new troops or military equipment, nor permit the establishment of foreign bases. Civilians, in addition to troops, were given three hundred days to move from one zone to another. An International Control Commission (ICC) with inspection teams composed of equal numbers of representatives of Poland, India, and Canada was to supervise the execution of these terms of the Cease-fire Agreement. Another document, known as the Final Declaration, emphasized that the demarcation line, the 17th parallel, was a temporary arrangement and called for general elections to be held in July, 1956, under ICC supervision with preliminary consultations regarding the arrangements for the elections to begin in July, 1955.

Both the Viet Minh, now officially reorganized as the Democratic Republic of Vietnam, and the Bao Dai side, known as the State of Vietnam, began to take steps each thought were necessary for its welfare. The DRV began removing its armies north of the 17th parallel, at the same time caching arms and leaving cadres, propaganda units, guerrilla units, and thousands of secret informants south of that border. France had moved faster than the Geneva conferees, and on June 4 granted the State of Vietnam full independence without reference to any arrangement for dividing the country that might be made at Geneva. On June 16, Ngo Dinh Diem took over the premiership of Emperor Bao Dai's newly independent country, and the United States government, with CIA in the key role, took over the task of guiding the steps necessary for the welfare of South Vietnam.

The first big step was for South Vietnam and the "observer" at Geneva, the United States, to refuse to sign any of the Geneva Agreements. This created the basis for political maneuvering to keep the Democratic Republic of Vietnam with its superior military power, elaborate nationwide clandestine support apparatus, and its appeal as a nationalist movement from taking over the entire country. This maneuvering would require the most experienced and able manipulators of Asian politics. Ed Lansdale was called back into action.

Giving CIA the leading role in the attempt to make South Vietnam a viable government was the inevitable and unavoidable result of the fatal flaw of the Eisenhower /Dulles policy of massive retaliation. This doctrine had helped win the election of 1952, for it seemed to represent the United States the way most Americans liked to think of themselves then and the way some still do. The United States, these people liked to believe, is always powerful, decisive, and forthright. Thus massive retaliation told the Russians and the Chinese we gave them fair warning (forthright) that in case of any further aggression anywhere we deemed of strategic importance to the free world we would retaliate directly against them with our nuclear strike force (decisive and powerful).

The massive retaliation doctrine collapsed with the French at

Dienbienphu. Before the French became imperiled at Dienbienphu, President Eisenhower had already declared that the fall of Indochina "would be of a most terrible significance to the United States of America," and he had warned the Chinese Communists that aggression in Indochina would incur "grave consequences which might not be confined to Indochina." John Foster Dulles made it clear in a statement on March 29, 1954, that we opposed not only open intervention but any indirect assistance to the Viet Minh, such as the supplying of arms, equipment, advisers, or training. "Under the conditions of today," Dulles declared, "the imposition on Southeast Asia of the political system of Communist Russia and its Chinese ally, by *whatever* means, would be a grave threat to the whole free community. The United States feels that the possibility should not be passively accepted but should be met by united action."*

The machinery of massive retaliation apparently had been set in motion in regard to Indochina. The rationale for the little story that Li Huan Li and I planted about Chinese intervention had been established. We had said boo. We even were willing to create the conditions for continuing to say boo, by stories like the one we sent out from Singapore. The Russians and the Chinese didn't care.

The reason they didn't care was that the corollary of the doctrine of massive retaliation was a policy of reducing expenditures on military forces, equipment, and hardware that could be sent to places like Dienbienphu. Funds were concentrated on the Strategic Air Command and on our nuclear weapons stockpile. This was called getting a bigger bang for a buck. The bang turned out to be just a big noise. When push came to shove, we had to step back.

The only assets the United States had that could possibly be used to deal with the situation we faced in Vietnam in the summer of 1954, in fact, were just Li Huan Li and I, and all the others like us. That is, CIA had the only manpower that the U.S. government had available to throw into the breach between the language of our policy toward the Russians and the Chinese and the reality of our effective power. Only CIA could provide the South Vietnamese the assistance they desperately needed to combat the cadres, the prop-

*Eisenhower and Dulles quotations are taken from John Spanier, *American Foreign Policy Since World War II* (New York: Praeger, Inc., 1960), pp. 117, 118.

aganda teams, the informers, and the guerrillas the Viet Minh left behind. CIA had men trained in counterintelligence and paramilitary activities who, hopefully, could organize what was needed. We also had our Philippine experience not only fighting a guerrilla war, but even more important, in organizing the political victory of Magsaysay, especially in creating the organizations that brought his government closer to the people, a rare phenomenon in Southeast Asia, and something that the French had never tried to do in Indochina.

If the United States had thin resources for coping with the task of nation building, which was the fearful enterprise upon which we were now to embark in Vietnam, they were mightily robust compared to those of the Vietnamese. The French had had no interest in training a Vietnamese civil service. They were content to let the old mandarins handle things, under careful French supervision. Only one university was established in Indochina. In 1939 it had 631 students. World War II and the postwar fight for independence did nothing to improve the capacity of the country to produce trained administrators. Less than 2 percent of the civil servants that greeted their new American advisers had university degrees and only 4 percent, including teachers, had completed secondary education.

We in Singapore were soon affected by the major concern the creation of the government of South Vietnam had become. Bob had to huddle with Fulton to discuss what help the British could provide in the way of intelligence reporting on North Vietnam, since our Saigon station had no assets at all that could provide any information. I was ordered to discuss what the British could do to support our new number one propaganda objective. This was to create the impression throughout Asia, and the world for that matter (thank God, we had to worry only about Asia in Singapore), that the new Diem government was a dynamic and viable entity that was going to resist successfully any effort of the Viet Minh puppets of the Russians and their Chinese allies to subvert its democratic institutions. The old inhibitions about discussing themes and mutual capabilities were loosened, although not totally relaxed. The caution about not revealing assets still remained in the instructions, but in a minor clause.

Bob traveled to Saigon, and on his return filled me in on what was happening at the station there.

178

"My God, Joey, you wouldn't believe it. New people are coming in so fast, they have two guys using the same desk. The really big thing, though, is that we seem to be going back to the old days and we're gonna have two stations in Saigon. It seems that Lansdale won't serve under the station chief, but no one, of course, wants to make Ed the chief. He's too damned independent. Seems, though, that he picked up contact with this Diem character when the guy was back in the States, and Eisenhower and Dulles both think Ed can do with him what he did with Magsaysay. So Lansdale's coming out as part of the huge military assistance group General Collins is putting in, and Ed's bringing his own hand-picked boys with him. He's also bringing over a whole gang of Filipinos that worked with him there. This is going to be great to watch."

It was. Soon the Filipinos had started Operation Brotherhood, a program to assist with the relocation of refugees who streamed down from north of the 17th parallel. According to the terms of the Geneva agreement, all persons desiring to move from one zone of the divided country to the other had to make their move within three hundred days. This migration, when completed, saw 900,000 persons from North Vietnam trek south to find new homes, new livelihoods, new roots. The old Magsaysay team organized all kinds of assistance from food packages to nurses, and found time to look for potential agent material on the side. Many of the refugees were Catholics who preferred to live under the reign of the scion of an old mandarin family that had been converts to their faith for three hundred years. This enabled the refugee effort to enlist the help of many Catholic relief organizations, which, unlike the Operation Brotherhood activity, did not require complete funding from the CIA budget. U.S. government funds were channeled also, of course, through the Mutual Security Agency to the fledgling departments of the Vietnamese government.

Our propaganda job was to emphasize that the significance of the refugee movement was that people were rejecting Communist rule in Vietnam. Thanks to the private efforts of the Catholic relief groups, who were active in so many places in Vietnam, it was possible to make Operation Brotherhood appear like another legitimate effort of humanitarian concern for brother Asians. Altogether the campaign to demonstrate to the world that a remarkable number of Vietnamese were making their decision to support Diem was a great success. The theme "they voted with their feet" was also useful when we helped Diem maneuver his way out of holding the general elections to unite the country required by the Final Declaration of Geneva. The steam generated by the great propaganda campaign about the refugees choosing freedom was enough, in fact, to supply energy for propaganda themes throughout the whole U.S. involvement in Vietnam we never dreamed then would be so long and tragic.

Soon our team in Saigon was busy developing Vietnamese versions of the mass organizations built for Magsaysay. Diem's brother, Ngo Dinh Nhu, and his wife, Madame Nhu, whom her case officer always called the Dragon Lady, proved to be as good at organizational work, if not better, than their Filipino counterparts. The National Revolutionary Movement took shape, the Civil Servants League was formed, the Popular Revolutionary Committee started, in addition to the building of propaganda and psychwar units for the government itself. Magsaysay's legal expert came over to write a constitution for Vietnam.

In Singapore I kept receiving propaganda guidance on Vietnam and the developing of the new government and popular institutions there for use by Li Huan Li in any ways we could think of to make them suitable for the wire service. I also activated the other press asset, who wrote for the *Nanyang Siang Pao*. One device we used was to have him run interviews with local officials into whose mouths we'd put praise for the amazing progress in Vietnam, the refugees' heroic rejection of Communism, etc., and then Li would pick them up for replay by the wire services. I also continued to furnish the British with material on Vietnam that they could use with their assets.

11
The Minds and Hearts of the People

Not only had my official duties become more interesting, but our living problems had been happily solved. When the Boylans left, we moved into their house, a Singapore version of a U.S. one-floor ranch house, only, since this was Singapore, it was considerably more spacious than most in the Fairfax or Montgomery county suburbs of Washington. It was adequately furnished and the few things we had brought fitted in well. There were swings in the garden, a big driveway for tricycle riding, and a large, level lawn that was perfect for badminton.

By the time the great events in Vietnam began absorbing my working hours almost completely, we had begun to enjoy the particular charm of being upper-class white residents of Asia. Mike Campbell began to think it was important that he show me what Malaya was really like before I became too impossibly spoiled. He said he wanted me to see how the "blokes who are fighting the bloody war with Chen Ping's Commie boys" lived. He began insisting we plan a trip to northern Malaya for the Christmas holidays.

I talked this over with Bob and he agreed that it would not be a waste of time because, "who knows, Joey, you might find out something. We sure as hell don't get anything from MI-5 about what's really happening except news handouts. Since Washington is so interested in Southeast Asia these days, we don't want to look stupid."

When I told my contacts at Phoenix Park about my trip, they obviously were not enthusiastic. They said they couldn't understand how I was really able to spare the time or what I was going to do.

I thought I would have some fun.

"You've told me many times you don't know where Chen Ping really is, so I'm going up to northern Perak and find him," I said.

By 1954, Chen Ping, the secretary general of the Malayan Communist Party, had been forced by the success of the British "new village" resettlement plan to make his central command headquarters a mobile unit. The systematic regrouping of Chinese squatters into villages where they were kept under the surveillance of British resettlement officers, supported by Malayan home guards plus British troops nearby, made it impossible for the Min Yuen, the supply units that kept the Malay Races Liberation Army in food and other provisions, to provide for the needs of a fixed headquarters position. It was a sore point with the British, however, that they were never able to locate him and that the war still went on after six years of expensive effort and the commitment of 65,000 troops.

The name Malay Races Liberation Army was only a propaganda invention, though the guerrillas themselves were not. The name had been made up to sound impressive and to hide the fact that there were no Malays, in fact, in the army, only Chinese. This was ultimately to turn out to be a decisive element in the British victory. It even seems, today, after the disastrous intervention of the United States in the civil war in Vietnam, that winning the war in Malaya was a rather simple thing. The British had only to take sides with the Malays against the Chinese. It was, after all, the Malays' country. Exploiting Malayan hatred of the Chinese was an intensive psychwar effort my friends in Phoenix Park were conducting in support of the High Commissioner of Malaya's staff in Kuala Lumpur. In 1954, however, it did not seem a very easy task and no one could dare to hope that the outcome was a foregone conclusion.

The Federation of Malaya, created by the British with the agreement of the Malay sultans of the nine Malay states, had a population of 5,300,000. Of that number, 2,600,000 were Malays and 2,040,000 Chinese. There were also 578,000 Indians and Pakistanis and 12,000 British and other Europeans in Malaya. The Malays were outnumbered in their own country.

Moreover, the Chinese controlled practically all the commerce and wealth, and had a number of long-standing grievances against the Malays. The Chinese could not own land, they could not hold citizenship, their children did not enjoy the benefit of the funds the government provided for the schooling of Malays. In addition, the war in China had ended in 1949 and the Malay Communist Party spread the word throughout the Chinese community that arms and perhaps even troops would soon be sent from the homeland to aid the cause in Malaya. The Chinese could remember what had been the fate of members of their race who had been known collaborators of the British when the Japanese army overran the peninsula. What might they expect now, if found to be disloyal to their own kind, when the mighty Maoist forces arrived?

What constantly concerned the British in 1954 was that they had another Palestine situation facing them, the solution to which could be reached only after prolonged and painful conflict. They could resettle more than half a million Chinese and thereby cut the supply line to the jungle warriors, but wasn't this only the beginning not the end of the struggle? It was Sir Gerald Templer, High Commissioner of Malaya when this important program was completed, who coined the phrase we were ten years later to turn into a tired cliche in Vietnam. "This is a struggle for the hearts and minds of the people," Templer said.

As good as his word, Templer made the sultans accept the fact that the Chinese had to be regarded as integral members of the permanent population. Land reform was the first concession wrung from the traditional Malay rulers. Work on this problem had been begun by Templer's predecessor, the unfortunate Sir Henry Gurney. All Chinese, but most important, the Chinese in the new villages, gained the right to long-term leaseholds on their patches of land. Legislation to create a common Malayan citizenship was pushed through, and in 1954 legislation to provide for national schools for all was pending. Another big concession was to open the Malay civil service to Chinese, Indians, and other non-Malay Asians on a ratio of one non-Malay for every four Malays. Hardly a giant step, but a move in the right direction. A National

Federation Regiment was established in the army for non-Malay Asians who were barred from the Malay Regiment. The propagandists called all this "Malayanization," a term that sounded odd to foreign ears unfamiliar with the realities and who thought that Malaya was a nation because its name appeared on the map. Deciding upon a national identity was what had to be settled in Malaya, and the jury was still out when Mike Campbell took me to see for myself.

"I'll show you some of the places this thing started, and I'll show you why it's so bloody hard to stop, and who knows, we may even find old Chen Ping when we get up to Kroh on the border of the country of your police chief friend, General Pao," Mike said when he met me at the airport in Ipoh. He had driven up from Singapore in his trusty Woolsey. I did not have the time for such a leisurely trip, although I would have greatly enjoyed the opportunity of seeing more of the country. Since Mike had explained the importance of Perak so many times before, I decided this state would be enough for one trip, and I made a plan with him to spend four days touring Perak and neighboring Kedah, ending up at Penang, from where I planned to fly back in time for New Year's with my family.

We stopped only a short time in Ipoh, the state's richest city before World War II. Ipoh was well on its way to recovery, since it is the urban center closest to the rich tin mines of the Kinta valley, when the Emergency slowed its pace. The streets were nearly empty when we made our way to Mike's favorite restaurant for lunch.

"I didn't bring you here because the food's so good, Joe. I wanted you to take a good look at the front door."

The door was covered with a steel-mesh screen, an odd enough sight to someone from Singapore who had become accustomed to no screens of any kind in the insect-free city.

"Tossing hand grenades in here was a favorite pastime of our Commie boys in the early days. They bounce off these screens pretty harmlessly now, though. Did you notice how we were let in the door and then the chap hooked it closed rather securely till the next customers appeared? Ipoh probably has had more trouble with the boys than most places, because they really wanted to paralyze business activity by scaring everyone.

"Actually," Mike continued, "it was up at Old Sungei Siput plantation—I'll take you past it by and by—where the boys first made their terrorist tactics plain. They came by one morning and picked up the manager and his assistant and two Chinese blokes who worked in the estate office. They tied the two managers to chairs and killed them. Then they said to the Chinese, 'We're only out for Europeans.' They didn't even rob the office safe, just killed the two poor devils to make their point. Nasty bit, what?"

At a carefully planned pace, we made our way north through the state of Perak. Mike had first been assigned here when he arrived in Malaya in 1939, and he had served as education officer for northern Perak for two years immediately before going on home leave in 1953, being assigned to Singapore on his return. He knew the area probably better than he knew his home country in Scotland. We stopped at plantations, we inspected tin mines, and we drove past miles of lush jungle. It was quickly quite apparent that any terrorists who cared to operate in these parts would have the upper hand.

It was also soon apparent that Mike had more on his mind than merely showing me what the handful of Europeans were facing in trying to survive against terrorist tactics. He wanted to relive with me the retreat from Perak of January, 1942. Again and again, he would swerve from the excellent hard-surface road and we would find ourselves on a jungle trail. These trails, which we inevitably ended up tramping on foot, would lead to where he would point out gun emplacements, remnants of whose works we would dig out of the elephant grass, or to stops where he would say something like, "Look, here's where they said we'd surely stop them. We'd stand and fight here, all right. Then we'd set up our machine guns and, about an hour later, our Malay scout would come in and tell us the Japs were already twenty miles south of us. They moved so fast we couldn't fight them properly because we couldn't catch up with 'em."

Mike had arranged for us to spend the first night at the government rest home in Taiping, where the British were running their experimental rehabilitation camp for captured guerrillas. First, however, he insisted on stopping at the royal capital, Kuala Kangsar. Here we had a drink at the rest house bar, where he had something else he wanted me to learn and perhaps to understand.

After the Chinese bar boy had blown the dust off the bar and

185

from the glasses into which he poured us meager measures of whiskey, and had started the ceiling fan on its creaking circuit, Mike asked, "What do you think of this place?"

"Well, it looks to me, Mike, as though not many people use it."

"They did. This was the scene of our Saturday-night bashes. That billiard table in the room over there was always in use. And you had to fight your way to the bar. Here's where your friends Dennis and Patricia Ambler first met. At one of those good old Saturday-night parties, you know. Old Dennis was head education officer. He was my boss, actually."

"Oh, was Patricia a young schoolteacher?"

"No, she was the wife of the District Officer, the chief British official in Kuala Kangsar."

"What you're trying to tell me is that a little hanky-panky went on, eh, Mike?"

"A bit more than a little, old boy. They started the worst scandal of the good old days in Perak. Very hot and heavy, indeed. The whole community was divided between those who supported the dashing Dennis and those who sympathized with the poor old husband. As for Patricia, she seemed happy with both of them, for a while anyway.

"Finally, the news got back to the Colonial Office. That sort of thing was not thought to be a very good show, in those days. Gave the service a bad name, you know. So they tried to pack Patricia and her husband off to Borneo. Patricia wouldn't go. She opted to stay with Dennis.

"Oh my, what a row. The husband finally went off to Borneo. He shot himself, eventually, I think. He not only lost his wife, it was a step down, a transfer to Borneo. You weren't supposed to lose your wife like that, you see."

I ordered us two more whiskeys to compose my thoughts or, at least, absorb the story better.

"I know you've read Somerset Maugham. But he never told the half of it. That's what I wanted you to know.

"Like a bridlepath building program of the Chief Resident, for example. That was our principle activity out here before the war. The Chief Resident liked to take parties picnicking in the jungle on elephant rides and he built hundreds of miles of these paths.

"A little Japanese photographer in Ipoh used to go out every Saturday and photograph the trails. He told everyone he was a col-

186

onel in the Japanese army, and everyone thought he was a bit cracked, you know. Well, those photos were what made it possible for the Japs to run through here in less than a week.

"Oh yes, the Sunday picnics figured in the Dennis and Patricia story too. They used to go off from the group and slide down waterfalls on huge palm leaves, in the nude, of course. One Sunday old Dennis's leaf slipped, and he came hurtling down the waterfall, legs thrown apart, and landed on a large rock. People thought this kind of accident would impede the romance. But Dennis recovered."

When we both had stopped laughing, Mike said he had a special person he now wanted me to meet. This chap, he said, was the oldest Englishman in Perak. He had come out from Cambridge with double honors in mathematics in 1885 to be the first British financial adviser of the sultan. In 1929, during the depression, he recommended his job be abolished to save the Colonial Office money. They accepted his generosity, but the sultan refused to let him leave. The Japanese were afraid of what might happen if they touched him, and he lived out the war in the sultan's palace.

We finished our drinks as Mike explained this to me. As we went out to the car, he said, "Malaya wasn't always like it is now, Joe, you see?"

The ninety-one-year-old financial adviser was enjoying the cool of the early evening on his veranda when we arrived. He gave me a rather penetrating glance when Mike introduced me.

"I've never seen many Americans in Kuala Kangsar," he observed, fanning himself with a straw fan like my grandmother had used on our front porch on a hot July night twenty-five years before, "What are you doing here?"

I explained I was from the Consul General's office in Singapore and was an official of the United States Information Services.

"What, you're one of those intelligence chaps, are you? I hope you're intelligent. Never met one of ours who was. I think that's why they use the term intelligence officer, close as they'll ever come to a quality they haven't got."

My cover was always terrible in this respect in Singapore and Malaya. No one could quite figure out what our propaganda agency was trying to accomplish by calling itself an information agency. As I tried to explain this, it made matters worse.

"What in the world are you going to propagandize the poor Malays about? They can hardly muck along now between what Chen Ping's boys tell them about the glories of the new Chinese revolution and what Kuala Lumpur tells them about how they should share their country with Chen Ping's countrymen."

I tried to explain the free world's burden to him. But he had never listened to the reasoning of John Foster Dulles before. He became very quiet, which misled me into going further into an explanation of the great ideological conflict that we were part of, and how the United States, humbly but determinedly, was assuming the role of leading the fight for the fundamental values of our civilization, because history seemed to have thrust this responsibility upon us.

After I stopped, there was a long pause before he spoke.

"Young man, I hope you really don't believe any of what you've just told me. I don't see how you possibly could, you seem to walk and move about like a rational person. No rational person could believe such utter nonsense. In any case, I implore you, don't try to tell this to the Malays. They are very polite people, so they won't harm you, but in their hearts they'll want to lock you up in some institution for the disturbed.

"The real world has nothing to do whatever with anything you've said. Look, you know what the old sultan said to me when he asked me not to leave Perak?

"The sultan said, 'Please never leave Perak. You are the only one who can make it work. I love only women and race horses. If you leave there will be no money at all in Perak, six months after you're gone.'

"There are struggles, great struggles in Malaya, in Asia, in the world. There are struggles for money, for power, for lust, greed, because of just plain meanness. But there is no such thing as the ideological struggle you talk about. If you're really going to come in here, to Malaya, to Asia, and take over, I pray to God you forget such absurd silliness. Unless you do, you'll never even learn what the real problems are. Good night."

If there were ever an occasion for Mike to give his nervous laugh this was it. Like me, however, he was simply too overwhelmed. We managed, all three of us, to say some pleasant farewells, and Mike and I drove on to Taiping, for the night.

It seemed obvious to me when we finally reached the village of

188

Kroh the next day that if Chen Ping was not hiding out in the mountains around there, he should be. Although we were able to make the trip from Taiping all the way by good hard-surface road, this was the principal sign that civilization might just perhaps extend this far. The road and one electric powerline were the sole modern conveniences that the village boasted.

There was another trusty rest house, however. Beside it the one in Kuala Kangsar seemed like the Raffles Hotel. One aged Chinese servant helped us with our bags and opened the windows of the musty room he showed us to.

"Old Cheng ought to be able to help you, Joe," said Mike, "he's been here for thirty years. I think Dennis used to pick up bits and pieces of information from him, in fact. If anyone in Perak knows where Chen Ping is, Cheng does."

We had arrived at dusk. Ah Cheng prepared us some fried rice, and we turned in right after dinner, there being nothing else to do and, besides, Mike had planned an early-morning tour of the tin mine, the *raison d'être* for Kroh.

Early the following morning we began our tour of the mine's property. The manager was a friend Mike had made during his days as education officer for northern Perak. He was a genial, youngish man, whose predecessor had been killed by the Communists, a weight he seemed to bear with ease. He arranged for us to tour the area in an armored Land Rover with one of his foremen and four armed guards.

"Really, there's nothing to worry about," the foreman said as we got into the Land Rover. "We just like to be careful, and besides, it's probably a good thing to keep in practice, so we keep our security setup functioning.

"Oh, there is one thing I might mention, though. If they do start firing, this damned buggy is a trap. Bullets ricochet like blazes in this tin lizzy. So at the first shot, jump over the side and roll as far as you can from the Rover. These blokes"—and he nodded to the four Malay guards—"will take care of returning the fire. The important thing is, jump out the far side, not the one against the hill they'll be firing from like old Gurney did."

The security briefing seemed not quite complete to me. What happened after we jumped out of the Land Rover and rolled down the hill? Then I recalled the ricocheting and decided he probably

189

didn't really think we would be doing much jumping if we actually were ambushed. This was a subject obviously best not pursued any further.

We traveled several miles down the hillside and the foreman pointed out various key sites and features of their operation. The tin mostly was dredged up from a stream bed at the foot of the mountain and transported via cablecar system to the processing area where we had begun our journey.

"The fascinating thing about these Chen Ping boys is the selectivity of their operations. They pop at us English blokes, and sometimes cut the wires of our telephone line to our outposts, but they never touch the cable that we move the tin by," the foreman explained. "They don't want any trouble with the townfolk. All of them depend on us for a livelihood. If they cut the tin car cable it would take us six months to get back into operation, and a lot of people would go hungry in the meantime. Cute trick, isn't it?"

Even a superficial glance at the hill and valley terrain with its thick jungle growth was enough to understand what he meant. If a clipped cable had flown off into that, the only thing would be to string a completely new line. I thought too, as I looked out over the jungle, what a great place for an ambush. I hoped the boys were not planning anything that morning.

When we got back to the rest house, we found a lanky Australian captain cleaning mud off his boots on the veranda. He looked up at us.

"Oh yes, you must be the chaps from Singapore, and"—smiling directly at me—"of course, you're the American. Welcome to Kroh. I heard you might be along."

He turned out to be the officer in charge of a Special Constabulary platoon of Malays whose job it was to search the area for signs of Chen Ping. He had just returned from a night patrol that, he sadly told us, had barely missed having some results.

"We found a fire still smoldering when we got to where we were going. They couldn't have left more than a couple of hours before. Damned problem with information around here. We get our tipoff, and then they get theirs."

He had been in Kroh just six months and they had been months of repeated similar frustrations. One big problem he had was that there was no well-defined border in the area between Malaya and Thailand. He said he frequently found himself in Thailand and ran into Thai police, who politely escorted him back into what they considered to be Malaya.

"These chaps are the real bastards, you know. There's a small Thai village not more than ten miles from here," he told us, "where we've seen the Commies dressed in uniform, mind you, buying food and enjoying a spot of beer and some words with the girls. The Thais claim they haven't been able to find a single guerrilla in the area. I'm afraid the police are being taken care of by someone, I'm sure you can imagine who.

"Doesn't your aid to the Thai police reach this far?" he asked me.

I said I didn't know, but as his experience showed, the funds we were spending to strengthen the Thai border patrols had probably stuck to someone's hands in Bangkok.

"Rotten mess," he said. "Well, if you'll excuse me, I've more gear to clean. Better luck with your try at finding Chen Ping." He went inside, content evidently that he could report he'd made contact with us. The arm of Phoenix Park was long.

Mike had another old-timer he wanted me to meet. We planned to leave on our way across Kedah to Penang in the morning, but before we left, he said he must introduce me to "old Keith," the first man to bring elephants to nothern Perak in 1925.

In the cool of the early evening we made our way to a modest house surrounded by a large garden and completely encircled by a wide covered veranda. The garden and veranda were swarming with Chinese children.

"Old Keith was the engineer who actually built the mine, and he had to bring in elephants to transport his heavy equipment. There were no roads in 1925. He married a Thai wife and settled down here when he retired. Some of the children may belong to him perhaps, but mostly to old employees, who are in jail because they are captured guerrillas. A strange sort of orphanage, in a way."

The old man was sitting in a large chair in the middle of the room. He was a huge fat man and two little Chinese girls were fanning him, supplementing the efforts of the ceiling fan directly beneath which he sat.

This time I omitted any mention of USIS and merely explained I was from the U.S. Consulate.

"You are the first American I have ever seen in Kroh in thirty-nine years, and I'm glad you're here. It's about time you chaps got out of your offices and stopped talking only with those ruddy Chinese rubber merchants and Tanglin Club members in Singapore," he commented.

We chatted about the old days and he told us some elephant stories. I could not resist asking him about the children. He smiled very broadly.

"Well, you see it's not that I particularly like children, nuisances really, but what can I do? Their fathers are all in jail and somebody must look after these tykes."

I asked how many he was taking care of and how long he thought he was going to have to.

"Never counted, of course. Must be about fifty of them. How long? Ha, that's a good question. How long are people going to be so damned silly? I mean, there probably will always be trouble between the government and the governed. No one's about to straighten that one out while I'm alive, I'm sure. Never have yet, probably never will. The thing is that, meanwhile, people have to live no matter what the crazy contest is called, especially children. It's none of their doing, the bloody nonsense.

"That's the worst of it, you know. The whole business is irresponsible. The governors are concerned only about themselves. They want power, but they don't want responsibility. I'm just trying to be responsible for these poor little ones. Someone has got to know how to be responsible."

We drank a beer with the old man, and talked some more about mining tin in the old days, and then we said goodbye.

Mike put me on the plane in Penang. He planned a trip back down the east coast. I was sorry that I was going to miss the additional education, but I thought that I had had about all I could absorb at one time.

As I sat listening to the rattling of the loose door of the Malayan Airways DC-3 that made its measured way toward Singapore, I thought I had been exposed to more than the realities of a jungle war with terrorists, more than area knowledge. I had met up with some wisdom in the words of the old men in Kuala Kangsar and Kroh. I didn't know how I could possibly use wisdom in my work. It was quick thinking my job required of me.

12

"It's All Right as Long as You Do It Professionally"

The new year was not very old before the election campaign for the Singapore legislative assembly began to attract attention. The new assembly would have a majority of elected members for the first time rather than be filled principally by appointees of the Queen's Royal Governor. Of the thirty-two members in the new assembly, twenty-five would be elected. The leader of the majority party would be the chief minister, heading a ministry of nine composed of six ministers chosen by him and three chosen by the governor. The governor was to be bound by the decisions of this council of ministers in all ordinary domestic matters, and the council, in turn, was to be responsible to the legislative assembly. Defense and security matters were still reserved to the governor and his staff, but it added up to a long step toward self-government for the crown colony.

The British seemed to believe that the election couldn't possibly bring any surprises. They had been priming certain candidates for eight years, when the first minority of elected members were chosen by popular vote. These Straits Chinese and Straits-born Englishmen called themselves the Progressive Party, which sounded properly forward-looking, and the British authorities felt certain should carry the day. They were so confident that this sensible, experienced group was going to win that they allowed automatic registration of all citizens. This quadrupled the number of voters as compared to the election eight years before and completely changed the racial composition of the electorate. The Straits-born Chinese were outnumbered by the Chinese Chinese, as the British called the more recent immigrants. The British thought was that many of them wouldn't bother to vote, and that those who did would be the responsible type, happy to follow the lead of the Straits Chinese and vote Progressive.

My two press agents, one Straits-born, the other Chinese Chinese thought somewhat differently. They kept telling me stories that made sense to me. The Straits Chinese were overconfident, the Chinese Chamber of Commerce was not happy to accept the Progressives as spokesmen for all the Chinese and were planning to field a ticket of candidates of their own, and the Chinese Chinese were being influenced by a number of ambitious politicians who saw this as an excellent chance to launch careers in politics hitherto denied them because they fell outside the charmed circle of Raffles Boys School graduates whom the British welcomed into civil service.

I talked this over with Bob. He had been involved in the initial meetings in Bangkok that attended the birth of SEATO. He had been back to Saigon before Christmas. He had personally briefed Secretary of State Dulles on what the British were providing in the way of information on Southeast Asia. He listened carefully.

"Well, Joey, we sure don't want to look stupid," he said, slowly. "Do you think we could get more information on our own about what's going to happen in this election?"

He knew I was going to say yes. I had one more agent prospect on ice. He had startled my predecessor by walking in the office one day and asking for work. He was an ex-Singapore policeman. He claimed he had quit, and was working for an obscure Chinese newspaper. Since it was the practice to submit all USIS and other prospective local consulate employees to the station for name checks of our counterintelligence files, he, as well as the other two agents, had been processed in that way. The station sent all such names to Phoenix Park for their checking for Communist or criminal connections. Mixed in with all these other names, our agent prospects did not call attention to themselves. All three had come back clean.

Bob and I were worried about this one's police background, because, if the British wanted to see whether or not we were trying to run independent operations without their knowledge, it would be logical for them to plant such a man on us. Naturally, his record would indicate he was an ex, not a current police employee. For that reason, and because his press credentials didn't seem in the same class as my first two agents, we had continued him on the inactive list. If the British had tried to plant him, after eighteen months of inactivity, they had probably given up the effort. We decided to test him out on reporting on election plans and activities in the Chinese community. If his test reporting seemed reliable, we could arrange a lie-detector test before getting into more operations with him to satisfy ourselves on the status of his connections with the British, as well as, of course, any Chinese Communist links.

Peter Lorre, as I liked to call my new agent because his manner always reminded me of that master at the portrayal of sinister intrigue, passed our initial tests, and he made us the only ones who didn't look stupid about the Singapore elections of April 2, 1955.

He and I developed a tradecraft pattern of communications that I was sure would have delighted Stan Archer. We found and used dead drop locations in the Singapore Public Library's stacks, and the men's rooms of the Adelphi Hotel and Robinson's department store. Into one of these drops one day he placed a full report on a new political party, the People's Action Party (PAP), whose leadership included at least one young man with a police record of long-time Communist membership.

The PAP's platform was designed to gain the party support for Malays and Indians as well as Chinese. The report also gave background information on the party's leader. He was a young Straits-born Chinese, a Raffles Boys School and double honors at Cambridge graduate, named Harry Lee, who had now dropped his anglicized name and was known as Lee Kuan Yew. The party was undertaking heavy organizational efforts in the largest poorer Chinese districts and support for the PAP was strong in these areas, the report said.

I was reminded of the mastermind solution to the counterintelligence targeting problem against the Nazis in New York that I had studied at the Farm, when the instructor had led us on about methods of sound targeting on agent prospects to insure the selection of the most potentially productive one and then had to admit that the perfect agent had been a walk-in, just like our Peter Lorre.

The report was very long and detailed and so completely at odds with what the official line on the election was that, I must admit, Bob and I faltered slightly. We decided not to write it up in intelligence report format for immediate dissemination to CIA's customers, but sent it in a regular dispatch, passing the decision on how to report it to headquarters.

It was the only report that came close to foretelling the election results. The winning plurality of ten seats was a coalition of leftists, who called themselves the Labour Front, but PAP won three seats, and the wealthy Chinese who was my neighbor across the street in Leedon Park and ran as a Progressive received less than 10 percent of the vote and had to forfeit his 200 Straits dollars election deposit. The election deposit is a British device used to discourage nuisance candidates with no chance of winning from participating in an election. The winner in the district in which my neighbor ran, in fact, was the young Communist leader in the PAP, twenty-two-year-old Lim Chin Siong, boss of the Factory and Shop Workers Union, and the one whose deposit was assumed would naturally be forfeited.

David Marshall, a Straits-born Eurasian of Mideastern ancestry, had no sooner formed his Labour Front ministry, on April 6, than the British were taught another lesson in the political realities of the colony. Since Marshall's leftist Labour Front did not have an absolute majority, he needed the support of the still more radical PAP in order to govern. The PAP apparently consented to go along with Marshall. Actually, it immediately began to rock the foundations of this temporary arrangement, using the mass-action strength of its young followers to achieve this end.

Chinese students began holding a series of meetings, without official approval from the authorities, to protest a number of alleged grievances. They also joined in rallies to support striking workers at the Hock Lee Bus Depot, with speeches, songs, food, and money. They rode around the streets in trucks singing a properly stirring Chinese revolutionary rendition of "John Brown's

Body." They also engaged in picketing, which was clearly illegal since they were not members of the striking force. Police tried to break up these picket lines. A riot followed.

Not only the British were unprepared for the night of April 12. Peter Lorre had not checked in with anything new, so my wife and I, the assistant air attache and his wife, and another consulate couple decided to try out a new restaurant we had heard was superb in the heart of what was called Chinatown, because no Malay face ever appeared there. It was located off colorful Bugis Street.

Bugis Street was almost empty. We saw two ancient mee sellers plying their trade. At the restaurant we were almost the only customers, certainly the only non-Chinese ones. We were served politely, but quickly and stiffly. On our way home we heard police sirens in the distance. As we passed the place where Tanglin Road became Holland Road, we saw a police car draw up, followed immediately by two more. Looking back, I thought they seemed to be about to form a roadblock.

Gene Symonds, the youthful bureau chief of UPI, had been having some drinks at the American Club at about ten o'clock that night when he received a call and the tip that students were coming in large numbers up Alexandra Road. He told his friends he was going to grab a cab and see what the action was. The taxi drove up to the point where the students were marching. On their shoulders, they were carrying a comrade who had been wounded by the police. When this crowd saw Symonds in the cab, they dragged him out and beat him mercilessly for half an hour.

We were no sooner home than Bob called to tell me the news about Symonds and to say that he had also heard an English man and woman had been beaten by the mob, and that they had been killed. There were road blocks on Holland Road, and we were not to leave the house. He said if I could contact any of my agents by phone, I should try to find out more, but I should not risk going out for a meeting. We would get together in the morning.

The next morning my new USIS boss and I rushed over to the Singapore General Hospital, where Symonds had been taken. We found him in an oxygen tent, hooked up for intravenous injections. He was a mass of bruises and was unconscious. We could learn no more from Gene. He died early on the morning of April 14.

As we tried to piece together what we knew about the situation, while we received reports from Phoenix Park, my agents, USIS reporters, and contacts of the embassy political officer, it was clear that the students had been shouting praise for Communist China, death to English and American imperialists, and other slogans that indicated pretty clearly the cause in which they were enlisted. They had made cruelly clear what they meant by death to Englishmen and Americans. It was a revelation to me that the conflict with Communists I had been engaged in only by means of verbal skirmishing through my press assets was a matter of life and death.

The death of Gene Symonds also affected Washington. Not only did the State Department spokesman say that the consulate in Singapore had been ordered to make a thorough investigation, there were words from the United States Senate.

Senator Lyndon B. Johnson of Texas declared that Symond's death was "a senseless, callous act of the kind that has made the word Communist hated throughout the world."

"I thought the British were giving our people protection over there," said Foreign Relations Committee chairman, Walter F. George.

The situation deteriorated rapidly and seriously from this point on for the next several months. Lim Chin Siong got busy organizing more strikes, and within a month a considerable amount of commercial activity in the city had been affected. A general strike was called for June 15. Initially the strike was supposed to be a sympathy action in support of the Harbour Workers Union's 17,000 members who had paralyzed the docks. When six Chinese were arrested for suspicion of subversive activities, including also the murder of Gene Symonds, the cause was changed to protest over these arrests. Before the end of June, 70,000 workers were out on general strike.

The events of those months set the pattern for the rest of my tour in Singapore, The great CIA operation that was creating the government of Ngo Dinh Diem in Saigon, from then on, had a strong competitor for my attention, the situation in the city where I was assigned.

In Saigon the great concern was establishing the political power base upon which the Diem government could rest its claim to legitimacy and, at the same time, create the basis upon which to avoid holding the nationwide general elections that the Geneva agreement demanded must be held the following year. Under brother

Ngu's leadership, the Popular Revolutionary Committee began calling for the replacement of Bao Dai by Diem as chief of state. Efforts then began to center on a referendum that took place in October. All the techniques that Quirino had tried to use to steal the election from Magsaysay were now used to insure the defeat of Bao Dai, who had to be replaced in order to distinguish the Diem regime from the discredited and despised French colonial past in order that Diem might have any chance at all of rallying genuine popular support for his new government. Although a National Intelligence Estimate that fall concluded that the Diem regime "almost certainly would not be able to defeat the communists in country-wide elections," a series of well-executed operations at least managed to give Diem 98.2 percent of the vote over Bao Dai in the October referendum.

On returning from one of his Saigon visits during this period, Bob told me, "Joey, they're spending money up there by the bushel basket."

"Did you find out what their budget is?"

"No, but I'll tell you, if we could spend that kind of money, we could buy every Chinese student in Singapore a first-class ticket to Shanghai and our troubles would be over."

The Chinese student problem was the one that we continued to live with. As the year wore on, it was compounded by the founding of an all-Chinese university. Nanyang University was the brainchild of the Chinese who was rumored to be the richest rubber merchant in Singapore, probably one of the richest Chinese in the world, as well as one who had concluded it was wise to side with the winner. Tan Lak Sai was rumored to be supplying the major part of the gold Mao's government needed. In a display of political acumen matching his shrewd business dealings, he chose Lin Yutang as chancellor of Nanyang University. The selection of this world-famous philosopher, supporter of Chiang Kai-shek, and long time resident of New York as chancellor was designed, of course, to reassure the British that Nanyang University would not be just a graduate school for subversion formed to complete the training and indoctrination of the Chinese middle school students who were terrorizing the colony.

The British were not only reassured, but concluded that Lin was our agent. He wasn't, which was probably unfortunate for all of us. Because of the concern for British prerogatives that affected all our

199

efforts in Singapore, and, probably, because of the heavy concentration on Saigon operations, no attempt was made to brief Lin in Washington before he got to Singapore or to arrange any kind of assistance for him in handling the situation he soon confronted. We were told to "monitor" the Nanyang University situation jointly with the British. Taking advantage of the vagueness of this word, I made it a point to meet Lin at one of the large international receptions held in his honor and was able to convey to him the idea that if he had any major problems, I was the person he should talk to about them. I didn't really expect to hear from him, but I thought at least I would try to do my monitoring first-hand.

One afternoon shortly after our conversation, Lin Yutang called me and asked if I would stay at my office after hours so that he could come by and see me alone.

Everyone else had left the USIS office when he knocked on my door. He explained that he had left his car in the Raffles Hotel parking area one block up Beach Road from my office. He said that he wanted to take every precaution that our meeting be as discreet as possible because he was in very serious trouble and, perhaps, even danger.

Lin explained that Tan and the board would allow him absolutely no decision-making power. This was not what really bothered him most, however; his concern was that the reason for this was that his views and theirs on the purpose of the university and how to run it were diametrically opposed.

"They want to indoctrinate the students not only with a love of China, that would be fine, I too love China," he said, "but they also want to concentrate all teaching on a love of Mao Tse-tung. Mao's teachings are to be the core curriculum of this college. I won't have it. I am going back to New York."

When pressed for details, Lin told me that he had been opposed not only on basic policy matters, but on selection of staff members, in which Tan refused to give him any say, and on books for the library, even on class hours. "They seem to want to leave the students plenty of free time to take part in strikes," he commented grimly.

My immediate reaction was that I must try to get him to change his mind about leaving and that I must get him some help to stick it out in order that we could not only monitor this new and potentially greater threat than any we had faced thus far, but hopefully find

200

a way to take some effective counteraction. Nanyang University, as its name implied, was intended to be a university not only for Chinese in Singapore but for Chinese from all the other countries of "the south seas." I could see it becoming a center for the training of Chinese Communist subversives for all of Southeast Asia, providing them with the marvelous cover of having been educated in Singapore and never having set foot in Peking.

I pleaded with Lin not to make a hasty decision but to allow me to consult with Washington and see what could be done to help him. He thanked me, but said he had made up his mind. I continued to try to change it. At last, we agreed that he would wait a week and we arranged for him to come by my house to talk things over further.

Washington told us to explain what had happened to the British and to continue to try to get Lin to stay, but would give no support to my specific proposal to assist him.

There followed a series of meetings with the British and between Lin and me. Given no resources to offer him beyond the philosophical probity of the free world, upon whose worth we agreed completely from the start, I was not able to convince the philosopher to stay. The man whose writing helped interpret China for me when I was a youth said this to me:

"It's not just that I don't agree with these people, I don't understand them. I cannot fathom their minds. I cannot tell what their actions are going to be, so I cannot be certain what I should do in response to them. Perhaps you do, or think you do. But I have enjoyed our talks and I don't think you are the kind of man who fools himself.

"I hope the United States government, and you, personally, will learn how to handle, how to deal with, the people of this new China, this new Asia." He smiled wryly. "My wife and I want to go back to New York. There are too many Chinese here for us."

These words did not seem as significant to me at that moment as the need to let the world know what was happening in Singapore, the enormity of what was happening to Lin Yutang, the threat to Southeast Asia that Nanyang University represented.

Lin readily agreed to my suggestion that he write an article about his experiences. The Time-Life representative in Singapore thought this was a good idea too. Soon *Life* magazine carried the story of Lin Yutang and Nanyang University.

Soon Diem won another overwhelming election in Vietnam. Not a single anti-Diem member was elected to the constituent assembly in March, 1956.

We continued to do a lot of things to fight against the threat of Chinese subversion in Singapore and all over Southeast Asia.

Postscript to Singapore

In early 1962 I was serving as desk chief for Venezuela. Among the duties I had was processing people going to the station in Caracas. One day a woman came into my office who was going to go to Caracas as secretary to the chief of station. We exchanged the usual introductory conversation. She was a newcomer to the Western Hemisphere Division, she explained. I said I was too, in fact, and I mentioned, among other past assignments, that my first one had been to Singapore. Her face dropped.

"Oh no, Mr. Smith, oh my God," she cried. "Oh, listen, could we please talk about it? I still have to talk about it. I spent the most horrible night of my life in Singapore."

I was, of course, a bit taken aback by this outburst at my mention of Singapore, and I said, of course, I would like to talk about Singapore very much. "What on earth happened to you there?" I asked.

"Haven't you heard of the Singapore flap, Mr. Smith?"

"Well, yes, I heard that some of our people got into trouble there with Special Branch, I think it was in 1960 or thereabouts."

"They didn't tell you that I was the girl in whose apartment it happened? No, I guess not, they're always very special in the way they handle me. You'd think it was my fault. Do you want me to tell you what really happened there? The shrinks say it's good for me to talk about it. That way, someday, maybe I'll forget it, they say. And you were in Singapore—I think you will really be able to appreciate it."

"Please do, please tell me all about it."

"Well, the station had this agent they wanted to give a lie-detector test to and they asked me if they could use my apartment. So, you know, I like to cooperate, so I said sure, yes, go ahead."

"Where did you live?"

"The Orange Grove Flats."

"Where?"

"The Orange Grove Flats. Right, Mr. Smith. Point one, a pretty wide-open place to use to put somebody on the box, but wait, they told me to go to the movies this night—"

"Night?"

"Yeah, at night. They said they'd be through by the time I came home if I went to the late show."

"You're sitting there and telling me that they tried to give a lie-detector test in an Orange Grove Flats apartment at night?"

"I am, Mr. Smith. Well, when I came home I saw a police car, two, I think, in the parking area. I looked up at my apartment, and somebody had closed the shutters. I should have run, then, I know. But I didn't, I went upstairs and two policemen grabbed me right away."

With tears in her eyes she told about how she had been interrogated for two solid hours by the policemen. When they weren't interrogating her, they were ripping up her chairs and sofas searching for God knows what. I tried to relieve her tension.

"Well, anyway, that was station or government furniture."

"Oh no, Mr. Smith, Singapore wasn't a furnished post anymore when I was there. These were my things, my precious things," she said with a sob. I had made matters worse, but she went on.

"Well, when they said they were going to body-search me, I would not let them. They insisted. I continued to refuse. So they said they'd call a policewoman to come over and do the job. We must have waited almost an hour for her. And my God, I had to go to the john, but they wouldn't let me go without one of them along. So I waited for the damned policewoman. I went to the john, all right, but I was body-searched too, really searched, if you know what I mean. Is there any wonder I still have to talk about it?"

I assured her there wasn't. I further said I couldn't believe it, but no one could invent anything so incredible. I said I knew now why people had once said something to me about trouble with Special Branch. Obviously, the man the station tried to put on the box had been a Singapore Special Branch source, a trained British agent. When he reported CIA was recruiting him and wanted to put him on the box, he had been told to lead the CIA officers on so that the police could catch them in the act of trying to subvert a Singapore police officer.

I said I just couldn't believe it and that it was a terrible experience to put a station girl through.

"That's another point, Mr. Smith. I wasn't a station girl. I was working for the overt office, the DDI liaison office we put in Phoenix Park. Do you remember we put a DDI representative and a secretary in Singapore?"

I told her that I did remember and that now I really had heard more than I could believe, even though she was sitting there telling me. An apartment in the Orange Grove Flats of an overt CIA secretary was used by the station for a lie-detector test!

"What happened to the guys doing the box job?" I inquired.

"Oh, they had tried to run before I arrived, of course, and of course, they were caught right away and put in jail. I understand the box man tried to chew up the graphs of the results he was getting and swallow them. Must have made him even more uncomfortable. I also understand we tried to offer the Prime Minister, Lee Kuan Yew, a couple of million dollars to let them out, and he said shove it."

"Good for Lee Kuan Yew," was all I could say.

Sometime after this girl told me this horror story, I heard that Bob Jantzen had received the highest award given by the United States government for outstanding intelligence work. His ability to get the complete cooperation of the Thai government in support of CIA's "secret war" in Laos won him the award. Bob, who by this time had been chief of station, Bangkok, since 1958, could get the Prime Minister of Thailand to do anything he asked. I also heard that Des Fitzgerald, who was by this time DDP, had called Bob "the greatest single asset the United States has in Southeast Asia." I was glad. I thought, "It's all right as long as you do it professionally."

13

Holding Sukarno's Feet to the Fire

One day in the fall of 1956, Frank Wisner, the DDP, said to Al Ulmer, the new Far East Division chief, "I think it's time we held Sukarno's feet to the fire." No one seemed to know the precise date when he said this, but Al made it plain to the officers of FE/5 the branch responsible for Indonesia, Malaya, and liaison with the Australian intelligence service, that if some plan for doing this were not forthcoming Santa might fill their stockings with assignments to far worse jobs. Thus began a year and a half of concentrated misadventures that ended with thousands of Indonesians dead, and an American pilot, Allen Lawrence Pope, in a Djakarta jail, awaiting execution. The last echoes of the matter reached well into the Kennedy administration, when the persistence of Robert Kennedy, who began trying to get Pope released in February, 1962, was finally rewarded with success in July that year. Within six months Pope was back at covert air operations with the CIA cover company, Southern Air Transport. The rest of us were scattered far from FE/5.

The way I got involved in these operations demonstrates how job assignments came about in the Clandestine Services. The way I got out, on the eve of the establishment of the rebel Sumatran government we supported, was also a good example of how people were disengaged from such operations. In between, I was involved in most of the fire-building and foot-holding activities. Our efforts, of course, had no more effect on Sukarno than the Spaniards had when they literally did anoint with oil and set fire to the feet of Cuauhtémoc, who followed his murdered uncle, Montezuma, to the Aztec throne. Something about the heirs of ancient civilizations of other races seems to escape the Western mind.

When I returned from Singapore in July, 1956, several assignments were available to me. I had once written a dispatch in which I had recommended that Cord Meyer's International Organizations Divisions should have a liaison representative in Singapore since the British had so much they wanted to discuss about his operations. This was bureaucratically stupid of me, because I was sticking my nose into the coveted business of suggesting new positions. Empire building is the bureaucrat's one unceasingly acceptable activity, but I was suggesting adding to Cord Meyer's domain and not that of my own division. I was promptly informed of the error of my ways. The incident caused Cord, however, to be interested in hiring me.

Kay strongly advised against this. She let me know that the soundings she had taken, which I always respected, indicated most important senior line officers considered his operations frippery that would come to no good. This turned out to be true, but not until February, 1967, when *Ramparts* magazine blew the entire labyrinth of IO operations out of the water. IO Division, in fact, probably would have been a better spiritual home for me. IO Division officers knew that we were involved in a war of ideas and that such a war cannot be won without being willing to pay attention to new ones—something that the Clandestine Services became increasingly afraid of as the years went by.

Kay had her own reasons too, of course, for giving me this advice. She wanted me to work for her again. I liked the idea except I thought after a tour in the field I should be moving on to something else. So did Al Ulmer.   When Al visited Singapore in the spring of 1956 on his get-acquainted tour he liked my briefing on Lee Kuan Yew. It had been a performance on which I had to rely heavily on the talents that won me the offer from the Province-town Players in my youth. Al and Bob Jantzen returned late one evening from talking with the British at Phoenix Park, but Al still liked working. He asked to see our file on Lee Kuan Yew. He had read, of course, both our station's and the Consul General, El-bridge Durbow's, reports about Lee. These expressed concern at Lee's close collaboration with known Communists, both in and out of his People's Action Party.

We didn't have a formal file on Lee. Bob Jantzen didn't like to bother with that sort of thing. Fortunately it was late, so Bob told him that our most confidential files were locked up in the part of the station that housed the communicators and their equipment, and he hated to disturb the late-duty communicator. I quickly vol-unteered to brief Al. He agreed that this would do. Remembering what such a file should have contained had we had one, I went to work and was a great success. In addition to my personal triumph, some real good came out of the briefing.

I made a lot of the fact that, for some months, a rather erratic free-lance British writer, named Alex Josey, had been almost con-stantly in the company of Lee. Josey, in addition to his prodigious beer drinking, seemed to like to travel around Southeast Asia at-tending things like the Socialist Internationale meetings in Burma and so forth.

"My God," cried Ulmer, "I know Josey. We were in the compos-ite OSS-SOE unit in Cairo during the war. I guess you haven't had time to send in all that stuff, or we could have checked it out for you. I don't think you have to worry too much about Mr. Lee any-more. MI-6 has a damned good case officer working on him. Josey's always been great at the vagabond leftist act."

Thus I found myself in FE/5 in October of 1956, just before we got the word to get moving on Sukarno. It didn't take from July until October to make the decision among the choices mentioned above. The person who was the Malaya desk chief had to be ma-neuvered out of the job. This was done, as always in those days, by arranging for the Office of Training to come up with an urgent re-quest for the services of an officer with qualifications for a special instructing assignment in training that only the person the bosses were trying to get rid of possessed.

I enjoyed my new job. I had a number of ideas about what we might do to improve our intelligence coverage of the volatile situation in Singapore and also to block the growing strength of the People's Action Party, and its Communist allies. For one thing, I had come home armed with a letter of introduction to a Chinese girl student who was secretary of the Malayan Students Association in the United States with headquarters in Chicago. These students, like almost everybody else in Singapore, were of course Chinese, not Malay. I proposed that I go out to Chicago with the cover story that I was a USIS officer responsible for liaison with foreign student groups. I would claim this was the assignment USIS had given me after my returning from my tour as USIS information officer in Singapore. I'd say that my special duty was to hear out their problems, especially any ones they had with U.S. authorities, and to try to help solve them. This would give me a chance to assess the girl and others in the group so that I possibly could recruit some young Chinese to help us follow the revolutionary youth when they returned home. The British simply were not giving us enough information to enable us to provide the Washington intelligence community with a meaningful assessment of the situation. We had to have more unilateral agents.

Ulmer agreed with me about the poor take from British liaison and approved my plan of action. After several trips, I did recruit the girl, and we soon had a good-sized file of potential agent material for Singapore. This pleased Ulmer.

Al Ulmer liked action. He had clocks on the walls of his office set for the correct time in the major European and Asian capitals so that he wouldn't lose track of the action going on anywhere at any time. Ulmer was one of the handful of OSS officers who had never left active intelligence service after the order came to disband the organization. He stayed on to wind up affairs in Vienna, and hence was on the spot when CIA was started. He had been chief of station, Vienna, Greece, and Madrid, before taking over the FE Division from George Aurell. Al had been an especially dynamic figure in the success of CIA's operations in Greece, so much so, he had been cooled off in stable Madrid for a few years. There was little doubt in anyone's mind where Al was going if he could get there—straight into the DDP's job whenever Wisner shed the mantle. Doing well as chief FE would help him greatly toward that goal.

FE was the biggest division and the one with the greatest variety of challenging situations. Not only did it have to deal with the number two world Communist power, China, but had to support John

Foster Dulles's pet project for keeping China at bay—the Southeast Asia Treaty Organization. This was no small task for, except for such Southeast Asians as the Americans, British, and Australians, no people in the area cared much for SEATO. We dragged in our client states, like Magsaysay's Philippines, but strong counterforces were at work. The most important opponent of SEATO was Sukarno. Hence, chief FE in 1956 was a job made for someone with ambition and drive. Opportunities to achieve operational spectaculars were as numerous as the countries the division was responsible for. The trick was to pick the right country and the officers who were willing to try.

The initiative I took in my own little corner, the Malayan desk, was appreciated. Soon after the word was passed to hold Sukarno's feet to the fire, I was told confidentially by Ulmer's executive officer, Sam, that Al wanted to move me up to deputy branch chief of FE/5 in order to get something going in Indonesia. Al planned to replace the branch chief too, as soon as he could find a senior officer he liked for the job. Meanwhile, he wanted me to move up to deputy to start the fire building beside the Reflecting Pool. I was to spend as much time as possible, beginning immediately, reading myself into the Indonesian political situation and getting fully acquainted with our operations in order to be able to propose a specific plan of action.

The first operation that had to be run, Sam explained, was the same one as in the case of my getting the Malaya desk job. Sam said he would handle it. This was the task of getting rid of the incumbent deputy. The special assignment in training ploy was used again. The victim balked, but was finally ordered to take the assignment. I felt bad about both these cases. I liked both people who were booted out to make room for me. But I did not protest. In the Clandestine Services the stepping stone to success was frequently the face of a friend.

As I read into the Indonesian picture I quickly discovered reasons why Wisner had given the word. For one thing, the PKI, the Communist Party of Indonesia, had made great gains since I had been in Djakarta in the summer of 1953, on TDY assignment to straighten out the bookstore. As for Sukarno, he returned from a visit to the Soviet Union, China, and other Communist countries at the end of October just as I was settling into my Malaya job and declared he thought all political parties should be buried. There was a lot of cause for the DDP to be upset with the way things seemed to be going from bad to worse the last couple of years in Indonesia—whose 90 million inhabitants made it the most populous country in Asia, aside from India and China.

For one thing, we had lost a million dollars in one shot on the Indonesian elections of 1955. This, of course, was not counting other related operational expenses. This was just the cost of the single big direct subsidy we gave to the Masjumi party—the centrist coalition of Moslem organizations which, before the elections of 1955, had looked like the largest and most stable political group in the country.

I had been told that we were supporting the Masjumi in the 1955 elections by my old friend from Linebarger's seminar, Curly, who was chief of station, Djakarta, when I was in Singapore. Curly always stopped off in Singapore whenever his business took him anywhere in Southeast Asia. He liked to check with Bob Jantzen on what the British were up to, but this was not his main reason for his Singapore stops. He always arrived in Singapore with a shopping list for his Indonesian station personnel and their dependents. The same import duties and surcharges that caused our bookstore grief made daily living in Indonesia something that even embassy duty-free import privileges could barely make tolerable. Nothing that Americans found essential for living, other than basic foods, could be purchased or even found in Djakarta. So Curly would arrive with a list ranging from shock absorbers for a Chevrolet to a nursing bra, and nearly everything else you wanted to name in between.

In the course of helping him shop, he kept me up on what was going on operationally for old-times' sake, because he knew that I had become friends with a number of his case officers during my brief Indonesian stint, and because he hoped I might be able to give the Masjumi party some of the propaganda support I was giving to Diem's struggling regime in Saigon. But he never told me the details of the Masjumi election operation.

As I looked through the file I found out there were many strange things about the whole election. Regarding the big one-shot campaign contribution, for example, the document that asked for approval to make the payment was unlike any I had ever seen. The normal request for a political action operation of such magnitude contained considerable required information, justifying the need, explaining the expected results, and giving details as to how it was

210

planned to achieve them. The Masjumi operation document was only a couple of paragraphs that said little more than we proposed to provide one million dollars to the party.

A glance at the approving officer's signature explained this. The proposal had gone directly to Kim Roosevelt, who at that time was special assistant to the DDP for political operations. He was considered a master of the art. His operation had put Nasser in power in Egypt. By 1956 this was beginning to look like a questionable accomplishment, but when the operation was pulled off, it was considered outstanding. I had heard in Singapore sometime in 1954 that Roosevelt was Mr. Political Action. Political action was big in 1954. It was the year of the Guatemalan operation and the establishment of the Diem government, and the year before, in 1953, we had elected Magsaysay. The Indonesian general elections were being planned then. Voters were registered in May, 1954, and the candidate lists of the parties drawn up in December, 1954. These were to be the first national elections ever held in Indonesia. A few paragraphs for Roosevelt's eye were enough to get the required approval of the topmost echelon of CIA for the Masjumi election operation.

Another startling thing about the project was that it provided for complete write-off of the funds, that is, no demand for a detailed accounting of how the funds were spent was required. I could find no clue as to what the Masjumi did with the million dollars. Hong Kong station, which in addition to its regular duties, had the job of procuring soft currency funds, like Indonesian rupiahs, at the going black market rate, kept flooding bags of currency into Djakarta. Officially the rupiah was pegged at 11.40 to the dollar, but the black market rate fluctuated in the 40 to 1 region. Forty-odd million rupiah in paper bills of any denomination is a lot of paper as well as a tidy sum of money. Running satchels of this stuff out to Masjumi contacts was a heavy task. Perhaps, I concluded, the Masjumi agents simply lost a lot of it after the transfer. It undoubtedly was dropped somewhere, but it didn't produce the winning votes.

The operation was not as reckless or unthoughtful as the above may sound, however. Indonesia was, in most ways, a more important country than Vietnam, the propping up of which we were contributing such great effort to at this same time. Stretching from Sabang, an island north of Penang, Malaya, to Merauke, a town almost on the border with Australian New Guinea, Indonesia is the world's largest archipelago. It consists of 3,000 islands large enough to mention, and 10,000 more that aren't. Its resources include tin, oil, bauxite, gold, silver, copper, and in the 1950s it was the world's largest exporter of natural rubber, as well as a leading copra producer. Java in the 1950s was the most densely populated place on earth, with approximately 1,250 people per square mile.

Unfortunately, Indonesia was just about the epitome of what we dared call an underdeveloped country in those days. Rubber, its principal export, suffered the most from price fluctuation of any agricultural product in the world. All underdeveloped nations depend for their existence on the sale of such products. According to a United Nations study of instability in export markets of underdeveloped countries from 1901 to 1951, rubber prices fluctuated by 36 percent. After the Korean War boom ended, Indonesia's national income plummeted precipitously. In 1951 the government had a surplus of 1,195 million rupiah. The next year it had a deficit of 5,362 million. It was difficult to determine exactly what happened. No Indonesian parliament ever got around to approving a budget. In 1956 the budgets for 1950, 1951, and 1952 had not yet been approved, let alone a current one. The cost of living went up 50 percent between 1953 and 1955 and the number of government employees and their cost grew at an equally disturbing rate.

In Indonesia, as in all underdeveloped countries, the number of qualified people necessary to run the country, direct its private businesses, and provide professional services was sadly below the country's needs. From 1950 until 1955, Indonesian universities graduated only 6 economists, 49 engineers, and 151 doctors. Yet more than 800,000 people were on the government payroll. The army alone had 150,000 civilian employees, which made up a large portion of the 42 percent of government expenditures that were spent on defense. An additional 40 percent of the rest of the floating national budget was spent for other government salaries. Under the circumstances, the government had hardly any choice except to print more paper money.

Political management of the country, below the level of Sukarno, who did little besides make speeches, and Vice-president Hatta, who didn't even do that, was as much of a hodgepodge as the economy. A cabinet form of government attempted to administer the affairs of state, and the parliament, a hold-over constituent assembly of revolutionaries that had formed the new federal republic, made laws when it could bring itself to take any action.

Political parties were mainly groups of officeholders who held rallies from time to time to pressure the government to act on matters of importance to their interests. These rallies, often partially financed by funds siphoned off from various government departments, gave a false impression of party strength, as the elections of 1955 would show. The Socialist Party, PSI, was the worse offender. The PSI was blessed with brilliant leadership and its members held important positions in the bureaucracy. The PSI also controlled the best newspaper in the country, *Pedoman,* and a Chinese-language newspaper, *Keng Po.* With this type of support to draw on, PSI always managed to hold the biggest rallies in the nation's capital. In the elections of 1955, however, the PSI all but disappeared.

The party that was closest to being a government party was the Nationalist, PNI, which bore the same name as the organization that Sukarno had established in 1927 when he began his revolutionary career. His cronies, indeed, still formed the party's old guard. They were basically as anti-Western in 1955 as they had been when they started their crusade against Dutch colonialism a quarter of a century before. All claimed to be better socialists than the PSI.

It was the amazing comeback of the Communist PKI that worried us most. The party had been almost wiped out when it had attempted a coup against Sukarno's leadership of the revolution in 1948. Even before then, however, the PKI had gained a foothold in the labor movement, and this was the basis of its strength. By 1955 the federation of labor unions of Indonesia, SOBSI, was completely controlled by the PKI. In the aftermath of an army-inspired cabinet crisis in October, 1952, the PKI gave full support to Sukarno's choice as prime minister, Al Sastroamidjojo, who formed an all-PNI cabinet in early 1953. As a result, a PKI/PNI partnership was formed. Sastroamidjojo remained a close friend of the Communists ever after. PKI's showing in the 1955 elections would be their biggest surprise and most disturbing result.

The Masjumi was an umbrella organization—a federation of Moslem social and religious groups formed during the Japanese occupation in 1943. It didn't organize as a political party until November, 1945. As a political party it was a strange animal. The Masjumi had two types of membership—individual and group. The

213

two most important group members were the Moslem reformists and the Nahdat'ul Ulama, an organization of Moslem traditionalist scholars—the wise men of the villages who believed everything, including politics, ought to be based on the canonical books of Islam. the older leaders of the Masjumi were anti-Dutch, and anti-West in general, believing that capitalism was anathema to their Islamic faith. Mohammad Natsir was the leader of the younger, moderate group, and, like a lot of the PSI intellectuals, pro-Western and anti-Communist. Like them, he believed Indonesia's only hope was some sort of an adaptation of Western industrial know-how in socialist frame, provided it was not the Soviet model.

A common denominator of all younger as well as most older Asian anti-colonialist revolutionaries in the 1950s was their belief that some form of socialism was their country's hope. They all arrived at this conclusion by the same syllogism—colonialism is capitalism; colonialism is bad; therefore, capitalism is bad. They were not nearly so clear about what socialism was. I remember the startled reaction of some British colleagues and myself to a statement at a dinner party by a rich young Chinese businessman/politician when he declared he was a socialist. When asked to define what he meant by socialism, he replied that socialism was a system under which everyone could get ahead in business without outside interference. The Dutch, the English, and the French in Asia were the "outside interference" that made all these young Asian politicians think they were socialists.

Our estimate of the situation in Indonesia on the eve of the 1955 elections was that the Masjumi was the counterforce the country needed to prevent the dangerous drift of Sukarno and his closest political associates toward a dictatorial government with strong PKI influence. All our training and the fundamental tenets of our cold war political philosophy told us that the kind of partnership Sukarno had with the PKI could lead only to the PKI's ultimate triumph. This had been the inevitable consequence of any partnership with Communist parties in Eastern Europe. What we thought we saw happening was the infiltration technique of the world Communist movement directed from Moscow at work to bring the rich Republic of Indonesia into the Soviet satellite domain, thereby sealing the fate of all the tiny countries in Southeast Asia. The largest Moslem country in the world falling under Communist control would also have fateful consequences far from the South China Sea.

214

At least, I thought, as I studied the files, in backing the Masjumi we had followed the country's own cultural and social pattern. We hadn't backed the Catholic party, as we did in Vietnam, although actually there was one and some of our best officers in Indonesia were Catholic. They had taken the trouble to learn something about Indonesia, however. They had even taken the trouble to find a rare American Moslem to use as the undercover contact with the Masjumi.

Two elections took place in 1955. The first one was held on September 29 to elect a new parliament, and the second was held on December 15 to choose members of a new constituent assembly to write a new constitution. The first one, of course, told the tale. The PNI won both in September and in December. Sukarno was so pleased with September's results, he campaigned openly for the PNI in the December contest.

Our postmortem of the Masjumi's defeat noted a number of possible reasons why our party lost. It had not gotten down to building good village-level organization. It had spent large sums on films, amplifiers, tape recorders (even though we had no detailed accounting) for mass rallies that the voters evidently found entertaining but not convincing. It was tagged by the PNI as being rightist and desiring a religious solution to the country's ills. This was unfair, but effective. The Masjumi's party symbol, a crescent moon and a star, was said to be a bad omen. (The PNI's symbol was the *benteng*—the Indonesian wild buffalo, long the emblem of the cause of nationalism and independence.) Most important of all, the Masjumi lost because its progressive leadership ignored the conservative Moslem segment of the population and gave this big vote by default to the Nahdat'ul Ulama.

Our reformist Moslem contacts in the Masjumi made their first mistake back in 1952 when they recommended a reformist for minister of religious affairs. The Nahdat'ul Ulama broke with the Masjumi on this issue. Our undercover agent working with the Masjumi was convinced by his contacts that this was not an important development. They thought the old-fashioned NU good riddance. This split lost the Masjumi nearly 7 million votes in 1955. They were cast for the reactionary NU. CIA lost a million dollars by supporting the progressive Moslems of Indonesia in 1955.

Worse still, the Communist PKI received over 6 million votes, just shy of the NU total. The PKI won heavily in Java, and it moved

215

quickly to consolidate its gains. As a result, in 1956, the Communist PKI was strong in local government all over the island of Java and controlled the city councils of four of the largest cities there.

The significance of the way the vote was split, with results in Java being so distinct from those in Sumatra, didn't impress me as much as it should have when I first reviewed the 1955 election. Although the Masjumi had come in a poor second to the PNI and was weakened and discredited on the national stage, it was still strong on Sumatra. When its defeated politicians and certain disgruntled military officers put their heads together an incipient separatist movement was born. This would be something that could shake up Sukarno.

Sukarno held seemingly unshakable sway over the Indonesian masses, but a number of specific incidents and actions of his caused Washington, not just Wisner, concern that he might be in the process of selling his charisma, if not his soul, to the Communist side in the cold war. Internationally, he organized the Bandung Conference in December, 1955, as an answer to SEATO. Chou En-lai was a featured guest as the doctrine of neutralism was proclaimed the faith of the underdeveloped world at Bandung. Sukarno followed this with his 1956 visit to China, Russia, and other Communist countries after which he repeatedly praised Soviet and Chinese economic models as guides for his country's future development. In local politics, as has been mentioned, his PNI and the PKI worked closely together and together had won the plurality of votes in the 1955 elections. By 1956, the PKI had one million members and was the largest Communist Party outside the Soviet bloc, France, and Italy.

John Foster Dulles was apoplectic and Manichean on the subject of neutralism. I was convinced that he did more harm than good to our cause by demanding that people around the world take a stand either for us (the side of Light) or for the Russians (the hordes of Darkness). Still, I found it difficult to accept Sukarno's brand of neutralism. I looked forward to the chance to try to do something to combat it, and I was happy the word had been passed to act. I understood the metaphorical language of the DDP about holding Sukarno's feet to the fire. I was sure it stemmed from some conversations between John Foster and his brother Allen Dulles. The colorful phrase meant that no one wanted to put any orders in writing. We who were closest to the situation, the Djakarta station and

216

FE/5, were supposed to discover some intelligence information that could be made into a plan that would look good enough on paper to justify NSC's Special Group approval of action to diminish or even destroy Sukarno's power in Indonesia and his influence in world affairs.

We knew a great deal about Sukarno and we knew nothing about him. He was an orator whose powers to melt the masses of Indonesians, who thronged to hear him, made Hitler's ability to stir Germans or Churchill's to move Britons seem paltry performances. I heard him on Merdeka (Freedom) Day in Djakarta in August, 1953. I could not understand *Bahasa Indonesia* but I didn't need to in order to appreciate his mastery. He began in what appeared to be an Indonesian version of the American country-boy style. The crowd tittered. He had them with him. Then he began to increase his intensity of voice and emotion. They were soon a mindless mass hanging on his hypnotic words.

Like many great orators, his ideas were vague and not too numerous, and those that were present in his ramblings do not translate or read well. Perhaps he made his greatest speech when still being supported by the Japanese as a diversionary force at a meeting of the BPKI, the investigation committee for the preparation of Indonesian independence, on June 1, 1945. This was his *Pantja Sila* speech, in which he proclaimed the "Five Fundamental Points" of Indonesian society. These were constantly brought up thereafter in every discussion of Indonesian affairs and served as a substitute for thought. The *Pantja Sila* were: nationalism, internationalism, democracy, social justice, and belief in one God. "In establishing an Indonesian state," Sukarno cried, "all should be responsible 'all for all.' If I press down five to get three and three to get one, then I have a genuine Indonesian term—*gotong rojong* (mutual cooperation). The State of Indonesia which we are going to establish should be a state of mutual cooperation. How fine that is! A *gotong rojong* state!"

Sukarno claimed his mother was a Balinese of Brahmin cast and his father a descendant of a Javanese sultan. His mother's uncle, according to his official biography, was the last king of Singaradja, in northern Bali. The Dutch said he was the illegitimate son of a coffee planter. Sukarno admitted, when the Dutch made this claim, that the last witness who could prove his true parentage had died. Like most Indonesians, Sukarno was casual about first names. He

217

preferred to be called "Bung" (brother) and was widely referred to by people all over Indonesia as "Bungkarno."

He was born in Java on June 6, 1901. He was an intense student and became a revolutionary by his late teens. He spent many years in jail in the 1930s, where he taught himself English by reading, among other things, the writings of Thomas Jefferson. He delighted in quoting to Americans verbatim texts from lesser-known Jefferson letters. In addition, he could, and often did recite the American Declaration of Independence, including all the lengthy charges against George III, and Lincoln's Gettysburg Address and First and Second Inaugurals. He also read Karl Marx in English.

Whatever his parentage, our sources all agreed he was a Javanese through and through as far as personality was concerned. The above recital of his proclivity for eclectic and odd bits of information indicates what they meant by this. The Javanese are almost as adept at assimilation as are the Japanese. They live comfortably with both a Hindu and a Moslem religious heritage. They are intent on trying to find compromises and fit loose ends together. They love to "push down five to get three and three to get one" in almost any situation in which they find themselves. When reality doesn't yield to this kind of pushing, they retreat from it. Perhaps this explains why Sukarno could live easily with the kind of neutralism he tried to promote—the best of both worlds. It was also the reason he found administering a government so distasteful. He preferred to talk and to enjoy the prerequisites of power to prodding parliament into passing a budget. "Sukarno wants only his palace," one of our reports on his personality said, "he dreams he is a Javanese sultan."

He had other dreams too, and he acted out as many of these fantasies as he could find time for. His greatest joy in life was amorous adventure. He once put it thus: "As an artist, I gravitate naturally toward what pleases the senses." He not only gravitated toward women, he stayed in orbit. He delighted in casual sex, and he delighted even more in serious love affairs. When I went to Indonesia on TDY in 1953, the gossip everywhere concerned Sukarno and a Mrs. Hartini Suwondo, wife of an oil company executive. It was widely known that Major General Suhardjo, one of the country's top military officers, was Sukarno's principal accomplice in arranging their liaison. Suhardjo flew Hartini on a military aircraft from Semarang to Djakarta for their lovers' trysts.

In 1954, Sukarno invoked his Moslem privilege and took Hartini as an additional wife. Fatmawate, Sukarno's second wife, would not divorce him as his first wife, Inggit, had done, when Fatmawate came along. Even when Sukarno boldly moved Hartini into the palace, Fatmawate refused to divorce him. So Moslem law solved the stubborn problem, and Sultan Sukarno took two of the four wives to which a man is entitled if he can afford it. Fatmawate, however, then moved out of the palace to a house in the new Djakarta upper-class suburb, Kebajoran.

Beyond the stories of his sexual exploits that everyone in governing circles in Djakarta talked about, and some similar gossip that claimed he had bad kidneys, unfortunately we knew no really inside information about Sukarno. We had no agent with direct personal access to him and had not really made much of an effort to get one. Our assets were concentrated outside his inner circle.

The major operation we were running in Indonesia in those days was a large amorphous affair that supposedly gave us coverage of all our main targets—the PKI, the links between the PKI and the PNI, and some coverage of Soviet and Chinese Communist activities as well. It involved liaison with people close to the Sultan of Djogjakarta, Hamengku Buwono. He had been a powerful figure in the Indonesian revolution when Sukarno and Hatta based their independence movement in his capital, Djogjakarta. The sultan, in fact, had figured in an important political crisis that we probably should have studied more closely because following its ramifications more carefully would have meant we would have been much better prepared to carry out Wisner's command in 1956 than we were.

This crisis began on October 17, 1952, when the army chief of staff declared his intention to pension off what he called unprofessional officers. This precipitated a parliamentary crisis that almost led to a military coup. Parliament bucked the army order and voted no confidence in the Sultan of Djogjakarta, who was defense minister at the time. The sultan retired from politics. The military, at least the army chief and his top officers, wanted to abolish parliament and wanted the sultan to lead a coup that would have changed the course of Indonesian history. The sultan was not anxious to move, and Sukarno's golden tongue rallied the masses behind him and parliament. One spillover from this event was our operation.

In other words, we were financing the efforts of some of the sultan's men to keep in touch with the ensuing political situation. In exchange for this help they shared their information with us. But we neglected to follow up the army officers and their subsequent planning and plotting. We thought these things peripheral so long as we knew the sultan wasn't planning any action. Thus, we didn't know the colonels who were then already thinking the thoughts that led to the revolt of 1958—support of which in the end turned out to be the only thing we were able to think of to accomplish the mission our boss had given us.

After the debacle of 1955, our deep-cover Moslem agent left Indonesia to try his hand at operations in Algeria, and our Masjumi contacts were withering by the end of 1956. We had no press assets that could help us harass Sukarno on the spot. *Abadi,* the Masjumi newspaper that had been an asset in the heyday of our Masjumi operations, was no longer being subsidized by us. It had lost its punch when the Masjumi lost its power in Djakarta's ruling circles.

We had one small operation that was always good to mention at briefings of top DDP staff officers. It looked like the kind of operation intelligence officers call "classic." We had a little man who regularly provided us copies of the secret minutes of all the meetings of the Indonesian cabinet. Nothing delights a covert espionage officer more than to hear that this kind of information is being collected. What we didn't mention when claiming credit for this classic intelligence coup was that, by 1956, no important matters were decided by the cabinet. All the important decisions were made by Sukarno and his henchmen in the palace before the formal cabinet meetings took place.

The other large activity on which we were placing our bets for future improved coverage of Indonesia was a police training program. We conducted this under cover of the Economic Cooperation Administration, ECA, as the foreign aid program was called in 1956. ECA was able to offer programs such as police training to countries where CIA had an interest in using them. CIA, in fact, had its own man, a former Counter Intelligence Staff officer, in a key position in ECA's office responsible for managing these programs.

The 105,000-strong national police force was second only to the army in size among the elements of the Indonesian defense establishment. Its responsibilities took it into every part of the country, and so training its key officers and then recruiting them to provide us the information we needed on Soviet, Chinese, and PKI activities and the links between these activities and the country's political structure seemed to offer promise of a most rewarding operational arrangement.

We had a retired U.S. Army colonel running the overt training show in Indonesia and a number of case officers under him who could fan out around the country to follow up police officers and activities of particular interest. From time to time, some of the ones identified for recruitment were sent to Washington for special training. This was a reward they cherished, and an opportunity for us to soften them up for recruitment. When police officers were recruited, they were sent back with specific assignments to carry out under the direction of the case officers under ECA cover in the field.

Participation in the recruitment effort in Washington was eagerly sought by younger officers on the desk. At least one important part of the process offered them very pleasant duty. Whether the police officers were bent on emulating their national leader or were just guys out for a good time away from home, I can't say. All had an absorbing desire to sleep with a white woman. They were convinced that this would be a different experience from enjoying the little brown maidens at home. So the Washington case officers hauled them off to the Oasis in Baltimore to accomplish this mission. This strippers' dive at Baltimore and Frederick streets offered them quick, direct action.

The CIA officers who worked the Indonesian beat were a special group in those days. The man who had been branch chief since the time of the OSO/OPC merger had been in Indonesia with the United States Rubber Company before the war. He had his limitations, among them that he had fewer scruples than any man I ever met elsewhere, but he had one good idea. He believed that the officers going to Indonesia, a country he felt he knew from long experience, should devote their careers to that country, learn the language, and accomplish both these ends by rotating assignments regularly between the Washington desk and the field. Thus, at any one time, there were in Djakarta men who had been there before supported by men in Washington whom they had just replaced. Al Ulmer made him take his own medicine, and sent him off to be COS, Djakarta, in the summer of 1956. Al thought Bob Jantzen should learn something about Washington after nine years in Singapore. He ordered Bob home and sent Curly to Singapore. Then he sent the Indonesian branch chief off to Djakarta to see whether he was the specialist on the country he claimed to be.

His replacement as branch chief, the man I was supposed to prod into action, was an amiable, affable chap and a great improvement over his predecessor as a human being in every way. He didn't know Indonesia, however. His only experience in the Far East had been in Japan, where nothing in either the national or operational picture prepared him for his new job. Since he was aware of this, his natural tendency to be cautious was considerably increased.

The key officers, just back from Djakarta, upon whom he had to depend more than made up for his lack of area knowledge and sense of adventure. I had known the desk chief, since my earliest days in FE. In those days, he was principally known as the youngest officer in the division—the only case officer under twenty-five. He was one of those individuals who would always seem to be that age and to seem to dash, never walk, down a corridor. A graduate of MIT, his spirit could never have been confined by an engineer's slide rule. But his mind was as alert and incisive as the shrewdest member of that exacting profession. If there was a point to anything, Dick always got right to it.

The officer who eventually bore the brunt of the work during the operation with the Indonesian rebel colonels was in Bethesda hospital at the time I was reading into the Indonesian scene. He was recuperating from his second nearly fatal automobile accident, which he had suffered in Surabaja as he was preparing to become chief of our base there. He had had his first accident when he was in Indonesia on his first tour of duty at the beginning of the decade. I had first met Ned when I became involved in Indonesian matters briefly in 1953. He had one leg in a powerful brace that enabled him to ignore his handicap completely. When he finally got out of Bethesda and came to work in 1957, he had to use two aluminum crutches. Otherwise nothing had changed. He made it clear at once that he was no worse off than before. Ned never asked and never gave any quarter.

He not only knew Indonesia and Indonesians, he could look the truth in the face more unflinchingly than anyone I have ever

222

known. Ned's whiskey was Johnnie Walker Black Label Scotch but his politics were straight Bourbon. Despite the fact that our political biases were polls apart, however, I have never worked with anyone more harmoniously. It was too bad that we had to share the ill-fated adventure that began in early April, 1957.

14

Sêlamat Sumatra

We had many problems dealing with the dissident colonels who defied Sukarno in 1957 and 1958. None was greater than the one we created for ourselves. We had a terrible time articulating our objectives in contacting the colonels because we hid the fact we were supporting their aspirations to form a separate state independent of Sukarno's government from higher authorities in Washington until we were certain we could win approval for this course of action.

It all began in early April, 1957. A top-priority cable came in from Djakarta saying that one of our agents had offered to give a case officer information from representatives of the Indonesian army commander in Central Sumatra, Lt. Col. Achmad Hussein. He and other local commanders in Sumatra and elsewhere in outlying islands had been defying the central government since the previous December. We had never been able to find out any details of what they were up to. We knew only that their general gripe seemed to be that they were not being properly supported by the defense department in Djakarta. They lacked equipment, supplies, and even provisions for their troops, they claimed. The cable wanted headquarters approval before making contact with these dissident elements. The COS, Djakarta, was good at rotating his case officers, but he was out of his depth in making risky decisions.

Dick, the desk officer, by standard operating procedure was the first one in FE/5 called by the weekend duty detail at the Cable Secretariat—the central unit for receiving all incoming messages—when the cable came in on a Sunday morning. He ran with it as he was wont to run with everything. By the time I heard about the request for headquarters advice, Dick had obtained approval for the contact to be made, had authorized further instructions that Djakarta should insist on direct case officer contact with Hussein's representatives rather than rely on our agent to relay the information obtained, and had the entire subject issued a special communications designation. This limited distribution of all incoming and outgoing messages related to contact with the colonels to only nine officers: the director of Central Intelligence and his deputy, the DDP and his deputy, chief FE and his deputy, the FE/5 branch chief and his deputy, and Dick. We were not going to handle this delicate matter in the usual manner, with every staff element in the Clandestine Services putting in its two cents' worth of advice.

I understood the reason for Dick's rapid action. I also understood that he knew why I had been moved up to the job of deputy branch chief. We were months past Al's deadline for producing a plan for Wisner. Dick was told of the impending change in the branch chief's office by Ulmer's executive officer, Sam, soon after I had been told myself. Dick and I had spent hours wracking our brains about what our limited assets in Indonesia might do to rock Sukarno's relationship with his Communist companions. We hadn't come up with anything so far. Dick saw the cable from Djakarta as something he could move on to show he was on top of the situation.

I was a bit worried by Dick's decisive move. I reminded him that we didn't know very much about the colonels. We didn't have a file on a single one of them. None of our agents had ever had any contact with them before.

"Well," Dick assured me, "it's true, we don't. But we soon will if the station understands this is what we've been looking for."

He could be right, I thought. We had let Djakarta know, of course, that Wisner wanted Sukarno's feet held to the fire. They had not come up with any bright ideas either, but the cable seemed to show that someone out there saw the same glimmer of opportunity for an action program that Dick had seen and that, of course, Al had grasped immediately when Dick rushed to Al's house the Sunday morning the cable came in to get the chief's stamp of approval for the reply he sent out. We would have to wait to see what happened.

In a couple of days we had the answer. A case officer had been taken to a meeting with Hussein's representatives. The dissident colonels were all working together, the case officer was informed, to bring pressure on Sukarno to desist from his drift toward Communism. They were also acting because they believed Sumatra and the other outer islands were paying a disproportionate share of the taxes and other costs of the corrupt, wasteful, Javanese-dominated central government. The colonels specifically opposed Sukarno's declaration on February 21, 1957, that Western-style democracy should be abolished in Indonesia in favor of something he called "guided democracy" and that a "national council," consisting of representatives of all segments of society, be installed to replace parliament. Sukarno had also called for the formation of a cabinet that would be founded on the "Indonesian *konsepsi* of deliberation and consensus—a *gotong rojong* cabinet." What this meant in plain language was that Sukarno wanted the PKI to be represented in the cabinet in the same proportion as the results of the 1955 election indicated. The PKI had obtained one-fourth of the votes in those elections. What Sukarno was proposing was that the PKI hold one-fourth of the cabinet posts.

Finally, the colonels explained that they had opened their own bank accounts in Singapore in order to obtain supplies that the central government was remiss in providing their troops. They suggested that these accounts might be useful to anyone helping them with any kind of assistance. They did not, in the first contact, come right out and ask for arms.

The message revealed that the rebel colonels had gone further than anyone had yet realized in developing the nucleus of a genuine separatist movement. The Singapore accounts and the news they were coordinating their actions was new intelligence. We saw this was put out to the intelligence community immediately, with the sourcing disguised so as not to show that a CIA case officer had gotten the information directly from representatives of Hussein

227

himself. This was both standard operating procedure for protection of sourcing and, in this case, also a hedge to enable us to figure out where we wanted to go from here in our activities with the rebels.

Hitherto, we had been able only to speculate about the meaning of various acts of defiance of central authority on the part of army officers scattered from Medan in North Sumatra to the Celebes and Borneo. The first trouble had begun on December 20, 1956, when Hussein had declared his autonomy of command and said he was taking over the civil administration of his area, Central Sumatra. Two days later, Colonel Maludin Simbolon, a thirty-seven-year-old officer considered one of the army's brightest, declared North Sumatra, his command, also no longer responsible to the central army chief. He took over the administration of the key port city, Medan, the largest and most important place in Sumatra. Two years earlier Simbolon had been beaten out for the post of army chief of staff by Abdul Haris Nasution, a slightly older Dutch-trained colonel.

When Dick made his run to Al Ulmer's house, the Indonesian political scene appeared to be unsettled but indolent—a condition Western observers following Indonesia had long since come to accept as more or less permanent. The cabinet of pro-Communist Ali Sastroamidjojo had fallen on March 14 under pressure from the unruly colonels. No new cabinet had yet been selected, although Sukarno had dismissed the PNI chairman as cabinet maker and taken on the task himself, "as citizen Sukarno," he said.

The dissident colonels had undoubtedly become a factor in the denouement of the Indonesian political situation, but no one up until now had produced any information that would enable our intelligence analysts or those of Defense and State to determine precisely what effect on the outcome of the story the colonels might have. So we could accomplish a lot before getting into the matter that really concerned Wisner—how we might manipulate that outcome. We decided our first presentation to Washington's higher echelons would give no hint of a future intention of mounting a political action program.

This was the crux of the matter. Not only were we far from ready to say precisely what this action program should be and what chances for success it might have, but at the first hint of any action program, we would have to begin the process of coordination with the ambassador, the Department of State in Washington, the Defense Department, and, before any direct action against Sukarno's position could be undertaken, we would have to have the approval of the Special Group—the small group of top National Security Council officials who approved covert action plans. Premature mention of any such idea might get it shot down at any one of these levels. If it fell to earth with a thud at the embassy in Djakarta, then it would never be revivable at the Department of State, and Defense would get scared off by word of this and nothing would ever reach the Special Group.

So we began to feed the State and Defense departments intelligence that no one could deny was a useful contribution to understanding Indonesia. When they had read enough alarming reports, we planned to spring the suggestion we should support the colonels' plans to reduce Sukarno's power. This was a method of operation which became the basis of many of the political action adventures of the 1960s and 1970s. In other words, the statement is false that CIA undertook to intervene in the affairs of countries like Chile *only after* being ordered to do so by the 5412 Committee, the Special Group, the 303 Committee, or the 40 Committee, the small group of top National Security officials who acted in the President's name under these various labels throughout the cold war. In many instances, we made the action programs up ourselves after we had collected enough intelligence to make them appear required by the circumstances. Our activity in Indonesia in 1957–1958 was one such instance. We also made a few special contributions to the technique of making a situation appear to require that CIA step in to correct it.

For instance, the statement that our intelligence collection effort was something no one could deny was a useful contribution is not quite accurate. The new ambassador, John Allison, who had just arrived on the scene in Djakarta, was not certain of this. He had been ambassador to Japan and assistant secretary of state for the Far East. He did not think CIA operations contributed as much to the overall effort of the U.S. government abroad as we did. He wasn't too sure their contribution was worth the risk entailed in having CIA officers under embassy cover in contact with dissident rebel colonels. This was really the reason the chief of station had cautiously sought headquarters approval for the first contact with the colonels in the cable he sent in. He could then, if required, tell the ambassador that he had been ordered to do it by Washington.

The solution we adopted to the ambassador's objection about a case officer under official cover contacting the rebels was to instruct the chief of station simply to deny that the contact was being made by such an officer and say we were handling the matter through a series of carefully compartmentalized cut-outs. The most efficient way to handle ambassadors who demand their rights as heads of U.S. missions abroad to be informed of CIA operational activities was to tell them plausible lies.

Allison continued to raise annoying questions throughout the development of the operation. He frequently made a point of writing Washington his explicit disagreement with our estimate of the situation as it progressed. We handled this problem by getting Allen Dulles to have his brother relieve Allison of his post within a year of his arrival in Indonesia. There was no objection from the embassy in Djakarta when the rebel colonels were ready to give Sukarno their ultimatum in February, 1958.

Events moved rapidly in Indonesia in April and May, 1957. Political pressures developed in Djakarta and the rebel colonels became more articulate in their contacts with our case officer. The first blood of the colonels' revolt was shed on April 6 in the distant Celebes. A clash occurred between rebel forces and Indonesian troops loyal to the central government about forty miles south of Macassar. Twenty-nine soldiers were killed. Three days later Sukarno announced his new cabinet.

The cabinet "citizen" Sukarno came up with was a compromise with his announced intention of bringing the Communists into the government. It was headed by a nonparty bureaucrat and consisted of twenty-three ministers who were described as "technicians." There were no PKI members in the cabinet but there were three well-identified fellow travelers and Communist sympathizers. This cabinet, Sukarno said, would undertake to govern in the interests of all Indonesians under the broad principles of a kind of state he had outlined in his February 21 speech. Obviously, Sukarno was not abandoning his objective of moving Indonesia into a closer relationship with the Sino-Soviet bloc. He had been slowed down a bit, however, by the anti-central-government movement in the outer islands. This boded well for the potential usefulness of the colonels' group as an instrument to thwart his plans to move from neutralist to satellite status.

The cabinet was in office barely two weeks when Kliment Voro-

230

shilov, president of the Soviet Union, arrived in Djakarta for a state visit. It was billed as a courtesy trip in response to Sukarno's visit to Russia in the fall of 1956. Over the course of the next fourteen days, however, he and Sukarno spent considerable time together both in sight-seeing trips and in the palace. We wished we had someone in the palace who could give us the kind of reporting we received on the unimportant cabinet meetings. The little coverage that we did get of Voroshilov and his entourage convinced us that Sukarno was being strongly influenced by the Soviets.

Voroshilov left on May 6, and two days later we were sure we saw the first results of his stay in Indonesia. On May 8 Sukarno announced the formation of his "national council." This was the step he had proposed in his outline for the new-style Indonesian government in his February blueprint. By the way he arranged for what he called "representation for all segments of the population," Sukarno showed his national council was meant to be the first step in strengthening Communist participation in the government— something he had not dared to propose directly when he formed the new cabinet. SOBSI, the PKI-dominated labor federation, plus the PKI-controlled youth organization and woman's group, all received representation on the council equal to that of traditional social groups. What the national council was going to do, exactly, was not as clear as the significance of its political makeup. As usual, Sukarno's rhetoric beclouded this point. We felt, however, another big step had been taken in the wrong direction by our shifty antagonist.

Sukarno then announced that district elections would begin in June all over Java and would continue for the next several months. A glance at the PKI's strength in Java showed us this was another disquieting development. In building up their party for the 1955 elections, the PKI had changed traditional Communist Party tactics. Traditionally, Party membership is supposed to be limited to a relatively small number of dedicated revolutionaries—the vanguard of the proletariat, Marx preached, should not be a large, mass organization. The PKI in 1954 and 1955 instituted a new category of membership, adding "supporter member" to the traditional Communist categories of "member" and "candidate member." On this basis, the PKI expanded from 7,910 members in 1952 to 165,000 in 1954 and more than one million members by May, 1957. The supporter members were key figures in attracting voters

231

to the PKI in rural areas in 1955. Now we thought this grass-roots technique of the PKI was about to be put to work to take over control of all rural local government on the island.

None of these developments was lost on the colonels. Our contact had continued and had steadily improved. Our case officer had met with Hussein himself and he was promised meetings with Simbolon and with the other leaders. Meanwhile the colonels kept providing us with intelligence that supported our worst fears concerning the direction that Sukarno was taking the Indonesian state.

Our reporting was well received in high circles in Washington. I don't know if it caused him to make the decision, but in May President Eisenhower turned down flatly Sukarno's invitation to visit Indonesia. Ambassador Allison reported that Foreign Office officials in Djakarta considered the refusal brusque. Senator Styles Bridges, chairman of the Republican policy committee in the Senate, singled out Indonesia for censure in a debate over foreign aid. Bridges backed a $3.5 billion cut in aid funds, saying that it was time do-gooders stopped spreading American dollars abroad among people who were not on our side. Indonesia, Bridges pointed out, was one country where he thought we should stop our foreign aid programs.

Our effort to determine the background of the colonels and the situation within the army's officer corps was making some progress. It was a great help when Ned came back to work. I suggested he be made branch chief of operations, and he took charge of our search for answers to the nagging questions we faced. He was no more a specialist on the Indonesian army than the rest of us, but he had a vast stock of Indonesian lore to draw on and he could recall things that others couldn't. He also insisted that we add to our team the deep-cover case officer for the big liaison operation with the sultan's friends. This officer had been in Indonesia for four straight years working as an arms dealer, and, Ned pointed out, if anyone had a feel for the military situation it was Bill. Bill was on home leave, and, as a deep-cover officer, was not supposed to enter the buildings by the Reflecting Pool. We convinced Bill to cut short his home leave and join us. We told him to avoid coming to work when other people did and sneaked him into the office as a visitor.

We were careful to clear this system for using Bill with Al Ulmer. Ulmer approved immediately when we explained what Bill could contribute. Arrangements such as the one we made to use Bill were nothing new to Al. When he had been chief of station, Athens, he added a large contingent of nonembassy cover officers to the station. He found a building adjacent to the embassy for their offices, and then had a passageway built so that they could slip unobserved into his embassy office when necessary, to confer with him, check files, or whatever else was required for the conduct of their business.

As soon as really serious contact had been established, the rebel colonels asked us for arms. We were careful not to mention this outside Al Ulmer's office, because it threatened to upset completely our strategy for putting an operation together that we could sell in Washington.

"Hell," said Ned, "what else did anyone think they wanted? They're big boys and don't need us to hold their hands while they say boo to Bungkarno."

Ned was right, of course. Nevertheless, it was tricky to face up to the fact. If word of the request for arms leaked out it might make our plan for continuing to avoid asking approval from the NSC Special Group unworkable. We had to do something and fast. If we didn't come across with this assistance, the colonels would stop talking to us and the intelligence collection on their plans and activities that we so proudly provided the Washington intelligence community and the White House would come to an abrupt halt.

The way out of this dilemma, we first thought, was to find some manner in which we could provide them funds to buy their own arms. We would claim ignorance and innocence as our defense if they got arms and began to use them. We would say that we merely had given money to them as payment for the intelligence they gave us. We would swear that we had no idea they planned to purchase arms and we had given them the funds in good faith in exchange for their services. The high security classification and limited distribution of the messages about our dealings with the colonels that Dick and Al Ulmer arranged that first Sunday would enable us to get away with this.

There were several flaws in this solution, we soon discovered. First, the colonels might go about their arms buying in such a flagrant way they would tip off Sukarno too soon as to what was going to happen to him and his government. They might get stung badly by some of the unscrupulous illegal arms merchants with whom they most likely would have to deal and get a lot of junk for

233

our good money. Then too, the colonels made it clear they wanted topnotch U.S. material. Enough of this kind of armament had been floating around the world since it had slipped through the hands of our Korean allies to make it plausible if they turned up with these high-class items, the colonels insisted.

So the next plan we tried to work out was how to furnish the arms as though they had been purchased through an honest broker. We rationalized our not telling about this scheme just yet to any of the authorities that might not approve by reminding ourselves that intelligence could also be obtained by giving the sources not money but what the tradecraft term called "exchange commodities."

Ulmer called me into his office one day to tell me he was turning over to me an interesting man who, as he put it, "the Australians have given us, but we haven't found any use for yet." He went on to explain that this man's background and current business interests were such that he should be of use primarily to Branch 5, if to anyone, and he wanted me to look over the case to see if the man might be the answer to how we could get the arms into the hands of the Indonesians.

The man was John Galvin, owner of the Malayan Mining and Metals Company Ltd., which had been supplying the Japanese with all the iron ore it had been using since the war to rebuild its steel industry.

Galvin was an Australian who had joined up with the British SOE in Hong Kong during the war. He had a newspaper background and worked on black propaganda and related activities. He took a keen interest, as a good propagandist should, in what the enemy, then the Japanese, were up to in their newly conquered territory so that he might uncover information for his propaganda efforts. He discovered one weakness of great value to his future fortunes. The Japanese were hauling all their iron ore from mines in eastern Malaya which the British had barely touched but which the Japanese quickly expanded as soon as they took over the former British dependency. Galvin made some quick plans himself. He found some Chinese moneylenders in Hong Kong and, as soon as the war was over, rushed to Malaya and bought the mines at a nominal cost as Japanese enemy alien assets. By 1957, Galvin was many times a millionaire. Here, indeed, I thought, is a man who should be of great use to FE/5.

First of all, given his stake in society in Malaya and Singapore, Galvin could help us out there. Every week that passed indicated Singapore needed attention, both for the success of any operation with the rebel colonels and also because of what was happening on the local political scene. The colonels had established bank accounts in Singapore and were counting on help coming via that great trading center of Indonesia's rubber and oil. They already had representatives at work there. One of these was Dr. Sumitro Djojohadikusumo, the Indonesian Socialist Party's most brilliant economist, who had also been the country's most capable finance minister. Curly had known Sumitro in Djakarta and had reestablished contact with him in Singapore to help us follow rebel plans.

Local developments during April, 1957, in Singapore indicated it might be very difficult in the future to talk to Sumitro or any other anti-Communist there. On April 11, Lim Yew Hock, the Singapore prime minister, signed an agreement with the British which established the former crown colony as a fully independent state. Lim was a labor leader who had replaced Marshall as prime minister when Marshall's efforts to negotiate such an agreement bogged down. He faced threats to his labor leadership from the Communist-dominated unions and threats to his political leadership from the People's Action Party. On April 30, the PAP dealt Lim and the new agreement a severe blow when they managed to get the Singapore assembly to strike out of the accord with the British a clause forbidding subversives the right to vote in the elections to choose the new assembly to be elected to govern the independent state of Singapore. If the PAP should win these elections, we would be in trouble.

We had to support Lim. To do this we needed cover for passing him funds to support his election bid. We also needed a good direct contact between him and the Singapore station. Our contact with Lim up to this point had been through an American labor leader, a collaborator in Cord Meyer's international labor operations. George Weaver, whom John Kennedy would name the first black assistant secretary of labor for international affairs, was at that time a high AFL/CIO official and he had made several trips to Singapore to assess Lim and to offer him international labor support for his non-Communist labor union. If we were going to get involved in an election operation, however, we would need a man on the spot the station could use as a contact. I thought Galvin should be able to provide us with cover for passing funds to Lim and a man in Singapore the station could use in the contact role.

As for helping us with the matter of getting arms to the Indonesian colonels, I thought Galvin should be able to do this too. He had considerable shipping activities going on in all Malayan ports, as well as Singapore. The straits of Malacca are a pretty narrow passage—at points the island of Sumatra and the west coast of Malaya almost touch—and I thought he could arrange for one of his captains to drop off some cargo somewhere along the Sumatran coast.

Al agreed with my plan to contact Galvin and sound him out about both the movement of arms to the colonels and support to Lim Yew Hock. The head of the Australian service had called Galvin to Al's attention because Galvin had decided to establish residence in California. He had an office in San Francisco and a ranch near Santa Barbara. So I took a trip to see him.

We decided also it was time we discussed the Indonesian situation with the British. Now that we were going to involve an ex-British SOE officer in our activities there was all the more reason for having a talk with them, as Al put it, "to give MI-6 in Singapore some first-hand Washington thinking." I thought it would be great if I went out to see Galvin and then on to Singapore to meet with Curly and the British. Sam, Al's executive officer, wanted to make the Singapore trip, however, and he won.

Sam, in fact, was an excellent choice because he not only had more experience than I, he had never forgotten anything that had transpired since his wartime service days. He would not be caught off base by any points the British might raise. We called him the human computer. He knew not only where all the bodies were buried, but who had arranged the burials and what the funerals had cost. Sam and I flew together to San Francisco. There I learned that Galvin was at his ranch not his office, and I took off for Santa Barbara and Sam for Singapore.

I had talked to Galvin on the telephone and identified myself through a recognition signal Al had established with him to indicate that one of Al's representatives was seeking an interview. Galvin had a station wagon waiting for me at Santa Barbara airport. His ranch was located in the beautiful hills outside of town, and it was a copy of a Spanish hacienda—main house, work buildings, chapel and all.

Galvin was a stocky, self-assured, pleasant man who introduced me to his wife and daughter and insisted on showing me around the place. His pride was his stable where he had a dozen beautiful horses. He made a point of introducing me to the groom. "He comes directly from the Spanish Riding Academy in Vienna," Galvin proudly explained. "I've known Alois Podhajsky for years, and the good colonel not only gave me a groom, but he has provided an instructor for Patricia ever since she was a tiny girl. I hope someday to get a Lippizaner from him." As a result of the world's best equestrian training, Galvin further pointed out, he expected Patricia to make the U.S. Olympic riding team. She was going to enter Sweetbriar College in Virginia in the fall, he said, because it was the only college that would let her bring her favorite horse with her. This was essential, of course, if she were to maintain top form as a rider.

After lunching on some trout from a stream on his property, perfectly prepared by a Chinese cook, Galvin and I retired to his den to talk business. I decided to bring up the Singapore question of support for Lim Yew Hock first, since it was less sensitive than the matter of providing arms for a rebellion against Sukarno. I went over our assessment of the situation and the background of Lim. Galvin concurred in our views and said he had several men on the spot following things closely. "You never forget your tradecraft, old chap. I have my own little intelligence service, you know," he assured me.

More important, Galvin assured me that he would be glad to cooperate fully in any plan we had to see that the pro-Communist PAP was defeated at the polls. "What do you have in mind?" he asked. I replied that for one thing we wondered if he could cover some funding of Lim's election expenses we would like to provide. "How much money are you talking about?" he wanted to know immediately.

I didn't have any figure to mention. No amount of money had been approved for the operation yet. To test his reaction, I decided that I would mention a figure I thought sufficiently substantial, and one probably greater than we would be willing to spend. "About a hundred thousand dollars," I said.

Galvin burst into prolonged laughter. When he could stop laughing, he said, "Really, my boy, I thought you were talking about *money*. I'll give old Lim more than that personally, so you don't have to give the matter another thought. I thought you had some serious sum in mind."

I was impressed, as I was meant to be, but I also began to reassess my pleasant new friend and the evidence he had been presenting me all day of his opulence and importance. I decided to go ahead with the discussion of the Indonesian arms deal but to be as circumspect as possible and be alert to try to separate fact from fiction.

We talked more than an hour about possible ways to ship arms and to cover the deal as a purchase from wildcat arms dealers. I came away with the idea that Galvin could undoubtedly arrange the matter but how securely I was not too sure. I told him we would be in touch.

As he said goodbye to me, Galvin remarked, "If you're ever in Hong Kong in this operation, let me know and you can use my place on Repulse Bay. Has its own beach. I lent it to Han Suyin and her British boyfriend. It's where all this 'many splendoured thing' business took place, you know."

I reported to Al. We decided that using Galvin could get us involved in an arms shipment deal even more flamboyant than one the colonels might arrange for themselves. Galvin had too much flair. The last I heard of him was when I read in *Time* some years later he had fled to his ancestral Ireland a few steps ahead of the U.S. Internal Revenue Service.

We also decided to wait to see how things developed during the coming weeks before going further with any plans for covert arms shipments. Events in Indonesia, especially the PKI local election victories on Java, and our own propaganda effort to raise the threshold of awareness of Sukarno's pro-Communist policies might just enable us to get Special Group approval for support of the colonels. As an approved political action mission, we would be able to count on cooperation from CINCPAC headquarters in Hawaii and the entire Pentagon establishment in getting arms and other supplies to the rebels.

We had been ringing as many changes on the theme of Sukarno's Communist proclivities as we could for the past several months. The Communist influence on the new national council and the growing power and importance of the PKI were favorite themes as was the insidious influence of the Voroshilov visit. We developed, in this last regard, the theme that Sukarno's well-known swordsmanship had trapped him in the spell of a Soviet female agent. His succumbing to Soviet control, we implied, was the result of her influence or blackmail or both.

238

Exploiting Sukarno's sexual appetite in this way was a tricky theme. His conquests didn't disturb Indonesians too much. In Indonesian society a woman's place is in the bed. And it was the Prophet Mohammed who promised his faithful warriors that he would furnish heaven with beautiful black-eyed houris to provide them eternal happiness if not eternal rest. However, what we were saying was that a woman had gotten the better of Sukarno. Being tricked, deceived, or otherwise outsmarted by one of the creatures God has provided for man's pleasure cannot be condoned. Also, we were interested in the impact of this theme outside Indonesia, for our purpose was to present Sukarno in as unfavorable and unsympathetic light as possible. If he were deposed by our friends the colonels, we wanted the world to agree with us that Indonesia would be better off.

Actually the theme wasn't something we invented simply by brooding about this obvious vulnerability of Sukarno. There had been reports that a good-looking blond stewardess had been aboard his aircraft everywhere he went in the Soviet Union in 1956. We had a report that this same woman had come to Indonesia with Voroshilov and had been seen several times in the company of Sukarno. This formed the foundation of our flights of fancy. We had, as a matter of fact, considerable success with this theme. It appeared in the press around the world, and when *Round Table*, the serious British quarterly of international affairs, came to analyze the Indonesian revolt in its March, 1958, issue, it listed Sukarno's being blackmailed by a Soviet female spy as one of the reasons that caused the uprising.

Our success went to our heads. I don't know exactly who thought of carrying the theme one step further, but one day Dick suggested I come with him to Al Ulmer's office. There I found Sam and Al and Ned getting ready to view a film. When the lights dimmed and the film began to flicker on the screen, it was a grainy and gamey exposition of genital activity between what looked like a Mexican man and a seedy-looking woman. The consensus was this wouldn't do.

What our special Sukarno committee was formed to accomplish was the production of a film, or at least, some still photos, showing Sukarno and his Russian girlfriend engaged in his favorite activity. We ourselves were going to produce some proof of our theme—the very films with which the Soviets were blackmailing Sukarno.

239

Movies that in those days were called blue films, which indeed they were when compared with the full-color, full-length features that have become standard viewing throughout the country today, were acquired for us by CIA's chief of security, Sheffield Edwards, through his close, friendly contact with the police chief of Los Angeles. Los Angeles's supply of blue films suited our purpose, we thought, because they included dark male subjects, like the Mexican, who might be made to look like Sukarno with a little touching up. The problem was the female partner. They did not use talent in blue films in Los Angeles in those days that could compare with that of a decade later. We saw no likely candidates for the beautiful blond Soviet agent.

We hadn't too much luck with a likely Sukarno either. One idea we had was to ask the Los Angeles police department to find us a dark and bald male lead. Sukarno never permitted himself to be photographed without his *pitji*, the traditional black cap worn by Malayan and Indonesian male Moslems, lest his balding head be seen. We figured he surely didn't wear his *pitji* in bed. We thought we would expose his vanity while we were exposing him. We saw a number of bald Chicanos but no Sukarnos. Finally, we decided that we would try to develop us a full-face mask of Sukarno. We planned to ship this out to Los Angeles and ask the police to pay some blue film star to wear it during his big scene.

Diverting as this kind of duty was, we had a lot of other things to do during the hot summer of 1957. We wrote our paper for the Special Group and got formal approval to support the rebel cause. Al Ulmer was very happy with this new development. "We'll drive Lebanon off the front page," Al said. We all got the message. If we could pull off the Indonesian operation successfully, all our careers would greatly prosper.

The PKI showing in the elections was a great help to us in convincing Washington authorities how serious the Indonesian situation was. The only person who did not seem terribly alarmed at the PKI victories was Ambassador Allison. That was all we needed to convince John Foster Dulles finally that he had the wrong man in Indonesia. The wheels began to turn to remove this last stumbling block in the way of our operation.

Within our own shop, Al had managed to ship Bob, the branch chief he thought was not with it, off to the Army War College. In the Clandestine Services in those days, places like top-level government training programs, such as the Army War College, that were coveted rewards for personnel of other agencies, were used to dump people who were considered not to be doing the job. Al also had found the man he wanted as a replacement. This was Joe Smith, who was returning from Bangkok, where he had been deputy chief of that key Southeast Asian station.

I had been told about this choice in advance, and Sam had asked me if I thought that Joe and I could work well together. I had known Joe since my earliest days in FE. He was then working in the office of the OSO Division Chief, Lloyd George. Joe had been with OSS in the China-Burma theater during the war. By an additional quirk of fate, we both had been born in June, 1921. A number of times in our careers this caused confusion, as when the medics gave me his file and not mine for a physical examination. I told Sam I thought we would be the perfect bureaucratic combination, able to confuse everyone who would have to figure out whether something had been ordered by one Joe Smith or the other. Actually, since he was six feet four and I was five feet seven, we were soon easily identified as Big Joe and Little Joe.

I learned before Joe arrived that he had a man in the Bangkok station whom he would like to have as his deputy. The man was not due back until the late spring of 1958, but I decided I had better act immediately before I too found myself on the way to a training assignment or some course of study I didn't particularly want. I began at once to talk about being anxious for another field assignment in order to be one step ahead of the pack.

Meanwhile, in addition to Joe's arrival on the scene, the new situation regarding the status of the operation began to affect everything we did. Before Joe was able to settle in the branch chief's chair, the top level of CIA was talking with Ulmer about forming an Indonesian task force. This was the panacea of the Eisenhower years. Every time a situation developed into a big operation, which, with Special Group approval, ours now was, there was talk of forming a task force. This meant bringing in a high-ranking chief for the operation and specialists from all over the Agency. Joe was angry at me for not trying to block the task force and let me know this at once. I think it was then that he decided to write the fateful line in my fitness report saying I was an excellent operator but not a good administrator.

Joe was right. I much preferred working with agents, trying to

241

recruit new ones, attempting to deal successfully with people like John Galvin, and writing stories about Sukarno's wenching with Soviet spies, to administering staff personnel, adjusting leave schedules so that not too many people would be away at Christmas, and seeing that the secretaries stayed at their desks instead of running off to the ladies' room to trade gossip. I didn't seem to comprehend that you couldn't make any operational mistakes being a good administrator. I caught on years later when I found that those who were good at these administrative tasks were named to all the top jobs in the Clandestine Services. One of them explained to me that my enthusiasm for operating did me no good. "Look," he said, "the way to get ahead in this outfit is to always be opposed, or at least on record as very doubtful, about any operation that's suggested. Never be enthusiastic. Almost all operations end up failures finally. If you get known as having been opposed to the idea from the beginning, people think you are very shrewd and must be a good administrator."

I was very enthusiastic about our Indonesian operational prospects, and while I waited to hear of a good new field assignment, I buckled down to some of the work we had at hand. While Big Joe and the task force conferred with Defense officials and tried to arrange for a submarine to move arms to a point off the Sumatran coast where the colonels' men could pick them up in small boats, I was arranging to get into Padang, Sumatra, a paramilitary specialist to train the Indonesians to use the arms when we were able to arrange the shipment, as well as a communicator to assist him. Padang was going to be the rebel capital.

We located a tough, but bright and resourceful paramilitary man. I suggested the commo man who had been in Singapore with me because he was good with commo equipment and I knew he would like to get into operations. He had told me that a hundred times. Both were bachelors so there were no family problems for them in accepting these rather risky assignments. The problem was to arrange to get them into Sumatra black—that is, without any record of their entering the country and as little record as possible of their trip from the United States to Indonesia.

The first thing I discovered was that the CIA, up to that point, had never insisted on obtaining a passport under a false name and identity from the State Department for any U.S. citizen. Of course, this was an illegal action, but I couldn't imagine how we were ever going to really hide the travel of these two CIA officers if they had to travel with passports issued in their true names. We had ruled out an airdrop as too likely to be spotted. We planned to have them go separately to Malaya by different routes, join up by becoming casual acquaintances in a bar in Penang, and cross to Medan, where rebel agents would pass them along to their people in Padang. But no matter what imaginative stories we made up about their background, one curious customs or immigration officer might note their true names on their passports and track them down. Both of them had been in various Asian countries before.

I found, try as I might, I could not fight this through normal bureaucracy. Finally, this matter too had to become something for the task force to settle. We eventually got our false-identity passports—another first for our Indonesian operation.

While I was involved in this, someone tried to kill Sukarno. On the evening of November 30, 1957, as Sukarno was leaving a fund-raising bazaar at a school attended by two of his oldest children, five hand grenades were tossed at him and his party. Sukarno ducked safely behind a car, but ten people were killed and forty-eight children were injured by the blasts. We had no idea who was responsible. We had never heard the colonels talk about assassination but we couldn't be sure some fanatics in their group might not have thought this would be the quickest way to solve their quarrel with the Indonesian president. At the same time, the Darul Islam, an outlaw Moslem group also opposed to the government, had been active in killings in other parts of Java. They might have tried to pull off the assassination.

I suggested we act fast, before our friends were blamed. Whether they were innocent or guilty we could try to find out later. So we quickly put out the story that the clumsy assassination attempt had been staged by the PKI at the suggestion of their Soviet contacts in order to make it appear that Sukarno's opponents were wild and desperate men.

Sukarno had his own ideas how he wished to exploit the incident for his own propaganda purposes. He blamed the Dutch, and during the first ten days of December all Dutch citizens were ordered out of Indonesia, all Dutch commercial and banking assets were seized, and even KLM flying rights to Indonesia were cancelled. Sukarno was furious because the UN General Assembly had fallen fourteen votes shy of the necessary two-thirds required to establish a commission in which the Dutch and the Indonesians would negotiate the ceding of Western New Guinea—West Irian, Sukarno called it—to the Indonesian government. The assassination attempt gave him grounds to be more forceful than he might otherwise have been able to be in his spite. The West Irian claim dispute was also an excellent ploy he could use to take his people's minds off the troubles he was having with the dissident regimes, now going concerns for almost a year, in Sumatra, the Celebes, Borneo, Bali, Timor, and Flores.

Between Sukarno's propagandists and ours, sight of the real assassins was lost, and they were almost forgotten. We were relieved, however, when evidence surfaced that it had been a Darul Islam operation and in no way part of the colonels' plans. Holding Sukarno's feet to the fire was a figure of speech. We didn't wish him any harm. We weren't too sure that anyone else could rule Indonesia any better. We just wanted to pressure him to change course. We didn't want to sink the ship of state.

After mounting his anti-Dutch campaign to his satisfaction, Sukarno announced at the end of December that he was going to take another foreign trip for "rest and friendly consultations." The moment of truth seemed to be drawing near. Curly reported that Sumitro said the rebels were forming their political plans, and assured us that by denying the central government the revenue from the resources of Sumatra and the other outer islands, the rebels could starve Sukarno into submission. The colonels were working closely with top Masjumi leaders and preparing an ultimatum for Sukarno. If he left Indonesia as planned, the rebels would demand that the prime minister be replaced and a cabinet formed headed by Hatta and the Sultan of Djojokarta.

Sukarno seemed blissfully unaware of how serious things were and continued making plans for his trip. So did we. Sukarno announced he was planning a five-week trip, to India, across the Middle East to Egypt, then Yugoslavia, and then would retrace his steps, stopping in Syria, Pakistan, and ending up in Japan. We asked the stations in those countries to do whatever they could to follow Sukarno's every move and report as fully as possible what he did with and said to the leaders in those countries and, especially, to be on the lookout for any Soviet contacts with him en route.

He left Djakarta on January 6, after declaring that the country enjoyed complete solidarity against all troublemakers. The official

244

spokesman for the Indonesian army issued a statement pledging the complete loyalty of the army to Sukarno.

The only station that was able to bug his telephone was, of all places, Cairo. Evidently, we had some remnants of the operational capabilities there that had helped Kim Roosevelt put Nasser in power, despite the fact that the Egyptian strongman himself had apparently drifted far from our fold. We learned nothing of any operational importance from the conversations Cairo cabled us after Sukarno's arrival on January 12. We did learn, however, that Gamal Nasser was a prude by Sukarno's standards.

Almost as soon as Sukarno had settled in his hotel room, he called Nasser. He greeted his friend effusively and suggested Nasser come right over to the hotel. "I have three gorgeous Pan American stewardesses here with me and they'd like to have a party," Sukarno said. There was an awkward pause on the other end of the line. Then Nasser replied curtly that he couldn't accept the invitation and slammed down the phone.

We had given some thought to recruiting one of the PanAm girls when we learned that he was chartering a plane from the company for the trip, but finally dismissed the idea as unproductive. We already knew enough about his sex life, and unless we had been able to give the girl a lot of training we figured we wouldn't find out much of intelligence value. We were relieved to know now that we hadn't missed an orgy involving Sukarno and Nasser with all the possibilities the mere thought of such a thing brought to mind.

Receiving the report of the phone call in Cairo marked my last direct involvement in the Indonesian operation. I was called into the front office and offered the job of replacing Gabe Kaplan in the Philippines. I accepted at once. Following in the footsteps of one of the main architects of the Magsaysay triumph seemed a great opportunity to be the kind of operator I liked to be. By this time, anyway, the task force, headed by the former deputy division chief, had taken full charge of the operation in Sumatra and there was little for me to do. I asked only one thing. Jeanne hated to fly and I requested we be permitted to travel by ship. This was approved, provided we could get packed and on the *President Wilson* just after mid-February. Jeanne said she could do it.

So I was in the middle of preparations for the trip to Manila when the colonels made their move. They sent a representative to Osaka, Japan, on February 5, where Sukarno was by this time, and warned him of their intentions. He ignored them. On February 10, they issued publicly the ultimatum they had told us they would. They gave the central government five days to respond. Sukarno was still in Japan.

I was at home when I read the paper on the morning of February 15. The colonels declared themselves an independent government and announced a cabinet that contained all the familiar names of the people who had figured so largely in my working life for the past year. They had been joined by Indonesia's other capable economist—Dr. Prawiranegara Sjafruddin, who resigned as head of the national bank on January 31 and announced his support for their cause. Sjafruddin was named prime minister. Simbolon was named foreign minister. Sumitro was minister of trade and economy. Another new recruit to the cause, who would turn out to be the bravest soldier of them all, Colonel Joop Warouw, was named minister of reconstruction and industry. He defected as Indonesian military attaché in Peking to throw in his lot with the new separatist regime.

The news looked good to me, and when I checked in at the office later in the day, I found even Ned optimistic. He was particularly pleased because it looked as though our efforts to defect Colonel Alex Kawilarang, the Indonesian military attaché in Washington, were being successful. Kawilarang, Ned thought, was the man who could command the rebel troops better than any of the others. Also, Secretary Dulles had prepared a good cover statement for issue the next day. Dulles declared the development an internal Indonesian problem, but added that "apparently Sukarno's guided democracy does not satisfy large segments of the population." Another satisfying development was that Ambassador Howard Jones was about to arrive in Djakarta, replacing Allison. Jones was fully cut in on the operation and his selection pleased all our officers.

The other big front-page news story on February 15, 1958, was the announcement by Harold Stassen that he was resigning as special assistant to President Eisenhower as disarmament adviser to run in the primaries for the Republican nomination for governor of Pennsylvania. In a little more than three months, I was to reflect on the irony of this parallel timing of the announcement of two equally hopeless political causes. They both collapsed at almost the same time. On May 20, Stassen lost the Pennsylvania primary to the Republican organization's preferred candidate—overwhelmed by a two to one vote. By that time the superior organization of the Indonesian army loyal to Sukarno had effectively crushed the colonels' revolt and we had cut our losses, as Ned told me they put it in Washington, when he and I postmortemed the affair in my house in Manila. Ned had come out to supervise the winding up of our Philippine-based support, such as the Clark Field operations that had put the ill-fated rebel air force in the air.

Sukarno returned from Japan the day after the colonels' government was announced. He showed more take-charge ability than we had given him credit for. Over the course of the next two days, the Indonesian navy blockaded the rebels, the air force strafed them, and troops began to move from Java to Sumatra. In two months' time, Padang had fallen and the rebel government had retreated to Bukittingi. Bukittingi fell on May 4, and the rebel leaders fled to the Celebes.

It was in the Celebes that Kawilarang, who had taken charge as commander in chief of the rebel forces, and Colonel Warouw put up the only real fight against the loyal troops. Unfortunately, it was in the same general area of this last rebel command, the port of Ambon, that Allen Pope was shot down, on a bombing run after hitting a church on Sunday morning, May 18, by mistake, and killing most of the congregation.

Warouw held on in Menado, sending frantic messages to Washington pleading for continued help. I still remember the wording of the message that turned him down for the last time. It was signed by Allen Dulles himself so our man in Menado would know he should not ask again. "Tell Colonel Warouw that we must disengage," the message said, and then added a lot of fine things about courage and so forth.

Government troops landed twenty miles from Menado on my birthday, June 16, 1958, and ten days later Menado, the last point of organized rebel resistance, surrendered.

At various times, the Indonesian government put out different statistics about the number killed in the rebellion. In June, 1958, they claimed the figure was more than three thousand. Later they increased this, and remnants of rebel units did fight on in different places in the outer islands for a couple of years longer. Whatever

247

had been the cost in lives and treasure, it had been too great, Ned and I concluded, as we finished a bottle of his favorite Johnny Walker Black Label.

"For one thing," Ned said, "the Sumatrans didn't have any guts. One young man told me that no one wanted a fight. One day he carefully planned a reception for one of our airdrops of supplies. The Sumatrans, as soon as they heard the sound of the plane, ran off in the jungle, our guy told me. They were afraid it was Sukarno's boys about to make a paratroop drop.

"Hell, the commanders had been told about the drop time and everything," Ned added. "Even worse, our PM guy had the whole area filled with bamboo stakes as sharp as bayonets. If any paratroopers had landed in the area, we'd have impaled more than half of them right away."

We agreed that even more fundamental had been our eagerness to support men we didn't know enough about to start with. We hoped we would learn all we needed to know about them as we went along, but we didn't find out what they were really like until they were on the battlefield. Then it had been too late.

"The whole damned thing was patch work," Ned said.

When he came to the office to say goodbye, Ned dropped a package on my desk.

"Here's the final result of our porno studio," he said. "You're supposed to be able to get anything at all printed in the Philippine press, maybe you can use these photos."

I never tried.

15
The Pieces of Mt. Pinatubo

When Nestor Mata, a reporter for the *Philippine Herald*, woke up he was lying on his back in damp jungle grass. He could see the moon shining through the trees on the hillside, but it was the smell of burning flesh that brought him fully to his senses. Pieces of fuselage and packages of personal belongings were scattered all around him. Fifteen meters away he saw the torn frame of the aircraft. He instinctively looked at his watch. It showed three o'clock. It was still running somehow because he remembered now they had taken off at one-fifteen after visiting a housing project past midnight. He crawled slowly over to the plane and saw two rows of charred bodies still strapped in their seats. He had forgotten to fasten his seatbelt and had been thrown clear of the plane as it crashed.

At one-thirty on Sunday morning, March 17, 1957, Ramón Magsaysay's presidential plane, *Mt. Pinatubo*, crashed on a mountainside just outside Cebu City. Twenty-six persons in the president's party, including the president, died—everyone except Nestor Mata.

I was busy helping with preparations for a welcome-home party we were giving a young colleague from Singapore whom I had persuaded Al Ulmer was the man to replace me as Malaya desk chief, and I didn't listen to the news that Saturday evening. Since Manila time is thirteen hours ahead of Washington, our friends had heard the news at seven o'clock and brought the sad message with them when they arrived.

The party was an office affair, so everyone was not only saddened by the human tragedy but knew that it was a great blow to our operations in the Far East. Magsaysay was the only really sure friend the United States and CIA could count on in Asia. My guests were Branch 5 people, so our reaction was to wonder whether our colleagues in the Philippines would now be faced with something like the confusion we had to deal with in Indonesia. Personally, I was too involved in thinking about the big responsibility I was going to assume on April 1, when I was to become deputy branch chief, to concern myself too much with the problems the other island branch might have to wrestle with in the wake of Magsaysay's death. We were also all glad to see our friend home, and, after a brief exchange of conversation on the subject, we let the death of the Philippine president drop.

When I got to work on Monday morning I found out just how deeply the whole division was shaken. Reports of possible sabotage were being checked out. Magsaysay had made a lightning trip to Cebu to solidify his position with the political bosses of that central Philippine island. In the fall of 1957 he would be trying to do what no other Philippine president had ever done—get reelected. His popularity with the masses was tremendous, but he had spent most of his first term fighting with the old bosses of the Nacionalista Party, Recto and Laurel, who had regretted from the moment of his inauguration that they had ever agreed to Lansdale's cleverly engineered pact that secured Magsaysay their party's nomination.

The president took off at one o'clock in the afternoon of March 16 to visit with ex-president Sergio Osmeña and Osmeña's ambitious son, Sergio Jr., the mayor of Cebu City, as well as ex-governor Manuel Cueñco, and the archbishop, Julio Rosales. What the Osmeñas didn't control of Cebu politics, Cueñco did, and the archbishop was a good man to be friends with.

Beginning at five in the afternoon, Magsaysay ran through a typically frenzied schedule—speaking at two universities, attending two dinners, dedicating a new people's recreation hall, visiting a forum of Philippine war veterans, and finally racing through a new housing project. He was more than a hour behind his scheduled flight plan when he shook hands with the last of the well-wishers at the airport and boarded his plane. Rumors that the delay had been deliberately plotted in order to sabotage the plane began to circulate at once.

The *Mt. Pinatubo* was an old C-47 that had been given to the Philippine air force. It had been refurbished for the president and named by him for the highest peak in his native province of Zambales. "Where we hid and fought during guerrilla days," Magsaysay said when he named the plane. My friends on the Philippine desk told me that, despite its age, they considered the craft thoroughly airworthy. They also said that the president's pilot had more air hours than any other Philippine flyer. They agreed with the efforts being made to check out the crash for foul play.

I lost track of the investigation because I was soon completely absorbed in our efforts to keep up with the activities of the Indonesian rebel colonels. I learned in time that the crash was said to have been caused by the failure of the plane's electrical system, which made the pilot crash blindly into the mountainside.

During my two years in the Philippines, the Osmeñas, Cueñco, Recto, and all the Magsaysay men would become contacts of mine. They, and a large number of other political figures in the Philippines, would cause me more concern and sleepless nights than the Indonesian colonels ever did. I never had to deal with the colonels directly.

When Magsaysay died, an elaborate structure of activities designed to help him turn the country into the showplace of democracy that Dulles wanted came rather quickly apart. Not only was the station in Manila engaged in these efforts to support our man, but a large number of activities were being run from Manila to try to use Filipinos as our alter egos to spread democracy throughout the SEATO security area our Secretary of State had put together in Southeast Asia. It was believed that the Filipinos would be more readily accepted by Asians than Americans in roles as political advisers and liaison officers with local intelligence services.

The most venturesome enterprise abroad was the so-called Freedom Company of the Philippines that was set up in 1954 by Ed Lansdale to help him establish the Diem regime in Vietnam. Magsaysay was the company's honorary president. The company was a mechanism to deploy Filipinos in Vietnam and possibly elsewhere, under cover of a public service organization having a contract with the host government. Freedom Company personnel helped write the constitution of Vietnam, trained the Vietnamese president's Guard Battalion, organized the Vietnamese Veterans Legion to tie in with one of Cord Meyer's schemes to use veterans groups internationally as an anti-Communist front, and ran the huge Operation Brotherhood activity.

Outside Vietnam, the Filipinos had less success, although they did get involved in Thailand and even got a toehold in Burma. Asians did not accept them as their own. They simply had been associated with Americans too long. As a Chinese told me in Singapore one time, "They have brown faces but they wear the same Hawaiian sports shirts the Americans do."

Back in Manila, the station tried to orchestrate the press of the capital and the provincial press to provide Magsaysay with a constant claque of support for his internal programs as well as his involvement in the anti-Communist crusade in Asia. They continued to supply him with the personal advice and comradely support in dealing with his problems that Ed Lansdale had established as a tradition when Magsaysay had been defense minister. They wrote his speeches too. In addition, they engineered a rural reconstruction system that was a combination of the program of providing land for the repentant Huks, which Lansdale had developed for his friend, and NAMFREL activities, which Gabe Kaplan had initiated.

The rural community development plan was Gabe's special project and he thought it would in time develop a truly democratic structure at the level of the smallest unit of Philippine society—the barrio country village. An ingenious scheme was worked out whereby the United States foreign aid agency supplied the bulk of the funds for the project while CIA paid the key officials and provided special funds for certain selective activities designed to build up future political leaders upon whom we could count. But Gabe's heart was in the grand design he had for teaching the lowly Filipino peasant how to help himself solve his urgent social and economic problems in order to be free from the control of the corrupt political bosses who tried to buy his vote but otherwise paid the peasant's plight no heed. I inherited the project involving the presidential assistant for community development (PACD), Gabe's intricate provincial press project, and a station chief who was wary of both.

George Aurell had been the cautious Far East Division chief who had presided over the election operation of 1953 in which the whole Philippine operational complex came into being, but he had done so in a sort of *ex-officio* way. Des Fitzgerald, his deputy, had run the show from Washington. Aurell was moved to Manila to make room for a bold division chief, Al Ulmer, as the situation in Asia required increasing attention in 1956. Fitzgerald had earlier gone out to Japan to head an ambitious field superstructure for Chinese operations, called the China command.

George had never been able to accept the fact that so much social engineering was involved in the activities of Lansdale and Kaplan. He had often complained about them. When he found himself after the crash in March, 1957, with no Magsaysay to support any longer, he became even more skeptical of the programs that had been designed for this purpose. He also, by nature, was a man who preferred to hedge his bets. The Magsaysay team immediately, when they recovered from their initial grief, began to plan a way in which their Camelot could spring again from the ashes, just as the Kennedy men would do in the next decade in the United States. Aurell hesitated to join in. He wanted to look over the new president, Carlos García. He also had another iron in the fire. While Gabe and most of the station were swept up in support of the Magsaysay administration and the new blood it brought into Philippine politics, a deep-cover agent had been encouraged to establish a relationship with a canny member of the opposition, Diosdado Macapagal. When the Lansdale-organized team trooped out of the Liberal Party to launch the Magsaysay for President Movement, Macapagal had stayed put. At the time of the election of Magsaysay in 1953, he had been for the past three years chairman of the house foreign affairs committee. The Liberals lost nearly everything in 1953. In 1955, when Macapagal tried for the senate, they lost even more. His home district kept him in the lower house, however. From this vantage point he was able to provide a different viewpoint on the political scene that Aurell liked. In 1957, the Liberals rewarded Macapagal with the vice-presidential nomination.

The election of 1957 turned into a four-man contest, and the station could not decide which one to support. Carlos García was sixty years old when he succeeded Magsaysay. He was a Nacionalist, a Party hack from the small southern island of Bohol. His dark skin and, many said, his darker political past earned him the nickname "Black Charlie." His selection as vice-presidential candidate had been a sop to party regulars given by our people who never expected any plane crash and who knew that the office of vice-president of the Philippines was even less important than vice-president of the United States. The Philippine vice-president did not even have the duty of presiding over the senate. Latin influence probably prevailed in providing yet another chief's position, that of president of the senate, when the constitution of the new republic was written. The vice-president of the Philippines had only whatever tasks to do that the president cared to assign him. Magsaysay made García foreign affairs secretary, which was, under the circumstances, a purely protocol post since all important decisions in the foreign affairs field were made between Magsaysay and his CIA station contacts. Consequently, no one from the station even knew García when he took office.

The Magsaysay men pointed out at once that he was a crook who would return the country to all the evil ways that President Quirino had practiced. They were, of course, right. García hadn't been in office six months before false bills of lading became standard at the Manila harbor, copra was being smuggled out of the southern islands in huge amounts, and a payoff system was put into effect for conducting any sort of transaction with the government. The story was that the president's wife, Leonila, took the payoffs so as not to burden the president with either the work or the guilt.

The Magsaysay men all resigned their government posts, and Manuel Manahan, who had proudly cleaned up Philippine Customs, which under García quickly reverted again to a major cesspool of corruption, became their candidate for president on the Progressive Party ticket. The group rallied again as it had in 1953, important leaders even coming back from Vietnam to organize the new party.

Aurell agreed that it would be the undoing of everything if García won a full term in office, but decided that the Liberal ticket of old Liberal faithful José Yulo and young Diosdado Macapagal would have a better chance than the upstart third party. Neverthe-

254

less, he could not renege on the station's long-established suit, so he also agreed that some support be given to Manahan.

The fourth man in the race was Senator Claro M. Recto. Recto had broken completely with Magsaysay before the latter's death. The aftermath of this quarrel would be another of my headaches when I got to Manila. Recto took a nationalist stance which included opposing the close relationship between the United States and the Philippines and advocated dealing openly with the new power in Asia—Communist China.

The station's election operation was, therefore, more an effort to make sure that Recto was soundly defeated, so that the reputation of our principal SEATO ally not be sullied, than the positive effort that had been made four years earlier to elect our own president.

The results were what might have been expected. García won a new full term as president. Yulo and Manahan split between them a total of more than 2,400,000 votes, enough to have elected either one or the other of them since García got only 2,079,000 votes. Recto was ignominiously defeated. The "father of the Philippine constitution," as he liked to be known, gathered barely 400,000 ballots. Our friend Macapagal was elected vice-president, receiving over 100,000 more votes than García.

The strange situation was not simply that the country had a president of one party and a vice-president of another, but that no one was pleased with the result. We had now no power base around which to center our operations. The new administration, which we had opposed, was not very likely to offer much support for what we had been doing either inside the country or elsewhere in Southeast Asia. The Freedom Company was renamed the Eastern Construction Company, which both made it seem less political and was an accommodation to the fact that its former honorary president was dead. Our other operations targeted abroad through the Philippine intelligence service also became more delicate. This, in particular, bothered Aurell, for whom these international operations meant that while he was no longer division chief he was more than the ordinary station chief. Thus, by the time I was assigned to the Philippines, we were "taking a new look at the situation" as the jargon of the Clandestine Services put it.

When I asked Al Ulmer what his instructions were for me, he said, "Find another Magsaysay."

The first thing I had to do in getting ready for my new job was to go over to the Pentagon—not for a briefing, but to arrange my cover. Cover backstopping had progressed considerably since I had been told simply to make up any plausible story about where I worked, but it still left a lot to be desired. I had been forced to surrender the USIS cover I had in Singapore shortly after I returned to Washington in the summer of 1956. I did manage to get approval to use it in making my contacts with the Malayan Students Association on a special dispensation basis. Actually, this was an arrangement with the USIS Far Eastern Division chief's office so that if any of my Malayan friends called or otherwise tried to check on my bona fides, USIS would backstop my claim by saying that I was indeed an employee. My credentials were taken away from me, however, because USIS did not want to carry a surplus CIA body on its rolls since this blocked a position for a legitimate employee, and, of course, they didn't much like anything else about the matter either.

The State Department felt the same way and officers who had Foreign Service Reserve status were constantly battling to keep it while they served tours of duty in Washington. A few Clandestine Services operators were able to do this for years, and they were greatly benefited by having a government position they could talk to strangers about. One disadvantage was that State would never give our officers a grade equivalent to their CIA rank, but usually insisted that it be several grades lower. This made things like obtaining mortgage money difficult, because when the standard formula of four times annual income was applied to an officer's lower State Department rank, it frequently didn't qualify him for the loan he wanted. My friend Ned, in disgust, actually demanded he be released from his State cover and given one of the so-called loose cover backstops with some Defense Department component. We both ended up, in fact, with one of the most widely used of these—we were documented as belonging to a service unit at Patrick Air Force Base in southeast Washington. A person under this cover backstopping was given a proper Patrick Air Force badge, and the name of a commanding officer and an administrative officer which could be used for credit references. No more Viola Pitts. When mortgage companies, banks, stores, etc., called to check with these fictitious Air Force officers, the phone rang in CIA Cover Staff offices and someone posing as the Air Force official provided the reference.

256

Cover Staff even had a system for handling any personal calls made by anyone to whom the story had been given that the CIA officer worked at Patrick. They would take the call, say they were checking whether or not you were in, and then they would call you on another line and patch you through to the caller.

There was nothing wrong with this, except that by 1958 Patrick Air Force Base had been abandoned by all units except a small housekeeping outfit. Another thing was that neither I nor Ned nor anyone else I ever knew who had this cover lived anywhere near Patrick Air Force Base. No one was supposed to wonder what so many people were doing working for a minute detachment at an abandoned Air Force base miles from where they lived.

My cover in Manila was to be that of a civilian Air Force employee of an organization known as the 13th Air Force Southeast Asia Regional Survey Unit. Therefore, I had to go over to the Pentagon to get 13th Air Force credentials. Jeanne and our daughters had to go along too in order to get dependents' documentation. After that, however, we all had to go back across the Potomac to have our physical exams and get our shots at the CIA medical unit in "K" Building beside the Reflecting Pool. Ruthven was very bright, but fortunately at twelve she wasn't curious about the stories her father told concerning where he worked. Julie was only five so she wasn't aware of anything except the fact that the shots hurt. Episodes like these, however, made me glad that I had told Jeanne all about my job after my first few months on duty in 1951. I wasn't interested in invoking national security in order to cheat on her, as so many colleagues did to their wives, and I didn't want to insult her intelligence by keeping silent about the kind of antics working for the Clandestine Services entailed.

The 13th Air Force Southeast Asia Regional Survey Unit was a large umbrella under which were sheltered the station administrative staff, various support units at Clark Field, and the covert action section of the station. The unit that was engaged in liaison with the Philippine Intelligence Service trying to position Philippine agents all over Southeast Asia was so large that another cover group of civilian Air Force employees had to be invented for them. Fortunately, the 13th Air Force was the major U.S. Air Force component outside Japan and could take the addition of this large number of civilian employees. There was only one problem with the arrangement.

It was strange that so many of these civilians were located in Manila instead of at Clark Field, where the commanding general and all the rest of his personnel were found.

There would be another problem for me, since I was supposed to work on the high-level political contacts among whom Gabe moved. In the U.S. armed forces in World War II and in the 1950s, an enlisted man was considered about the lowest form of human life. There was only one lower species—a civilian employee. Their social life was expected to be limited to service clubs and the high point of their lives was supposed to be Friday-afternoon happy hour when they could get two drinks for the price of one. They certainly weren't considered eligible for cocktails and dinner with people like Philippine congressmen and senators.

Gabe Kaplan's cover was an enviable concoction. Unfortunately it was something not likely to be put together twice so I never had a chance at replacing him in his cover capacity. He first came out to the Philippines under Asia Foundation cover. It was the Committee for Free Asia in 1952, and its president was Gabe's classmate at Swarthmore, Dr. Alan Vallentine. Alan Vallentine had enjoyed a distinguished academic career, as dean of Swarthmore, master of Pearson College at Yale, and president of the University of Rochester before entering government service in 1950. He was one of Paul Hoffman's key administrators of the Marshall Plan, chief of the program in the Netherlands, before taking the presidency of the Committee for Free Asia. Vallentine was the first of the heads of that organization who caused the coordination nightmare I had with British liaison on Asia Foundation affairs when I got to Singapore. It wasn't possible for Gabe to function well under this set-up despite his old friendship with Vallentine, so after consultations in the States, Gabe returned to Manila in April, 1952, with his new cover.

The core of this cover was the Catherwood Foundation of Bryn Mawr, Pennsylvania. Catherwood continued to be a CIA funding mechanism down to the *Ramparts* exposé of this kind of cover arrangement in 1967. Thanks to the fact that Gabe had been associated with Judge Samuel Seabury and Mayor Fiorello LaGuardia in reforming New York City's legislative program and legal assistant to the New York City Council, it wasn't difficult to add a number of distinguished names to the new cover organization established

258

especially to enable Gabe to engage in the wide-ranging political action he accomplished in 1953 and afterward. Ostensibly, former ambassador to the Philippines Myron Cowen joined Cummins Catherwood in persuading a few staunch friends of the Philippines, such as General Leland S. Hobbs, ex-Joint Military Advisory Group chief; Charles V. Griffiths, the publisher; and General Hugh Casey of the board of Schenley Distillers, to set up the Committee for Philippine Action in Development, Reconstruction and Education. Somehow this just happened to form the acronym COMPADRE—the one word that held more meaning than any other for a Filipino. Gabe was resident director of COMPADRE, on the spot to carry out all sorts of good works, backed by a bankroll the size of which Filipinos could only guess.

As if this were not enough blessing for one man, the arrangement had a personal bonus of considerable importance in living well on the restricted Philippine postwar economy. Since Gabe and his family had no official status, they were granted only a six-month visa. Every six months Gabe, his wife, and daughter had to make an all-expenses-paid trip to Hong Kong in order to renew their visas from outside the country as the law required. In those days, if there was a heaven on earth where everything could be purchased at a price so low as to encourage the most parsimonious person to spend his last cent, it was Hong Kong. The Kaplans missed no amenities.

The cover was just too slick and it wore thin as the years went by. After the change of administration had been sealed by the election of García as president in his own right, it was decided Gabe should leave and his replacement come out in a less conspicuous position.

My civilian Air Force employee status was certainly inconspicuous. I learned to live with it mostly by ignoring its limitations. I'm afraid, however, that long before my tour was up my cover was as thin as Gabe's had ever been when the decision was made to abandon the fiction of COMPADRE.

On the voyage out to Manila, however, I found at least one person who not only bought my cover but congratulated me on my status with the U.S. government. General Robert E. Wood, chairman of Sears, Roebuck, and his wife were among our fellow passengers. One morning at bouillon time, he and I had a brief chat. He asked me, almost in so many words, what I was doing on the ship, strongly implying that he thought I was too young to be whiling away my time on a Pacific cruise. I told him I was with the U.S. government and being assigned to Manila. This was not the right thing to say to General Wood, who thought that the U.S. government was a socialist conspiracy against private enterprise. He asked if I were a State Department officer. I said no, I was a civilian employee of the Air Force.

"Well, that's good," said General Wood, "the Air Force and the whole Defense Department are the decent parts of the government. The only ones that are doing anything worthwhile. You didn't look like one of those damned pinkos in the State Department, but there are so damned many of those useless bastards around, you can't ever be sure when you'll meet another one."

General Wood was one of the principal financial supporters of the extreme right in American politics, I realized. He was rumored to have been a contributor to Senator McCarthy's campaign to rid the government of Reds. I was strongly tempted to tell him what part of the government I really worked for, but I resisted the impulse and was content to bask a bit in the glow of the general's approval of me as a member of the military establishment.

We arrived in Manila on Monday, March 10, 1958, with the tugs easing us into a dock at South Harbor at two in the afternoon. We were met by a station officer and taken quickly around the Luneta and down Dewey Boulevard to the Hotel Filipinas. The hotel was far from luxurious but it did have a swimming pool, and the afternoon was as humid and hot as it could be expected to get in the worst of tropical weather. The Filipinas was also just across the street from the American Embassy, and right next door to the U.S. foreign aid mission building where the 13th Air Force Southeast Asia Regional Survey Unit had its offices.

Manila is said to have among the most beautiful sunsets in the world. This is possibly the only thing of beauty about the city. I have not been there in fifteen years, but people I have talked to who have been more recent visitors have told me nothing to change the opinion I formed almost immediately in the first days in March, 1958. We arrived in Manila in the dry season, which meant that, in addition to the heavy tropical heat, the town was covered with dust. The streets were crowded with cars, buses, and garish jeepneys— old World War II jeeps converted into a kind of low-cost fixed-route taxi fleet, each one decorated to the driver's taste and usually featuring a number of shiny stolen hubcaps festooned around the chassis to catch the gleam of the brutal sunlight. There were also a large number of horse-drawn Spanish *calesas* plodding along. When the on-shore breeze in the afternoon moved the air but failed to relieve the heat, a by-product of this ancient mode of transportation made its contribution to the swirling dust the breezes stirred. Shreds of dried horse droppings blew about abundantly. I tried to tell myself that this was not symbolic of the atmosphere in which I was going to work.

Housing in Manila was rebuilt very slowly after the destruction of the final days of World War II. The first Americans who had come out to Manila in the late 1940s lived in Quonset huts set up on U.S. government property. By the time we arrived, housing starts had been made in the Manila suburbs but at enormously inflated prices. Homes for the country's elite were naturally built first, and although they were the only kinds of shelter that resembled U.S.-style living, they were too expensive and ostentatious for U.S. employees. To satisfy the desires of the large number of U.S. aid mission personnel, embassy personnel, veterans administration employees, and others, as well as the growing number of representatives of American business that came into the crowded city in the 1950's, some enterprising Filipinos got the idea of duplicating Southern California ranch-style homes just for Americans. They built a development that looked as if it had been copied from an aerial photograph of the most densely and unimaginatively constructed suburban nightmare in Los Angeles County.

San Lorenzo Village was the only place to go house hunting, however. Hence, before the first week was over, we found a place to live. Thanks to the station's generosity we had air-conditioned bedrooms and I was permitted to exceed my housing allowance on the grounds that I would use my home as a meeting place for contacts. Thus we were able to settle into a house that was comfortable. We missed the spacious grounds of our previous home. We couldn't play badminton on the minute lawn, but we grew to like the high walls which surrounded the small property—a Spanish whim that provided privacy which we enjoyed and which was also important in my profession.

The most rewarding thing about the house, I have already mentioned. Our landlady was the mistress of former senate president Fernando Lopez, a steadfast Recto follower and, together with his brother, Eugenio, publisher of the Manila *Chronicle,* among the most vigorous anti-U.S. voices in the Philippines. Thanks to their custom of visiting her various properties together, I met Senator Lopez on the first day we moved in. He seemed to me to be a pleasant person, and I was glad to meet right away one of the targets that our station's Magsaysay propaganda support apparatus had spent many hours and many dollars trying to denigrate. No one had ever dared to talk directly to the villain. I thought that I just might have a chance to develop contacts with the Recto group thanks to this naturally friendly relationship I found myself involved in with Senator Lopez. A first-hand knowledge of what they thought could only help to clarify the picture of Philippine politics I had been hastily briefed on.

George Aurell was pleased when I told him I had met Lopez and what I thought I should do about it. Aurell had known me when I worked for Kay and we had always gotten along very well. I think he thought of me as somewhat academic at times and of himself as a model of shrewd common sense. He seemed glad that now I seemed to him to be showing a shrewd streak.

"You know," he said, "the old Lansdale crowd had a tendency to indulge themselves in the good old American fantasy that the world is divided into the white hats and the black hats. You know that's just not true. Most of the world is really pretty gray, and for an intelligence officer not to recognize this means he's not going to be able to do a very good job.

"I want you to follow up on what you've told me," he continued, "and I want you to take a very hard look at Gabe's operations. Hell, they're costing us almost a quarter of a million dollars a year, and frankly I'm not sure we ought even to be involved in some of them. Gabe is a great operator but he's also a great crusader. I'm not sure CIA ought to be involved in any crusades. Of course, he got that from Lansdale, who's a crusader too."

He thought a moment and then he added rather vehemently, "At least Gabe's not smartassed, and that was a characteristic of most of the Lansdale bunch. Do you know what I found out they were doing to me when I was division chief? They were sending in cables in their own secret code and getting approval for things and

262

for spending money that I would never have approved of, if I had known.

"They used to send in admin cables instead of operational cables when they wanted approval of new operational expenses. They'd call money for political funding, propaganda schemes, and so forth, requests for new filing equipment or air-conditioning repairs. Of course, they got these approved without any staff review or my review. Hell, naturally I wouldn't oppose new files and air-conditioners. I didn't learn about this damned trick until I got out here and looked at some things in the records.

"So, Joe, go to work. Try to find us some new approaches, honest ones."

16

Democracy Begins in the Barrio

No one introduced me to Gabe Kaplan. He introduced himself. On the third day I was at the office in Manila, busy with my travel accounting and dozens of similar administrative details that must be taken care of on arrival at a new post, a short, stocky figure appeared suddenly in front of my desk. He was dressed in gray slacks and a white Filipino *Barong Tagalog*—the informal sheer embroidered shirt Magsaysay had made the uniform of his administration. At first glance, the most distinguishing feature of his face was an enormous cigar clenched in his teeth.

"I'm Gabe Kaplan," he said, extending his hand and smiling.

I soon learned that the cigar was Gabe's trademark. He loved to smoke the special product of the Tabacalera company—an eight-inch, dark-leaf, richly aromatic number that was called "The Churchill." I quickly developed a taste for them myself, and I remembered my father had always said Manila cigars were much better than Havanas.

"Since community development is the business of the U.S. aid

265

program, I figured I could walk into their building. I'm kind of well identified with community development activities around here," Gabe said, adding, "I'm a short-timer so I don't think it matters too much about my cover, and I thought we should get together right away so you can meet my boys and get to work."

I agreed with him, except I was hoping to have a little more time to read into project files before meeting the key figures involved. We set up a meeting for the following morning at his house.

"I know you'll have to change the meeting pattern to something more covert, but the boys are accustomed to meeting me at my house, where I also run the COMPADRE office. I think it makes sense for you to meet there the first time."

At ten o'clock the next morning Gabe met me at the front door of his house and escorted me to a secluded screened porch at the rear which looked out on a large garden. The high garden walls shut out the neighbors completely. There were three men on the porch, all either glancing at magazines or reading newspapers. They seemed to be trying to ignore each other's presence. Two were skinny youths, one tall and sporting a narrow moustache that modified a bit his somewhat simian features, the other was shorter with a slightly Chinese look. The third man was a good ten years their senior, with a rounded figure and features that were an almost perfect blend of Malay and Chinese. Gabe made the introductions.

"Ramón Binamira, presidential assistant for community development," said Gabe, indicating the tall young man, "and this is Teddy de los Santos, his right-hand man," indicating the shorter of the young men.

"And this," Gabe said slowly, "is Colonel Ferrer."

Gabe explained to the group who I was and then went on to say that he realized this was rather unusual procedure, bringing together three people who worked on different types of programs, but saying that there were sound historical reasons for a meeting of this kind.

"Jimmy Ferrer, as you undoubtedly know, Joe, was the chief organizer of NAMFREL. These two bright young guys are a testimony to his talent. They already know I think they're the brightest and best young men in the country, so I can't swell their heads any more by what I say now. Jimmy found them and they ran the best NAMFREL chapter in the country in Cebu. Ramón is, I'm sure, the

266

youngest man with as high responsibilities as he has in any government in the world. He was only twenty-nine when Magsaysay named him to his present job two years ago.

"As for Teddy, he almost got elected to congress last year, but it's pretty hard to buck both the Osmeñas and the Cueñcos in Cebu and 1957 was a tough election.

"Jimmy has a world reputation as a veterans leader and, of course, he was Magsaysay's undersecretary of agriculture and helped organize the Community Development Planning Committee out of which Ramón's office, PACD, developed.

"They're all going different directions now, but you might say they grew up together. Most important of all, these men are not agents. They're loyal Filipinos who find us a source of help financially and morally in their efforts to make this country work and free it from corruption. Remember that."

I always did. The situation did not fit the CIA tradecraft manual. Stan Archer would never have made any sense out of it. I saw at once that I must try. I sensed immediately from the reaction of all three to Gabe's words that the key to any success we had ever had in the Philippines lay in the mutual trust and respect that had existed between them and Gabe. I decided then and there that I would have to try to establish the same kind of relationship with them. And I thought that it would make sense if I tried to do the same with all the Filipino contacts I hoped to make. It would be difficult to explain this to George Aurell, although I thought he probably would understand. It would be impossible to explain to headquarters, especially if someone from Jimmy Angleton's Counter Intelligence Staff heard about it. They believed the only sensible way to get along with anybody was to read his mail, tap his telephone, bug his bedroom, and to distrust him even more when you knew all the intimate details of his life.

Our conversation that morning was strictly get-acquainted chitchat, and rather stiff at that. I made proper tradecraft arrangements to meet them all separately in a station safehouse and set dates for these individual first meetings. We talked for about an hour. I think I was the one who got the most out of the meeting. In addition to appreciating the basis on which Gabe had worked so well, I caught a glimpse of the dream they all had for the future of the Philippines—a country free from the political and economic bondage that ageless poverty brings.

I did not see Gabe Kaplan, who left the Philippines just two weeks after I arrived, for many years. In 1967, after the *Ramparts* flap I got the job of reorganizing CIA's training in covert action to try to teach how propaganda and political operations might be conducted successfully and securely. I asked Gabe to be one of my guest seminar leaders. He had retired but was still a consultant to the Far East Division on ways to "de-fuse insurgency," as he called it. By this he meant building peasant communities that would want to resist Communist insurgents' blandishments because they had already made a better life for themselves than any utopia the Communists might offer. He was still at his trade, in other words. Unfortunately, he was also dying of lung cancer. I don't know whether or not too many Churchills had brought him low. We never discussed this. Ill as he was, he bravely worked the covert action seminar with me until he died in 1968.

As I have already pointed out, Gabe's dream did not impress George Aurell, and my instructions were clear. I was to examine the operation with the office of the presidential assistant for community development (PACD) with the idea of seeing how we could reduce our expenditures and decide whether there was anything about the operation that we wanted to keep. I was to do the same thing with Teddy de los Santos's provincial press mechanism, which had promoted PACD and other parts of the Magsaysay program throughout the country. Jimmy Ferrer was, at the moment, considered to be an asset on ice. His great organizing talents had helped create the Progressive Party of the Philippines out of nothing. Manuel Manahan, its candidate, had gotten over a million votes, just 250,000 less than Yulo, the candidate of the established Liberal Party, the official opposition, thanks largely to Jimmy's great work. Aurell didn't want to do anything about the Progressives, however, except watch them. This made my relationship with Jimmy initially rather artificial. And the directives I had for dealing with Binamira and de los Santos didn't make working with them a picnic either. It certainly made it difficult for me to put into practice my resolve to imitate Gabe's method of dealing with Filipinos.

De los Santos's project was my most immediate concern, because it demanded so much attention due to its size, cost, and the way it worked. The project involved a couple dozen writers, like Teddy himself and Binamira, mostly old cronies from NAMFREL days and fellow Cebuanos. They were a self-styled "propaganda workshop" and produced a large number of articles each week for small local newspapers scattered from northern Luzon to Mindanao. At the same time, they produced a "Digest of the Provincial Press" monthly. This was sent to all congressmen and to other opinion leaders in Manila. It was supposed to be sold by subscription, which it was in a number of cases due to the generous slush funds the congressmen voted themselves for expenses, but a lot of copies were simply given away. The "Digest" reprinted the articles which the station wanted in particular to emphasize (and which had, of course, been written by the workshop in the first place) and to represent to the Manila opinion leaders as the opinion of the people in the provinces.

The operation had been considered a very important and very useful mechanism for helping Magsaysay's administration put its program through congress. It had also, along with the rest of the Magsaysay operations, been well publicized in Washington. Stations everywhere began to develop their own copies of this outstanding provincial press operation. When I got into the Western Hemisphere in later years, I found them all over the place, and had to live with another one of them in Argentina. As good as they looked in Washington, they all had several significant flaws, as did this original model in the Philippines.

First, it was almost impossible to cover them. The figleaf of the Philippine operation was that the activity was a spinoff of the good-government crusading spirit left over from NAMFREL days. In Latin America cover was frequently a phony and insolvent local press service. The provincial press in the Philippines and most Latin American countries, in the second place, is hardly an impressive medium. Almost all the papers resemble more a U.S. fraternal organization's handout to members, or, at best, some high-class high school paper than they do the Cleveland *Plain Dealer* or the Denver *Post*. Like the school paper, they are mostly read for their local gossip and important announcements of local events. They certainly cannot afford to pay for services such as CIA provided them in operations such as the one I inherited in the Philippines. This is the third big flaw—no legitimate news-peddling outfit could afford to stay in business based on the income derived from such an operation.

On the other hand, these same flaws made the operations tempting. The poor local press gladly printed what we sent them each week to fill up the space between the births and deaths and marriage announcements. Thus these projects showed a healthy amount of production. That is, it was possible to bundle together each month an impressive number of clippings and send them off to Washington as proof that something was being accomplished. This was very important, because these projects were expensive and their costs had to be justified. Our Philippine project was running around $100,000 a year when I arrived in Manila. The writers, the workshop, the "Digest," and the air freight costs of distributing the articles all over the country were sizable items. Some cynics at home were beginning to ask what the large bundle of clippings proved. They wanted to know what impact the stories had on their readers.

Throughout my entire career in the Clandestine Services I remember someone was always asking these kinds of questions, and no one ever answered them clearly. For one thing, in regard to propaganda operations, the obvious way to answer these questions with some reasonable accuracy was to run an opinion survey. Such surveys were themselves so expensive that the cost-conscious administrators didn't want to spend this additional amount to get the answers.

In regard to intelligence report collection, the claim was always made that "we are not in the numbers game." This expression meant that it was the intention of the management to measure the value of intelligence reporting not by the volume of reports sent to Washington but by their quality, that is, accuracy, timeliness, and importance. However, let the number of reports sent in drop by any significant amount and headquarters would scream that the station was falling down on the job.

I realized that I was going to have to find something about the project to cut that wouldn't impair its existence and jazz up the reporting of accomplishments with some new gimmicks until the critics lost interest in complaining. I would suggest an opinion survey too, so they could react in horror to the prospect of this expense, and thus find the cost cuts I would recommend entirely acceptable, modest though they might be. The only alternative would be to suggest that the entire project be terminated. However, the same wise officer who advised me never to be enthusiastic about an operation also counseled never to terminate a project. This, he said, was considered a negative attitude. The longer I looked at this operation, however, the less I cared about whether I would be considered negative as long as I could look myself in the mirror and know I was honest.

The original purpose for the project—generating support for Magsaysay's programs—no longer existed. The writers were reduced to inventing subjects to talk about that were not themes we had ordered them to take up or were even interested in their discussing. Although it was a poor way for me to start trying to build up the same kind of human relationship that Gabe had with Teddy de los Santos, I decided to terminate the old project and to try to save Teddy and the best of the writers to use in the metropolitan press. We had other press assets for planting news items in the Manila papers, but what I thought Teddy and his writers could contribute were columns and longer articles on major topics. The fiction that the old project had impact because it represented provincial opinion, I didn't think worth even considering. I soon discovered that the opinion leaders in the provinces ignored the local gossip sheets and waited for Philippines Airlines to bring them the morning papers from Manila. So painful as it was, Teddy and I were soon busy taking apart his old project.

Ramón Binamira and the PACD were something else. Ramón was a very bright man and Gabe had him spotted for a great future. When Gabe had steered NAMFREL into the community development business and Ferrer had begun organizing community centers in 1953 and 1954, Binamira had been moved to Manila as executive secretary of the centers' project. After Ferrer went into his subcabinet post and pushed through the creation of the Community Development Planning Council, an interdepartmental government agency, Binamira became its executive director. After continued tinkering to find the most effective mechanism, the proposal was made that Magsaysay have on his personal staff a presidential assistant for community development who in turn would have a staff to carry out an effective program and cut bureaucratic red tape. Binamira was named to this PACD post in January, 1956.

Meanwhile the U.S. aid mission was involved in the project. In December, 1955, at about the same time the executive order creating the PACD was signed by the Philippine president, smooth coordination got an aid mission project proposal approved for $4.2 million for Philippine Community Development and tentative approval was given for support for community development activities in

271

the Philippines for the next five years in a total amount of $42.5 million.

Although everything had been predicated on the continuation of the Magsaysay administration, President García was not about to turn aside such generous aid, and the station got the aid mission director to insist that Binamira stay in his job, because Gabe had great plans both for his protégé and for the project.

Gabe sold it to CIA as a long-range investment in Philippine democratic institution building and as a mechanism for developing future leaders with whom future stations could collaborate. He even got in the idea that pleased George Aurell so well—he suggested that Philippine-trained Community Development Workers could assist in other Southeast Asian countries. The training program was the core of the CIA part of the project.

Binamira had been in the PACD job only two months before he was able to get this program off the ground. In March, 1956, an agreement was made to train PACD workers at the University of the Philippines Agricultural College at Los Baños, in Laguna province. The ambitious goal was to train a total of more than 7,000 PACD workers with 2,700 of them located in rural barrios, the rest filling municipal and provincial coordinating posts. It was fascinating to listen to Binamira explain the training program and the concepts of group dynamics the barrio-level workers were taught to use in order to take complete control of these basic units of Filipino society without the peasants or the old-style political bosses realizing what was happening. Also, students were chosen by competitive examination and thus hundreds of application forms were filled in by young Filipinos providing the delight of an intelligence officer's life—hundreds of dossiers to pore over looking for potential agents.

Unlike the case of the provincial press operation, the cost-consciousness advocates were pleased with the PACD project. After all, the aid mission had been maneuvered into paying the bulk of the expenses and picking up all the big-ticket items. We provided Binamira with flexible funds for manipulating the training program. Obviously, Gabe had in mind building Binamira up through this job for an even higher one someday. I quickly gathered he was convinced we had another future Philippine president in our grasp.

Ramón could and did handle himself well with both Philippine officials much older than he and American aid mission personnel.

272

He knew the jargon of modern sociology and when to use it to his advantage and when not to. He tried his best to initiate me into the mystique of his profession.

He had a number of goals he could enumerate to impress upon his various listeners the key role his department was playing in the evolution of a new and better Philippines. These included assisting in the development of self-government in the barrios, increasing rural productivity, constructing feeder roads so that peasant products could enter the money economy, improving government services and coordinating existing government services in the rural areas, improving the morale of the barrio residents, as well as improving education, health standards, and similar basic matters related to moving the peasant population beyond their nearly stone-age cultural level. To me he emphasized that PACD was involved in strengthening community organizations, that is, barrio councils and the next higher level of governmental organization, municipal and provincial councils, and the significance of the Barrio Community Development Worker. He liked to say, "These workers are multipurpose catalysts in inducing the barrio people to undertake self-help projects." When I asked him what this was supposed to mean to me and the CIA, he got down to brass tacks.

He explained that his barrio workers would in time change the power base in the Philippines. "Philippine society," Binamira told me, "is based on what sociologists call dyadic alliances, that is, mutual aid arrangements between pairs of individuals under which each partner helps the other pursue his own personal goals. We don't function well as groups. Everyone seeks a *compadre* with whom to form one of these helpful alliances. As a result, we have no labor movement to speak of, and the peasants in the barrio don't cooperate for the common good. That's what we want to teach them how to do."

He went on to tell me that the barrio lieutenant, although formally an elected official, was merely someone whose *compadre* was a local political boss at the next higher level. "He buys the votes he needs to get elected," Ramón said, "and then the barrio is his to exploit as his *compadre* wishes him to. I want to change all that."

This is what he was training the Barrio Community Development Workers to do. They were taught how to use group dynamics to this end. They would first study a barrio, decide what its needs were, and select a man they thought should be barrio lieutenant.

273

Then they'd suggest a meeting of the villagers. At the meeting they would carefully steer the conversation around to the needs of the barrio they thought should be attended, and they would get the barrio folk to discuss the characteristics of their ideal leader. It turned out the man they had in mind for the job fit these characteristics perfectly. The villagers would "discover" that their ideal leader was in fact already in their midst. After that, they could not be swayed even by the money that the political boss's candidate for lieutenant offered them. Binamira explained they had already held several barrio elections and the barrio worker's choice had won every time.

"In time," he said, "the people in the barrio will be politically alive and we will have a force that will mean there will be solid reform undertaken in this country. Once they know how to vote for what they want and need, and elect the capable people we hope to provide as their candidates, the Philippine peasants will be the key to all future elections. They'll vote for results and we'll make sure they get results. A handful of sugar barons, copra kings, and Chinese merchants won't run this country ever again."

All this was pretty heady fare. I enjoyed listening to it, but I hesitated to report it to Aurell or Washington. I was rather thrilled to think we were supporting a social revolution, but what would Angleton think of this? I couldn't readily decide how I was going to handle the matter. So I continued to listen and be noncommittal. Meanwhile I turned my attention to my plan to do something different about the Recto crowd.

I boldly had my driver take me to Senator Lopez's house one morning to see if I could invite the senator to lunch as a first move in exploiting this interesting contact in the Recto camp that had fallen into my lap. I saw the Philippine political system at work firsthand.

The front yard of the Lopez home was swarming with all sorts of people even though it was only eight-thirty in the morning when we drove up. Not only the yard was full, but as I made my way up the path and entered the large center hall of the house, I saw that it was just as full. The people inside, however, and the people outside were different. Outside the house were gathered peasant men and women, children, and even their family pets—a parrot, dogs, and even pigs. One family had brought its Mongolian idiot and the

274

poor creature's enormous head was sheltered by his mother's apron. Inside were a number of men in *barong tagalogs,* some with briefcases and all with sunglasses and large wristwatches—the two symbols of success for striving lower-middle-class bureaucrats, clientless lawyers, and aspiring technicians all over Asia. I gave my card to an attendant and was told to wait. The senator would see me soon.

In about twenty minutes, Lopez appeared. He had a word for everyone in the room and then he went outside and spoke briefly with everyone there. He patted the Mongoloid child on the head.

Lopez was cordial to me and said he was honored by my invitation, but he was going on a two-week trip to his home state of Iloilo and asked that I contact him again when he returned. A polite brushoff. But I considered I had enjoyed a lesson in Philippine politics, I had seen the *compadre,* the *patrón* at work.

As for my plan to use Lopez, I temporarily abandoned that for another approach. In looking over the files we had on the Recto group, I discovered that the son of Senator Lopez's brother, Eugenio, who published the Manila *Chronicle,* had attended a semester at the Harvard Business School and listed himself as a member of the Harvard Club of Manila. I found the Harvard Club's number in the phone book and let them know they had a new member candidate.

The Harvard Club of Manila was the main interest in life of a semi-retired real estate broker who, I learned, had served as club secretary for twenty-one years. This was fortunate, for he not only welcomed new members warmly, he ran an excellent series of luncheon and some evening meetings featuring the country's important media leaders and politicians as speakers. Nothing could have been more helpful for me.

It wasn't long before I met young Hennie Lopez. He was a pleasant, open young man who talked freely about himself and his work. It seemed from what he said that his father had given him responsibility for the day-to-day operation of the *Chronicle.* This perked my interest considerably. I told him I had been a reporter in my youth and we joked about the old saying that once you've got a whiff of printer's ink in your nostrils you're hooked. He invited me to visit him at the paper to see his operation whenever I wished. We exchanged cards and telephone numbers.

As quickly as I thought enough time had passed so that I wouldn't appear too eager, I called him at his office and asked if I might come over.

On his home ground he was completely self-confident and he showed more curiosity about what my real interest might be. I had to invent an explanation of what the 13th Air Force Southeast Asian Regional Survey Unit did and what its responsibilities could possibly have to do with the Manila *Chronicle,* because he wanted to be satisfied who I was before he'd go any further in our conversation once we had finished the usual pleasantries. I told him that my office concentrated on compiling complete data on all the countries in Southeast Asia—geographic, political, social, and economic—so that Air Force personnel of U.S. missions in these countries would be fully briefed before they were stationed in any of them. "The Defense Department wants to make certain that Americans know how they should conduct themselves abroad," I assured him.

"You mean, you're trying to do something about the wild conduct of your airmen when they're off base from Clark Field?" he asked. He had taken the bait.

"Precisely," I replied. "We hope to alleviate the problems in the Philippines and make sure we don't have similar ones in the other countries."

"You realize you couldn't come to a better place than the *Chronicle* to get the true picture of how the Filipinos feel about Clark Field and all its annoyances?"

"I certainly do. And I hope you will be brutally frank with me."

"Well, that's refreshing. You know, most American officials here call us 'Communists' for what we write," Lopez commented with an ironic smile, "but they'd never even set foot in here."

"All I can say," I answered, "is that I can't help it if there are so many bureaucrats who were brainwashed by Senator McCarthy. As you get to know me better, you'll find out I'm not one of them. Hell, this is a free country, the *Chronicle* certainly has a right to say whatever it pleases whether Americans like it or not."

A basis for continuing the interview had been established. Lopez proceeded to tell me how the paper functioned. He then took me to the editorial room to meet I. P. Soliongco and Ernesto Grenada, the paper's bitterest anti-U.S. columnists. "I want these guys to see you and to listen to the way you talk," he said. Unfortunately, neither of these top targets of station propaganda assets' attack were

276

in the office that morning. But I said goodbye to Hennie well satisfied with the start I had made.

Just a week later, he called.

"Would you be free to go deep-sea fishing with me and some friends this weekend?" he asked.

I said I thought so but asked him to let me check with my wife to make certain she had not accepted any social obligations for us. I promised to call him back promptly.

Actually, of course, it was George Aurell I wanted to check with to see if he wanted me literally to jump into Lopez's boat so fast. One of my colleagues was convinced it was a trap. He was certain Lopez planned either a sex orgy with which to blackmail me, or more direct action to neutralize me, such as throwing me off the boat with a lead weight around my neck one night. Neither George nor I could accept such fanciful flights of imagination, and it was agreed that I would accept the invitation.

When I called back, I did try, however, to ascertain that this was to be a serious fishing trip. Hennie said that while he wasn't a great fisherman, one of his other guests was probably the sport's most avid devotee in the Philippines. He said the intention was to fish quite seriously.

The Lopez yacht was an old World War II PT boat, and I hadn't been on board an hour the Friday night we chugged out of Manila harbor before I was glad my myopia had disqualified me for the Navy V-12 program which had rounded up so many of my college friends for PT boat service during the war. We were in a storm by the time we were passing Corregidor, and we tossed about like an empty bottle floating in the water. Hennie was right about the fishing interests of one of his guests, Joaquin Roces, publisher of the rival major paper, the Manila *Times*. Roces fished all night. I knew because I didn't sleep. Watching Roces fish and the other guest retch were my diversions from my back deck bunk throughout the long hours until morning.

We sailed seeking ever more promising fishing grounds all day Saturday and didn't return to Manila until late Sunday evening. Roces never stopped fishing, but Hennie and his other guest and I had a number of interesting conversations about Philippine politics. The other guest was also named Lopez, although he was no relative. He was, however, leader of the youth movement of Recto's party.

277

I caught nothing, but Hennie insisted on driving me home when we got in on Sunday and giving me three barracuda. So my wife would know I really had gone fishing, he said. Jeanne was only slightly consoled by the return of her fisherman and his unearned prizes. She had spent a Friday night more harrowing than mine.

She had gone to a party at a neighboring station officer's house where the man who was convinced I had fallen into a trap proceeded to tell her his fears. While she was mulling over these ideas, our houseboy appeared in the doorway covered with blood. He had not found my battered body somewhere, as my colleague's concerns at first inclined my wife to think. His brother, Pedro explained, had been knifed in a fight and Pedro wanted to borrow money for medical expenses. So Jeanne went home with him to arrange the loan. No sooner had she arrived than the lights went out. She got rid of Pedro and gathered up Ruthven and Julie. They all slept in one bed as the storm raged through the night.

The operational results of the fishing trip were worth the trauma, however. I had evidently been looked over carefully and the decision made by Recto's friends was to continue contact. We decided at the station that Roces had probably been along to see whether he knew me or could identify me. He had been a friend of Gabe's and associated closely with Gabe and Jimmy Ferrer in the early days of NAMFREL. We had, of course, never met before, so Roces had nothing to contribute to their curiosity.

By an amazing piece of good fortune, it turned out that Lopez, the Recto youth leader, was a *compadre* of the agent who arranged our news placements in the Manila press. This agent, we found on checking the files, had once mentioned his relationship with the Recto follower, but no one followed up the lead. Our employee, who was manager of the Manila press club, now reported that his young *compadre* had come around to the bar full of interest in me. Lopez asked our agent to find out all he could about me, saying he knew the agent had a lot of American friends and should be able to get him some information. He further observed, "He must be an intelligence officer, because he's so intelligent. He knows too much about Philippine politics." Nonetheless, he added, he liked me and was terribly curious. He said he planned to try to see me soon again.

The flattering observation I naturally enjoyed. I was amused, however, at his confusion about intelligence. A victim of overtraining in nominalist philosophy, I thought. He mistakes things for their names. I knew quite well that to confuse the title intelligence officer with an intelligent man could be a serious error. That he wanted to see me again was the important fact.

He surprised me, although he shouldn't have, when he called up and insisted on coming to my office to see me. Fortunately, there was a side door from the office next to mine opening directly onto the outside hall, so that it was possible to enter my office without going through the other offices in the section. Normally we kept this side door locked and everyone went in and out of the section's premises through one common entrance for better security control. We opened the side door for my new friend and closed off my office from the rest of the section by shutting the door I normally used. It now appeared I had a private office and one for my secretary, who was "out" when the cagy follower of Senator Recto came to see me.

He tried obviously to get as good a look as possible at my office surroundings. Apparently he decided they were not too suspicious, for he inquired whether I would like to meet Recto. I said this would be a great honor and asked if he would see whether Recto and he could have lunch with me the following Tuesday. He said he would let me know as soon as possible.

I dug hurriedly into the Recto file. I wanted to review the great quarrel he had with Magsaysay and to pick up whatever useful information I could in preparation for my meeting with him. The man I was about to meet was sixty-eight years old and had been chairman of the Philippine constitutional convention, named to the post specifically at the request of Quezon, father of Philippine independence. His complaint with Magsaysay and the Americans seemed to rest on three things. First, he thought that Nationalist leader Laurel, president of the Philippines during the Japanese occupation, had promised him the party's nomination in 1953. This had been usurped by Magsaysay. Second, he considered himself a foreign affairs expert of long standing and was furious when Magsaysay ignored him. Finally, he objected to close relations with the United States, a country that unfairly, he thought, arrested and detained him after the war. As Magsaysay supported one U.S. project after the other in Asia—the Diem regime, SEATO, the Formosa Straits Resolution by which the United States pledged to defend the offshore islands against Chinese Communist attack—a resolution Recto called "a pre-dated declaration of war"—the gulf between the president and the senator widened. As a result and as I already knew, he broke with Magsaysay completely in 1955 and joined Senator Tañada in the Citizens' Party—the two of them running for president and vice-president respectively in 1957.

The station had helped Magsaysay fight this formidable opponent every step of the way. He had been labeled a Chinese Communist stooge, an agent infiltrated into the Philippine Senate (shades of Senator Joe McCarthy), and, I discovered, he had been subjected to various dirty tricks. As I went through the files, I found something that absolutely astounded me. I saw a sealed envelope marked "Recto Campaign." I opened it and found it filled with condoms, marked "Courtesy of Claro M. Recto—the People's Friend." The condoms all had holes in them at the place they could least afford to have them.

I tried to find out what purpose the condoms had been supposed to serve. The best I could do was to learn that they were distributed to show how Recto would let you down. This crude locker-room prank made me feel a little better about my days as a pornographer. Our Sukarno pictures, after all, could have well been real if anyone had ever been able to hide a camera in a hotel room he occupied.

On the appointed Tuesday, I arrived promptly at the Army Navy Club. My choice had been very deliberate. It was the citadel of American imperialism in the Philippines, or had been. In the days of MacArthur and young Colonel Dwight Eisenhower, no Filipinos had been allowed in the club except as waiters and cleaning women. My new young friend assured me, however, that "Don Claro," as he called his mentor, would appear. After ten minutes and no Recto, I went into the reading room to wait, feeling both conspicuous and possibly stood up. In another few minutes, the club manager came tearing into the room. He dated back to before the war in his position, having been a prisoner of the Japanese between his tours running the club. He was terribly flustered. He asked if I were Mr. Smith and when I said I was, he said, "Hurry, hurry! Don Claro Recto is here and he's asking for you."

It was, of course, the first time Recto had ever set foot in the club, as the manager knew only too well. If possible, it was a bigger day for the manager than it was for me. He always showed me the greatest respect, tinged, I thought, with a gnawing uncertainty, thereafter.

Recto was a pudgy man, with drooping eyelids, but he greeted me most cordially and the manager personally ushered us to a table with the best view of the grounds.

"I'll bet you thought I wouldn't show up," Recto opened the conversation, "but I figured if you could invite me here I could come."

He was clearly in a mood to talk. This we did for more than two and a half hours. My mind was spinning with the dual task of countering his thrusts without offending him or arousing his suspicion and trying to remember all that he said in order to write down the conversation for the record.

"I don't really hate the United States, you know, despite what General MacArthur tried to do to me after the war. I once rather liked Americans. But you seem to be obsessed these days. And the way you manipulated poor ignorant Magsaysay was shameful, really," Recto said by way of introducing the topic that we both knew interested us the most—the future of his relationship with the United States. "You should know," he continued, "that I've always been known as the great oppositionist. It seems to be my fate, and I have to confess I rather enjoy it."

I made the obvious point that this would be a pretty dull world without oppositionists, in addition to which no democracy could function without them.

"Well, you must know my quarrels with U.S. Attorney General Brownell's idea that you have ownership of the base sites are an affront to sovereignty and a display of total ignorance of international law."

"Mr. Brownell, in my opinion, isn't much of a lawyer. He's just a sidekick of Tom Dewey," I commented.

Recto looked at me hard and said, "But he's your attorney general."

"He's not *my* attorney general," I replied, "he's the Republican Party's attorney general. More people than you enjoy the right to be oppositionists."

We continued from this point on with a discussion of the weakness Eisenhower had shown toward Joe McCarthy, even to the point of keeping silent when McCarthy attacked the man to whom Eisenhower owed his entire career, General George Marshall. Recto soon found that he and I could agree on a number of points.

"It's rather unusual to find a government official who dares to speak his own mind the way you do," Recto remarked.

"I'm not an official, in my own mind," I said. "I am an American citizen first, and I'm out here trying to get to understand the Philippines."

"Good," he said. "I think that we ought to get together often. I especially think that it's a fine thing that you and both the young Lopezes know each other. The new dialogue has got to start with the younger generations. I think you're perceptive enough to play a part in this. Like Franklin Roosevelt—he's the last American I liked—now he was extremely perceptive.

"Do you know," he went on, "when I presented him the constitution we had written, he glanced at it, and immediately picked out the clause I thought was the most important in the document and said to me, 'I think this is a great document, because of this one clause.'

"I'm not going to flatter you by saying I think you're as perceptive as Roosevelt, but you have possibilities."

I did not know whether or not Recto was pulling my leg. As an experienced politician, he must have realized that FDR had been given a good briefing as to what Recto thought was important. Was he trying to say that he realized I had briefed myself pretty well for this meeting?

During the course of the long conversation, we covered most of the points that Recto was concerned about. We parted with the understanding that I would come to visit him in his law office whenever it was convenient for me to have his youth leader escort me. "I want to show you my collection of *Foreign Affairs*. I have every issue from the first number." I rushed back to the office and wrote down all I could remember of each of Recto's fine points and sent the memo over to George at the station office.

Late the next afternoon George called and said, "Come right over. Ambassador Bohlen wants to see you."

George explained that he had sent my memo up to the ambassador. "Don't worry," he commented as we walked to the ambassador's office, "he liked the memo. What he wants to know is whether you think you can keep up the contact."

On perceptivity, I would give Charles Bohlen the same kind of marks Recto gave to FDR. He wasted no time in making clear that he knew precisely what I was trying to do, and that he enjoyed reading my account because it reminded him of his greatest delight—parrying and thrusting with the Soviets. He also made it clear that he thought it was a useful service CIA could perform by having an officer take a renegade's stance with a determined U.S. opponent. "It's a real contribution you fellows can make," he said, "and it's obvious that Recto enjoys it. He knows, for example, that he and I could never talk that way because of our positions. How do you propose to keep it up? Needless to say, I want you to."

I replied that I hoped to keep it up basically by more of the same kind of conversation, hoping that I could eventually reach the point of real acceptance. Then Recto might trust me with something truly serious he had on his mind.

Ambassador Bohlen said he wished me good luck. He sighed and added he wished he could get to know the Philippine leaders a little better. "I don't think anyone ever did as well with Filipinos as William Howard Taft, the very first American to try to understand them. I want to tell you something I don't want you ever to let Recto know. Do you realize that the selection of Rizal as national hero for the Filipinos was Taft's doing?

"Taft quickly decided that it would be extremely useful for the Filipinos to have a national hero of their revolution against the Spanish in order to channel their feelings and focus their resentment backward on Spain. But he told his advisers that he wanted it to be someone who really wasn't so much of a revolutionary that, if his life were examined too closely or his works read too carefully, this could cause us any trouble. He chose Rizal as the man who fit his model."

On the way back to the station offices, Aurell remarked, "You know, Bohlen feels that Dulles exiled him by sending him here and taking him out of Moscow. He's not trying too hard. He's coasting."

"It's too bad," I said. "Obviously he could easily do as well as William Howard Taft."

Years later in his memoirs Bohlen called his chapter about the Philippines "Exile in Manila," and he wrote, "I whiled away two years in the Philippines thinking ever of the Soviet Union and America."[*] He devoted, in fact, only a page and a half to talking about Philippine problems. This was mainly concerned with the matter that annoyed Recto most specifically—the bases agreement of 1946. The agreement provided a unique bit of extraterritoriality rights, namely that U.S. servicemen must be tried for crimes com-

[*]Charles E. Bohlen, *Witness to History* (New York: W. W. Norton, 1973), p. 456.

mitted off base not in Philippine courts but by military tribunals back on the base. The Pentagon would not budge on this issue. Perhaps this was one reason why Bohlen liked my contact with the Philippines' great oppositionist. We both, in our hearts, thought Recto was right.

If Bohlen was half-hearted in his ambassadorial role in the Philippines, he was a great improvement over all of his recent predecessors, not only because even when he wasn't trying he was a great diplomat, but they had been nonentities. The first ambassador Eisenhower sent out after Ambassador Spruance and the Lansdale team departed was Homer Ferguson. Ferguson had been defeated in his try for reelection to the Senate from Michigan. Ironically, Ferguson had been one of the chief tormentors when Bohlen, at McCarthy's insistence, was challenged as ambassador to Russia in 1953. He kept harping on the fact that Bohlen's role in the Yalta Conference showed that Bohlen was soft on the Russians and made much of a point that showed how little he understood international affairs. He argued that it had been wrong that Chiang Kai-shek had not been invited to Yalta. The reason of course was very simple: at the time of the Yalta Conference Japan and Russia still maintained diplomatic relations and no war had been declared between them. It was for this same reason that Stalin had not been invited to the Cairo Conference when Roosevelt and Churchill met with Chiang, who had been at war with the Japanese longer than any of the allies, to discuss the Far East.

The kindest word to describe Ferguson's ambassadorship was that he was unprepared. His idea of relating to a foreign chief executive was to show his warmth by swatting Magsaysay on the seat of his pants after the president delivered his state of the union message. His wife's contribution was to ask "Raymond," as she pronounced the president's first name, if he could arrange a trip for her to Zamboanga to see the monkeys without tails. She hadn't bothered to check out the ancient ditty sung by American soldiers at the turn of the century when they suppressed the Filipino insurrection, and didn't know the monkeys without tails reference was the punch line of this insulting song.

Small wonder that CIA performed so many of the normal functions of an embassy in relationship with Magsaysay in those days—someone had to represent the United States properly. That we continued to be the principal link with the Philippine

284

political leadership after Magsaysay's death did not bother Bohlen. This led almost inevitably to the kinds of activities I became involved in my second year in the country and will describe in the following chapter.

My contact with Recto blossomed richly for a time. Soon his young follower had me dropping in at Recto's law office every other week, and he introduced me to Ernesto Grenada and Soliongco. I also continued to see Hennie Lopez from time to time. All this was very fine except that I felt I was not making the progress toward the goal of full acceptance I had promised Ambassador Bohlen I would reach. I began to evolve a plan to achieve this which turned out to be a disaster.

The Southeast Asian Regional Survey Unit story I had concocted concerning trying to develop ways to handle the serviceman situation was effective with Recto, but he kept insisting that the only real solution was for the United States to give up its position regarding the trial of offenders caught off base by Philippine authorities. "I admire your objective of trying to make these men behave better by teaching them more about how we Filipinos feel," Recto said on one occasion, "but this doesn't solve the problem of what you are doing to our national sovereignty."

I decided to make up a document, supposedly a survey report on attitudes of Americans toward Filipinos. This, I intended to pretend, was a classified document revealing such misconceptions that I was showing it to Recto both to let him know how outraged I was and to ask his help in doing something to correct the situation. My plan, in short, was to demonstrate to him that he was winning me to his side to the point I would provide him classified information. In return, I would expect him to reveal to me his confidential plans and ideas.

When I had the paper ready, I chose a day on which he had invited me to be his guest at lunch as the moment to spring my surprise. When I arrived at the law offices, as he had suggested I do so we could go to lunch from there, Don Claro was surrounded by several lackeys, including his speech writer. The speech writer was working on a speech for Recto to deliver in Tagalog, the official national language, which Recto couldn't speak. Recto preferred Spanish and was a member of the Academy of the Spanish Language. He spoke perfect English, of course, because the Americans had made this the language of Philippine politics since 1901. We greeted each

285

other warmly, as was by now our habit. I said I had a very disturbing document I wanted to show him because I was certain that only he could help me do something about it. I gave him the paper.

As he read it, Don Claro's face turned white. He looked at me with anger in his eyes and threw the paper down. "So this is what you really think of us, is it?" he demanded.

I was stunned. "No, Don Claro, it is not what I think. It's what the ignorant airmen I have to try to educate think. I want you to know just how big my problem is. Look, it's classified information. People would be beside themselves if they knew I was showing it to you. But you are my friend and the man I hope will help me rectify the situation."

He didn't seem to hear me. "You Americans are all alike. This is what you think of us deep down. Hear this"—he turned to his speech writer—"they call us 'greedy, inherently dishonest, untrustworthy.'"

I could not make him understand what I was trying to do by showing him the paper. I made a bit of progress, finally, I thought, in making him see I did not agree with these ideas. But he didn't really seem to get the point that they were not my characterizations of the Filipinos. I prepared to leave, but he insisted we continue with our plan to have lunch. We got into his car and drove to a small Spanish restaurant he liked.

We had a very stiff and uncomfortable mealtime session. He paid more attention to his speech writer than he did to me, concentrating on his effort to pronounce the Tagalog words correctly. We said goodbye with formal politeness.

On the way back to the office, the only consolation I could find for myself in the midst of my horrible mistake was that I felt his performance had not been an act. I realized now that almost certainly he did not realize Franklin Roosevelt had been briefed to point out to him immediately that he considered the best part of the Philippine constitution the very clause which Recto liked the most.

Almost as rapidly as my contacts with the Recto group had expanded they now began to dry up. Grenada, who liked to come over to my house to drink after the *Chronicle* was put to bed at midnight, stopped showing up. I couldn't reach the leader of the Recto Youth by phone anymore. Hennie Lopez agreed to have lunch with me. Then he called and cancelled the appointment. I never saw Don Claro Recto for lunch or at his office again.

At least I had learned how the word was passed within a Filipino political group and how well it was obeyed. This would be of help to me in the activities in which I soon found myself engaged.

Jimmy Ferrer had been taken off the ice. He and I began trying to put together an opposition coalition that could bring to an end the corrupt regime of Carlos García by the time the next presidential elections rolled around.

In the summer of 1958, Des Fitzgerald took over as Far East Division chief. Al Ulmer went to Paris as COS. Des told us to "get the Philippines back on the track."

17

The Grand Alliance

I don't know who thought of it first, we or the Filipinos, but by the time the year 1959 began the idea that the senatorial election that November could be a momentous challenge to President García had taken possession of all of us.

The Philippine senate in those days consisted of 24 senators and the house of representatives numbered 104. The congressmen were elected for periods of four not two years, as in the United States, but like their U.S. counterparts, they were chosen to represent geographical districts. The senators, as in the United States, served for six years and also, as in our country, one-third of the senators were elected every two years. The important difference, which made the Philippine senate elections extremely significant, was that the senatorial candidates ran at-large. They were not chosen to represent the various Philippine states. Hence every senatorial election was a truly national affair—a test of the party in power and a chance for senate candidates to become national political figures. The candidate who received the largest number of votes of all those running for the eight senate seats became at once a national political leader, a potential president.

For this reason, all the Filipinos concerned about national politics and we in the station, who had our orders to get the country back on the track, concluded that the 1959 senate contest was the golden opportunity to have García and his cronies repudiated on a national scale, and to have the voters of the whole country indicate the new man who would throw García out of the presidential palace in 1961. I would learn in the next few months that there were at least seven men who believed they should be the next president and I found myself caught between them all and trying to decide which of them would be the winner.

Two of them, in particular, were the most convinced that the choice could only possibly be they. These were Diosdado Macapagal, the Liberal who had startled everyone by winning the vice-presidency when García and the Nationalists won the election of 1957. He thus emerged as the leader of the Liberal Party and considered that a change in administration must obviously mean the Liberal Party with him at its head would return to the power Magsaysay and the CIA station had taken from them. As I have already noted, he also thought himself covered on this last point. He had been furnishing the station political information through a deep-cover agent cut-out for a number of years. That Macapagal should want station support was a bit ironic. It was he who had been the bitterest objector to American intervention in the Magsaysay election in 1953, quoting time and again from Section 56 of the Republic Act of the Philippines 180, "No foreigner shall aid any candidate directly or indirectly or take part in or influence in any manner any election." He conveniently ignored that law in 1959 as he sought to win our as well as his party's blessing. There was one man whom he couldn't ignore, however.

This man was, of course, our half-heartedly supported third-party candidate in 1957, the man who considered himself to be the natural heir of Magsaysay, Manuel P. Manahan, president of the Progressive Party of the Philippines. Manahan had long-standing ties to the station. He had been the principal figure in arranging the surrender of the top Huk leader for Magsaysay and the Lansdale team. At thirty-eight, he was named by Magsaysay to head the presidential complaints and action committee, PCAC. The PCAC was another bit of the brilliant structure erected to help Magsaysay

290

and the station run the Philippines efficiently. The PCAC was the president's direct link with the people. Anyone having any problem with the government bureaucracy at any level had prompt access to Manny Manahan or his two young top assistants, Frisco San Juan, thirty, and Antonio Villegas, twenty-six, or to someone on their staff. Action was taken on these complaints. The PCAC proved that Magsaysay really was the people's president. It also collected a large mass of files that were of great use to all station operations, especially intelligence collection. Manahan was subsequently named chief of Philippine customs and he engineered a thorough cleanup of this number one center of corruption.

Even more important than these achievements was the fact that Manny Manahan was almost the double of Magsaysay. He took full advantage of this and copied all the late president's mannerisms. One final advantage Manny had was that no one could make any jokes about his intellectual capacity, as they did of Magsaysay's. Manahan was a very bright young man, eight years younger than Macapagal.

Macapagal was not the undisputed leader of the Liberal Party that he thought he was. One who considered himself more endowed with both ability and money was Senator Ambrosio Padilla. Two years older than Macapagal, he had been another surprise victor in 1957, sweeping into the senate as a Liberal. He was his party's senate floor leader. Still another was the Liberal Party's leader in the house of representatives, Ferdinand Marcos, like Manahan only forty-two years old.

Among the Nationalist younger leadership were three men, all of whom had supported Magsaysay, and all of whom had solid local political bases which made each one feel that if he should play a role in dumping García he could also reasonably expect he should be considered the choice to head the future presidential ticket that might be brewed in the political pot in 1959. One was Sergio Osmeña, Jr., heir to his father's political fiefdom in Cebu. Another was Emmanuel Pelaez, heir to his father's domain. His father had been governor of Misamis Oriental, the most important state on Mindanao. Pelaez had also been a Magsaysay supporter in the senate and was known as "the father of the barrio home rule law." The third was Mayor Arsenio Lacson of Manila, no one's heir but already finishing his second term as mayor of the country's main metropolis, and who was about to try for a third term in the fall of

1959. He controlled the city with an iron hand which was never more than inches away from the forty-five he always carried stuck in the belt of his trousers. By July, 1959, I had personal relationships with all of them except Mayor Lacson. I didn't care to meet him. To me, he typified what we were against and why we were breaking Philippine law against foreign intervention in their elections in order to change the country for the better.

The city Lacson ruled was the heartland of the vice and crooked politics we convinced ourselves had to be corrected. He controlled the city because he made his own personal arrangement with the system. He was a colorful figure. In fact, he was just about the first person I saw the first day we arrived at the Filipinas Hotel. At four o'clock that afternoon there was a stir around the swimming pool, where we were trying to get some relief from the heat after unpacking. Lacson and his bodyguard strode by, with several other men in tow, heading for the bar. I found out later that Lacson visited the Filipinas between four and four-thirty every day for what he called his "Chinese tea." Every day the people who ran such things in Manila provided a lovely young Chinese girl for the mayor's pleasure. Sometimes more than one. He eventually died of a heart attack during one of his tea parties on an afternoon in the early 1960s.

There were a few other young Nationalist Party figures of consequence, but they were not yet straining to enter the presidential race. They were inclined to follow the party's top leadership and enjoy the prosperity that power had brought the party. Most of the top leadership were old men, like Recto and Laurel, veterans of the prewar, pre-independence political wars.

Each of these old warriors was the political boss of a state. José Laurel, Yale graduate and Japanese puppet president, was perhaps the most distinguished. He and his son, José Junior, ruled Batangas. The party's most accomplished political power manipulator was seventy-one-year-old Eulogio "Amang" Rodriguez, ruler of Rizal, the provincial state that surrounded Manila and contained all the suburbs of the metropolis. Amang had arranged, among other things, that the nation's capital should be moved into his political and personal real estate, Quezon City, outermost of the Rizal suburbs of Manila. The government granted Amang his big real estate development deal, but congress continued to sit in downtown Manila and the president to rule from Malacañang Palace, where the

American High Commissioner had maintained his residence. As far as I know, the Philippines in those days was the only country whose capital city was not the seat of the national government. Amang was credited, in addition to this unique achievement, with coining the phrase that summed up the nation's political system. "Politics," Amang was reported to have declared, "is addition."

Other important clan leaders were old men like Mariano Cueñco of Cebu, Daniel Romualdez of Leyte, and Fernando Lopez of Iloilo. These men headed up a graft machine that politicians were so eager to join they would spend 300,000 to 700,000 pesos to get elected to congress, where their annual salaries were only 7,200 pesos. They gladly made this outlay because each congressman and senator enjoyed participating in what was frankly called the "pork barrel" bill. This was an annual piece of legislation each one of them could have approved for the expenditure of between 250,000 to 500,000 pesos, at their discretion, for "public improvements." What was improved most frequently was the pocketbook of the congressman or senator who proposed the legislation. Hence, an expenditure of 700,000 pesos to get a job in which you would write yourself a piece of legislation that would provide you 500,000 a year for four years, if you were a congressman, or the same amount for six years, if a senator, was not a bad investment.

The campaign funds, moreover, were usually raised not from the aspirant's own resources, but from businessmen, especially Chinese (about whom the Filipinos had the same antagonistic feelings as did the Indonesians and other Southeast Asians) who were easy targets for extortion. That is, all business dealings with the government were subject to a "tax," which could be alleviated by a contribution to a congressman's or senator's campaign fund. The Chinese were also expected to pay a regular retainer to a politician's law firm whether or not the firm provided any legal services in return.

The García administration used all these devices and as many others as the imagination could possibly devise. Juan Pajo, the president's secretary, was, next to the president's brother, Cosme García, and the president's wife, Leonila, the most important arranger of deals.

A man who wove his way daily through the network of payoffs and chicanery was an American citizen named Ted Lewin. Lewin operated under cover of being a sports promoter and lived this cover occasionally by arranging a visit of the Harlem Globetrotters or a prizefight. His main enterprise was running a gambling casino in Pasay City, the suburb closest to downtown Manila. His clientele were the high officials of the administration. Officially, gambling casinos were against the law, but Lewin had that and many other things arranged. He was also king of the black market, and ran a network of Filipinos with PX privileges acquired on the basis of their alleged guerrilla services during the war. These regularly siphoned off from the nearby Navy PX at Sangley Point and the great shopping center for service personnel at Clark Field hundreds of choice items unavailable in Manila's markets, where imports were few because of tariffs and because the peso was artificially pegged at two to the dollar when the world free rate of exchange for Philippine currency was four to one.

He provided all kinds of other services. There was a story that when the wife of one of Senator Lopez's sons left her husband and took her small boy with her to the United States, Lewin arranged through his friends in organized crime back home to have the child kidnapped and returned to the Lopez family. He and Pajo were close friends.

Because of his being an American citizen with criminal connections, the station helped out the FBI by having Lewin's penthouse apartment, in the Shellburne Hotel across the street from the embassy on Dewey Boulevard, bugged by the Philippine National Bureau of Investigation. The tapes of his phone conversations were regularly read by some of us in the station for various reasons. I read them to try to pick up leads on political deals that might be being arranged with Lewin's help. The Philippine National Bureau of Investigation Director, Colonel José Lukban, readily agreed to this type of cooperation because he believed in emulating his hero and model, J. Edgar Hoover, and carefully maintained secret dossiers on indiscretions of high Filipino officials to make sure he kept his job. His aim was to stay in office by this means as long as Hoover had been able to by following the same practice.

The trouble with reading such phone conversation tapes is that there is the temptation to fall into the Lukban/Hoover pattern and begin to pay more attention to the peccadilloes of the person whose life is being listened to than to the operational matters that are the supposed justification for the bugging operation. Soon we were all fascinated by an affair Lewin got going with the wife of a major in

294

the Counter Intelligence Corps. While her husband was busy snooping on servicemen, the bored housewife got enticed into enjoying evenings at Ted's casino. Next thing, we were listening to them arrange their bedding-down dates on Lewin's phone.

This diverting pastime that provided a pleasant break from our serious business activities suddenly turned into a matter of real concern, if not directly for us, for the husband's Counter Intelligence outfit. Lewin's PX purchasing operation depended on his Filipino network having a plentiful supply of U.S. Military scrip, which was used in all PXs in order to try to prevent precisely the kind of black market supply operations Ted was running for himself and his Filipino friends in the García administration. The scrip was supposedly tightly controlled and its use, rather than the use of normal currency, was supposed to limit the amount of goods that any one person might buy at a given moment. Ted's group, of course, counterfeited a large enough supply to circumvent this restriction. The same thing went on all over the world, and the armed forces, from time to time, tried to break it up by cancelling old scrip and issuing new, thereby catching the offenders when they came into the PX with their no longer valid paper money. The operation could work only if the date on which the change was to take place was kept Top Secret information so that the black marketeers would be taken by complete surprise.

The major's wife tipped Ted off one day to one of these impending changes in scrip. It was probably more valuable to him than any of her other services. He got the word out to his entire net, and when the change took place not a single offender was caught.

We had no recourse but to tell the CIC what we knew about the cause of the complete failure of their operation. The major and his wife shortly left Manila. We had sacrificed something too, of course. Ted guessed that his girlfriend's departure was the result of her help to him being discovered and assumed correctly that his phone was tapped. We got no more interesting information from that source again.

We had other sources, of course, on the rampant corruption of the García administration. One was Binamira, whom I kept clinging to his PACD post, still unable to make up my mind what I should do about his social revolution. He had many lurid stories to tell about abuses in the agencies of the government that had been established to provide credit to rural areas and to market the peasants' commodities—both agencies being ones his PACD workers regularly dealt with.

What we were witnessing was the total collapse of the showplace of democracy that had been the pride not only of CIA but the Eisenhower administration. Important activities such as the work of the Eastern Construction Company in Vietnam and Thailand might soon be in jeopardy as the greedy politicians got the idea to extend their "taxation" tactics to this organization. Besides, we had saved the Philippines once, couldn't we possibly save it again, particularly since there seemed to be ample talent to do the job? The task again was to organize this talent effectively. It seemed almost tragic to see so many fine men frustrated. Des Fitzgerald, who had presided over the creation of the Magsaysay era, certainly thought so. I did. We did not think that we were interfering in the political life of the country. We were, as Gabe would put it, engaging in pump-priming. We were providing the means to help the Filipinos help themselves to make their country a better land in which to live.

Colonel Jaime Ferrer was delighted when I told him of our intentions. I explained that we wanted to be realistic and not simply carried away by the ideal he and his friends had of transforming the Philippines into a real democracy where the little man had a chance to be heard and to receive a decent living as the product of his labor. The political reality was that, as the Progressives had learned, a third party couldn't win in the Philippines because it could not build the grass-roots organization required. Local leaders don't want to take the chance. They want to be with the winning president. If they lose one election, they want to be sure to come back the next time. In short, we wanted the Progressives to merge with the Liberals so that there would be the kind of organizational base that was required to win. Practical politics must be mixed with our idealism.

I was presenting him the kind of practical plan his years as an organizer had taught him made sense. I was also telling him, in effect, that his organizing efforts for the Progressives in 1957 had been a failure. He took this in stride because he was a soldier. I never met another Jimmy Ferrer again in my career.

Jimmy combined qualities that usually don't go together in the same man. He was an activist, a doer, and at the same time a completely disciplined person. His heart and his head were well met. He always explained his great talent at organizing action by saying

296

he liked to "fix-up" things. Unfortunately, I knew no Spanish then, and I could not fully appreciate what he meant when he used this expression. He was translating the Spanish verb *arreglar*. When an American thinks of something being fixed up he thinks perhaps of the clock, the washing machine, or the car being made to run again by having been successfully tinkered with by someone with the right mechanical knowledge. When a Spanish speaker thinks of *arreglar*, he is thinking that the final result will work only if he remembers always just how sensitive and transitory is the way all the components happen to work together properly.

Like the others of the Magsaysay group, Ferrer had been a guerrilla leader during the war. I learned, in time, that he and his men had had more control over Parañaque, the suburb just to the south of Pasay City, than the Japanese occupation forces and the Japanese commander feared to leave his quarters at night lest Jimmy's men assassinate him.

"I think a coalition makes good sense, all right," Jimmy agreed, "but Manahan will be afraid that if we join the Liberals and win the senate elections Macapagal will claim he did it all himself and insist he should be the presidential candidate."

"Can't we take one thing at a time? Let's worry about the 'fifty-nine elections now and the 'sixty-one elections later," I tried to argue.

"You don't understand how things work around here well enough yet," said Jimmy. "Everyone is thinking about nineteen sixty-one right now."

"Well, do you think there is a way to work this out somehow?"

Jimmy had an idea. He said he knew Liberals close to Macapagal and they all knew that he was a loyal Manahan lieutenant. His scheme was to sound them out about whether some agreement could be reached with Macapagal that the presidential candidate decision be deferred by common written agreement, if possible, or a solemn oath of some kind until after the coalition had worked together in the 1959 elections. He said he'd find out what Macapagal would demand from Manahan in the way of a pledge to the same purpose. He would also try to find out what Macapagal's ideas were concerning Manahan and other Progressives being on the senate ticket. Thus the first round of negotiations began.

The station also was able to get to Macapagal through the cut-out and ask the same kinds of questions. We also had an officer under embassy cover who was in contact with Manahan and his best friend, Raul Manglapus, former under-secretary of foreign affairs and an unsuccessful senate candidate for the Progressives in 1957. These contacts were handled very gingerly, lest these two principal Progressive leaders get the idea we were about to consider any help to them in their political careers.

On the basis of this overall effort and thanks to Jimmy's ability to fix up things, a loose general agreement was arrived at on April 23, 1959. The Progressives and the Liberals were to merge and to work together to plan a senate ticket for the coming elections. Washington was extremely pleased and sent commendations to all of us who had anything to do with the arrangement. Ambassador Bohlen told Aurell that this was the most exciting development he'd seen since arriving in the Philippines. "There's no doubt," Bohlen told a meeting George arranged between the ambassador and the station officers involved one night at George's house, "you've brought together the best men in Philippine politics. I hope they can work together as a team."

They couldn't. Within less than two months the coalition was coming apart on the question of the senatorial candidates and just who had said what to whom when the agreement had been made concerning who was going to be the campaign director. Macapagal insisted this be he. He also wanted to give only two places on the eight-man ticket to the Progressives, naming Liberals to the other six spots. The Progressives argued that this was not a fair merger—if two parties join to run eight candidates, each one obviously should have four slots, they insisted. The only concession the Progressives would make was that they would consider that two of the four places they demanded could be filled by other strong candidates who were opposed to García's gang but not necessarily Progressive Party men. They thought that Emmanuel Pelaez and General Jesus Vargas, recently dismissed as secretary of defense by President García, should be added to the ticket. Both Pelaez and Vargas had played major roles in revealing what was known as a Nationalist Party "white paper" on corruption. They were thought to have helped Senator Cueñco prepare his speech announcing the existence of this top-secret party document on May 19 on the floor of the Philippine Senate. As a result Vargas had been fired as defense secretary, and strong hints were made that Pelaez, who was up for reelection, would not be one of the eight candidates that the

298

Nationalists would run in the November elections. Since Macapagal was already committed to run Ferdinand Marcos for the senate, he was afraid that all these stars on the ticket, while they might mean victory, would also surely mean that his prominence in the presidential firmament would be consequently diminished.

As Jimmy put it, "We haven't got enough things fixed up."

George Aurell decided that I should take over contact with Manahan so that no one under embassy cover would be so close to these political machinations and because he thought that, backed up by Ferrer, I could keep Manahan in the coalition.

I met Manny for the first time at a station safehouse I used on A. Mabini, the second street in from the bay parallel to Dewey Boulevard. A. Mabini was a street of small nightclubs and small hotels. The safehouse was a good eight blocks down the street past most of them, in an apartment building one door away from the last of the small hotels. The cover story for using the place was that it was an apartment which the Air Force kept for people who came in from Clark Field on business so that there was no need to make hotel reservations for them, especially since their visits were often made on short notice. This cover story sounded great from the point of view of explaining the irregular times it was used to the landlord, but there was no safehouse keeper, which violated good tradecraft. When I wasn't using it, it was almost never used. The fact that there were some goings and comings at the small hotel next door was supposed to enhance the legend. That is, transients were no strangers to the neighborhood.

The first thing Manny said was, "My God, why did you bring me here? This place is next door to a Chinese whorehouse—that's the main business of that hotel. If I'm spotted in this neighborhood, there goes the reputation of this honest family man in politics."

That was the first and last of our meetings there. We had just settled another mess concerning the safehouse a few months before. We fired the cleaning woman because her husband had begun hanging around the place saying he was looking for the American who had gotten his wife pregnant. The only person whom we had ever housed there semi-permanently had been the commo man we had brought out of Menado in the summer of 1958 after the final collapse of the Indonesian rebellion. He had stayed for a fairly extended period in Manila being debriefed and taking care of odds and ends as well as enjoying rest and recuperation. Whether he was the father of the child or whether the husband was trying to shirk responsibility for yet another unwanted offspring, we didn't know, but it had been a sticky situation for a while. Why no one of my other contacts had told me about the Chinese whorehouse I didn't know. Anyway, from that night on, my negotiation sessions with the string of political contacts that grew steadily during the rest of the summer of 1959 were held late at night in my own house.

I liked Manahan, but I could see from the start that he would continually try to press me to side with him for old-times' sake. I didn't think this would be a sound basis upon which to make any of the decisions that would have to be made by all parties concerned. I told this to Jimmy the next time I saw him. He agreed with me. I said that I thought I needed a broader approach than being, in effect, just another spokesman for the Progressives. He immediately suggested that he could introduce me to Ambrosio Padilla, an important Liberal with his own presidential ambitions, he explained, who wasn't about to accept Macapagal's unquestioned leadership. Perhaps we could get some ideas on how to handle things from Padilla. He would at least give me another angle of the picture to ponder.

A few nights later we went to see Senator Padilla in Jimmy's prewar Chevrolet that for some mysterious reason managed to run reasonably well that night.

Ambrosio Padilla greeted us on the terrace surrounding his swimming pool where his houseboy had asked us to wait. Padilla could trace his ancestry back to Spanish colonial arrivals in the eighteenth century. They had fraternized with the natives enough, however, that he was quite sufficiently Filipino. But the fact that he represented old money made him distinct from all the rest of the politicians, who were either making their fortunes at that moment or adding to those their fathers had made from their political careers just one generation before. Padilla thought this was important and so did I. He had been asked to enter politics for the first time, when he had successfully run for the senate in 1957, because the much tainted Liberal Party needed the kind of new face and fresh image he represented—a man never involved in the scandals of the Quirino administration, the mess Magsaysay had tried to clean up, and who obviously had no need to line his pockets from the public treasury.

Jimmy explained who I was by saying that I represented the peo-

300

ple who had helped Magsaysay and that I now was trying on their behalf to bring honest government back to the Philippines again. He didn't mention CIA. Padilla understood. He said he was most anxious to help and told us succinctly what he thought of the situation.

"Obviously, you want a strong ticket for the senate, one with the kind of men who stand for Magsaysay's ideals, but you have two problems." Padilla put it plainly: "One is that some hitherto loyal Nationalists, like Senator Cuenco, who can hardly claim a reputation for political probity, need to be elected again this year and he is afraid that García has such a stench attached to the Nationalist administration he can't win on the Nationalist Party ticket. The other is Macapagal, who can't think of anything except getting elected president next time.

"Macapagal doesn't want the senate ticket filled up with men who might be big enough to challenge him for the nomination in 1961, and he doesn't even care whether the ticket wins so long as he gets recognized as the Liberal Party's number one leader. That's why he'd rather make a deal with Cuenco and put him on the ticket, than a person like Manny Pelaez, who also has broken with García but who is a brilliant young man with a future. Cuenco's too old to worry Macapagal, but his votes in Cebu, which he'd owe Mac in 1961's presidential election if Mac put him on the Liberal ticket this year for the senate, would be very valuable.

"Do you know what Macapagal said to me?" Padilla asked, looking at Jimmy and me in a way that indicated he wanted to be sure we understood he thought this was the most important thing he had to say. "He said that if I'd help him get Cuenco on the ticket and not let Pelaez on and also try to dump Manahan and Manglapus, he'd make sure I would succeed him as president after he was elected in 1961 and served just one term."

Padilla readily agreed that he would do all he could to help us with our plan, which was not only to insure Manahan and Manglapus places on the ticket but also make certain Pelaez and General Jesus Vargas were also included. This, we had decided, was the essential hard core of a ticket that would assure repudiation of García. A myth that had taken shape in the short time the Philippines had been independent was that if four of the opposition senate slate won an election, the administration in power had been repudiated.

"I'm certainly happy and relieved to meet you," Padilla said when we parted. "Young Osmeña is going around saying he's the broker in arranging the senate ticket whom the Americans have chosen to speak for them. I consider his political morals lower than Macapagal's. I'm glad to know this isn't true."

"Senator," I said, "we do our own work."

I didn't tell Padilla that just a week before I had met with Sergio Osmeña Jr. to tell him the same thing. After the Cueñco "white paper" speech on May 19 the political climate had undergone a steady rise in temperature until we had reached the feverish period which began at the time I met Padilla. A special session of congress had been called to consider an administration proposal to add a 40 percent tax on all foreign exchange. Thus all the leading actors in the coalition ticket drama were in town and anti-García elements daily gained headlines by pointing out the new legislation was just another scheme to line the pockets of the president's henchmen. In addition to Cueñco and Pelaez in the senate, Sergio Osmeña Jr. in the house of representatives joined the hue and cry. Even Mayor Lacson, who was up for reelection in Manila that coming November, broke with the García administration. When the political columnists got word that the Liberal/Progressive coalition was quarreling over the list of candidates they were to run for the senate, young Osmeña made his move. He leaked to his press contacts that he was playing a leading role in the coalition negotiations and added for good measure a hint that the Americans were concerned about their outcome because they were worried that corruption was getting out of hand and were hoping that the better men in Philippine politics would unite to halt the trend.

George Aurell called me into his office and said that we must do something about Osmeña. He explained he had been introduced to Osmeña and Osmeña knew he was the station chief. Obviously, George reasoned, he couldn't personally talk to Osmeña because their contact might be discovered and this would only confirm that CIA was working with Osmeña when not only wasn't this true but we wanted to scotch the rumors the ambitious young man was stimulating. He said he could get the word to Osmeña that a man who represented him was coming to talk over the situation and he gave me his card to prove my bona fides. That afternoon I went off to Osmeña's house with George's calling card.

"Serging," as he was always referred to in the Philippine custom of forming nicknames from a syllable of a given name plus a diminutive that sounded felicitous, met me in the library of the Osmeña family's Manila mansion just off Dewey Boulevard. He impressed me at once as someone who had been trained from boyhood to take charge of everything and everyone with whom he was in touch as befitted the son of one of the country's two principal founding fathers—an impression he made certain I received by calling his secretary on the house intercom to tell her he was not to be disturbed indefinitely and ordering her to pass the word along to his office in congress, his downtown law office, and his office in Cebu City.

I thought the only way to handle this situation was to adopt an equally imperious manner. I told him flatly that I was the only person in the Philippines authorized by the United States government to discuss political negotiations with anyone. I said that I would of course appreciate any help he could give me as long as he understood this and made no statements or took any actions without clearing them with me.

I guessed right. He warmed up immediately to that approach. "Serging" and I began that afternoon a strange and wonderful relationship that added a strain to my nervous system greater than that which the face-to-face negotiations I soon began with Vice-President Macapagal caused me.

I first talked with Serging Osmeña on July 1. He promised to make no more public statements but to work hard behind the scenes to see just how things stood with Emmanuel Pelaez and with old man Cuenco, his family's rival in Cebu. On July 7, Cuenco publicly announced that under no circumstances would he run for reelection as a Nationalist. The same day the newspapers reported Pelaez said Amang Rodriguez had assured him a place on the Nationalist ticket but that he had received feelers from the people who were planning a coalition. I saw right away that Osmeña may have kept his mouth shut about making public announcements, but that privately he had probably told people of our conversation, for I had told him we would like to see anti-García Nationalists on the senate ticket. That is why Jimmy and I met with Padilla immediately on the evening of July 7, to find out if he were a reliable ally on the Liberal executive committee and, if so, that he understood we and not Osmeña were the ones trying to make the necessary arrangements.

Jimmy called me at midnight the day following our meeting with Padilla. "Don't go to bed," he said. "I'm bringing someone around to see you." Forty-five minutes later he was in my living room with Senator Emmanuel Pelaez. He introduced us, and then said, "I think you two should talk. I'm leaving."

Pelaez was noticeably nervous. I was not exactly at ease myself. My fixer had really fixed up something this time. I asked Pelaez if he would like a drink and he said yes. We retired to a secluded alcove of my living room and talked until three-thirty in the morning.

I told Pelaez that I had become involved in this matter only with the greatest reluctance, that I didn't want to interfere in the internal affairs of the Philippines, but that, on the other hand, the country deserved far better leadership than it was getting and anything that anyone could do to further this end I considered a worthwhile cause. Pelaez said he was surprised that the American Magsaysay group would talk to him, especially an American official, since he had taken a stand on the bases question that was so close to Recto's. I assured him this was his right. Personally, I told him, I thought the Pentagon position was outrageous. The Philippines was an independent nation and the U.S. military had no right to try to reserve a piece of the country forever for themselves. Our concern, his and mine, was the future of that independent nation, not the United States' imagined prerogatives. Gradually, we both began to feel more comfortable and soon were talking about many things besides the immediate political situation.

Emmanuel Pelaez had an impressive grasp of his country's fundamental problems. I soon realized why he was known as the "father of barrio home rule." Like Binamira, he saw clearly the reality that there could be no real chance for the Philippines to break out of the vicious circle of mass poverty until efforts to develop the country were undertaken at the bottom of the pyramid. He too had a dream of a Philippines free from economic and political bondage to a small self-perpetuating elite. Looking outward at the world, he thought that the ideological struggle between Communist imperialism and John Foster Dulles's free world was an unreal contest. Freedom, for him, rested on an honest respect for each country's peculiar needs and desires and a leadership in each that saw they were properly attended to. He was as wise as the old Englishman I had met with Mike Campbell in Malaya, I thought. At the same time, he understood the realities of Philippine politics. He seemed immediately to me to be the man who could and should lead his people. Within a few more days I would meet the rest of the important aspirants for that role, but I never changed my mind about Manny Pelaez.

Just at this point, an important change took place in the people who were significant for me. George Aurell was replaced as chief of station by John Richardson. George's health had been deteriorating for the past year. Also, Des Fitzgerald wanted more decisive action. Jocko Richardson had been chief of the Southeast Europe Division and served in important posts in that region. Most recently he had been chief of station in Athens. He was a decisive man. He quickly sat me down and debriefed me carefully on all I was doing and all I knew about the political situation. When we were through, he said he was satisfied that I had a feel for politics he thought he could trust and remarked, "I'm going to give you your head, just be sure to keep me fully informed of everything you do."

He immediately had the chance to be as good as his word. The deep-cover agent with indirect contact with Macapagal reported that the vice-president insisted that he talk with me. Just as happened when I had become involved with the Recto crowd, the word was now being passed about my contacts with the Progressives, with Serging, Padilla, and Pelaez. When I later came to know Latin America I learned what the process was called—*media palabra*, the half-word, literally, but what we would call the inside word. There are no really covert operations possible in a Latin society. The only kind of information that anyone cares to exchange is secret information. Jocko said, "Go meet him."

On July 9 the Liberal/Progressive coalition had clashed head-on. The Liberal executive committee met with the leadership of the Progressives at the home of Amelito Mutoc, a young lawyer who had headed the Macapagal vice-presidential campaign and who before that had been a NAMFREL executive—in fact he had taken over the top executive post from Jimmy Ferrer when Jimmy became involved in other tasks during the Magsaysay election operation. His place should have been acceptable neutral ground on which to meet and negotiate. The meeting began at noon and lasted well into the evening. As a result, I had another midnight visit from Ferrer. He said Macapagal would not budge on his formula—six Liberals and only two others. If Manahan and Manglapus didn't want these two places, they could give them up in favor of the Nationalists they were urging be added to the ticket. Jimmy said, with some satisfaction, that Padilla had at one point been about to punch Macapagal in the nose.

When I got to the office late the next morning after Jimmy and I had gone round and round on the problem until five o'clock, I learned about Macapagal's desire to see me. The meeting was set up for breakfast at Mutoc's on Saturday, July 11.

Promptly at eight o'clock a car drove up outside my gate. I sent Pedro to answer the bell and he returned with a young man whose handsome features I recognized from newspaper pictures. He smiled and held out his hand. "I'm Ferdinand Marcos. Macapagal has sent me to escort you to meet him."

After we got into the car, Marcos immediately began giving me his ideas about how I should handle Macapagal. "If you just remember, he has an exaggerated opinion of himself and his own importance," he said, "you should be able to reason with him. We really want American help to win this election, and all of us really want a good strong ticket. Also, we don't necessarily think Macapagal must be the presidential candidate in 1961. Only he does."

Mel Mutoc's house was not far from mine. About a mile down the road to Quezon City, known as Highway 54, was the entrance to Forbes Park, the deluxe development of the affluent Filipinos, surrounding the most exclusive club, the Manila Polo Club. Mel lived not far from this center of the community. Forbes Park was not only beyond San Lorenzo Village, where I lived, it was on the opposite side of Highway 54 in every sense. When you arrived at a home in Forbes Park you knew you were on the other side of the tracks.

Mel Mutoc, the host, met us at the door and took us into the dining room, where the vice-president was already seated at the breakfast table, surrounded by five of his party leaders. Ambrosio Padilla was not one of them. I felt that I was alone with the enemy. Manahan, Osmeña, Ferrer, Padilla, Pelaez, and just now even Ferdinand Marcos, the messenger he had sent to fetch me, had all given me the impression that the man I was about to meet was the ogre of Philippine politics.

He wasn't. Macapagal rose to shake hands with me with a warm smile on his face. This seemed a very special sign of goodwill and also an unnecessary honor for the man who was a heartbeat away

306

from being president of his country to show me. It set the tone for the entire meeting, and, of course, gave the clue to his team. They immediately insisted we talk on a first-name basis. They let me know they called Diosdado Macapagal, "Dadoy." I was careful not to.

Our meeting lasted until noon. We both agreed that it was "exploratory." The main thing Macapagal wanted to explore was how much money we would put into the campaign if the ticket were mutually satisfactory. Unarmed as always with specifics to lay at the end of the string trailing out from Washington and yet unwilling to be defeated by this before even starting our negotiations, I replied, "Substantial." He naturally wanted me to define that term. I could counter only by suggesting that we talk about the ticket, and if we arrived at a mutual understanding, he could then give me a budget estimate.

We went over the senatorial candidate question for some time with no results. I had by now learned all the arguments my Progressive friends had to offer, and I had studied the results of the last four elections carefully. I made the best use I could of these. Macapagal seemed surprised that I could talk statistics state by state. He was very gracious. "I thought I knew more about our politics than anyone," he smiled, "but I think you're doing better." After all the flattering exchanges, the trading of serious information on future political prospects, analyses of past election returns and bargaining, we came merely to the conclusion that we should continue our talks.

"But you announced yesterday that the slate was final," I reminded Macapagal as we agreed to break off the session.

"That was merely for newspaper consumption," he said with a large grin. "You know, sort of like what Wendell Willkie once said, 'just campaign talk.'"

With that morning's meeting began a period of three weeks of almost ceaseless activity. The six presidential hopefuls I had met didn't know what I meant by substantial support, but they all had a stake in finding out which made it worthwhile to keep in constant touch with me. I met Manahan, Osmeña, Pelaez, Padilla, Marcos, and Macapagal in meetings for breakfast, for lunch, for dinner, after dinner, after midnight, in the early morning, and in the middle of the afternoon. It was exhausting, but, I must confess, it was tormentingly exhilarating. Assessing character is supposed to be something vital to any operation an intelligence officer undertakes. I never again had a chance to assess so many talented men under conditions that gave me such an opportunity to find out so much about them.

I also learned a great deal about the nature of decision-making in the Philippines. All the interested groups tended toward the same process. They seemed to work best as sort of clan meetings. They almost never arrived on time, and they never concluded any meeting when they had agreed their schedules showed they should have been through. The same group would meet and unmeet over the course of many hours. People wandered in and out. This was most frustrating to an American who was trying to get something definitely decided. As the cast changed the decisions changed. In other words, if a reasonable quorum finally started a scheduled ten o'clock meeting by eleven o'clock, and had reached a decision by noon, then a new important figure would show up. The decision was almost immediately unmade. By two P.M. it had been made once more. Someone or two would leave and be replaced by others, and the same business was repeated. I learned to be very careful about what I reported to Jocko as having been decided. Too many times, I would get a telephone call a half-hour later telling me someone was coming around to tell me the decision I had just reported had been changed.

Jeanne was affected by the whole matter almost as drastically as I was. For my numerous contacts did not content themselves with business meetings with me, but insisted on our taking part in their social lives. This began when I got the word from the Army Navy Club one afternoon that General Macario Peralta was at the club and wished to see me there urgently. Thanks to Jimmy, I knew who Peralta was. He and Ferrer had worked on veterans affairs many years before. Macario Peralta was one of the truly great guerrilla leaders. But the distinction of which he was most proud was that he had attended the U.S. Army Command and General Staff College at Ft. Leavenworth just before World War II began. He received the highest marks of anyone who had ever attended Leavenworth up until that point, except for one man—Douglas MacArthur.

Peralta told me he was Macapagal's intelligence chief. He said he had an important suggestion to make. "You must make a good impression on Mrs. Macapagal if you are going to succeed with your plan," Peralta explained. "I love Dadoy, but he's a bit under the influence of his wife, I'm afraid. You and your wife must have the Macapagals over to your house for a quiet private dinner."

When I told Jeanne she should get ready to have the vice-president and his wife to dinner, she gave me a long hard look and then exclaimed, "For eighteen months I've been creeping around trying to be invisible with only office parties and movies for entertainment and now I'm expected to have the Macapagals to dinner!"

Singapore had been a very social post and we had been encouraged to make the most of it. In Manila, with my "sergeant's file clerk's cover," as Jeanne called it, we were told to be very inconspicuous. "Well," she added after a moment, "it sounds exciting, in a dull sort of way."

Jeanne had no trouble getting back into her hostess role even though she had to suffer General Peralta's advice. He took it upon himself to drop by the house the afternoon of the dinner party to try to give her some helpful hints. She kept her temper and even offered him a drink. He stared at his scotch and water in the roly-poly glass she gave him. "We don't use glasses like this," he muttered disdainfully. "We do," she said.

I came home early to prepare for the party, for Peralta had also passed some last-minute tips to me by phone, and found my wife not in the best of moods as a result of the general's visit. "Who is this guy? What's his claim to fame?" she asked, after she told me what had happened.

"My dear, he's the man who got the highest marks next to General MacArthur they ever gave anyone at Ft. Leavenworth," I said. "Do you know what he told me? He wants us to have Ruthven rush out when Macapagal gets here and say she must have his autograph because she can't sleep with such a famous man in the house!"

I regret to say we did prostitute our twelve-year-old daughter by making her go through with Peralta's ploy, but we needn't have. The Macapagals were delightful and comfortable guests.

They apologized at once for arriving late. "We had car trouble," said Macapagal. "Our car is a wreck and I had to borrow Mel Mutoc's. You've seen my letter in the newspaper about why I turned in my official car, haven't you?"

I had. It had given me my first good laugh during my first weeks in the Philippines. On March 29, 1958, just a few weeks after I arrived, Macapagal's letter to the man in charge of the Malacañang garage had appeared in all papers. The vice-president had turned back the official car given him for business use saying that other vice-presidents had refused to use it and he knew why. He recited a long list of problems he had suffered with the aged vehicle that always seemed to break down at crucial moments—when he was riding in the parade welcoming President Diem, when he was due to make a speech at a college in the provinces, when his wife had substituted as official hostess, representing the First Lady at a meeting of the Catholic Women's League, when he and his wife were due at Ambassador Bohlen's for a diplomatic reception.

"Worst of all was the time we were going up the zigzag road to Baguio. You know what a dangerous mountain road that is?" Macapagal continued.

"Yes," Jeanne said, "that's why I've only been to Baguio twice."

"Well, I don't know how the driver managed to roll to a stop with no brakes when the road dipped," said the vice-president, "but he did. We had to hail a truck. The driver took us as far as he was going, to the outskirts of town, and then we took a jeepney to our official vice-presidential cottage."

Macapagal had other complaints about his treatment by President García. "The air-conditioning in my office is the only air-conditioning system in Malacañang that ever breaks down. And it breaks down about every other day," he told us. He also pointed out that his salary was smaller than that of the chief of the supreme court, the supreme court's associate justices, and even the senate president. "He gets sixteen thousand pesos a year and I get only fifteen," he said with a smile. "Of course, it's true I'm not doing anything, but that's García's fault, not mine."

We had several rounds of drinks, and were having a contest to see who could get out of our exceptionally deep chairs without using hands when Pedro announced dinner. After dinner, Jeanne and Eva Macapagal managed to have an interesting talk together not limited to girls' party chatter, Jeanne told me later. Macapagal and I retreated to the privacy of our master bedroom, whose air-conditioner provided excellent soundproofing, for a business talk. Pedro brought us in a bottle and some ice, and we sat together on the sofa. Macapagal asked to be allowed to take off his shoes.

As a result of this stocking-foot session, we agreed to putting Pelaez, in addition to Manahan and Manglapus, on the ticket, and Macapagal said he'd think hard about Vargas.

Serging Osmeña was the person who bothered me most. He

would call me at odd hours, even one time getting the American consul in Cebu out of bed to reach me for an "urgent message." He arranged meetings between him and me and Marcos. One night he called me to say, "We're at Marcos', and I'm sending a car to pick you up." I thought of course he meant the home of Ferdinand Marcos, but instead it turned out to be a restaurant run by a man named Marcos. He was with Senator Padilla, Congressman Cornelio Villareal, the number two Liberal in congress, and several newsmen to whom he paid subsidies for good stories about himself. From there he insisted we all go at his expense to one of the nightclubs on Dewey Boulevard and enjoy the services of some of the hostesses. As soon as I could I whispered to him I was expecting a call from Manahan and made my escape.

Another ploy he used to identify himself with me was to call me from his law office where he had one of the first amplified telephone receivers in the Philippines. These devices enable busy executives to keep on writing while answering the phone but also make it possible for everyone else who may be in the office to hear the voice of the person on the other end of the conversation.

The sessions between him and me and Ferdinand Marcos were interesting. In addition to the first breakfast, I had several other meetings with Macapagal at Mutoc's with Marcos present. Marcos and I both kept this secret from Serging. While always extremely affable, Marcos was terribly inscrutable in both houses. I could not really tell whose side he was on. Did he want a strong winning ticket, as he told Serging, or six Liberals no matter who they were so long as they included him, as I gathered when he was with Macapagal? Once I tried to get a rise out of him, and I did. I remarked at Serging's one afternoon that I had heard reliably that Macapagal had promised to serve only one term if elected president and then to support Padilla as his successor. "Ha," said Marcos, "he said the same thing to me too. God knows how many others he's said it to. Remember what I told you about him the first day we met? He'll do anything, absolutely anything, to get his own way." I didn't realize the man who was telling me this was the man who would destroy democratic government in the Philippines fourteen years later in order to get his. But I trusted him even less than I did Serging. Osmeña was transparently trying to enhance his position. Marcos wouldn't make his position clear.

I can't say for certain whether Osmeña's constant efforts to get on center stage caused it, but by the final week in July both sides were hardening their positions. Macapagal asked me to a night meeting to reconsider our earlier agreement. Meanwhile, Manahan demanded a showdown on the ticket decision publicly, although I had advised him not to. I had talked seriously a number of times with Pelaez and with Padilla and grown increasingly impressed with the sincerity and ability of both. They thought that even though a third party was not feasible in the Philippines for the reasons I have already mentioned, an independent senate slate was. Since the senate race was a free-for-all, individual arrangements could be made with leaders all over the country so that a few men, even the magical four, half a ticket, might win by a series of swaps for votes in key areas—some with strong Nationalists and some with strong Liberal leaders. Jimmy Ferrer thought so too, and showed me the arithmetic. The idea was now gaining momentum that if Macapagal insisted on trying to treat the question solely from the point of view that the 1959 election was but a prelude to his election to the presidency in 1961, an alternative was possible—form a small, four- or possibly six-man slate, elect Pelaez, Manahan, Manglapus, and maybe even General Vargas, and force a realignment of the entire opposition in 1961. I was attracted to the idea.

For one thing, I never heard from Macapagal any ideas about what kind of a country he wanted the Philippines to be. He was an intelligent man and a very capable politician but was he anything more? When I told Jocko I was beginning to think, like my Magsaysay friends, that "Macapagal is just a politician," he held up his hand.

"Let me tell you something," Richardson said. "I went to a small college in California with a man like Macapagal. The college was Whittier, and my classmate was a man named Richard Nixon. Look, Nixon was running for President of the United States even then.

"Nixon wanted to be president of the student council at Whittier. All the successful candidates for that office had always come from a jock-strap fraternity. Nixon reasoned he had to make that fraternity as step number one. So he went out for football. Hell, he couldn't begin to play football, but even though he fell all over himself, he managed to make the scrub team. That got him in the fraternity.

312

And he got elected president of the student council. If you're in politics, Joe, you have to be a politician all the time."

I disagreed. Or rather, I felt that while a successful politician had to work full-time at his job, a president of a country, to be worthy of the job, should be something more. Jocko's Nixon story didn't surprise me. I had heard the Checkers speech in 1952—the most repulsive display of chicanery I had ever listened to.

If there had been a lack of talent, a limited choice, I would have picked Macapagal hands down. It simply seemed to me that there were better men available—men who were politicians, but who had vision and integrity. If our purpose was not merely to enjoy playing politics in a country where it was easy to do so, but to revitalize the movement that had begun with Magsaysay so that one day the Philippines would be the showplace of democracy our propaganda operations had tried to make people think it was, Macapagal was not the man. Certainly, I couldn't see spending the U.S. taxpayers' money in an off-year election for the purpose of enhancing his chances of being president someday.

When Macapagal and I had our last evening negotiating session, it was as friendly as always. We met in a house in Pasay City where Mutoc said Macapagal held his most secret meetings. Macapagal said he was afraid that unless I could restrain Manahan's public utterances, he might have to renege on our earlier tentative agreement. I said he shouldn't worry, I'd take care of that, but I said I would have to insist on the four men being on the ticket—Manahan, Manglapus, Pelaez, and Vargas. He quickly said he would agree to the first three but simply couldn't go any further and maintain the position he felt he must have in the Liberal Party. I said I understood, but since that was the case, we might as well conclude our talk. We looked at each other a long moment, then we said good night.

It was the moment when I exercised the case officer's lonely responsibility of making a decision that only he could make and which he could report to his superiors any way he wished. It was my moment of arrogance—the quality the congressional investigations have revealed as a characteristic of a CIA operations officer.

The Grand Alliance, as my friends chose to call their independent senate candidate slate, was proclaimed on July 28. A six-man ticket was put together by adding to the basic four for whom I had been negotiating with Macapagal, two Liberals whom Macapagal had rejected in favor of even lesser-known politicians to whom he owed favors. The Grand Alliance thus represented all three parties—Nationalist, Progressive, and Liberal. Macapagal quickly moved to complete a Liberal ticket after I broke off our talks, and the Nationalists held a convention in Manila and named their slate on July 26. The campaign was ready to begin.

There was no question about the fact that the Liberal ticket, except for Marcos and Villareal, was undistinguished. The Nationalists', except for Amang Rodriguez and my landlady's lover, Fernando Lopez, was, if anything, worse. García had insisted that his notoriously corrupt secretary, Juan Pajo, be on the ticket—a fact that made for much rejoicing on the part of all the opposition elements. One figure remained in the balance, swaying between the Grand Alliance and the Liberals. This was Mariano Cueñco, the battle-scarred politico who had helped bring matters to a head with his May 19 speech denouncing corruption in the García administration.

I received a phone call just before the Grand Alliance was announced inviting me to breakfast with Cueñco. Part of the *media palabra* that went out on me among the politicians was my telephone number. Cueñco could by no stretch of the imagination be considered a fitting partner for the reformist Grand Alliance to court, but he had a lot of clout. Osmeña had promised me he would support the Grand Alliance, so that Cueñco's additional support for the GA should assure these candidates a huge vote in Cebu. Cueñco had, according to Macapagal's announcement, accepted a "guest slot" on the Liberal ticket, after the Progressive/Liberal coalition broke up. Why did he want to talk to me?

What he wanted was to arrange a deal to cover himself all around. He said he had heard that I was going to provide substantial support in the campaign so he wanted to assure me that, while he was apparently going along with Macapagal and accepting a slot on the Liberal ticket, his heart was really with the Grand Alliance. So, he said, he would drop all the Liberals from the ballots in Cebu except for Marcos and Villareal and replace them with Pelaez, Manahan, Manglapus, and General Vargas. He said he hoped we'd stay in touch during the campaign, especially in order to talk over financial problems as they might arise. I thanked him for his offer

314

of support and said it was an honor for me to be asked to join in the political activities of one of the country's distinguished veteran politicians.

The Cueñco conversation was my baptism in the campaign. It represented all the problems that would mark our effort to elect the independent candidates as well as the dilemma we never did resolve. As I have said before, the senate race was a free-for-all. It did not really involve any party tickets. It involved the efforts of twenty-two men to get themselves elected one way or another—eight Nationalists, eight Liberals, and six candidates of the Grand Alliance, each one needing to put together the best deal for himself. This I saw as our great opportunity, but convinced that our mission was to support the men who would reform the Philippines, I wondered just how many deals and what kind I could honestly support in the name of more decent politics.

Jimmy Ferrer, joined by Johnny San Juan—who, as he did in 1957, returned from supervising Eastern Construction Company activities in Vietnam to help—thought that if we would give them enough funds they could reconstruct enough of the old Magsaysay for President Movement to elect Manahan, Manglapus, Pelaez, and, just possibly, Vargas with a minimum of deals.

We didn't have that much money, and, once again, we followed the policy of hedging our bets in spending what we had. Jocko insisted we give some funds to Macapagal. Macapagal and I had not parted bad friends, and the old channel to him through the deep-cover agent still existed. If the Grand Alliance won, we would have the exciting prospect of helping the Filipinos rebuild the progressive government of Magsaysay and, hopefully, go on to even greater things. If Macapagal and his Liberals won, we would still have the prospect of a change of administration led by a friend.

This was not Indonesia in 1954 and we didn't have a million dollars to use in our efforts. Our election project was approved for only $250,000. I used all my persuasive talent and finally got Richardson to agree to let me spend $200,000 on the Grand Alliance, while he arranged to give $50,000 to Macapagal. Jimmy and Johnny presented me with a well-drawn-up organizational plan that would cost a minimum of one million pesos. In addition, I had promised help on a direct personal basis to Pelaez and to Padilla, who had been named campaign manager. Fortunately, station pe-

315

sos were acquired in Hong Kong at four to one instead of the official Philippine rate of two to one. But even this black market money would not stretch far enough to meet the commitments I had made during my days as Mr. Substantial Support. Osmeña, naturally, asked me for money too. I didn't give him any money because I thought that in my financially embarrassed state he should have helped me and not vice versa.

Putting aside politics for the moment, Serging just at this point ran a little operation on the stock market that, when I found out about it, I thought he should have cut me in on for the benefit of the Grand Alliance. I told him so when I refused to give him any funds. Osmeña had floated stock of an oil company several years before. There was no oil anyone had ever heard of in the Philippines, and in the summer of 1959 the stock sold for ten cents a share. Serging's operational mind went to work. He hired an American geologist to come to the Philippines to check on oil deposits and launched a propaganda effort about this geologist's visit that produced results. While the geologist disappeared in Cebu, newspaper reports about his explorations flowed like the oil that wasn't there. The stock rose to one dollar and fifty cents. It fell back again to its old rate when the geologist left, his exploration a failure. I told Serging that if he had been a true friend, he would have tipped me off about this operation and I could have stretched my budget to cover all our campaign costs.

A week after the Grand Alliance was announced I met Jimmy and Johnny in the A. Mabini safehouse and gave them 500,000 pesos to start the campaign. "Did you walk down A. Mabini with that much money on you?" Jimmy asked.

"Sure," I said.

"Look, I've been worried about you for some time," Jimmy said. "You're pretty exposed. It's not carrying money that worries me so much, it's President García. The way Serging has blown your cover I'm sure the president must have heard about you. Don't you know, you can get a guy murdered in Manila for just ten bucks? I'm going to get some of my boys in Parañaque to give you some protection from now on."

After that, street vendors of various types began to pass regularly by my house. Street cleaning crews would linger to take breaks on the corner. Jimmy again was fixing things up.

As November 10 grew closer, Jimmy became increasingly concerned that the election was something that could not be fixed up. I juggled other funds at my disposal and managed to reach the million-peso mark called for by his operational plan. I also was able to give some help to Pelaez and Padilla. Padilla contributed from his own personal funds. He was hoping to play an important role in the 1961 elections if the Grand Alliance won in 1959 and forced a realignment of opposition leadership. I was hoping so too. He won my heart when, after the night Osmeña forced us together in the nightclub, he expressed his contempt for the tactic by telling me of the fight he had with his press secretary. "He's always telling me to give him large sums of money so he can give it to newsmen to spend on nights on the town like Osmeña does. He says that's the only way I can get the kind of good press coverage I should have," Padilla explained.

"I tell him that if he wants me to give him money to buy the newspaper guys' kids some shoes, okay, but I'm not going to give them money to waste on nightclub hostesses. If they need money, like he claims, surely it must be to help with basic expenses."

My secret ticket for 1959 was Pelaez for president—the man I thought had the broadest vision and quickest mind of all the talented men I had met, and Padilla for vice-president—the only man in Philippine politics who refused to waste money on the whoring habits of the newsmen who made the senators and congressmen look good in the morning press.

Padilla's involvement in the Grand Alliance provided us the only cover we had for our funding since he was known to be wealthy. The expense we couldn't afford to spend enough money on, even with Padilla's help, was sample ballots. As Cuenco had explained to me, they were the key to obtaining the kind of ticket-swapping deals that won senatorial elections. The Filipino voters had to be able to write their names and also be able to fill in blank ballots with the names of the persons they were voting for. This was the level of functional literacy required for voting. Candidates, therefore, printed and distributed sample ballots with their own names at the top of the ballot, filling up the rest of the blanks with the names of those other candidates with whom they had made deals.

Since the Grand Alliance was not an officially listed party—only the Nationalists and Liberals were—they did not have poll watchers supplied free of charge by the government. This was a large item in Jimmy's budget, paying for GA poll watchers. Without them almost anything one might think of could happen to votes and voters that the GA might attract. Hence, there were not many funds left for sample ballots. So Jimmy began to work on deals. Some I thought met the test of probity we set for our reformists who were to bring a new ethic and a new hope to Philippine politics. But when he proposed making a deal with Amang Rodriguez and Fernando Lopez, I felt I had to say no. This may have lost the Grand Alliance the election.

The first returns from Manila late on the night of November 10 were all that we could possibly have hoped for. With one-third of the vote counted, only Rodriguez and Lopez were in the winning eight column. Pelaez, Manglapus, Manahan, and Vargas, plus Marcos and one other Liberal, appeared to be winning the other six senate seats. I checked with Jimmy, feeling we should probably begin planning a victory party. He was glum. "Manila isn't the Philippines. Lacson helped us here. You see, he's so far ahead of the García candidate for mayor the guy has already conceded. Lacson put us on his sample ballot. We'll be in trouble when the provincial vote comes in."

The Lacson deal was one I hadn't heard about. I hoped now Jimmy had ignored my puritanical instructions elsewhere. He hadn't.

By the next morning, it appeared that maybe Pelaez and Manglapus might pull through. By Thursday they had dropped to tenth and eleventh. And that is where they remained. Manahan finished thirteenth and Vargas eighteenth. Our two GA Liberals were number twenty-one and twenty-two—the very last positions in the race.

Ferdinand Marcos won the election. He topped the list with almost 300,000 votes more than the second-place winner, who was Genaro Magsaysay, the late president's younger brother. Genaro had not only broken with the family tradition and the idealism of his late brother's friends, he had married the daughter of Amang Rodriguez, the man who knew that "politics is addition." Fernando Lopez came in third. Cueñco, of course, won. Also one more Liberal candidate made it. The man the station considered the winner at that point, however, was Macapagal. He did too.

Soon Jocko and I began a series of meetings with all the princi-

318

pals. Jocko's point was that the election had proved García could be beaten in 1961, and that the quarrel over who would lead the opposition to victory was over. Macapagal had won the right to lead them all.

Several months later Des Fitzgerald came out to Manila and so did Richard Bissell. Bissell had replaced Frank Wisner as DDP the previous year when Wisner suffered a nervous breakdown. They came partly to review the election operation but also for the Far Eastern area chiefs of station meeting. In those days these meetings took place annually in the John Hay Air Force Base, the U.S. Armed Forces Rest and Recreation Center for the Far East, in the lovely mountain town of Baguio.

I talked to both Des and Bissell about the election operation.

Des said to me, "We've paid our last debt to the Magsaysay boys. They'll have to join up with Macapagal or we'll have to forget them." Jocko wanted me to stay on in the Philippines through the 1961 elections. Des thought I had been overexposed and wanted me to come back to Washington and be chief of the Philippines desk.

This was not welcome news to me. I had not thought I had been paying any debts to anyone for past deeds or services but that I had been trying to create something new and better. I did not want to have anything further to do with the Philippines on the terms he offered. I told him I did not want the Washington assignment.

Bissell was more flexible in his view of what happened. Of course, to him the Philippines was only a relatively minor responsibility. He was, I thought, a more likely college professor than a man of action of the Fitzgerald type. Bissell was a noted economist, in fact, and had been one of the architects of the success of the Marshall Plan before coming into the CIA. He and I had a pleasant talk about the election. He told me gently, "Don't worry about it. We don't always win."

On an April evening in 1961, I would see Bissell when he too had lost. His defeat—the disaster of the Bay of Pigs—was terrible in every conceivable way—for a thousand brave Cubans, for the U.S. government, for the Kennedy administration, for the CIA, and for his career. He was almost as calm then as when he consoled me on the defeat of the Grand Alliance.

I was not calm about the Grand Alliance defeat for a long time. If only I had been given the funds I needed, if I had let Jimmy make some more deals—these kinds of regrets stayed with me.

I went about the tasks assigned me as best I could. I not only worked with Jocko in joint meetings to try to heal the wounds, he let me try my own hand with the relationships we both thought I could handle best alone as a result of my work of the last several months. We didn't worry about exposure. Thus, I got together with both Macapagal and Pelaez at a Lions Club luncheon. This went so well that Macapagal, when his turn came to speak, beamed at both Pelaez and me and said, "When I lost a senate race as closely as Senator Pelaez just did, I never dreamed that in only two years I would be vice-president. I think history may repeat itself." The crowd applauded warmly.

In 1961, the winning ticket was Macapagal and Pelaez. Manahan and Manglapus won senate seats. The new coalition we started working on after November, 1959, swept the elections. Four years later, Macapagal's ploy of promising the presidential succession to every rival backfired. Ferdinand Marcos demanded his promised chance to succeed Macapagal be honored. So did Pelaez. Macapagal, who never intended to honor his word, would yield to neither of them. He wanted to run again. Pelaez and Marcos bolted the Liberals and fought it out for the Nationalist nomination. Marcos, with the help of his powerful father-in-law, Daniel Romualdez, the boss of Leyte, and the other old Nationalist clansmen, won. He easily defeated Macapagal in November, 1965. After one term as president, Marcos ran again and was victorious. He then declared himself the dictator of the Philippines.

I read about these events in Washington and in Argentina. I couldn't help thinking things might not have taken this turn if the Grand Alliance had won. I was in Mexico City when Marcos declared Philippine democracy dead. I was sorry I had not been able to stop his being elected to the senate in 1959.

When I thought of the wreckage of political institutions in the Philippines, I thought of Jimmy Ferrer's car. His country was now as bad off, it seemed to me, as his car had been, and I hadn't done enough about either. Jimmy had begged me to sell him my car when I left Manila.

As in Singapore, my car in Manila was a quasi-personal vehicle. Regulations forbad me to sell him my Ford. I couldn't tell Jimmy

320

this, the station administrative officer insisted, I had to pretend I had found a better buyer. I ignored this nonsense and told Jimmy the truth.

Typically, the last time I saw Ferrer and we had said goodbye, he returned and knocked on my gate five minutes later. As usual, he couldn't start his car. I backed my Ford out of the driveway and had to push him for two blocks before his engine turned over.

18

"There Will Be No Communist Government in Latin America While I Am DDP"

One day in late November, 1960, an old college friend, who was working with the Kennedy talent-search task force, asked me to lunch. Knowing I was a member of the Clandestine Services because he had been one once himself, he wanted to talk to me about a possible future Deputy Director Plans.

"You know," he said in opening the conversation, "after the President, the DDP is the most important man in the U.S. government. When you consider the money he can spend from unvouchered funds and the kinds of operations he can get into, he could easily get the country so deeply involved in a situation that started out as a simple covert action activity we couldn't get ourselves out of it."

I realized exactly what he meant and thought immediately that since coming back from the Philippines my major concern had been just such a thing. I was producing worldwide propaganda guidances about Castro's Cuba to make sure that CIA's Wurlitzer was playing with all stops out on the theme. Frank Wisner always referred to CIA's worldwide propaganda assets as his Wurlitzer, and a unit of the senior Covert Action Staff, known as the Propaganda Guidance Section, of which I was now chief, produced guidance for all stations to provide the score for this great organ. Although Wisner was gone, the new DDP had not changed Wisner's concept or method of operation in this regard, except that what had been the Psychological and Political Warfare Staff was now called the Covert Action Staff.

My friend's evaluation of the importance of the DDP was not only accurate, in my opinion, but undoubtedly explained why the mild-mannered, professorial Bissell had not only made no changes in the operational style and methods of the flamboyant Frank Wisner, who liked to be called "Wiz," but had reportedly made a remark that seemed completely out of character with the man I had talked to in Manila. I had heard that, in discussing the precipitous pace at which Fidel Castro seemed to be turning his revolt against the brutal dictatorship of Batista in Cuba into a Communist revolution since coming to power in 1959, Bissell had declared, "There will be no Communist government in Latin America while I am DDP." That I recognized as the language of a man who knows he has great power and is affected by its intoxicating qualities.

I knew that Bissell was now directing a supersecret operation designed to bring down the Castro regime—a version on a larger scale of the Guatemalan operation of 1954 that had deposed Arbenz by armed intervention. As we talked, I was disturbed to discover that my friend on the Kennedy team seemed to know something about this too. The Cuban task force's existence could not be hidden from Clandestine Services' employees, but every effort was being made to keep its purposes secret. Naturally, a task force had come into existence as the Cuban situation took on more ominous tones—everyone in the offices in the Clandestine Services had come to expect this—but the story was put out that they were engaged in planning and analysis, while, of course, running what intelligence collection operations and undertaking what propaganda activities they could. Only a very limited number of people who had a "need to know," as I did in my particular job, had been told the truth. One of the ironies of the Bay of Pigs, CIA's greatest fiasco, was that so few of the Agency's professional staff knew anything about the preparation and launching of the operation while almost every Cuban exile in Miami knew practically everything.

From what Tom was saying, I felt that not only had the Presi-

324

dent-elect been briefed since November 8, but probably before that. Tom was not so close to the new President that he could know as much as he seemed to unless the "secret" information had had time to trickle through some layers of Kennedy staff. The reason Tom was interested in talking about a future DDP was, as he said, "We expect Bissell to be named Director of CIA after he pulls off the Cuban operation." I remembered that late in the campaign Kennedy had startled me, and many others, by coming out for aid to Cuban exiles and other Cubans who might wish to rebel against Castro. He seemed to be anticipating the Cuban operation, I thought, fearing perhaps that it might come off before election day and if successful cost him the election.

Nixon would write two years later in his book *Six Crises* that he had thought so too. He would complain that the matter was an excellent illustration of the "disadvantage that confronts a candidate who also represents an incumbent administration."* At the time, I credited Nixon with doing a good job of maintaining cover when he denounced Kennedy's statement, pointing out that we couldn't intervene in Cuban affairs because of our treaty commitments to nonintervention in Latin American affairs and because of the UN charter. It was Nixon's job to uphold the principle of presidential plausible denial of covert operations—the principle that meant that we would carry out such activities in such a way that the top level of the U.S. government could deny any involvement and the denial could be believed because of the smoothness of our execution of the task.

As I knew, the Cuban operation had been approved through the usual Special Group process of the National Security Council and okayed by President Eisenhower. Nixon, I also knew, had been a principal advocate of its approval. I had even been allowed to read the Covert Action Staff's copy of the approval that had been given on March 17, 1960, when I had been briefed about the role that it was desired our staff propaganda guidance should play in its support. Sworn to secrecy as I was, and since the Vice President of the United States had gone to the lengths he had to dissimulate during the campaign, I figured the only thing I could do in the face of my friend's provocative remark about the Cuban affair was to lie like Nixon.

*Richard M. Nixon, *Six Crises* (New York: Doubleday, 1962), p. 351.

"Well, I don't know what you're talking about, Tom," I said, "but I think that someday Des Fitzgerald should be DDP. He would understand how to use the power of the office and he would enjoy doing it."

This would not be the last conversation I would have with friends on President Kennedy's staff about filling top jobs in CIA. After the Bay of Pigs disaster swept both Allen Dulles and Richard Bissell from their high offices in the Agency, I was amazed to have another old college chum, who was on the White House personnel selection staff that engaged in locating people for top positions, ask me whom I would recommend for Director of Central Intelligence. On the phone he had asked me over to his office in the old State Department Building that had been converted into White House Executive Staff offices to talk about something important, but I never dreamed it was going to be something that important.

Before I fully recovered from the shock of what he had asked me, he produced a class list of our fellow members of Harvard '44. He was class secretary. Glancing at the list for a few moments and then up at me, he said, "I'm just thinking out loud, but what about your old roommate Bill? I see he was in OSS and he's running his father's manufacturing business successfully these days. I know the Boss and Bobby are looking for someone from the business world, but some OSS experience seems important to me."

I knew the administration was looking for new faces, younger men for high positions, but being asked to suggest the guy who had been my roommate after freshman year to be my own big chief rather took my breath away. Not that I didn't like the idea—I certainly liked my old roommate, with whom I had remained friends ever since, but to have the chance to help him achieve his ambition to enter government service, which had been frustrated when he had gotten out of Harvard's Littauer School of Government and failed to find a job in pre-Korean War Washington, by making him head of CIA, boggled me. "Yeah," I answered, but I'm afraid rather weakly in my condition.

John McCone, another businessman, got the job. I don't think that my failure to support Bill vigorously enough had any deciding influence on the ultimate selection. For one thing, there was quite a difference between John McCone's multi-million-dollar enterprise built during World War II and Bill's hospital and hotel linen manufacturing business. Nevertheless, the way Kennedy's team went about fortifying the New Frontier and otherwise doing the business of government was always surprising. It was also stimulating if they were friends of yours, as many were in my case. If they were not, the reaction was usually one of stuttering rage, as was the case of most Clandestine Services officers who were on the front line during the Bay of Pigs.

The Bay of Pigs was a terrible trauma for everyone involved. It was an event that so severely crippled U.S. foreign policy that the Soviets felt free to bring the Berlin situation to a point of tension that hadn't been known since the early days of the cold war and the Berlin airlift of the Truman years when they had first shut off the city. Khrushchev also began to undertake a series of adventures in Africa confident he couldn't be stopped. The image of President Kennedy and his idealist team come to revitalize the country after eight years of drift under the rule of a sick and aging President, whose major concern seemed to be his golf game, suddenly was so tarnished that no amount of rubbing seemed likely to remove the stain.

The confident atmosphere prevailing the day I talked with Tom and the sense of great things in the making that prevailed in the offices of the Cuban task force, which I visited almost daily in the summer and fall of 1960, evaporated so completely that it was almost impossible to recall that there ever had been such a time of hope and heroics.

The result naturally was that all those concerned with the catastrophe came forth with explanations assigning the blame to someone else. Perhaps nothing that the Agency ever did has had so much written about it. Paul Blackstock, whom my old Harvard professor sent me to see about a job in the Pentagon when I first went to Washington seeking to be an intelligence analyst, made a case study of the Bay of Pigs in his scholarly investigation of covert political operations, *The Strategy of Subversion.* David Wise and Thomas B. Ross began their exposé of CIA, *The Invisible Government,* with four Bay of Pigs chapters. Dozens of magazine articles were published, including an article in *Fortune* by Charles Murphy that the CIA inspired in order to whitewash its role. The Kennedy team returned the fire with a series of self-serving accounts designed to dissolve the whitewash. Of these the one written by Arthur Schlesinger in his story of the Kennedy years, *A Thousand Days,* I think, is the least misleading. Howard Hunt, after his arrest in the Watergate affair, wrote *Give Us This Day,* an apology from a warrior who was on the line. He reveals more about the reasons for the failure than he intended to, in my opinion.

I do not want to add to the welter of words written by so many interested parties. From my position on the fringe of the operation I believe I saw some things about it then which I still think now deserve to be recorded. There were many reasons why the operation failed. There are always many reasons why any operation does. One may well have been the Kennedy men, whose ability to cover their lack of substantive knowledge on national security and a host of other matters with a lofty, ringing rhetoric, was probably unmatched in American history. Our officers involved in the operation thought so almost to a man, cursing them and blaming them for the "failure to approve the second air strike" at Castro's air force to which they liked to assign nearly sole responsibility for the failure. To me a large measure of fault lay in the character defects of my fellow cold warriors. Perhaps it was my recent failure in the Philippines, which at the time of the Cuban operation was still such a sore wound, that enabled me to see these defects in them for I saw them in myself.

The first of these defects is arrogance. This had led me to feel I could bend the reality of Philippine politics to fit the hopes I had. It made me think I couldn't lose and led me to ignore the signs of impending failure. It was clear to me that the Grand Alliance could not win without making deals with Amang Rodriguez and Fernando Lopez, but I chose to ignore it and continued to provide funds for sample ballots for the fledgling organization Ferrer had formed and trusted somehow things would turn out right. The Cuban task force claimed that when President Kennedy and his advisers had ruled against the involvement of any backup U.S. air support on April 5, 1961, they knew the doom of the invasion forces had been sealed. This was ten days before the brigade hit the beach. Why didn't they tell the President they thought they would fail? Why didn't they tell him that, in view of this decision, the invasion should be called off?

A second flaw in us all, in those days of great adventure, was career opportunism. Someone said to me during the Philippine election campaign of 1959, "If you win, you'll be known as the second Ed Lansdale." My friend Tom was right when he said that Bissell would be the next Director of CIA if he successfully engineered the

Bay of Pigs operation. Everyone involved was saying this. They were also saying that Tracy Barnes, the man who had directed the Guatemalan coup in 1954 and was directing the Cuban show, would succeed Bissell as DDP. All the officers further down the line were keenly aware of what a victory over Castro would mean to them. Dave Phillips, the propaganda chief of the task force with whom I worked in preparing my worldwide propaganda guidances, tried to recruit me to go to Miami by saying, "It will be good for your career. You better join us before it's too late and you've missed the boat."

I think that both these blemishes had as much to do with the failure of the Cuban invasion as the decisions in the White House. I saw them cropping up at a number of points during the summer and fall of 1960 and the fateful spring of 1961.

My being involved in any way with these events was a direct fallout of my Manila experience. When I did not accept the Philippine desk chief's job, I heard nothing for a number of months about what my next assignment would be. Then came the news. I was asked to take the position of covert action chief in Korea. This was even less welcome than the first offer. What could I do in such a job? I asked myself. What covert action were we undertaking in a police state? In addition to being a political situation I found extremely distasteful, the personal situation, the living arrangements, would be even worse. If Manila had too many overtones of U.S. military mission life to suit Jeanne and me, Korea was an armed camp. The PX, the commissary, the officers' club, the base movie would mark the boundaries of our lives. I decided that it was probably time for me to leave the Far Eastern Division, and with Jocko's permission, I wrote and told Des so. Meanwhile, my friend Curly came through Manila on a business trip. He had recently been named chief of the senior Covert Action Staff. He said he had a good job for me. Thus, I ended up in the propaganda guidance role.

The propaganda guidance section was part of a larger unit that provided various kinds of support to propaganda operations around the world. The chief of this propaganda branch, as it was called, through whom I was supposed to report to Curly, was one of the authentic originals who cropped up here and there in the Clandestine Services. Henry was a huge fat Austrian, who as a young man had been a follower of the Austrian Socialist leader Engelbert Dollfuss, whom Hitler had murdered in 1934 on his way to annexing Austria to his Third Reich. He had tangled with treacherous Communists who helped betray the Socialists. He had served time in jail as a political prisoner, and had successfully fled before the outbreak of World War II and served with distinction in OSS morale operations against Germany throughout the war. He was one of the first OPC men in Germany. Unfortunately, he tripped up in organizing large-scale anti-Communist activities, and fell into a mire of ex-Nazis and Soviet infiltrators and had to be pulled out. He never served overseas again.

Henry generated animosity daily. He was convinced that he knew more about Communism, about propaganda, and about the proper techniques of propaganda operations than anyone else in the Clandestine Services, or the world for that matter. As a staff officer his role was supposed to be limited to giving advice and assistance when sought. This was something his own view of his competence and his German soul both found unbearably restrictive. Thus, when his advice was sought, he gave more than anyone wanted to hear, and whenever and wherever possible he sought to impose his ideas although they were unsolicited. Because he was fat and dogmatic, he reminded me of my first boss, Dr. Wing, the chairman of the Dickinson history department. The trick of getting along with both of them was to ignore them without letting them realize you were.

Not all of Henry's ideas were bad, however. Some were remarkably good. This was the tragedy of his fate—he should have been heeded many times when he wasn't. For example, his great interest in the summer of 1960, when I returned from Manila and joined his office, was the rift that was growing between the Soviet Union and the Chinese. He was convinced it was the most significant development of the cold war and should be the major preoccupation not only of covert operations, but intelligence and the entire policy-making structure of the U.S. government—the State Department, the Defense Department, and the National Security Council. At his insistence a study group had been formed to examine the matter. Members of the group consisted of representatives from China operations, from Soviet operations, from the Communist Branch of the Counter Intelligence Staff, from the Office of the Deputy Director for Intelligence, the overt analyst side of CIA, and Henry, plus experts on different aspects of the problem who joined the group from time to time. As long as I was associated with him, while he made progress with the China operations' representatives, and, of course, had the complete support of the DDI intelligence analysts, he could never convince the representatives of Soviet operations or the Counter Intelligence Staff that the "world Communist movement," in the existence of which they believed with the fervor of early Christian martyrs or Mohammed's desert warriors, could possibly split. Until I retired from the Agency, in fact, there were many members of the Counter Intelligence Staff who insisted the whole thing was a mammoth deception operation designed to catch us off guard—the arguments they used against Henry's ideas in 1960.

Another good insight Henry had, I learned the first time we discussed my new responsibilities, was that the Cuban task force's plan to destroy Castro would lead to disaster.

The man I was to replace as chief of the guidance section was having some problems working out his new assignment, Henry explained to me, so that during the overlap period, he had a special operation he wanted me to handle. He said it was so secret that of all the officers on the Covert Action Staff only he and Curly and the chief of the Paramilitary Branch had been briefed on it. This tightly held secret was the actual purpose of the Cuban task force. He said that when he was finished briefing me, he would let me read the CA Staff's copy of the NSC directive that had ordered the overthrow of Fidel Castro.

"The first thing you must understand," said Henry, "is the special nature of our Western Hemisphere Division. Colonel J. C. King, the division chief, has the unique distinction of being the only division chief in the Clandestine Services who has held his job since CIA was organized. The reason for this, as far as I can make out, is the special nature of our relationship to Latin America. I'm afraid it's the one place in the world where, as much as I hate to admit it, the Communists' propaganda claim that the United States is an exploiting imperialist power can't easily be denied. U.S. business interests have huge investments in Latin America, and the U.S. government's policy seems to be that the protection of these interests should control completely what we do in Latin America.

"Colonel King was an Army attaché in Buenos Aires during the war, and he has many links with the area. Among them are the close relations he developed with the FBI. As you know, the FBI was responsible for counterintelligence operations against the Nazis throughout Latin America during the war. When we came into existence, they reluctantly withdrew. Colonel King was able to convince a number of their officers to join him, and he's manned his division almost entirely with these FBI men. They and he all are close to American and Latin business leaders. They also are in with the police forces and local intelligence organizations. Of course, they supported Batista to the hilt. Fidel Castro's victory was a shock to J. C.'s men and their American business friends in Havana, who owned everything of consequence in the country either directly or through Cuban associates, from which they'll probably never recover. Before Castro had settled into office, the businessmen ran to Washington to tell President Eisenhower Castro was a dangerous Communist who had to be overthrown at any cost. J. C. ran right along with them. And so we have the Cuban task force."

Henry said he didn't want to get into the question of whether Castro had always been a Communist or not, although, he said, Castro simply didn't seem to fit the model of a disciplined Marxist Communist Party leader that thirty years of experience with Communists had taught him to expect. It was too late now to worry about this, we were committed to a course of action, and, as good soldiers, we must do all we could to carry out our orders successfully. He was bothered about the chances of success, however, for several reasons.

"First of all, as in the case of Guatemala, when the director had to see a covert action program carried out, he has had to push J. C. and his officers aside. They know only how to talk with police chiefs and to exchange information with security officers of American companies. Sophisticated political or propaganda operations, they are not good at.

"So again, Tracy Barnes is really running the operation and the task force, as he did our Guatemalan operation. He's brought in many of the old team. I did the propaganda on the Guatemalan operation, and Tracy asked me to do it again, but I said no."

The reasons Henry had refused the assignment were, first, he thought that, although J. C. King had been pushed aside again, he would continue to try to assert the interests of the old Batista followers and agents, since American business interests in Cuba were vastly greater than they had been in Guatemala and, hence, the businessmen would hound J. C. to put their Batista friends back in power. Henry was sure that there would be continual problems as a result, the most serious being that any attempt to put Batista or any of his followers back in power would doom the operation to failure. "The reason Castro won," said Henry, "was that everybody in Cuba, except J. C.'s friends, hated Batista. Any invasion force that goes in for the purpose of putting him back just won't have the support of the Cuban people. I think a lot of good propaganda operations, but they can't produce miracles."

Henry's second fear was, in a sense, an extension of his first. He wasn't sure that Castro didn't have a much greater following than WH Division liked to think, even though he had been brutal and killed and imprisoned hundreds of people. "I'm afraid he may have a real power base. This was something Arbenz didn't have. I think we must not fool ourselves that Cuba is another Guatemala."

Finally what bothered Henry was that the whole operation was going to be almost impossible to hide. "In the case of Guatemala," he pointed out, "we worked from a neighboring country. Now we're working out of Miami. I don't think it's enough to say that, historically, Cuban revolutionary movements were supported by Americans and call that cover." More seriously, he was concerned that the signs of preparations could not be kept out of the American press. It was not like planning an invasion of Guatemala from a neighboring police state, he observed. Above all, the basing of such an operation in the United States, if not an outright violation of CIA's charter, was skirting too close to it to suit him.

"For all these reasons, I'm afraid it just won't work," he concluded, "and if it's blown, it could destroy the Agency. I hate to see that happen, especially over a tiny Latin country, when so much needs to be done about China and Russia."

This attitude, naturally, had led to another of his excursions into the realm of offering unsolicited and unwanted advice. He was more or less *persona non grata* with Tracy and the task force. He wanted me to see what I could do to help them as we had been ordered to do. (He also wanted me to find out what was really going on since no one would tell him.) He figured I was a new face who might be accepted.

Our propaganda guidance section divided its workload by assigning an officer to assist each area division. I was assigned the Western Hemisphere Division, in addition to my responsibilities reading into replacing the chief. We produced "Bi-Weekly Propaganda Guidances"—a booklet that took up significant developments in the various areas of the world which the divisions considered all stations should be aware of so they could produce newspaper or magazine articles or broadcasts, depending on assets available, that would make it appear that independent world opinion was supporting the position regarding such developments that CIA wanted given support. Copies of such articles were mailed to cover addresses each station maintained. Thus, an article about Berlin might be printed in Buenos Aires and a copy mailed to Berlin. Berlin would get it reprinted or, at least, mentioned in a German paper or news analysis broadcast and German readers or listeners would then think that the Argentines, not Americans, were saying whatever it was CIA wanted said.

The responsibility of the chief of the propaganda guidance section was to have these guidances coordinated with the State Department and with USIS. This directive had been given by the Operations Coordination Board, OCB, established by the National Security Council to insure all operations of all U.S. agencies working abroad achieved some common purpose. The OCB was one of the clumsiest bureaucratic devices anyone ever devised, but it fitted President Eisenhower's style of making decisions by committee. As everyone knows, this is about the poorest possible way to make a decision. I recall sitting on OCB panels on Indonesia and Malaya. Each agency representative had obviously been briefed that whatever the proposed U.S. objective toward the country of concern might be, his job was primarily to safeguard the role his agency wanted to play in regard to it. The result was that every point was compromised so that, in the end, no one's toes were tread upon, but no action responsibilities were ever put in forceful terms or even very clearly. As the CIA representative, I was always instructed to say nothing specific but to insist that what we might do about any matter was to be subsumed under some such clause as "other agencies will take appropriate action."

The clearance process for the propaganda guidances was the same sort of farce. After the section's officers had discovered what the divisions wanted to discuss in the guidances and had written these topics up and had them okayed again by the divisions, I would bundle them over to the State Department, where they would be circulated to cleared State desk officers and to USIS. I would take one two-week batch with me each time I went and receive the comments on the batch I had delivered two weeks before. The only thing I enjoyed about the business was that the State Department officer who had been assigned the task of supervising the clearance procedure had been the economic officer when I first arrived in Singapore; Bob Boylan introduced me to him the first time he took me to the consulate general's offices and told him he was going to have to introduce me to Jantzen's special people. The man never caught on to the fact that I was CIA. He was astounded to see me bring the guidances. I think he always wondered whether or not USIS might be up to some tricky business, assigning me to such a job.

Even though I stressed each time that these guidances were intended for use by assets not attributable to the U.S. government, and, which, therefore, were trying to make oblique points and not merely mouth the words of the USIS press officer or the State Department spokesman on the subject, the guidances were always watered down so they were as nearly like the official statements as my State and USIS friends could make them. Playing safe was their primary professional skill.

The worst job of all was trying to clear themes on Cuba. I knew the themes were intended to provide a long-range buildup for the day the Cuban brigade hit the beach and liberated the country. None of the officers with whom I cleared the guidances knew of the brigade's existence. Furthermore, when I began to work on the Cuban problem, we still maintained diplomatic relations with Castro. These were not severed until January, 1961. Thus the heavy dose of "Castro Communism" that I tried to make them swallow was especially difficult for these diplomats to take. All I could do was continue to try.

The day after Henry briefed me, I read the NSC directive of March 17, 1960. This ordered two types of activity be undertaken by CIA. The first was to form a unified Cuban exile political group which would be capable of replacing Castro and in whose name the operation would be undertaken. The second was to train a Cuban guerrilla force which would be able to establish a foothold on the island and enable the new government we had formed to proclaim itself. A fundamental assumption of the paper was that the Cuban people would rally to the new cause, once it had shown its strength. The paper suggested the formation of the new Cuban exile group

335

be completed within six months. No specific date was mentioned, but presumably the operation would get under way in August, I thought.

I next made myself acquainted with the covert action chief on Colonel King's Western Hemisphere Division staff because I was supposed to work not just on Cuba but to cover all topics of interest to WH Division. I explained, however, that I was also supposed to support the Cuban task force and asked to be introduced to the appropriate officer.

Paul, my new acquaintance, was the kind of down-to-earth Pennsylvania Dutchman I had grown up with. We immediately formed not only a business relationship but a friendship. He was never taken in by any of the con men on the Cuban task force, of which there were more than a few. Paul and I lived through the whole experience consuming all their bluster and dramatics like so much Philadelphia scrapple.

Paul suggested, before I really got into things, I read up on Latin America and become familiar with the U.S. stake involved. I recalled Henry's briefing. I soon had digested the statistics that bore out what he had said concerning J. C. King and his business friends.

In 1960 American private investment in Latin America amounted to $8 billion. The total U.S. private investment in Europe at that time was less than $5.5 billion. One-fourth of all U.S. exports, I found, went to Latin America, and one-third of our imports came from there. Of the seventy-seven articles listed as strategic materials to be stockpiled in World War II, thirty were produced in large amounts in the countries to the south of us. Ninety percent of all quartz crystals, two-thirds of the antimony, half the bauxite and beryl, one-third of the lead, one-fourth of the copper that we needed came from these countries. Zinc, tin, tungsten, manganese, petroleum, and iron ore also were found in substantial amounts in Latin America. Two items, not strategic materials, but staples of every American household, coffee and sugar, were very significant. Almost all of these two products consumed in the United States came from our good neighbors of the hemisphere. Annual trade, both ways, totaled more than $8 billion.

Like many people born and raised in the northeastern part of the United States, I had never given much serious thought to Latin America. Its image was for me the one that Hollywood presented with Carmen Miranda and Wallace Berry as Pancho Villa portraying the people of the area. I was educated to think that Europe was the only area outside the continental United States which was of any great concern to America. World War II and nine years in the Clandestine Services had made me appreciate Asia. Now I was learning that Latin America, economically speaking, was far more significant than either of these parts of the world. I may not have been paying any attention to Latin America, but a lot of people had, and they had gotten rich in the process. I was very eager to become involved in what we were doing there, and what we were doing was getting ready to throw Fidel Castro out.

Paul introduced me to Dave Phillips—the head of the Cuban task force's propaganda branch. I had heard of Dave from the man who had come out to Manila to be Jocko's deputy the latter part of my tour there. Bill Caldwell was one of J. C. King's FBI men and had been chief of station when Castro had taken over. Although he was certainly in no way responsible for this bad turn in the affairs of the U.S. ambassador's good friend Batista, Bill had to leave Havana, and a place was found for him in the Philippines. He had told me one day, in the course of discussing our propaganda operations in Manila, that he was surprised at how sophisticated they were. He said, "When they told me I should get some propaganda writing started in Chile, I went out and recruited a young American who was bumming around putting out a small newspaper—a guy named Dave Phillips. He sure was a help. Dave's not only a good writer, he's a great snake oil salesman. I brought him to Cuba and he was doing my propaganda work for me when Fidel took over. I don't know what he's doing now. Since he was under unofficial cover, I hope he got out all right."

Dave got out. He was now running the propaganda show like a newsroom. He had a number of telephones on his desk—one for office calls, one for Coral Gables, where the Florida station was located, one for New York, one to talk directly to Tracy Barnes. He welcomed me warmly. His manner with me and with others reminded me of Bob Jantzen. Dave, however, did not limit his remarks to the clichés that were Bob's trademark. Although his manner was Rotarian, he had a quick mind bursting with ideas. His enthusiasm and energy were not theater, they were real.

He said he was happy for any help the staff and I could give him, and we got down to the business of discussing his propaganda ob-

337

jectives, what assets he had for his own direct use, and what he thought the worldwide guidance system might do to support them. From that first day, we had a relationship that I thought was productive and certainly one that I found a great pleasure.

Dave's principal activity was seeing that Swan Island radio was supplied with material, also that Cuban exile media men were put to proper use. He did a lot of work also through a New York public relations man who had worked for Wendell Willkie.

The Swan Island radio was an amazing operation for me. I had stretched my cover very thin in Manila, but a fifty-kilowatt radio station owned by something known as the Gibraltar Steamship Company broadcasting propaganda to Cuba as a "commercial venture" was an eye-opening experience for me in how the WH Division went about its work. Evidently, I mused, any type of business venture, even a New York-based steamship company running a radio station from an uninhabited island in the Caribbean, was something that Latin Americans, conditioned to living with all sorts of American business activities in their midst, could accept as legitimate.

Dave and I decided that the most useful thing the staff could do was give maximum publicity to every shred of evidence that Castro was converting his revolution into a Communist model, and his country into a police state and a Soviet satellite. The rapidly unfolding events in Cuba in the summer and fall of 1960 and in early 1961 provided ample material to use.

Cuban Communists, who had actually opposed Castro's tactics when he was fighting Batista, had by 1960 become prominent in government affairs. By far our favorite example of Communists in the Cuban government, however, was Ernesto "Che" Guevara, the Argentine medical student who had joined Castro in Mexico at the very beginning of Fidel's great adventure. Guevara took over the National Bank on late November, 1959, although he had no known qualifications as an economist. He had a plan, however. Batista had left the country practically bare of cash. Guevara proposed that funds be raised by taking away the assets of the middle class. He also froze wages and imposed "revolutionary discipline" on the workers. His trump card was to turn to the Soviet bloc for economic assistance. We pushed in all our guidances, the theory that Guevara was the man who made Cuba Communist, aided by Fidel Castro's brother Raul and Raul's wife, Vilma, her sister Nilsa, and Nilsa's husband, a well-known Cuban Communist. Everything Guevara did, we pointed out, was part of a pattern—destruction of the middle class, destruction of workers' union rights, and reliance on the Soviets for aid was not just an economic policy, it was a blueprint for a Communist state. The emphasis on Guevara was supposed to raise resentment when played back to Cuba over Radio Swan because a "foreigner" was dominating their government. The emphasis on Raul Castro and his clique was intended to diminish Castro in the eyes of the world and of the Cubans.

Events in 1960 provided us the drift toward satellite status as ammunition for our "Bi-Weekly Guidances." In February, Castro signed a pact with the Russians which provided him $100 million in credit over a twelve-year period. Then Soviets also agreed to buy a million tons of sugar a year and to send technicians. There was a point about the sugar-purchasing arrangement that we delighted to make.

The Soviets agreed to buy the Cuban sugar at a price of .0278 cents a pound, one-half the price the U.S. paid. The Soviets then sold the sugar to their own citizens at forty cents a pound. This was an example of Communist economic exploitation that made the worst kind of dealing the Communists could ever accuse capitalist imperialists of look good by comparison. Also, we liked to point out that the Soviet exploitation of the Cubans went one step further— the Soviets agreed to pay 20 percent in cash and the rest in Soviet goods.

In May, 1960, the two countries agreed to resume diplomatic relations, which Batista had severed at our request. Two months later, the first Soviet ambassador arrived. This was a priceless opportunity for our propaganda treatment. The new ambassador was Sergei M. Kudryavtsev. He had been first secretary of the Soviet Embassy in Ottawa in 1947 when Igor Gouzenko, the code clerk of the Soviet military, GRU, office in Canada, defected in one of the great spy sensation cases of the 1940s.

Kudryavtsev had to leave Canada as a result of the revelations of his connections with Soviet intelligence exposed by Gouzenko. Subsequently he had served in Vienna and as minister counselor of embassy in Paris. He was a representative of the international section of the Soviet Communist Party as well. His appointment, we said, proved that Castro was now a Soviet puppet with an experienced Soviet spy sent to Havana to watch over his activities.

Meanwhile relations with other Soviet bloc countries, who usually played a key role in promoting Soviet foreign policy objectives as well as supporting Soviet intelligence operations abroad, kept pace with the evolution of the Cuban-Soviet axis. Czechoslovakian technicians poured into Havana. Poland agreed to supply equipment for a shipyard capable of constructing 10,000-ton ships. On September 2, Castro announced that Cuba recognized Red China and that China was buying 130,000 tons of sugar.

By mid-fall 1960, as the presidential campaign began to climax and the two contenders added Cuba to their topics of debate, as I have already noted, a disturbing note began to creep into Cuban and Soviet announcements, I thought. Raul Castro, touring Soviet bloc countries, was quoted as saying he was delighted to learn that "the Soviet Union would use every means to prevent any U.S. armed intervention." On October 27, Khrushchev declared "Soviet rockets are ready in case the U.S. attacks Cuba." These were not the first signs that the Cubans evidently had gotten some wind of our task force plan. As early as July, there had been talk of Soviet defense of Cuba against U.S. attack. Khrushchev had mentioned his rockets and Che Guevara had declared, "Cuba is now defended by the greatest military power in history." But more than words was involved. Between August 1 and October 27, when Khrushchev again rattled his rockets, 22,000-tons of arms, we knew, had entered Cuba from the Soviet Union. Soviet technicians had also arrived. The military aid totaled about $40 million, we estimated. I recalled that the operational approval which President Eisenhower had given indicated the new Cuban exile political front should be formed within six months. Presumably by now the operation to overthrow Castro was under way.

Even before the chilling prospect that Castro and his giant ally might be getting ready for us became so apparent in October, 1960, I had tried to find out what was wrong with the timetable. I got nothing out of Dave Phillips, but did get a clue from Paul. He admitted that he understood plans for the unification of Cuban exile political groups had run into trouble. "With Howard Hunt and this guy they brought in from the German desk running the show," Paul said, "as you might imagine, the political action group is behind schedule, all right."

I had heard about Howard Hunt, it seemed, all my career, but I had never met him. I had met the "guy from the German desk"

340

several times back in the days I worked for Kay and coordinated propaganda themes occasionally with him. His operational alias for the Bay of Pigs activity was "Frank Bender," but as Arthur Schlesinger pointed out in *A Thousand Days,* his real name was Droller. From what I knew of him and what I had heard of Howard Hunt, I couldn't imagine them functioning well together. Paul told me that Gerry Droller was in charge of the Political Action Branch at headquarters and that Hunt was "working in the field" directly with the Cuban exile groups.

Gerry Droller was a man I would be associated with rather closely when I myself eventually joined the WH Division after the Bay of Pigs. I also met Howard Hunt in time. My original reaction when Paul told me these officers were the key figures in arranging the most delicate piece of the operation—the political basis that would justify the invasion and become the foundation of the post-Castro Cuba—was stunned amazement. How these two could put together a coalition of Cuban exiles, involving the constant soothing of egos, I could never imagine. Hunt, almost the epitome of the kind of WASP that is not appreciated in Latin America—a man who naturally would talk down to Latins—and Droller, who always seemed to go out of his way to try to be the caricature of a Jew invented by Goebbels' propaganda ministry and who in addition couldn't speak a word of Spanish—negotiating with Latin political leaders just did not make sense to me.

When Howard Hunt wrote *Give Us This Day* he made clear how correct my insight was. No one, not even Paul (from whom they might well have been mostly concealed), gave me any of the details of the mess of bickering that Hunt and Droller made of the Cuban political exiles because of their personal problems and because of Hunt's extreme political conservatism and Droller's constant opportunism. Hunt does not give too many details in his book, but enough of the essentials for anyone who knew the two men to be able to see pretty clearly why the exiles were not united by August, 1960.

First of all, Howard Hunt would have liked to have used in a key role a Batista follower who was a friend of J. C. King and especially of former ambassador to Cuba, William D. Pauley. Pauley also, incidentally, owned the Havana Gas Company. Pauley's protégé was Dr. Antonio Rubio Padilla. Hunt tells how Droller fended off Rubio Padilla in an important meeting in the spring of 1960 when the operation was just getting under way. Gerry, of course, was following the line laid down by Tracy Barnes—the official position of taking care not to remove Castro in order to bring back the Batista gang, which was the reason the task force had to be established under Tracy Barnes's control and not left to J. C. King. I could picture Gerry Droller "fending off" the Cuban. He did not know how to fend off anyone without being insulting.

Throughout his book and, obviously, throughout the operation, Hunt speaks up constantly in favor of a number of other right-wing adventurers who made the task of uniting the Cubans so terribly difficult. He praises to the sky Captain Pedro Luis Diaz Lanz, whose daring personal leaflet drop when he defected as Castro's air force chief he admired. Diaz Lanz wanted to be air chief of the Bay of Pigs operation to the disruption and dismay of the officers in charge of this phase. Hunt relied heavily in his liaison with the exile political leaders on an ex-Marine, Frank Fiorini. Fiorini accompanied Diaz Lanz on the leaflet drop run over Havana. Fiorini worked for Hunt in Coral Gables under the name of Frank Sturgis, the name he was using when he broke into Democratic Party headquarters in the Watergate Apartments to find the proof that the Soviets were financing the Democratic Party which Hunt told him was there.

After August, 1960, the operational planning of the Cuban task force changed course. Since Hunt and Droller couldn't form a political organization sufficiently coherent to confront Castro, the emphasis shifted to a larger-scale military action. Napoleon Valeriano, Ed Lansdale's man, who had been training the Cuban exile guerrilla fighters, was dismissed and $13 million to train a full-fledged fighting brigade was approved. John Kennedy didn't know it, but there was no chance that the operation which had been originally approved in March, 1960, could be undertaken before the November elections.

When Kennedy was elected and briefed, he asked to have the operation thoroughly reviewed. His closest advisers especially wanted the Batista group completely out of the picture. This caused Hunt severe pangs of doubt, but not Gerry Droller. He quickly became an advocate of the Kennedy line on Cuba—the "revolution betrayed" theme that became our number one propaganda tune both covertly and overtly. Arthur Schlesinger, just before the invasion,

342

would give this line its most eloquent expression in the State Department Cuban White Paper, issued April 3, 1961.

The Kennedy group was especially impressed by the credentials of Manolo Ray, a U.S.-trained Cuban architect who for eighteen months was Castro's minister of public works. Ray did not defect until the end of 1960, when his escape was arranged by CIA. He was brought by ship to Tampa, where he was met by Gerry Droller. Ray formed the Movimiento Revolucionario del Pueblo, MRP. He wanted to join the overall exile political front we had formed. Kennedy's advisers strongly favored this. Hunt was so disturbed by the possibility of this dangerous leftist becoming part of the operation that he quit as case officer for the front and went to work for Dave Phillips's propaganda shop.

One morning in mid-March, 1961, Curly called me into his office. "Joe, Tracy wants us to do a special job to help out the task force," he said. "The White House wants to put out a policy statement on Cuba. It will be both an analysis of the situation as the United States views it and a rationale for what's going to happen. In other words, it will be an explanation of why the brigade went in."

He explained that the White House wanted us to prepare a first draft and provide all the information that would help make it a strong document supporting the revolution betrayed theme.

"Of course," he added, "they want all we've got on Communists in the Castro government and growing Soviet influence on Cuba, the kind of stuff you've been putting out in the guidances.

"Dave Phillips's shop is too busy to do this kind of research paper. Since you're closer to the situation than anyone outside Dave's shop, would you please take a crack at it?" He told me that Tracy said he understood Arthur Schlesinger would do the final write-up and it would be put out as though it were a State Department White Paper policy statement.

I knew now that things were coming to a climax, and I went to work feverishly to produce the best draft I could. The Cuban invasion evidently was going to be the counterpoint of the Alianza para el Progreso theme that the Kennedy administration had just launched on March 13. How they were to be woven into a harmonious whole I didn't quite see but obviously the Cuban White Paper was to be an effort in that direction.

I peppered the draft with the names of Cuban Communists in key positions: President Osvaldo Dorticos, Raul Roa, Major Antonio Nuñez Jiménez, head of the National Agrarian Reform Institute, Dulce Maria Escalona Almeida, director of primary education, Pedro Cañas Abril, director of secondary education, Valdés, the cruel G-2 chief, the sinister Che Guevara, of course, and many others. I put great stress on the Soviet military equipment theme. I noted that since mid-1960 30,000 tons of equipment worth $50 million had arrived in Cuba from Soviet sources and pointed out that in the parade on January 1, 1961, the annual Castro Revolution anniversary celebration of the takeover of Havana in 1959, Soviet JS-251 tanks, Soviet SU-100 assault guns, Soviet T-34 35-ton tanks, Soviet 76 mm, 88 mm, and 122 mm field guns were seen. I also pointed out that Cuba was becoming a military police state of frightening proportions, noting that proportionately more Cubans were under arms than were either Soviets or Americans—1 out of every 30 Cubans, as compared to 1 out of every 50 Soviet citizens and 1 out of every 60 U.S. citizens, were in some kind of military service.

Curly and I went to Tracy Barnes's office to clear the document with him. I had already checked it with Dave. We waited. Gerry Droller, we were told, was having a conference with Tracy. "Oh good," said Curly, "we'll get his comments too."

After a while the door opened, Gerry was coming out, but Tracy had a few final words to say. "Tell Manolo Ray that, damn it, we want no more discussion. Tell him he's either in or not. Tell him we are going with the formation of the Revolutionary Council. If he's not in now, he never will be. If he's not, tell him he'll be sorry."

I remembered shouting something very like that over the phone in Manila, when someone suggested still further negotiations with Macapagal after I had made up my mind to go with the Grand Alliance. Not a very good way to save the Philippines or to save Cuba, I thought to myself.

"Gerry," said Curly, "Joe and I have a draft for Schlesinger's policy paper on Cuba. Would you like to take a look at it?"

Gerry took the paper in his hands. He glanced at it but didn't read it. "What's dis? Words, words, making mit de lips. You guys got time to schlepp around with this policy paper crap but I'm a busy man." He rushed out the door.

On March 22, the Cuban Revolutionary Front was publicly announced at a press conference at the Belmont Plaza Hotel in New York. Its leader was declared to be José Miró Cardona, who had been Castro's first prime minister. Ray and the MRP were in. The bulk of the front consisted of the Frente Revolucionario Democratico which Hunt and Droller had formed originally in the spring of 1960 at a meeting in another New York Hotel—the Commodore. From then on, until the invasion flopped, the Miró Cardona group was used to put out all statements—it was fulfilling the role originally planned for such a group in the NSC paper approved on March 17, 1960.

The story of the failure of the invasion at Playa Girón, Bahía de Cochinos, on the Zapata peninsula, Cuba, has been told many times, as I have said. I will recall only the small part of it that I saw at headquarters from Monday, April 17, until the early evening of Wednesday, April 19. The Saturday before the invasion an air strike was flown from Puerto Cabezas, Nicaragua, attacking Castro's air force parked on the ground in Havana. Reportedly, 60 percent of the planes were knocked out. Two of the Cuban exile pilots who flew for us landed in Florida, claiming to be defectors from Castro's forces they had just been shooting up. Their thin cover story was torn apart by Raul Roa in the UN and Adlai Stevenson was forced to tell a bad lie. Nevertheless, my propaganda shop was geared up to repeat the cover story around the world. President Kennedy meanwhile cancelled a second air strike because of the embarrassment.

Long before this point was reached, however, the operation had been badly blown. In October, 1960, a Guatemalan newspaper, La Hora, had run a story on the training site at a remote Guatemalan coffee plantation. In November articles by Ronald Hilton in the Hispanic American Report and then The Nation told the tale to the American public. Don Dwiggins, aviation editor of the Los Angeles Mirror, wrote about the "secret" air base that fed the camp with men and supplies. Paul Kennedy elaborated further on the front page of the New York Times on January 10, 1961. The Miami Herald, which had been cooperating by not telling the story that everyone in the Cuban exile community who cared to know had known for months, resented being scooped and followed with two stories, one on the camp and one on the air traffic between Florida and Guatemala. In addition, Time Magazine in January talked about Gerry Droller, the mysterious "Mr. Bender" and his activities. It discreetly called him "Mr. B" but it was less discreet about describing what he was up to with the Cuban exiles.

Why did no one take pause at all this? For the reasons I have already mentioned—the arrogance, the opportunism, the momentum of the operation carried it onward to its doom. These factors were given further impact when President Ydigoras, of Guatemala, dispatched Roberto Alejos, owner of TRAX, the training camp, to see President Kennedy to tell him he thought it was time to act. I learned this later. At the time, however, I heard he had told our chief of station in Guatemala to tell us "to get these Cubans out of here as fast as you can." Ydigoras was sensitive to the implications of the widely blown activities if no one else was. Finally, although all the Cuban exiles knew about the operation, anyone who cared to read about such matters knew about it, and Castro knew about it, in Washington the final fateful decisions were kept tightly controlled by the little group of men who had been running the operation.

I didn't know what was happening that weekend of April 15 and 16, 1961, because I had been shut out of the task force area on Friday, before the fateful air strike of Saturday, April 15, got under way. I had seen cots being brought in when I was refused admission, however, so I assumed that D-Day was near. I learned later, as did everyone else, that the top officials of CIA spent Sunday, April 16, pleading with the President to change his decision cancelling the second strike at Castro's planes. My friends on the task force spent a nervous day and a sleepless night.

The Cuban Revolutionary Council issued a press bulletin on the morning of April 17, announcing "before dawn Cuban patriots in the cities and in the hills began the battle to liberate our homeland . . ." Dave Phillips's prose. Brigade 2506, as the Cubans called themselves, taking this name from the serial number of the one trainee who had died in a practice parachute jump, had landed. All that day and the next, I could learn very little, except, on Tuesday, Paul sounded very glum, and he said, "Don't bother Dave. Things are going badly."

Wednesday afternoon, Al Cox, chief of the paramilitary branch of the Covert Action Staff, called me into his office. His eyes were glistening. "Joe," he said in a choked voice, "the brigade has been lost." I couldn't believe him. "You mean they're in trouble?"

"No," said Al, "I mean they're gone. I've just talked to the task force. They need help. Everyone is in a state of shock, but Bissell wants to send out a cable. No one over there has the heart to write it. Please go over and see what you can do."

When I arrived at the task force building, located among the Agency temporary buildings across Independence Avenue from the Reflecting Pool area, a secretary, who had been alerted to my arrival, admitted me to the war room. I saw J. C. King, holding his head in his hands, and a couple of officers I didn't know. I thought I spotted Howard Hunt in the back of the room. I asked for Dave Phillips. Someone said he had gone home. Richard Bissell was talking on the telephone.

"Yes, Mr. Ambassador," he was saying, "yes, I'm sorry, but it's true. There is nothing more we can do. I'm afraid we've lost. No, we have nothing else to throw into it. Well, I'm sorry you're distressed. We all are. Yes, I'm sorry too that you weren't better informed. Well, good evening, Governor."

Bissell had been giving the news to Adlai Stevenson. I approached him slowly. I was caught up in the mood of the room. With difficulty, I managed to explain I had been sent over by Al to do a cable for him. I asked if he had anything special he wanted me to say.

"No," he said, "nothing special, just tell everyone what happened. Here, I'll sign as releasing officer on a blank cable form so the commo people will know you have the proper authority. Remember, I want this message sent to every station and every single base in the world."

I went over to Dave's shop and found one of his stunned subordinates. I asked him if he had any ideas about what I should say. "Well," he replied, "I think we should do what we can for those men. They fought like hell. Say they were overwhelmed by Soviet tanks and fighter planes."

I did. I found out later it wasn't true. Old used U.S. tanks and planes had done the job for Castro. I didn't regret giving these men an unearned increment in the odds which they had faced. They had been undone by a series of shortcomings that were not theirs. I thought that perhaps even I might have contributed my small share.

All night long I kept being awakened by calls from the communications people. They had never received instructions to send messages directly from Washington to a number of our bases around the world. Evidently the DDP didn't know any more than I did just how many bases he had around the world nor that many of them received their messages only by relay systems too involved and insecure to receive the kind of direct communication I had ordered.

The night of April 19, 1961, was not like any other for many officers in the Clandestine Services. In the offices of the Cuban task force that evening I had the feeling all those there felt almost that the world had ended. Actually, it was just one more operation gone wrong. Soon the Kennedy brothers would have CIA back in the business of overthrowing Castro again. All the officers involved in the new venture would be working at the task "with vigor," as the President liked to say of many things.

19

South of the Border and Beyond

Six weeks after the Bay of Pigs disaster Paul called me and asked me to come to see him. He said he had something important to talk about. He did. The conversation we had that morning set off a series of events that shaped the course of the rest of my career with the Clandestine Services.

He explained when I arrived that he wanted to block the latest scheme Dick Goodwin's White House Latin American task force had proposed to WH Division. Two afflictions plagued the division in the aftermath of the Bay of Pigs. One was the investigating commission the President had established to look into the causes of the failure. The other was the Goodwin-Schlesinger task force. My friends who had been involved in the Cuban operation sat staring blankly at the wall, waiting their turns to be called to testify to General Maxwell Taylor's commission. J. C. King and his deputy, Ray Herbert, spent much of their time dodging a bombardment of proposals for new approaches to Latin American problems that came from the White House task force. The Goodwin group had fathered the Alianza para el Progreso program which President Kennedy had announced to a convocation of Latin American diplomats on March 13, 1961, just slightly more than a month before Brigade 2506 hit the beach. In the wake of CIA's failure, the White House advisers seemed to think they should tell the Agency how to spend its covert funds.

J. C. King and his crew of former FBI men were more disturbed by Goodwin and Schlesinger than by General Taylor's investigating committee. They believed they had a chance with Maxwell Taylor—he and King had gone to West Point together—while they thought there was no hope with Goodwin and Schlesinger. Those two relied on consultants such as staff members of Luis Muñoz Marín, the reform governor of Puerto Rico. On his trip to Latin America to get ideas for the Alianza, Schlesinger had spent too much time with Latin political leaders whom the old hands in WH considered dangerous leftists—men like Romulo Betancourt in Venezuela, José Figueres in Costa Rica, and Eduardo Frei and Salvador Allende in Chile.

Not all the officers of WH thought this way. One who didn't was my friend Paul. Paul was far from being a leftist, but he had a feel for people. He also loved to hunt and fish and when he had served in South America he traveled to remote places in pursuit of his hobbies. He not only saw the impoverished peasants, he looked at them. Therefore, he didn't fear men like Betancourt and Figueres as his colleagues did. He knew that change had to come to Latin America. On the other hand, he didn't like the idea of Dick Goodwin trying to run the hemisphere and WH Division. Goodwin's claim to area expertise was that he had written some editorials on Latin America occasionally for the Washington *Post*.

"Ray Herbert just came back from the White House with a real live one from the geniuses over there," Paul said. "Pepe Figueres wants to start some kind of school for political leaders from all over the area and Goodwin's boys want us to pay for it. Not only that, they want to put their pal Alexander on the faculty."

Robert Alexander was a political scientist who specialized in Latin America and who taught at Rutgers. I was familiar with his work, especially the book *The Struggle for Democracy in Latin America*. This pointed out the ties of American business with Perón in Argentina, the Trujillo dictatorship in Santo Domingo, and the more recently

350

deposed strongman of Venezuela, Pérez Jiménez. Alexander suited the Goodwin task force well. He certainly would be totally unacceptable to the old guard of WH division, I was sure.

"Ray thinks we may have to go along," Paul continued, "but he'd like to figure out some way we can control the project. He doesn't want to give those guys in the White House our Agency money for a pet scheme of theirs we get nothing out of. Of course, he fears Figueres himself and his friends, like Betancourt, and he's scared to death of Alexander. However, as he says, now is hardly the time for us to fight city hall. He wants us to come up with a counterproposal, you know, agreeing in principle and that sort of thing, but with a candidate of our own to replace Alexander as the American participant."

What bothered Paul and his superiors almost as much as the Goodwin task force proposal was that Cord Meyer might hear about it. His International Organizations division had aggressively assisted labor activities in Latin America as part of its international labor program with the AFL/CIO. As a result, Cord's people were in touch with many of the political leaders of the democratic left in the area and all 10 Division officers were reported to be studying Spanish. "I've told J. C. that his old crowd has let him down," Paul pointed out. "The day is over when contact with the police chief can be called a CIA station in our area. We've given away all the important contacts with the new leadership group in every country to Cord's people. Now it looks like the White House will finish the job. If Cord Meyer and they get together on something like this proposal, they'll put old WH out of business."

Paul said he wanted me to help prevent this. "If there is going to be any such project as Goodwin's boys want, it must be a WH project. So I've told Ray Herbert about you. How about you're being our candidate for American participant in the school?"

This sounded to me like the old Rangoon branch of the Johns Hopkins School for Advanced International Studies idea come to life again, only better. The initiative was coming from Latin American leaders. It was their idea to start the school, not something that was being sold to them by Americans. There was the possibility, of course, that Alexander had been whispering in Figueres's ear, I realized, but I chose to disregard this cloud. I was flattered, and I was more than ready to volunteer. I told Paul that the proposition

351

sounded great to me, but I didn't know any Spanish and there was no way I could be compared academically to Alexander.

"We'll teach you the Spanish, and I think we can make you look pretty good to the White House bunch. You went to Harvard, didn't you? Isn't this a Harvard administration? Besides, you'll come with a big bag of money attached."

Negotiations began. I started trying to get Curly to release me from my Covert Action Staff job, and Paul and Herbert commenced putting together a written counterproposal for the Goodwin task force. I met with Ray Herbert to discuss the matter. He was another ex-FBI man but considerably more suave, urbane, and polished than most. He told me he had ways of introducing me to Figueres but didn't say what they were. He said I should get my passport in order and check my shot record. He and I would probably soon be taking a trip to Central America.

Within another six weeks I found myself transferred to WH division, but the Figueres project had somehow been shelved. Herbert told me that the White House had lost interest so, naturally, he wasn't going to take the initiative on the matter. "We'll have you on the back burner, ready to go, if they bring it up again," he said. "We have a darn good job for you meanwhile. We want you to be chief of the Venezuelan desk. Venezuela's an interesting country and one the White House is watching closely to see whether Betancourt can make it. They consider him the answer to Castro."

I never heard anything more about the Figueres project. Several years later, when I was in Argentina, something that bore a close resemblance to it was started in Figueres's country, Costa Rica—a political training institute supported by Cord Meyer's 10 Division.

When I took over the Venezuelan desk in August, 1961, it was not yet clear what was going to happen regarding Cuba, but the President had ordered that the Agency make certain that Castro's efforts to export his revolution throughout the hemisphere be stopped. Venezuela was one spot Castro had picked out as a top-priority target to be revolutionized. The reason was obvious—oil. Not only could Castro use the oil himself, the thought that a Marxist government under his influence would deny the United States its major source of foreign crude was sweet. When I looked over the assets of the Caracas station, I frankly despaired of our chances of stopping him.

Most of the Caracas station's effort before Betancourt was elected

352

president following the overthrow of Pérez Jiménez had been consumed in support of the strongman's security police. They were gone, and our station chief, another ex-FBI officer, was going about getting to know Betancourt's policemen very slowly. He didn't trust them. He was on record as saying he still thought Betancourt was a crypto Communist. Betancourt had professed Marxist ideas in his youth, and our man in Caracas belonged to the large school of CIA officers who were convinced that Communists, like leopards, can't change their spots. They even used this cliché to express this profound idea.

The strangest thing to me, when I looked up the true names of all the encrypted agents and contacts of the station, was that I found no Venezuelans. The cryptonyms led only to former FBI men working as security officers for American companies or to American businessmen, some active, some retired. The station's major covert action project was run by a retired American, an old friend of J. C. King, who was a permanent employee of the American Chamber of Commerce. Each year the station provided a large sum in support of the Chamber's Fourth of July celebration and called this a propaganda effort to cement good relations between Americans and Venezuelans.

Because President Kennedy had ordered action, however, the chance to change all this was at hand. When the new fiscal year began on July 1, 1961, WH Division found itself with an additional $10 million in its budget for the purpose of stopping the spread of Castroism. Unfortunately, in all the countries in the area, including Venezuela, there were no specific projects to spend the money on in order to accomplish this objective.

We did have in Caracas a group of Basques who had fled Franco's Spain. They had penetrated the Venezuelan Communist Party for us, a task made easy because the Communists hated Franco almost as much as they did and an excellent common bond existed between them. This project, however, couldn't accomplish what needed to be done to satisfy President Kennedy's wishes. New, sophisticated political operations and additional intelligence collection were both needed. Above all, we needed links with the Betancourt group, with his Acción Democrática, AD, Party so we could help them help themselves fend off Castro's efforts.

Two phenomena intrigued me in the weeks following my entering on duty in WH, one that was most uncommon in my CIA ex-

353

perience, and one that was very familiar. The uncommon experience was asking, pleading, begging the field station to come up with additional ideas for spending more money. Usually, a desk officer's fate was to tell the field station it had to find new ways to cut costs, not new ways to spend more money. The familiar experience was seeing all those who had been directly responsible for the Bay of Pigs operation being promoted. Being part of a major disaster always led to success in the Clandestine Services for officers below the very top. Thus, although Allen Dulles and Richard Bissell lost their jobs before 1961 had ended, Tracy Barnes had a new division created for him, Domestic Operations Division, and Howard Hunt went to work for him. Jake, the man who directed all daily operations of the Cuban task force, serving directly under Barnes, was made chief of operations for the entire Western Hemisphere Division. Dave Phillips went off to a senior field assignment in Mexico City. Gerry Droller became a special assistant for political operations to J. C. King and began traveling around Latin America to drum up projects for spending our new funds.

I recalled that the case officer who had made the first contacts with the Sumatran colonels, providing us all the information which misled us so badly, received an immediate promotion when he returned from Indonesia and was given his choice of assignments. He chose London. No more jungle duty for him. Whether this practice of rewarding an officer for his contribution to horrendous mistakes resulted from a guilt feeling on the part of the top echelon at involving their subordinates in such questionable activities or stemmed from the same motivation as hush money does, I could never decide. Unfortunately, I was never close enough to a disaster to benefit. I got out of the Indonesian adventure before it failed, and the Grand Alliance defeat was swallowed up in the victory of the coalition we put together for Macapagal.

The most interesting thing about my new job was a proposal which our insistence on developing new projects finally brought forth from Caracas. Some friends of Betancourt wanted to start a new daily paper which would be an unofficial mouthpiece of the AD Party and publicize the land reform program and other parts of the Venezuelan president's democratic revolution formula. The station chief didn't think too much of the idea, but I saw it as exactly the kind of activity we needed.

This kind of newspaper was precisely what Paul Linebarger meant when he defined gray propaganda. A paper associated with a leftist-inclined party which frequently opposed U.S. policies would have considerable weight when it occasionally supported us. More important, I saw this as a mechanism for access to AD political leaders. Since they, in turn, had ties with men of like mind in other countries, I could envision our supporting the newspaper as a means of following the plans of this group and trying to influence them.

One of the Venezuelan proponents of the plan was an importer of U.S. and other foreign cars. If he hadn't been involved I was sure the station would never have heard of the idea. A businessman of his sort was the only kind of Venezuelan our people in Caracas were ever apt to meet. He was putting some of his own funds into the scheme. This made cover for funding easier. I thought we should also ask him to provide cover for an officer to run the project under the guise of being a man who had come to Caracas to work with him in his auto dealership. I saw myself in this role.

I was looking for an opportunity to get out of Washington and into the field again. After serving in a field station and dealing directly with people a headquarters officer only has the chance to read about, I never liked a Washington assignment. Most of the work done at headquarters seemed not only dull, but something which could be done by far fewer people than the number who wrote each other memos and consumed hours in pointless conferences, or else something that need not be done at all.

I gave the proposal that we subsidize *La Republica* my fullest attention. Soon I had a project proposal ready for approval by higher echelons. President Kennedy had tightened controls after the Bay of Pigs. The Special Group of the NSC, although the persons who comprised it—the President's assistant for national security affairs, the deputy secretary of Defense, the undersecretary of state for political affairs, and the director of CIA—remained the same, its charters had been strengthened and reissued as NSC Directive 303. Support to a newspaper such as *La Republica,* with the political implications this involved, now had to be approved by the 303 Committee before the Clandestine Services could undertake the activity.

The project cleared the division and staff levels and then I got a

355

telephone call from the man who conducted liaison with the committee. He said he wanted me to present the project personally to Allen Dulles. Dulles was now only a lame-duck director since he had resigned and McCone had been named to replace him. McCone was not able to assume his duties immediately because of his wife's death so Dulles continued in his job and continued sitting with the 303 Committee. The liaison officer explained he wanted me to talk to Dulles since I was the man who would go to Caracas to be the deep-cover project officer, the car dealer's "business associate." Dulles would thereby get a briefing for the committee and also be able to tell them honestly he knew the officer concerned.

I hadn't seen Dulles since before I went to Manila. He hadn't changed. In spite of the Bay of Pigs disaster, he still puffed his pipe serenely. As usual he made me feel I was in the presence of a kindly old uncle who took a rather keen interest in his nephew's schemes. He remembered I was "little Joe" Smith, and I told him a Joe Smith story. When Serging Osmeña had visited Washington at one point in 1959, he had met "big Joe" Smith, the Philippine and Indonesian branches having been merged. When they were introduced, "big Joe" told me later, Serging exclaimed, "Now wait a minute. I deal with Joe Smith in Manila." He paused. "Or do you all use that name?"

Dulles laughed. He had only a few routine questions about the project funding and then he signaled the end of the meeting by holding out his hand and saying, "I think you've got a very good project here. I wish you all the success in the world with it."

That would have been the only assignment I ever had on which Allen Dulles personally gave me his blessing, but I never got the assignment. Although I had cleared the project with all the appropriate elements, it was approved by the 303 Committee, and Dulles himself wished me well, I didn't clear it properly with J. C. King's old-boy network.

At an early stage, long before I saw Dulles, I had sent a dispatch to the station explaining the way the project was being set up, along with a background sketch on me and a summary of my past experience. Caracas sent back a message saying the station agreed with the project's objectives, and that more detailed comments would follow. A number of weeks went by without further word. The project was approved by the 303 Committee and still there was not

356

further word from the station. In the meantime I became involved in an activity which the branch chief and I agreed would make possible a trip to Caracas. This activity concerned British Guiana, as Guyana was known in those days. Although it was not yet independent, obviously British control of the tiny country on the northern shore of South America would soon be ending. In addition, a man named Cheddi Jagan, whom we considered a dangerous Communist, had beaten his closest rival, Forbes Burnham, and was prime minister. We had no representative on the spot in British Guiana, but my colleague in the branch who was responsible for following events there didn't let a thing like this stop her.

Virginia had been in the thick of things since World War II began. She lost a leg parachuting into France during the war. This slowed her gait a bit but did nothing to damage her spirit or dull her keen, inquiring mind. She had developed contact with a young psychiatrist from British Guiana whose brother was a trusted lieutenant of Forbes Burnham in order to prepare for the day she was certain would come when we would be taking action to defeat Cheddi Jagan.

The psychiatrist worked in a hospital in Baltimore, which was convenient. He heard frequently from his brother, and Virginia felt the time had come to make this contact more professional. With Jagan in a position to control the mails, relying on family letters as sources of information was risky. She devised a plan to meet the brother outside British Guiana to discuss the situation with him personally and to provide him a secret writing system to use in sending future reports to Baltimore.

Male chauvinism prevailed over Virginia's war record and it was decided that, while her plan was excellent, she couldn't carry it out herself. I was chosen to meet the psychiatrist's brother and do the briefing and secret writing training. Virginia was more amused than angry. She told me when she took me to Baltimore to meet the psychiatrist, "I really think J. C. just can't bring himself to send me off alone with two black men."

The doctor and I flew to Barbados from New York one Saturday morning in February, 1962. His brother could manage to get away from British Guiana only for the weekend, and this was also the best timing for the doctor. Their cover story to their acquaintances and employers was that they had to meet urgently in Barbados on

357

family business. I was supposed to be someone the doctor met by chance on the airplane. We counted on a quiet British hotel being somnolent enough to be a safe place for our meetings and training sessions. It was.

The small hotel where we stayed reminded me of an up-country British resthouse in Malaya. Like the resthouses, nothing about the accommodations, food, or service had changed since before World War II. The brothers had a room on one floor and I was on another. I had no trouble slipping up the stairs to meet them undetected. If I had shouted "fire" while going up the steps, I don't think this would have aroused any of the staff from their apparent permanent immobility.

I had a wonderful time. I enjoyed being face to face with a political leader again. It seemed ages to me since I had left Manila. I also enjoyed teaching him the secret writing system. It was a simple carbon type that is as easy to teach as it is to learn. The message is transferred to a cover letter (in his case, the usual letters he wrote to his brother in Baltimore) by the use of a chemical with which a piece of what appears to be normal bond paper has been impregnated. The only possible problem is that the user will mislay this innocent-appearing stock of paper and take up some other blank page for his valuable secret-writing tool.

This would be a one-way system. His brother would send him no secret messages from Baltimore. We did not want to risk his having the incriminating developer solution in his possession in British Guiana. He would have to remember all the points I covered in my briefing. These would be his intelligence requirements to report on for the next six months. By that time we would have a man on the spot in Georgetown and we would have another meeting in Barbados so they could get to know each other and arrange how they would do business.

After two very satisfying days, I took off for Caracas. I used my Agency language-school Spanish to get me to the Tamañaco Hotel. This, of course, was a conceit on my part. Taxi drivers in Caracas had handled enough Texas oilmen to be able to get any American to this expense-account palace. I called the station and was told to come over to the embassy immediately and announce myself to the Marine guard.

"What the hell are you doing here? Defying me? I sent orders

that you were not to come here," the chief of station bellowed at me
as soon as I entered his office. He was a tense, pinch-faced Irishman. I had expected to have to use a lot of my diplomatic skills in
order to get along with Jack but this was more than I had bargained
for.

"I told J. C. I didn't want you. I have another man picked for the
job and he's been approved by J. C. so there was no need for you to
come here whatsoever. Who the hell signed your travel orders?"

"Ray Herbert."

"That figures." Jack now became less disturbed. "The old right
and left hands not coordinating again as usual. I'm sorry I yelled at
you. We both have reason to be upset."

That was putting it mildly. I was furious, but what could I do? It
was his station and he and J. C. King had made their decision. I
told him I'd take a plane back to Washington the next morning. He
said I could stay longer if I wished and said he would like me to talk
to all the people in the station since I was their desk officer. I
agreed to talk to the people but insisted I'd leave on the first flight
out in the morning.

I knew now what the "other details" were the chief of station had
in mind when he sent the cable concurring in the project. Obviously, Jack had sent an "eyes only" message to Colonel King. Ray
Herbert, my branch chief, not to mention me, had never been
shown the message. J. C. had simply written directly back agreeing
to Jack's candidate and that settled the matter.

I remembered Gerry Droller had come to see me two days before
I left and engaged me in a strange conversation. He showed great
interest in the project but seemed to be trying to persuade me I
shouldn't. I also remembered that one day J. C.'s secretary came
into the office and asked who "Arthur H. Toohill" was. This was my
official pseudonym and all correspondence to Caracas about me
had used it. When I told her I was "Toohill" she had given me a
strange look, but she said nothing and left.

Everybody was most apologetic and sympathetic when I got back
to Washington, but neither Colonel King nor Ray Herbert talked to
me about it. Gerry Droller made a point of commiserating with me.
"Joey," he said, "I knew you were in trouble going to Caracas but I
couldn't tell you. Look, I know you're in a state of shock. Let me tell
you, that's the way I've been ever since April, 1961." The old divi-

sion hands told me to forget it. This was the way J. C. ran things. He made decisions like this whenever his favorites asked him to. It was something they had become accustomed to living with. Jake, the chief of operations, called me in to say he would personally see I got the best assignment he could find which suited my background as fast as he could find one.

Paul pointed out things were changing almost daily in the division. "This may be the last trick of this kind J. C. pulls," he said. "You see what is happening. They've taken Cuba away from him again and given it to Des Fitzgerald, the Far East Division chief, for God's sake. The word is out for everyone to hire new people as many and as fast as possible. Everyone knows you can't change J. C., so he's just going to be ignored. Pretty soon most of the division will be made up of people like you whom he doesn't even know."

This was true. Soon I received a phone call from Curly. He had left the job of chief of the Covert Action Staff and was attending the National War College at Fort McNair. He called to say that when he finished his course in June his next assignment was going to be chief of station, Buenos Aires, and he wanted me to go with him. "See Jake," he told me. I did, and Jake said this was the kind of assignment he had in mind when he promised me a good one. "Buenos Aires is the Paris of South America," he said.

My major responsibility in Buenos Aires would be to handle the hundred-thousand-dollar-a-year propaganda project that we ran jointly with the Argentine government's top security agency, the Secretaría de Información del Estado, SIDE. I knew the project. One of the responsibilities I had when I was chief of the propaganda guidance section of the Covert Action Staff was to review all propaganda projects from all over the world once a year to see how they made use of our guidances. Henry, as chief of the entire Propaganda Branch, also looked over all such projects and gave his opinion on their general effectiveness. He rated this Argentine project, I recalled, "the best project of its kind in the world." Henry had made a special trip to Argentina in 1959 to assist SIDE in creating it. Naturally, he couldn't possibly give it any other kind of rating.

In 1959 President Arturo Frondizi of Argentina came to Washington. Frondizi had won the first national election following the overthrow of the dictator Juan Perón. He won it by making a deal with Perón which netted him two million votes and gained him the lasting enmity of Argentine military men who had played the important roles in deposing the dictator. From the moment of his election in February, 1958, Frondizi engaged in a tug-of-war with these opponents. He also launched an economic policy which freed his country of its international balance of trade debt but which infuriated Argentine nationalists. Although Frondizi himself was the author of the most widely read nationalist tract denouncing foreign oil companies, when once elected he reversed himself completely and contracts for oil drilling were signed with various American companies and adventurers. As a result Argentina was soon producing enough petroleum to change its bleak economic picture but the scene still looked dark to those Argentines who suffered from xenophobia.

Hence, Frondizi was a man beset by many local enemies when he visited Washington in 1959. During his stay he paid a call on Allen Dulles. Dulles offered to do anything he could to assist him. Frondizi told Dulles he would appreciate help in developing capabilities for fending off foes whom he labeled the "anti-democratic elements." As a result of this conversation Henry was sent to Argentina to help SIDE establish its propaganda branch. Henry set up the project so that a permanent adviser could be assigned by us to continue to assist SIDE's propaganda efforts.

Curly assured me that he would have more for me to do than just hold hands with SIDE. He said he had been told by the White House staff that President Kennedy was even more impressed with Frondizi than the Eisenhower administration had been. "The decision has been made to make Argentina the showplace of the Alianza para el Progreso," Curly said, "and we're responsible for developing all the covert assets we can to help accomplish this." Thinking of the Philippines, I felt good at the prospect of being back in the showplace business again. I accepted.

I was also happy to detach myself from Venezuela. The man Jack and J. C. King had selected for the job of adviser to Betancourt's friends' newspaper was a Puerto Rican translator. He was not an operations officer. No interesting political action was going to get under way with the AD Party if they could help it. I said goodbye to the problem and enrolled in language school.

If the cover arrangements for my Manila assignment left a lot to be desired, they were handled with consummate skill as compared to the way I was processed for Argentina. Because the cover was unrelated to any U.S. official installation, the administrators in the Clandestine Services considered it "deep cover." What was deep cover about an arrangement which not only was known to the local intelligence service but actually established thanks to their cooperation, I couldn't understand. But if the administrative staff couldn't place an officer under official cover with some government agency, then they couldn't think of any other way to classify him except as a deep-cover employee. This meant I had to resign from CIA, signing all the forms that would erase my name completely from all agency records. Then I signed a contract as "Arthur H. Toohill" which showed I really hadn't resigned at all.

After that, getting to Argentina was mostly up to me. The station had SIDE send a notice to the Argentine consulate in Baltimore indicating they had cleared me to accept a position as an adviser to the Instituto de Estudios Científicos y Técnicos de las Fuerzas Armadas. I took Jeanne, Ruthven, Julie, and our fifteen-month-old son, Andy, to the State Department and applied for regular passports. I listed my profession as "public relations," but since I had been forced to give up my Andrews Air Force Base cover address, I had to list myself as a contract employee of the Argentine armed forces. When we finally got the passports, I took them to Baltimore to get the visas SIDE's note entitled us to have.

Then back to official Agency processing again. I was instructed to bring my family to the new CIA building in Langley for our physicals. By now Ruthven was definitely interested in the strange goings-on in her father's career, especially when we were pulling her out of high school right after the junior prom to drag her off to another foreign country and another strange school—her tenth school in eleven years of education. Up to this point I had never told my children what my profession really was. It wasn't necessary after we walked across the great seal of CIA in the floor of the foyer at Langley on our way to the medical staff's reception room.

Our trip to Argentina was as much a misadventure as our processing had been. As usual, we planned to travel by ship but when we arrived in New York the evening before our scheduled sailing, I found a message from Moore-McCormack Lines telling

362

me its workers were on strike and the SS *Argentina*'s voyage had been cancelled. We had no choice but to transfer to PanAm.

We arrived at Ezeiza Airport in Buenos Aires well past midnight in the middle of June, 1962. June is winter in Argentina and we landed in our summer clothes. Our winter things were in trunks in the belly of the plane. We had expected to put them on at the appropriate moment as the SS *Argentina* sailed on into the southern hemisphere. We were not able to open the trunks in New York. I was fortunate to be able to get them transferred from the dock to Idlewild in time to be put on the same plane as excess baggage. Cold in the bedraggled clothes we had been wearing for three days while I cashed in the ship tickets, bought PanAm tickets, arranged the transfer of the trunks and a crate to ship Julie's cat she refused to leave behind, we had to struggle through customs without a diplomatic passport and without the help of a welcoming station officer. SIDE sent no one to assist either. The customs officer threw up his hands and let us go when he came to Moe's cage. PanAm had told me that Moe, the cat, had to have a visa to enter Argentina. I decided to ignore this idiocy. I made the right decision. The odor from the crate was enough to make the customs officer decide he was finished checking us and to overlook Moe's not having a visa. He didn't even care that Moe didn't have a passport.

None of us knew that we would stay four years in Argentina. If we had, I think we would simply have sat in the airport until time for the first flight back to New York. Very little about Argentina and the Argentines proved attractive. By the time I left Argentina, I also had begun to have doubts about the usefulness of a cold warrior's career.

I found Argentina a sad country and the Argentines sad people. By the time I arrived the man whose country I was supposed to make into the showplace of the Alianza para el Progreso had been deposed. Frondizi had become overconfident and permitted the Peronists to run in state elections against the advice of the military. The result was the Peronists won all the major contests. The military reacted at once, and, like Perón before him, Frondizi left the Casa Rosada a prisoner and was put away on the fortified island of Martín García.

On the day Arturo Frondizi was overthrown, March 29, 1962, a handful of supporters of civilian rule quickly grabbed Senate Presi-

363

dent José María Guido and swore him in as president under the Argentine law of *acefalía*—an apt term meaning headlessness. Constitutionally, with the president forced from office, the government was "headless" and the senate president legally entitled to supply this missing part. The story was that General Raúl Poggi, who led the coup against Frondizi, had to go to the bathroom just before he planned to have himself sworn in as the country's president. The advocates of constitutional civilian rule seized this natural pause in Poggi's official activities to prevent the installation of military dictatorship.

They might as well have saved themselves the trouble. The entire time I was in Argentina the government continued to suffer from *acefalía* and was either getting over the effects of a failed coup d'etat attempt by one group of military officers or engulfed in rumors of a planned coup by another group. Guido was completely ineffective and the country was even more headless when another Arturo, Dr. Arturo Illia, a country physician from Córdoba, was elected president on July 7, 1963, by what my friends in SIDE liked to call "our legal fraud." By this they meant the way in which they and the armed forces found a legal technicality that frustrated Peronist participation in the election. After Illia became president things were smoother for a short time but soon the coup plotters were back in business. I left Argentina as I found it, settling back after another major coup d'état—the one that made General Juan Carlos Ongania president.

Undoubtedly the political atmosphere helped make the country and its people seem sad to me. There were other, deeper reasons. The Argentines were constantly looking back over their shoulders at a happier time in the past. They seemed unable to face the present and to have no idea how to prepare for any future. They were right, of course, to think that things had once been better. In all the early decades of the twentieth century Argentina had been neither broke nor misgoverned. The country had been counted among the significant middle-sized nations of the world. When I lived among them from 1962 until 1966, the Argentines didn't know whose fault it was their fortunes had fallen so low. The anti-Peronists, consisting of the military, whom he had prostituted, the upper classes, whom he had disappropriated, and most of the middle class, whom he had despoiled by inflation, said it was Perón's fault. The working people, for whom he had robbed the rich and the

364

middle classes to gain their support, said it was the fault of these same old foes Perón had fought—the anti-Peronist coalition which overthrew him in 1955 and had failed to solve any of the country's problems since.

Another cause of low morale was the failure of the large immigrant population of Argentina ever to integrate. Only the United States has enjoyed a population growth by immigration of the size and scale of Argentina's. But third- and even fourth-generation Germans, Italians, and Englishmen in Argentina insisted they were Germans, Italians, or English. An Argentine was hard to find. The Argentines, in sum, suffered from a severe identity crisis.

If the Argentines suffered from an identity crisis so did the Buenos Aires station. Whether we should mainly concern ourselves with Argentina and its crises, or work on the Soviet and Czechoslovakian embassies with their spy contingents, or spend most of our time fighting Castro's efforts to export his revolution, never seemed to be resolved. We were always doing a little bit of all three and never enough of any one. What made matters worse for me was that I couldn't get used to the idea of not putting Argentina and its many problems first on the agenda at all times. It may have been my early days writing plans for every country in the Far East when I worked for Kay or, perhaps, because I was, after all, a believer in the American Century, but I couldn't see any sense in being in Argentina and being primarily concerned about Castro or Soviet intelligence services. I thought we should try to help the Argentines make their country a stable, democratic one. Later, in Mexico, I came to appreciate how important the Soviet target was and why we had to try to recruit a Soviet intelligence officer. In Argentina I was thankful that, at least, I didn't get involved in that business. But my efforts to concentrate on Argentina were always frustrated and I was continually yanked back into involvement in concern with Castro. I believed I could have prevented the Ongania coup if given the chance to work more closely with a contact I developed and should have been allowed to try. I came in the end to doubt whether this or anything else in Argentina really did matter or should matter to the United States.

20
How the Hemisphere Looked from Upside Down

I was always required to pay more attention to Castro than to Argentina because by the time I arrived in Buenos Aires John F. Kennedy had decided Castro had to be destroyed. In early 1962, just about the time of my disastrous trip to Caracas and my decision to accept the job in BA, the President selected Des Fitzgerald to head a new CIA task force to do the job. Bobby Kennedy was in charge of overall U.S. government coordination of the activity and Ed Lansdale was back in the picture as White House adviser on unconventional warfare.

Fitzgerald quickly reestablished a big station at the University of Miami's old Navy blimp facility in Coral Gables. An enormous effort began to put intelligence agents, sabotage teams, and, I heard but could hardly believe, assassination squads into Cuba. The extra $10 million WH Division received in 1961 was dwarfed by the $100 million plus budget for Cuban operations. Cuba began to be treated as a priority equal to the Soviet Union and China, and the tactics and strategy used to deal with these two major Communist powers, who were called "denied areas" since all our efforts to penetrate them had failed, began to be applied to Cuba.

If Des had had the funds and the full White House support Kennedy gave him for Cuba, he would probably have achieved his goal of starting an uprising against Mao Tse-tung when he backed Li Mi and the Chinese Nationalist remnants in Burma.

Cuban operations specialists were assigned to stations not only in the Western Hemisphere but all over the world. Thus, at the same time I was processed for my job as adviser to SIDE on propaganda, another officer was assigned as an adviser on developing joint intelligence operations with the Argentines against Castro, and I had the Cuban target written into my project as a priority propaganda effort. A specialist on the Soviets and another specialist on the Czechs, plus a man to translate tapes of conversations SIDE helped us bug from the conference room of the Czech Embassy, were already in Buenos Aires when I arrived. They too were "contract employees" of the Instituto de Estudios Científicos y Técnicos de las Fuerzas Armadas.

I found myself, in effect, a member of a substation of the main Buenos Aires CIA establishment involved with SIDE on matters that didn't concern Argentina directly but which were dear to the hearts of senior CIA officials and the President of the United States.

I had little to do with the Soviet and Czech concerns but more than I cared to have to do with Cuba. The Czech specialist spent a lot of time trying to connect Czech Embassy officials with Communist activities in Argentina. While I was in BA his efforts did lead to the expulsion of several members of the Czech Embassy for spying in Argentina. He turned over leads he got from listening to the tapes showing contact between embassy officials and local Communists to SIDE for interrogation. One time he ran into trouble. SIDE couldn't get a confession from a stubborn suspect even with the help of their favorite interrogation aid—an electric rod they attached to his testicles to give his memory a jolt. He finally told them, "Look, I've been an electrician for forty years, I've been shocked at least ten thousand times—a few more just don't bother me."

The first thing I learned about our relations with SIDE was,

368

while the organization might send cables to the consulate in Baltimore to help us get visas, that was the extent of the assistance they provided. They did not provide us office space. They did not help us get our household goods into the country, and through customs. They didn't even give us proper credentials. The armed forces institute did really exist but we weren't introduced to its chief or any of its officers. Our credentials were forged by a SIDE sergeant who obtained some of the institute's documents and copied them, signing a fictitious name. We must have given SIDE's administrative staff training on how to establish cover jobs, I thought. This was Andrews Air Force Base all over again, only in Spanish.

Before I arrived the Soviet and Czech specialists had found us all a small apartment on Solis Street, around the corner from the Argentine Congress, to serve as an office. It was a convenient place for the SIDE liaison officer to drop off his tapes from the Czech Embassy, but it was on the opposite side of town from the Casa Rosada, where the Argentine president conducted affairs of state and near which SIDE had its headquarters, where a colleague and I had to go regularly—he to talk Cuban intelligence collection efforts and I to discuss propaganda operations.

Our Soviet and Czech specialist colleagues had done a better job of solving the problems of personal housekeeping. They had found an Argentine customs broker who was a genius in his field. Since SIDE had not properly documented us as officials we could not bring household goods into the country without paying exorbitant fees, but the broker knew exactly whom to bribe and just how much to pay. As a result we were better taken care of than embassy personnel. He got my trunks delivered from the airport the afternoon after we arrived. No American Embassy official ever was able to get air freight from the customs area in less than two weeks.

Housing was a terrible problem because Art and I arrived just when the Ford Motor Company's Argentine subsidiary tripled its American personnel. They had housing allowances double ours and outbid us on every house. Art had preceded his wife in the hope of taking care of all these settling-in details before she arrived. He couldn't find a house he thought would suit her for six months. We couldn't wait for just the right thing.

As soon as I had met with the SIDE officers I could tell we did not look at the mission of combating Communism the same way. They made the men in Angleton's Counter Intelligence Staff seem soft on Communism. At first I hoped my rudimentary Spanish, in which we had all our discussions, caused me to misunderstand them. As my language skills improved, I found their views even worse than I first imagined. They seemed convinced that absolutely any political development contrary to their way of thinking was somehow the result of Communist machinations. The greatest irony was that these men were the team that Henry had briefed in order that they might become a propaganda arm of Frondizi's progressive regime. They hated Frondizi. They hated Frondizi's sidekick, Rogelio Frigerio, who had made the deal with Perón that got Frondizi elected, with even greater vengeance. Frigerio was a Jew, they told me. He and Frondizi were both secret Communists, they swore.

Acción Psicológica, the department our assistance had brought into being, was an outgrowth of SIDE's special anti-Communist operations department—Departamento de la Guerra Revolucionaria. Before CIA got into the act SIDE officers had gone for training to France. Their thinking forever after was affected by the French military's version of the war in Algeria. Behind every Algerian anti-colonialist stood a Communist conspirator, these French officers were convinced. If you don't want trouble in Argentina, they taught the men from SIDE, you better root out all the hidden Communists in your country.

One of the principal advisers of my contacts in Acción Psicológica was a Corsican Nazi collaborator who had found his way to Argentina and who was a leading exponent of the French military view. His name was Alberto Falcionelli. Fascist Nelly, as I always thought of him, was in a way my counterpart. He was supposed to help the Argentines develop propaganda programs and ideas just as I was. This frightened me. I was frightened even more when I read his book, *Sociedad Occidental y la Guerra Revolucionaria*. His thesis was that the United States was a soft-headed society whose economic system was dominated by Jewish international bankers who really were engaged in weakening the country's capitalist system so it would be ripe to fall into Communist hands. While they appeared to be capitalists, these bankers were actually sucking the blood from the capitalist system. John F. Kennedy was surrounded by Jewish advisers. Falcionelli's prescription for the salvation of the capitalist world was a coup d'état by the Pentagon or, failing this,

370

rejection of U.S. leadership in the struggle against Communism by the other nations, like Argentina, who were valiantly resisting the Marxist foe.

If their ideology appalled me, I found Acción Psicológica's operations even worse. Part of our funds were being spent on support of a series of spot radio announcements—stinging anti-Communist slogans I was certain resulted only in a crescendo of clicks all over the country as sets were turned off when the announcements came on. They had also dubbed in Spanish *I Led Three Lives*, the Herbert A. Philbrick TV series telling the story of that great hero of the McCarthy era who served as an informer for the FBI. They were feeding dozens of articles to provincial newspapers—the old provincial press operation ploy which produced hundreds of clippings for me to send to Washington and to other stations for replay. This proved how much production we were getting for our money. Newspapers from Salta, Jujuy, Tucumán, Mendosa, Córdoba, La Plata, and dozens more the uninitiated might not realize were completely insignificant were running our stuff, making it appear we were covering Argentina with a blanket of clever anti-Communist propaganda. They also had a team that ran all around Buenos Aires pasting on walls a variety of anti-Communist posters they considered eye-catching. I saw Henry's hand in this one. He loved wall posters. In my experience they were only items kids drew moustaches and wrote dirty words on, but he insisted that in Europe they were effective. Argentines thought of themselves as Europeans. I reluctantly had to admit that good-sized crowds frequently gathered around SIDE's wall posters.

Nevertheless, the first task I set myself was to reduce the amount of money we were spending on these operations. This met with station and Washington approval because I proposed to use the money saved to encourage special anti-Cuban efforts. The SIDE officers naturally resisted. They couldn't get excited about the Cuban threat.

"You know we're one hundred percent anti-Communist, Pépé," they told me, "but how can you take Cuba so seriously?"

To them Cubans were a joke. "They make good cigars, fairly decent rum, and lousy love to women," they said. "They can't possibly export their revolution to Argentina. Look, the only real revolutionary in Castro's gang is an Argentine, Che Guevara."

The missile crisis in October, 1962, changed their minds. They

371

responded with a will to my suggestions for editorials in major Buenos Aires dailies strongly supporting President Kennedy. I proposed they emphasize that when the President said, "The price of liberty is high, but we have always paid it," he obviously meant by "we" all Americans, the descendants of San Martín as well as George Washington. That was the kind of feeling they enjoyed expressing and I don't think we were ever closer. Even Fascist Nelly told me he admired John Kennedy's guts and perhaps the man was capable of leading the free world after all.

As the Argentine spring turned into summer in December, SIDE proposed a leaflet drop over the beaches in Mar del Plata, Argentina's seaside summer capital. They had an excellent cartoonist who did a great job of depicting a disgraced Castro and Khrushchev scurrying to get the missiles out of Cuba. We used funds from some of the radio spots I had discontinued to pay for these anti-Castro leaflets and they took me along for the drop.

SIDE had a Beechcraft we had helped them acquire at a second-hand aircraft sale and I and my three principal SIDE contacts piled into the plane for a weekend of seaside leaflet dropping. Besides dropping leaflets, the SIDE officers had some other business with the local military in which they did not wish to include me. My main contact, Juan Carlos, said he would take his wife along to show me the town. Bibi was a stunning woman and I found the prospect quite agreeable. I was particularly intrigued when I mentioned this to another Argentine who knew Juan Carlos and Bibi. "Oh yes," he said, "it's interesting all right. Personally, I can't stand a man who pimps for his wife."

Unfortunately, when the pilot found out Bibi was going on the trip he decided to take his wife along too. Thus a pattern of association between the two women naturally developed, and the amount of time Bibi could devote to me was severely limited. I never had the chance to find out whether this remark about Juan Carlos was anything more than merely nasty.

SIDE personnel spent many hours in secret business with Argentine army and navy officers besides the time they devoted to the meetings in Mar del Plata to which I was not invited. SIDE officers were, in fact, either former or current army or navy or air force officers, on loan to the intelligence organization. It was only natural, therefore, that the concerns of their colleagues were also theirs.

372

Their principal common interest was coup plotting. The trouble was that there were a large number of different factions in the armed forces. This produced a great deal of confusion and usually more conspiratorial meetings than action, but not always.

From the time I arrived in June, 1962, until the end of the year, there were four abortive coup attempts, at least three others that never got out of the talking stage, and one serious conflict. In September, 1962, a major confrontation between the two most powerful factions in the army took place. On Saturday night, September 22, 120 soldiers lost their lives in a tank battle in Avellaneda, the industrial suburb of Buenos Aires. General Juan Carlos Ongania emerged from this clash as the champion of continued civilian government. Ironically, in 1966 he would be the man who would agree to lead the coup forces that threw President Arturo Illia out of office. This was because of the way the rules of the coup d'état game worked. By early 1963, I thought I had figured out these rules and that we should support the efforts of Frondizi's followers and the moderate Peronists to win an overwhelming victory at the polls. This would put an end to the hopes of the military schemers and the country on the road to political stability without which its economy could never hope to recover. I was overruled.

I learned how the coup game worked from listening to my friends in SIDE. After the Mar del Plata trip, we took other junkets around the country on the Beechcraft. I don't think our propaganda missions achieved much but I got to know a lot of officers whose coup plotting efforts had caused their early retirement. The secret of the coup game was that everyone could play and no one lose. Officers whose plots failed were forced to retire by the winners, but they retired at full pay. So if your coup succeeded, you might rule Argentina. If you failed, you could retire at full pay and start a second career.

We drank a lot of wine late into the evening on these trips, and I heard of more coup plans than I could keep straight. I remember one air force major in Tucumán telling the story of how his retirement came about. He had been in charge of the air force security guard at the military airfield in Palermo on the night that President Frondizi flew back from Montevideo after the Punta del Este meeting in August, 1961, which made plans for the Alianza para el Progreso. The major was supposed to line up an honor guard beside

373

the presidential plane. When Frondizi reached the bottom of the steps, the major was to order the guard to open fire, "and kill the damned Communist bastard."

"I remember our final briefing," the major told us. "I could see the coup chief going chicken. He suddenly realized we planned to murder our country's president and turned pale. He asked me whether my men would comply with my order to shoot. The son-of-a-bitch. I said, 'Look, colonel, I command these men. When I give an order, they obey.' He finally said he wanted to reconsider the plan. He reconsidered, all right. The next day I was arrested and then retired."

The coup game resulted in many changes in SIDE throughout my stay in Argentina. After the September, 1962, affair, the chief of Acción Psicológica was retired and a jolly fat Italian took his place. I learned still more from Colonel Poli about how things worked. His sympathies lay entirely with the side that lost on September 22, but he had been able to keep out of the fray directly and now found himself in a powerful position where he could work to undermine the civilian government General Ongania had pledged to support. He concentrated on sabotaging the plan to hold free national elections in the summer of 1963 which President Guido promised the people.

One of Poli's gimmicks was to use his position as chief of Acción Psicológica to run opinion polls. These he carefully doctored so that the Peronists appeared to be completely uncompromising. This information he fed into the president's office and to the secretary of interior to upset their plans for permitting the Peronists to participate in a coalition ticket. President Guido and his minister of interior realized that unless the Peronists were permitted some form of participation the elections would not achieve the healing of wounds essential to a new political start for the country. They were trying to come up with a formula that would let the Peronists be involved but still not win complete power in a new civilian administration. This was perhaps an impossible task but Poli's purpose was to make failure certain.

I would not give Poli any of our funds for these polls but I did agree to provide money for another of his plans. This was a training school for anti-Communist activists who would infiltrate student groups, women's groups, and similar organizations to combat

374

Communist influence. I went along because of the constant pressure to fight the spread of Castro influence. The University of Buenos Aires was a major target of both the Argentine intelligence service and the station. We agreed the university was the principal center of pro-Cuban activities in the country. The station was also under constant pressure to spot likely candidates to send to Cuba posing as pro-Castro students in order to have what Des called "on-island reporting assets." Poli's trainees would be able to do this kind of spotting and recruiting after they had been taught how to gain control of a leftist student so that he could be convinced to do this kind of work for us.

I was with Poli at the inaugural session of the training school the night before the April, 1963, coup began. He was remarkably cheerful that night but not terribly communicative. The next day I knew why.

In going over the curriculum with Poli and the faculty members he selected for the school I discovered why the officers who were planning the coup were anti-Peronists and learned that obviously another coup was close at hand. I didn't dare ask them the date because nothing explicit enough for me to hang such a question on was ever said. There were two major anti-Peronist elements, I discovered. One were navy officers who felt that their leader, Admiral Isaac Rojas, who had engineered the overthrow of Perón, had been maneuvered out of power by the army. The other major anti-Peronist group were army officers who were disciples of officers who had supported Perón in his early pro-Fascist and pro-Nazi days. When to Perón's surprise the Germans lost the war, he dumped these men and began looking for a new inspiration for his patchwork Peronist ideology. Perón had no political ideas of his own except a desire for power. First he borrowed his ideas from fascism. When fascism failed he found support for his basic totalitarian inclinations in the totalitarian system that had won the war. He ignored the fact the Soviets had won in partnership with Britain and the United States. Hitler had taught him to dislike the British and disliking the United States is the birthright of every Latin American.

I could hardly contain myself when Poli and his fellow Fascist ideologues described themselves as the "democratic elements" in opposition to Peronism and complained that the efforts of Guido

375

and his interior minister to hold free elections must be defeated at all costs. Unfortunately, CIA had accepted this distorted definition of the political forces in Argentina and alone I couldn't change it.

On Tuesday morning, April 2, a column of General Ongania's tanks was attacked by Argentine navy jets at Magdalena, thirty-five miles southeast of Buenos Aires. Navy-controlled marines took over the downtown section of the city. Vessels from the fleet stood off the harbor and threatened to shell the capital.

I rushed over to the Acción Psicológica's offices to find out just how serious things were. By this time, my reaction to seeing tanks in the streets was the same as most Argentine citizens'. "Payasos militares"—military clowns—people shouted that morning at the tanks which were blocking traffic making driving to work even more difficult than usual. Except for the September, 1962, affair, no shots were usually fired when the soldiers were in the streets.

As I got to the door of the building Acción Psicológica occupied, two men rushed past me with bundles of the tabloid Noticias Gráficas under their arms. There were stacks of the paper in the entry. Full-page headlines declared "The National Revolution Triumphs!" Noticias Gráficas was the one newspaper in the metropolitan area which always printed whatever material Acción Psicológica prepared. I knew what I would find when I got upstairs.

All my SIDE contacts were bubbling with enthusiasm. The special edition of Noticias Gráficas was theirs, as I realized. Their men were also in the city's radio stations proclaiming victory. Poli said, "I'm sorry I didn't tell you last night, Pépé, but we couldn't afford any slips." The air force officer in the group was talking about the reported strafing at Magdalena. "My service did it," he shouted, "we're all in this together. We're backing the navy and Admiral Rojas to the hilt."

He was mistaken. The air force remained with Ongania and his commanders, who stood loyally by President Guido. It was the navy's air arm that attacked the pro-government forces. The loyal Argentine air force destroyed twenty-five of the navy's thirty-three planes in the next two days and Ongania massed tanks and 25,000 troops around the marine barracks in the Belgrano section of Buenos Aires. Acción Psicológica's bit of psychological warfare with Noticias Gráficas and the radio proved to have been premature. The last important coup d'état during my stay in Argentina, save one, was over by early Friday morning, April 5, 1963.

376

A CIA station is supposed to provide Washington early warning of all coup d'états. I was angry that Poli had not given me the word on Monday night. He was, after all, spending a lot of CIA money. I soon found that our having goofed on coup reporting was more inexcusable than I first thought.

On the Monday morning following the coup I had a visitor. He was a tall man past middle age with iron gray hair and a neatly trimmed moustache. His suit looked as if it had been freshly pressed five minutes before. His appearance and bearing were those all Argentine males who possibly could affected. The amount of equipment to aid in their grooming my SIDE colleagues packed aboard the Beechcraft on our trips always made me feel like a bum.

"I'm Navy Captain Eduardo Lynch," he introduced himself. "I've been wanting to meet you."

I knew who he was. His name had come up in discussions of the University of Buenos Aires, although I had never seen him before. He was the Guerra Revolucionaria department's specialist on university activities.

"Who is Mr. Connelly?" he asked.

I didn't recognize the name, but I evidently showed my apprehension in my face. I was wondering if this was the true name of an officer under cover in the Moore-McCormack office whom I knew only by pseudonym but who, I knew, worked on operations in the University of Buenos Aires which were not disclosed to SIDE.

"He's the freight shipment supervisor at Moore-McCormack Lines," Lynch continued, adding somewhat archly, "but he really seems to be more interested in student affairs at the university for some strange reason."

The compartmentation practiced in order to protect operations CIA doesn't want to admit to local intelligence services was working pretty well, because I could honestly say I knew nothing about the man's activities.

"Let me tell you what happened during the recent events which brought Mr. Connelly's activities rather forcefully to my attention," Lynch pressed on.

"Mr. Connelly is great friends with a chap who provides money for a student social center and, I also know, to certain student political groups. It seems this chap has an apartment on Maipu, just a few blocks from your embassy, as a matter of fact. Although he doesn't live there he and Mr. Connelly meet there rather often.

"Now, several navy officers who were involved in the coup have just been found in that apartment, and, I hate to say, arrested. I'm retired, as you might assume, but my heart was really with those chaps. I don't like the drift our government is taking very much. However, the point is I think I must warn someone that Mr. Connelly's activities may soon be very closely investigated. I know you talk to Acción Psicológica about our Communist problem at the university and so I thought I'd better see you. I don't know anyone in the embassy with whom I could speak."

Lynch was very politely saying he suspected either I was Mr. Connelly's case officer or that someone in the embassy was. The embassy station was supposed to be completely unknown. Its personnel were not disclosed to SIDE. Lynch was letting me know too, very nicely, that SIDE knew the undeclared station was there.

As quickly as I could I got rid of him, promising to call with a complete report as soon as possible. Then I checked into the station and told my story. As a result, we determined that I would take over Connelly's university contacts since they had now been blown to SIDE. Fortunately, he was leaving in a short time on reassignment. We decided that I would tell Lynch I was coordinator for all elements of the U.S. mission in Argentina on student affairs, and he should always deal with me about any questions he had, and no one else. I'd explain that Connelly's activities were ones I had thought his superiors had been told about. In any case, from now on I would keep him fully posted.

We tried to forget the horror story of our safehouse being used as a hideout for coup plotters. It wasn't easy since not only did this seem to link CIA to the coup but the embarrassment of our not even knowing Connelly's agent was involved and not receiving from him one advance word about the coup was even worse.

When I looked further into the so-called "unilateral" student operation, I discovered it was a remnant of a type of large-scale activity popular in the 1950s. I also learned that the project had been started a few years after Perón's overthrow by Hans Tofte. Tofte had founded a large umbrella anti-Communist group which was supposed to cover every conceivable sector of Argentine society. As in the case of Tofte's guerrilla operations behind North Korean lines, the organization's work proved to be fictional. The principal agent flunked the lie-detector test when asked what was happening

378

to the funds. Hundreds of thousands of dollars were missing. The operation was cancelled. However, several members who were active in university student political affairs passed their box tests and were retained.

By the time I took over, the principal agent of Connelly's was well past university student age. Professional students were common in BA where the university was a commuter college. It cost practically nothing to enroll and claim to be a *"universitario,"* a significant status symbol. Nevertheless, I thought our cover for operating through this man extremely thin. Then I found out it wasn't the poor cover that had revealed his activities to SIDE. Connelly's agent's best friend was Captain Lynch's assistant in the Guerra Revolucionaria department. Somehow we hadn't known this either. I discovered this fact quickly by comparing the man's true name with that of Lynch's aide. Lazy case officers frequently did not read files carefully and almost never bothered to look up the true names of encrypted agents, if they didn't have to meet them personally. Lynch had not been lying when he said his heart was with the coup plotters. His assistant had hidden the navy officers in our safehouse. I insisted we drop Connelly's "unilateral" contact.

Lynch and I became good friends. His views were conservative but not Fascist like many of his colleagues', and he appeared to have a wide range of contacts which could serve our legitimate interests, especially our preoccupation with Cuba.

Lynch smiled very broadly when I first mentioned our great concern with Cuba. "You want me to work against my nephew Ernie, is that it?" he asked. "He's the black sheep of the family, all right." Having had his fun, he added, "You know him as Ernesto Che Guevara. It seems he thinks Ernie Lynch isn't a very appropriate name for a Latin American revolutionary, so he uses his mother's maiden name. It also embarrasses him to think he's really an Irish Argentine with one uncle in SIDE and a branch of the family prosperous businessmen in the state of California, U.S.A."

Lynch provided me with a lot of information on Che Guevara's early life which Washington seemed pleased to receive. By the mid-1960s we had a group of psychiatrists who attempted to analyze targets like Guevara on the basis of such reporting in order to recommend the best means of dealing with them. I sent in with

379

some reserve the details about the seriousness of Che's asthma, fearing I might one day hear Guevara had mysteriously choked to death.

If the aftermath of the April, 1963, coup led to some interesting new activities for me, in particular the relationship with Captain Lynch, it led to the end of any chance for the kind of election I hoped Argentina would have that year and in which I thought we should play a part. Although Ongania's forces proved superior to the navy's, a negotiated settlement was made and President Guido pledged a strong anti-Peronist stand. This meant a coalition of Frondizi forces and moderate Peronists would not be permitted to put a presidential candidate in the field. I had developed some excellent contacts in this group on my own initiative. I thought we should put some serious money behind this coalition, but I could not sell the project even though I pleaded its success would mean once again we might be able to make Argentina the showplace of the Alianza para el Progreso.

I was overruled because it was said the operation was too risky. The real reason was that George Meany hated Peronist unions. Without dealing with the Argentine Confederation of Labor it was impossible to deal with the Peronists who controlled this organization. The Argentine labor confederation, furthermore, was the key to the kind of big vote the coalition needed. Meany's clout with the U.S. government and CIA's world labor operations was so great Washington didn't dare entertain my proposal. We couldn't be allowed to talk to Peronist labor leaders.

The following year, 1964, CIA spent $3 million to elect Eduardo Frei president of Chile. Then I knew another reason we did not get approval for a serious election operation in Argentina—one that I estimated would cost no more than $1 million. American investment in Argentina was minimal. Ford and Kaiser had assembly operations and American tire companies were operating in Argentina as well as some meat packers. Auto and tire people were also in Chile and many other places. They didn't count for much, when compared with the U.S. mining investment in Chile. Chile's copper mines, producing one of the largest copper outputs in the world, were almost entirely an American business. Americans were also deeply involved in other mineral-producing activities—nitrate, iron, gold, silver. Henry's initial briefing to me about Latin America came back to mind. Despite the idealistic Alianza para el Progreso prattle, U.S. policy and CIA activities in Latin America were shaped by U.S. business interests and investments.

Between the Argentine elections in 1963 and the Chilean election of 1964, my attention was once again focused on Cuba. Gerry Droller had become branch chief of the countries of the "Cono Sur," the southern cone of Uruguay, Paraguay, Argentina, and Chile. He came down to Buenos Aires to remind us Cuba was more important than any of them.

"Listen, this guy Des is a genius and he's got the inside track to the White House," Gerry explained. "I also think J. C.'s going to retire soon and Des will run the whole division in name as well as fact. Already we got dozens of old FE hands in the division and more guys from Germany too. WH Division is now all chopstick users and umlaut speakers. And we're all supposed to concentrate on Cuba."

The matter we all concentrated on from December, 1963, until the summer of 1964 was making the discovery of a small arms cache on the coast of Venezuela seem important enough proof of Castro's interventionist intentions that the OAS would declare Cuba an outlaw nation and refuse to allow OAS members to have political or economic relations with her. I initially paid little attention to the news of the discovery of these arms that came from Caracas just after John Kennedy's assassination. I still hadn't gotten over the terrible shock of the President's death when I received a cable saying headquarters wanted maximum press coverage given to the announcement on December 3, 1963, that the OAS had agreed to investigate Venezuelan charges the arms had been secretly delivered by Castro's forces for the use of Venezuelan leftist guerrillas.

SIDE wasn't interested in giving such a story all-out coverage. The attitude of SIDE officers was "what else is new?" They also did not share U.S. enthusiasm for Betancourt or his AD Party successor who had just been elected on December 1. They felt, as did Jack, the Caracas station chief, that Betancourt and all his colleagues were crypto Communists. We soon had another visitor from Washington to set us straight.

The new chief of covert action operations for WH came down to Buenos Aires just before Christmas to explain how important the

381

Venezuelan arms cache discovery was considered. Dramatically, he related how much the discovery had meant to John Kennedy. "The President had been pressuring us for months before he was killed to come up with some solid proof that Castro was exporting his revolution. He wanted to make his anti-Castro crusade a Latin American cause not just a U.S. mission. He wanted to have some really convincing evidence of Castro's interference in the affairs of Latin countries so that we could get the OAS to take collective action against Castro. This discovery is what he was looking for."

Herb explained that the news of the discovery had come in from Caracas just the day before President Kennedy left for Texas. He and another officer rushed over to see Bobby Kennedy with the cable. Bobby called the President and he ordered them to come immediately to the Oval Office. "President Kennedy was extremely pleased and excited about the prospects," Herb said. "It was very late in the evening when we left the White House. I think this was the last piece of business he took up before he left Washington. We all like to think we're running this operation for him."

Herb presented us the case against Cuba. The arms had been found on a remote peninsula served only by one secondary road and with no large settlements nearby. Local fishermen had discovered the cache by accident. No Venezuelan guerrillas ever had come near the spot. Herb's story was that on such a coast a boat could land at night with little chance of being detected, the stuff stashed in the dunes, and picked up some subsequent night by the revolutionaries receiving Castro's assistance.

We were working very closely, Herb said, with the Venezuelan authorities to establish complete proof the arms had come from Castro and investigations were going on in Europe and Canada. Some of the arms had been traced to a Belgian manufacturer and Belgian security officials were helping us find records that would show when they were purchased by the Cubans. The Canadians had already advantageously found us proof that a sixteen-foot aluminum boat found hidden with the arms had been sold by a Canadian firm to the Cuban Agrarian Reform Institute just one month before the arms were discovered.

He was most excited about a story from a Venezuelan leftist in the custody of the Venezuelan security police. The prisoner confessed that maps found in his apartment showed where attacks were to be made in Caracas, using these arms, on the eve of the December 1, 1963, presidential elections. Also found in his apartment were instructions on how to use the arms found in the cache. They were a type of weapon which hitherto had not been used by any Venezuelan rebel groups.

The story of the maps sounded familiar to me. I couldn't remember anything about arms instructions, but I remembered the maps were found in this man's apartment way back when I had been Venezuelan desk chief.

"Aren't these the maps we found the other year and couldn't make any sense of?" I asked.

"Yes, that's right," Herb replied. "Our intelligence assistant on the Venezuelan desk got the material out again right after we found the arms and she came up with a beautiful research job we sent to Caracas for the police to use in questioning the suspect. He's confessed."

I was not too impressed with this evidence of the Venezuelan guerrillas' intended use of the arms. It sounded to me as though we might have manufactured it to meet President Kennedy's requirement for an OAS case. I was especially unimpressed by the confession. There are few prisoners of security police in Latin America who refuse to confess. If they don't confess they usually have died in the process of making up their minds, having thought too long about the matter with their heads under water or something similar.

"I like the touch about the boat's being sold by Canadians to the Cuban Agrarian Reform Institute. Makes it sound as though Castro's trying to be real spooky, using a cover like the Agrarian Reform Institute to deliver arms," I couldn't resist saying. "How did we actually get the arms there?"

Herb looked at me very hard. "Joe, you are too fond of black operations. Of course, we didn't put the arms there ourselves. Come on."

We had three things to do: first, show all the evidence to SIDE and ask SIDE to push the matter up to the top of the Argentine government to gain Argentina's support for Venezuela's charges in the OAS; get the pictures in the Argentine press, plus editorial and other comment supporting the Venezuelan case; try to uncover anything similar we could to show that the Cubans were giving direct support to revolutionaries in Argentina. The first two tasks were easily accomplished. My friends in Acción Psicológica particularly liked the pictures of the arms. We had no luck for some months in finding any Argentine guerrillas.

In early March, 1964, we got a break. The Argentine gendarmerie, the border police, found eight young people in a camp in the far northern province of Salta near the Bolivian border. Seven men and a girl were picked up. They had some weapons, a copy of Che Guevara's book on guerrilla warfare, and a stack of Communist propaganda tracts. My SIDE friends suggested we all take the Beechcraft to Salta to see whether or not this might be the evidence of Cuban support to guerrillas we were looking for.

We went to the gendarmerie post a few miles outside the provincial capital where the prisoners were being held and their confiscated arms and possessions were stored. The arms were clearly old Argentine army rifles. The Communist propaganda was similar to that which could be obtained under the counter at bookstores near the University of Buenos Aires. The public sale of such literature was prohibited, but Captain Lynch's men were picking it up all the time and I had seen before most of what I saw in Salta. Lynch had also given me a copy of his nephew's book, also easily, if not legally, obtainable. I sat quietly in the back of the room, posing as another "European" Argentine, while the SIDE officers talked to several prisoners. They were middle-class kids and were awaiting the arrival of a lawyer one of their fathers had arranged for them. They were polite but not communicative. The SIDE officers tried no persuasion.

A week after my visit to the camp, Des Fitzgerald came to Buenos Aires. As Gerry Droller had predicted, Des was now WH Division chief and this was his first swing around the hemisphere to visit his new stations. He gave us all a short pep talk—the theme of which was the importance of the success of the OAS sanctions operation. He also briefed us on the overall status of other operations against Cuba being run from JMWAVE, but he sounded a trifle discouraged.

"If Jack Kennedy had lived," Des said, "I can assure you we would have gotten rid of Castro by last Christmas. Unfortunately, the new President isn't as gung-ho on fighting Castro as Kennedy was."

384

"What do you mean by 'gotten rid of,' Des?" I asked. "Assassination?"

"Well, you know, Joe, we don't use that language," he replied. "Just say I mean he wouldn't still be doing business in Havana."

Des asked me what I thought about the guerrillas in Salta. I told him I didn't think there was a shred of evidence that they were receiving any support from Castro. "They're just a bunch of bored middle-class kids, Des, who maybe had a fight with their parents."

I didn't know that unhappy middle-class kids would soon be throwing bombs all over the world, from Montevideo to New York, Paris to Tokyo, and almost everywhere in between. These kids would help drive Lyndon Johnson from office, but not before he had ordered CIA to violate its charter and get busy trying to stop dissent in the United States. They would push Richard Nixon's paranoia to the point where he couldn't rest until he had expanded Johnson's covert operations against them so that fighting the kids was a top priority of Mexico City station when I got there in 1969.

"Well," mused Des, "maybe we have enough friends in Argentina that somebody important might just say he thought Castro was helping them."

General Julio Alsogaray, commander in chief of the gendarmerie, declared on March 26, 1964, that there were at least twenty guerrillas in Salta and adjacent Jujuy province and that some of them had fired on his troops. Two guerrillas were killed trying to cross the border into Bolivia in the encounter. "These guerrillas," said Alsogaray, "are being aided by Fidel Castro, who is trying to export revolution to all of the continent."

The OAS convened a meeting of foreign ministers in Washington from July 21 to July 26, 1964, to decide on Venezuela's charges. They concluded that Castro had sent arms to Venezuela for the purpose of disrupting the Venezuelan elections of December, 1963. Diplomatic and consular relations with Cuba were severed by OAS members and economic sanctions enforced. Only Bolivia, Uruguay, Chile, and Mexico opposed these measures. The rest of Latin America evidently had been convinced of the validity of the Venezuelan charges and the threat of Cuban subversion in the hemisphere.

By that time I had agreed to serve another two-year tour in Argentina. Curly asked me to and promised I would have more responsibility and more interesting work. Ruthven was now at Wellesley and living on the Argentine pesos the station bought on the black market in Montevideo helped me save enough money to pay her way.

It was a mistake to stay another tour in Argentina. Before I left I felt like an Argentine myself. In addition to their other complexes, Argentines feel that they are alone at the bottom of the world and that their problems and interests are ignored. It seemed to me after two more years in BA that no one was paying any attention to Argentina or to any ideas I had about it. Washington could send an army to Santo Domingo, spend $3 million on an election in Chile, send hundreds of JMWAVE sabotage crews into Cuba and other Cuban exile mercenaries to fight in the Congo, even start a major war in Vietnam, but nobody cared whether or not the Argentine government could be made to function well enough to avoid further civil strife and military dictatorship.

Curly was transferred to Panama. He was replaced by Nick, a Greek who was comfortable with dictatorial regimes from his years of service in his family's homeland, Vietnam at the height of Diem's power, and in South Korea, from where he was sent directly to Buenos Aires. He was especially proud of the fact he had never served a tour in headquarters. Consequently, he didn't understand the game of promoting a situation into something that would win NSC's Special Group's approval for a political action program. He wasn't inclined to support my ideas for action in Argentina in any case. His view of our job was a journeyman intelligence officer's. Producing as many reports on as many aspects of the country's problems as possible was his goal. At least this kind of leadership got me more fully involved in what was going on in Argentine politics, which naturally I liked, but I was frustrated because I couldn't do anything to shape the events I was reporting.

I was happy to be told to gather more information from other sources than my SIDE contacts. For one thing, it gave me a chance to use the full talents of my one good unilateral propaganda partner. Antonio Ángel Diaz was owner of the nation's largest newsreel company and had years of advertising and public relations experience as well as the wide range of influential connections that a shrewd operator such as he develops in this line of work. His wheeler-dealer skills had enabled him to obtain passage of a law making it compulsory for all movie houses to show newsreels. He

386

also handled a lot of the contract work when Frondizi decided to reverse himself and ask for American oil drillers' bids to increase Argentine oil production. Diaz's oil contract deals made him and some Texans a lot of money. Naturally, Diaz found CIA, we didn't find him.

Diaz did all the filming of President Eisenhower's visit to South America and he worked on the Punta del Este conference in 1961. He became friends with Jim Haggerty when Haggerty was Eisenhower's press secretary and continued his relationship when Haggerty became head of ABC. At Punta del Este he came to know Dick Goodwin and he had fine relationships with USIS officers in Buenos Aires and Montevideo. When he thought the time was ripe, he came up with a proposal to slant his newsreels—something he knew full well USIS could not handle. With the kind of friends he had, by the time I arrived in Argentina it had been strongly suggested that CIA should pick up the Diaz proposal. I did.

I liked Diaz from the moment I met him. I knew at once what his interests were and he understood mine immediately. We worked out a business arrangement that was uncomplicated and effective. I paid him $40,000 in quarterly amounts and for this I selected one newsreel item a week for special treatment. These were sent to all theaters throughout Argentina and I received from him a report on the size of audiences which satisfied my requirements for reporting on how our money was spent. Diaz required theaters to provide this report so he could show it to clients who paid to be included in his newsreels. Hence, no change which could cause suspicion was required for him to get what Washington wanted.

One advantage of being a $40,000 client of his was that we held our meetings in his home, which was the finest safehouse I ever knew. Diaz had the penthouse of an apartment building in Palermo with a roof garden that included a swimming pool, a well-stocked bar, and an enormous barbecue pit on which he loved to grill us steaks of two-inch-thick Argentine baby beef. I spent the pleasantest hours of my tour in Argentina at my monthly meetings with Antonio Ángel lunching on our steaks and a couple of liters of Argentina's best red wine. The penthouse not only met the needs of the flesh admirably, it was an ideal arrangement as far as security was concerned. Once I had made certain I was not under surveillance when I entered the building, I went up to the apartment whose single entrance was a completely private double steel door.

Long before Nick told me to go out and get more intelligence in 1965, I had discovered how extensive my host's contacts were as we quickly finished our newsreel business and settled down to enjoying our lunches and talking about many things. He knew Peronists, Frondizi followers, military commanders, newspaper owners, nightclub proprietors, and hundreds of businessmen.

He told me how he had set up the drilling contracts. His favorite deal had been the one he made with Southeastern Drilling Company for a man named William Clements. He said they were making so much money that Clements's U.S. intermediaries had skipped the country to avoid paying U.S. income taxes. "Clements's company was nothing until I made this deal for him," he boasted. "We're great friends." They were splitting profits fifty-fifty. Evidently, something happened to this friendship, because I read when Richard Nixon appointed Clements deputy secretary of defense in 1972, that Diaz had sued Clements, claiming total profits had been $25 million not $18 million as Clements insisted. Clements had destroyed his Argentine records so the auditors could not swear to the books and the newspaper account didn't say what the ultimate outcome had been. I don't know whether my friend Diaz and the U.S. Internal Revenue System were cheated out of their share of $7 million or not.

Diaz's New York contacts were with U.S. firms who put together a large private lobbying effort in the 1960s to contribute to the success of the Alianza para el Progreso, they claimed. The week before Senator Robert Kennedy was to arrive in Buenos Aires on his South American tour in 1965, I was having lunch with Diaz when one of these New York contacts called. Diaz spoke almost no English and he had trouble with the call. "Will you please talk on the phone," he asked me, "this is very important I think. They want me to help out with the Kennedy visit but I can't get exactly what it is they want me to do." I took the phone.

"Look, tell Ángel," the caller requested, "that we want him to help out Dick Goodwin. Goodwin is coming with Kennedy's party. He's supposed to be an adviser on cultural affairs. Tell Ángel we want to arrange the kind of cultural contacts Dick likes. I mean some really good-looking brunettes, and some blondes and redheads, if he can get them down there."

When I had translated this message, Diaz was delighted. "Tell him I'll arrange the best damned assortment of cultural contacts the man has ever enjoyed."

Obviously Antonio Ángel could provide me with the kind of contacts Nick wanted me to develop. I decided that the one I most wanted to make was Roberto Noble, owner and publisher of *El Clarín*, the largest-circulation morning newspaper in Buenos Aires and the most anti-U.S. Noble was a close adviser of ex-president Frondizi and now that Frondizi had been moved from his island prison to the relatively free life he was enjoying in a chalet in Bariloche, the Argentine alpine resort in the southern Andes, Frondizi men were extremely active at their old game of arranging pacts with Peronists.

Diaz was happy to introduce me to Noble. I decided this time I would not make the kind of mistake I had with Claro Recto in the Philippines. I told Noble I was a CIA officer who needed to know what was going on in Argentina. I said I could not possibly meet my responsibilities without contact with him—the man I considered the most knowledgeable person on progressive political developments in the country. The fact he frequently attacked the United States' policies made me all the more interested in talking with him. I said I would offer him the chance to express his views, via me, to the highest authorities in Washington and in return I would get him equally frank replies. Thus, without the subterfuge of diplomacy, we would open an honest dialogue which I hoped would bring about intelligent understanding, which is more important than agreement. "In short, Don Roberto," I concluded, "I want to learn."

Noble bought this flattery and began to educate me right away. I will always remember what he said because it seemed to me the clearest statement I ever heard of the dilemma Latin Americans face in thinking about their great northern neighbor.

"I know your embassy considers me pro-Communist because of the editorials I've written attacking President Johnson's putting troops into Santo Domingo to force the political decision there he wants to see," said Noble. "You must understand something. I have to say what I have said about this kind of interference in Santo Domingo's domestic affairs. I must. However, let me assure you, if I were president of Argentina and Communists tried to take over in Uruguay tomorrow, I'd have the Argentine army over there the next day."

Don Roberto and I developed a fine relationship. Unfortunately, his varied business interests frequently took him out of the country so he was often not available to discuss things as the crisis mounted leading up to the Ongania coup d'état. He was in Paris, in fact, when the coup took place, but he contacted the American Embassy there two days before it occurred to tell us it was inevitable.

The other contact I had Diaz arrange was with his close friend Brigadier General Eduardo Castro Sanchez, who became secretary of war in November, 1965. Castro Sanchez's appointment to this job caused the resignation of general Ongania as commander in chief. Ongania said he could not serve under an officer of inferior rank. To no avail, Castro Sanchez resigned his commission to become a civilian before accepting the job in order to try to prevent Ongania's resignation. The resignation would be the first step on the road to overthrowing the elected government and anyone following the Argentine scene realized this. The excuse of rank was too flimsy even for proud Argentines to swallow. The question was what the next step would be and when it would be taken. I thought a good way to find out was to talk to the man who would lose his job as secretary of war when the coup took place.

Nick was extremely pleased when I told him I had met Castro Sanchez at Diaz's apartment. He said he would like to come along next time. Nick and I first met together with Castro Sanchez in April, 1966, and we continued to see him frequently during the next three months. We quickly learned that he knew a lot about the moves of the coup plotters and was carefully planning his countermoves.

There was little doubt that Arturo Illia's government was drifting badly by the time we first met Castro Sanchez to talk about the problem. Illia's policies since he took office in October, 1963, had brought the country much economic grief. Illia's main accomplishment had been to cancel the Frondizi oil drilling contracts. This soon forced the country to import oil again and by the time Illia had been in office a year the Argentine government was heavily in debt. Castro Sanchez's plan was to have the government begin to act vigorously enough to stem the tide favoring the coup plotters.

Castro Sanchez finally persuaded the president to call a full cabinet meeting on June 10, 1966. It was only the second general cabinet meeting Illia had called in his two years and nine months in office. He called the first one when Kennedy was assassinated. That was devoted to deciding what kind of condolences to send. Castro Sanchez really ran the June 10 meeting, which issued a strong statement against Communism (something the generals were saying Illia was soft on) and pledged to control the labor unions who had been paralyzing the country with repeated widespread strikes. Thus, he struck directly at the two big issues being used to rally people to the cause of the promoters of military dictatorship. He also advised the president to keep the cabinet in session and hammer out other decisions as fast as possible. Meanwhile, he would try to split the ranks of the pro-coup officers, even placing some under house arrest if necessary.

I thought we had in Eduardo Castro Sanchez the man who could hold off the coup and revitalize the civilian government. I knew Illia was a weak reed, but if we gave Castro Sanchez full support, I was sure we could keep Argentina on the road to political recovery. Surely we could find the talent to assist Castro Sanchez. If we had been able to keep a man like Diem in business for nearly ten years, we could keep Illia going long enough for Argentina to have another presidential election. I told Nick I thought we should do everything possible to help Castro Sanchez.

"Don't be ridiculous," said Nick, "what can we do? Anyway, why should we save Illia?"

"First of all," I replied, "we could get Eduardo some funds. I'm sure if he had some money he'd have success with his plan to divide the coup group."

"We're going to be content to just listen," said Nick. "Does what kind of government Argentina has affect any U.S. vital interest?"

I pleaded it would be psychologically bad to let the coup occur. The United States was already in trouble in Latin America because of our action in Santo Domingo and Brazil. I also pointed out Ambassador Martin had publicly declared the United States wanted to see elective government kept alive in Argentina. Hence we would have no trouble getting policy approval to support Eduardo.

"You're talking like an old psychwarrior. Who cares about psychological effects as long as Argentina has a stable government? I'm sure the military will provide that." Nick would hear no more.

I knew Nick had a young station officer in touch with General Julio Alsogaray's staff. Alsogaray, who had said the right things about the Salta guerrillas, was now commander of the First Army and a leading coup plotter. Nick figured we couldn't lose. Anyway, I'm sure he also felt the situation would be more the kind he was used to handling if the military took over.

Castro Sanchez tried one last move. On Friday, June 24, he met with a general whose brother was a Peronist deputy in Congress. If he could get Peronist support and have their labor unions cooperate voluntarily in keeping their workers on the job instead of the government's needing to take control of the strike situation by force, there might be enough social peace for a while to remove the excuse for a coup. It was the wrong move. General Pascual Pistarini, who replaced Ongania as commander in chief, called the army's top officers together on Saturday morning and the coup plan started in motion. By Monday afternoon, June 27, Pistarini had forced Castro Sanchez to resign, pointing out that the army simply would take no further orders from the secretary of war. President Illia responded by firing Pistarini, but no other officer would agree to be commander in chief. By early evening, General Alsogaray was moving into town from Campo de Mayo and truckloads of his troops had surrounded the Casa Rosada. Nick thought we should stay up all night to see what happened. It was my turn to tell him his idea was ridiculous. I had lived through the September, 1962, coup and I knew that with the troops from Campo de Mayo in action against the government this time, rather than for it, the coup was over. Illia had no counterforce.

In the early morning hours of June 28, General Alsogaray walked into the president's office and ordered him to leave. Illia's cabinet had joined hands and sung the national anthem at midnight and then they had the sense enough to go home. Without a strong man like Castro Sanchez to advise him, the poor old doctor had trouble with his last decision. He couldn't decide whether to accept the car Alsogaray offered him or take a taxi to his brother's house. He finally decided to leave by cab to show his contempt for his disloyal generals.

Juan Carlos Ongania was sworn in as president the next day, June 29, and political parties were abolished. It was announced there would be no more elections held in Argentina for the foreseeable future. By July 1, the new head of SIDE was arresting Jews and by the end of the month all universities were closed by the government. Rioting students were fired on by the army, but the U.S. government had forgotten that its policy was to stand by civilian government in Argentina. Ambassador Martin, who had declared this policy, was out of favor with the new government, but the United States recognized the Ongania regime. Repudiating Ambassador Martin posed no problem. Nick, of course, was very happy.

I now saw that he was a wiser man than I thought. What kind of government Argentina had didn't matter to Washington. We had no vital interests there. I decided it was time for me to think very seriously about this. Perhaps I had been wrong all these years in thinking we should have a policy for saving every country in the world—one which would include covert action where necessary.

Jeanne, Julie, Andy, and I sailed home on August 29, exactly two months after Ongania took office. We were looking forward to meeting Ruthven in New York. We could see Punta del Este as we sailed by the Uruguayan coast. Through our binoculars we could pick out the Edificio Vanguardia where we had spent two wonderful vacations.

"It's too bad," said Jeanne, "if we had to spend four years on the Rio de la Plata, we spent them on the wrong side of the river."

21

We Don't Spy on Fellow Americans Unless They Disagree with Us

Career State Department Foreign Service Officers are fond of saying there are only two good posts—your last and your next. Mexico is the exception that proves the rule. After only one week in Mexico City Jeanne and I decided we didn't want to leave. I began to think about asking for early retirement as the way to achieve this goal. Nothing happened after our arrival in June, 1969, to make me want to continue my CIA career. A lot happened to convince me I should not. I have already mentioned the things that made me decide to take the final step when I did in June, 1973. Between June, 1969, and June, 1973, one of the things that bothered me most was finding CIA spying on the people who were protesting the Vietnam War.

I discovered my old trainer, Stan Archer, in charge of the Mexico City station's MHCHAOS program, and I learned the program was top priority. Before coming to Mexico I had only a few hints that MHCHAOS existed. CIA cryptonyms use a digraph, two letters at the beginning of the word, to help process the material the cryptonym covers. Sometimes the digraph indicates a geographic location, sometimes general subject matter. MH stood for matters relating to internal U.S. security. Someone evidently thought CHAOS appropriate for the specific subject. This was because MHCHAOS involved spying on fellow Americans—something CIA employees were always told we did not do. I and, I'm sure, the majority of my colleagues believed this. We believed it for a number of reasons.

First of all, the initial orientation lectures for all employees pointed out that the CIA's charter expressly forbid the Agency to have "police, subpoena, law enforcement powers or internal security functions inside the United States." Second, it was important for Clandestine Services officers to believe this when they served in U.S. embassies abroad. They faced almost universal suspicion on this point from State Department personnel, USIS officers, aid mission employees, and people from all the other components of the U.S. mission. These people simply couldn't believe the illogical story that an Agency devoted to national security had no security interests in the American people it was supposed to protect. You couldn't believe this unless you had the language of our restrictive charter drummed into you. We had, and we tried to convince them. We often quoted the charter's language. Many were still skeptical because, unlike us, they did not appreciate fully how much power J. Edgar Hoover had in the U.S. government and how thoroughly he resented CIA. It was to placate Hoover that the CIA's charter was written the way it was. CIA's responsibility for national security ended at the water's edge and Hoover's men took over.

Another reason a lot of CIA employees believed that we did not spy on fellow Americans was that relatively few really knew what James Angleton's CI staff was doing. Most Clandestine Services employees were aware of the mail-intercept program and had some idea that our extensive capabilities to bug installations and tap telephones might be used sometimes to follow particular cases in which we were tracking down Soviet or other agents operating from outside the United States into our country, but not many realized the extent of the violation of people's mail which the investigations of the Agency uncovered in 1975. They didn't because only a few knew exactly how we worked in this field. Angleton's staff handled liaison with the FBI, and officers with a "need to know" got information they had to have, but never learned precisely how it had been produced. For one thing, the bad blood between the FBI and CIA was reason enough for the CI staff officers to be closed-mouthed.

The source of most of the illegal information the Agency acquired was the National Security Agency, however, and this material was guarded by an extremely strict security system. The National Security Agency's worldwide code-breaking and information-interception results flowed into our Agency via the CI staff's special unit known as "Staff D." No one got a Staff D clearance unless Angleton's men were satisfied that the officer absolutely had to have access to the NSA information in order to carry out his responsibilities. The counterintelligence paranoid personality was nowhere more prominent than in the Staff D clearance procedure.

I didn't get a Staff D clearance until I became involved in our Indonesian operations in 1957. It was decided then that I couldn't hold Sukarno's feet to the fire without access to Staff D. I was notified one day to go to a certain corridor in "L" building. I wasn't able to enter the corridor when I got there because I was stopped by a man who peered suspiciously at me from a window in the bolted door that blocked the corridor from the central passageway. After verifying I was who I claimed to be, I was admitted to an anteroom shut off from the rest of the offices in the corridor and given a security briefing which included reading a brief history of code-breaking activities in World War II and which stressed I was to guard the secrecy of the very existence of the National Security Agency work with my life.

The briefing material told how the British film star Leslie Howard had done exactly that. The quiet courage with which he faced Humphrey Bogart in *The Petrified Forest* he displayed in real life as he met his death. A British intelligence officer in World War II, Leslie Howard had access to information from the German coded-message system—the breaking of which was a tremendous triumph for British cryptologists. He learned the mission he was about to fly into France had been blown and German planes would be in the air to shoot him down. If Howard did not fly the mission, however, the Germans would realize the British had cracked the code. Howard died to keep the secret.

None of the Indonesian messages, mostly police calls, I soon was reading were worth anyone's life. Neither in 1957 nor at any other

397

time did I ever read any NSA intercepts in Staff D that were of much use to me. This may have been bad luck, but there was a growing suspicion by the time I left CIA that most of NSA's material was of little value.

I never saw, of course, the kind of material that the congressional investigating committees uncovered in 1975. The sensitive material on Americans was even more tightly restricted. The Staff D spooky clearance didn't automatically give an officer a chance to see this information.

Angleton's stringent control of his staff and their secrecy was a special feature of Clandestine Services life. I remember the first time I ever went to Angleton's office. It took me a day to get over the experience. I found Angleton tucked away in an inside office which was completely draped in very heavy curtains. His desk sat amid a dozen various gadgets. Some of them I could identify as photographic apparatus, but I had no idea what purpose most of them served. Angleton himself was peering at some documents under a strong desk light. He was very pleasant and we had a good business talk, but I felt I had been admitted to an inner sanctum whose existence I must never mention to anyone for the same reasons I was never to tell the circumstances of Leslie Howard's death.

When I left Argentina I was full of doubts and questions about my work. I had begun to think that there was no need for cold warriors anymore. At the time I thought that my mood was shaped by living in a country as sick as Argentina. When we reached Washington in September, 1966, I found the United States was almost as sick. Racial tension was vibrant on every street in town. The Vietnam War, which I had even talked Roberto Noble into editorializing about as an example of how the United States stood by its commitments, was a subject of debate, not consensus, as the propaganda guidances from Washington had assured me in Buenos Aires.

Because I wanted to think about where I was going, and because my old boss in Manila, Jocko Richardson, whom I considered the wisest, most supportive man I ever worked for, was chief, I asked for an assignment in the Office of Training. It was in the Office of Training that I got the first hints of the existence of MHCHAOS. I first believed the premises of such a program to be sound, but later I came to doubt they were.

In June, 1968, I was running a seminar on black propaganda operations and techniques for a group of Army officers who were re-

398

turning to Vietnam to be part of a jointly sponsored Department of Defense–CIA unit engaged in these types of operations. Paul Linebarger unfortunately was dead and I was on my own. I drew on talent among old friends in FE Division who had served in Vietnam, some Vietnam specialists in the CIA director's office, and the CI staff. The CI staffers were supposed to help the class understand how to analyze Communist propaganda and appeals and also how to protect their unit from penetration by the Viet Cong or North Vietnamese army agents.

When I began the class, I was a hawk. When it was over I certainly hadn't become a dove, but I was very worried about the way the Army officers and the CI staff officers looked at Vietnam, our mission there, and at those people in our country who thought differently than they did.

The Army officers looked at the Vietnam War as a practice session which gave them a chance to try out new weapons and lead troops in combat. "Do you realize," the colonel who commanded the unit said to me one day at lunch, "the Russians haven't been in combat since World War II. Thank God for the Vietnam War, it gives us a chance to get some live action experience." As I tried to develop in class the theme of the importance of understanding the people who are targets of propaganda appeals, black, gray or white, it was obvious that the colonel and all his men considered the Vietnamese to be live range targets rather than people.

Regarding Americans who were questioning our role in Vietnam, they were apoplectic, and even sinister. "You haven't been out there, so you don't realize what it's like to be being sold out by these antiwar bastards, Bobby Kennedy, and the rest of the thimbleheads," they told me. "Look, if these people don't shape up, they better watch out when the troops get home. We can't have a government that won't support us. We'll have to see we have a strong anti-Commie government here if we have to take it over by force." I had read *Seven Days in May* and a friend of mine who knew the author had sworn when he asked Fletcher Knebel where he got his idea for the book, Knebel had replied, "From the files in the Pentagon while I was working there." Now I believed him.

When the CI staff officer was lecturing about Communist penetration techniques, the students insisted on getting him to comment on antiwar activists. The CI officer was as rabid on the subject as they were. He hated Bobby Kennedy and he told them an interagency, FBI, Defense, and CIA group had been formed to deal with the opponents of the Vietnam War. "The top level of the government," he assured them, "shares your concern and we're gonna see what their links with the Soviets and Chinese are, not to mention the North Vietnamese." The MHCHAOS program was what he was referring to. I assumed he meant collating data on protestors, not penetrating their groups.

Although these attitudes were disturbing to me, I couldn't help using an old teaching trick to put the class in a good mood to start the day, and I also thought it was a pretty good example of bumper sticker art, so I wrote on the board one morning what I had seen on a car on my way to work: "First Ethel Now Us." It produced the desired effect.

The following morning I was listening to my radio tell the unbelievable news of Robert Kennedy's assassination. I could hardly control the car. It was barely two months after the assassination of Martin Luther King. Only a few days before King was shot, my barber in Potomac had said, "Somebody'd better shut up that nigger." My class had told me of their thoughts about a coup d'état only a few days before Kennedy was shot. America seemed far worse than Argentina to me that morning when I met the class.

"Congratulations," said the colonel, "now it won't be us. You guys are great. Only, for Christ's sake, having your agent use that small-caliber weapon is taking an awful chance. He's not dead yet."

I told the colonel and the class that they made me ashamed of being an American. I assured them that CIA did not run assassinations. "We did not kill President Kennedy, nor his brother, nor Martin Luther King. We never operate against Americans in any way," I added. "What's happening in the United States these days makes us worse than a banana republic. It seems to me our political system is coming apart. We're turning into a government by assassination. I'm sorry, there's not going to be any class today."

I believed and meant every word I said. Now, just a couple of weeks more than a year later, I was finding out in Mexico City that at least the part about not operating against Americans had been a lie. I had mixed feelings about MHCHAOS from my first briefing by Stan Archer, but I was still enough of a cold warrior to accept the MHCHAOS activities as a gray area. I soon had an experience that showed me how ridiculous and cruel the consequences of a MHCHAOS mentality can be.

Stan Archer, I had to admit to myself, was the ideal man to handle such a program. He was a counterintelligence officer through and through. His response to any idea, especially a new one, was a reflexive reaction of doubt. MHCHAOS gave him the opportunity to doubt every long-haired kid who came by the embassy to ask for tourist information. In particular, directing this program provided him the opportunity to practice the tradecraft that he loved so well.

It was easy to tell when Stan had an operational meeting scheduled. On those days he always showed up at the office with his trench coat and his hat. He had the MHCHAOS files divided among several safes so that if anyone should come across the material in any one safe what was discovered would be unintelligible without the content of the others. He alone could put the puzzle together.

I had to agree that if the hypothesis President Nixon believed was correct, then giving great importance to MHCHAOS in Mexico City made sense. If you were convinced, as Nixon was, that opposition to the Vietnam War in the United States had to be something that was generated and supported by our enemies, it was logical to look for links between American protest groups and Mexico City. For one thing, the Soviets and Cubans both had embassies in Mexico City whose staffs consisted mostly of intelligence officers. Also, Mexico is one of the world's leading champions of the right of political asylum. Dissenters representing all sorts of radical convictions are welcome in Mexico. After my Vietnam black operations seminar I thought that the premise that Vietnam protest had to be of foreign origin was suspect because I considered many of the people who believed this were as sick as the protestors, whom I still did not understand. Nevertheless, I knew we had far from figured out what all our Soviet and Cuban counterparts were doing in Mexico and had little idea what all the hundreds of Latin American and Caribbean radicals in Mexico City were up to.

Stan admitted that he wasn't making any progress. He spent a lot of time trying to get pictures of the Venceremos Brigade, the young Americans who passed through Mexico City en route to Cuba at sugar harvest time to help Castro get in his crop, and he worked closely with the large FBI staff in the embassy.

I was initiated into the mysteries of MHCHAOS because of a request the labor attaché, Jack O'Grady, made of me. Jack and I were coffee-break buddies at the embassy cafeteria, and we also had a small bit of business together. One of my responsibilities was to meet with the headquarters case officer for the ORIT labor training school in Cuernavaca when he came to Mexico from time to time to check into the school's operations. As labor attaché, Jack also had to keep an eye on the school. The Interamerican Regional Organization of Workers (ORIT are its Spanish language initials) was one of the earliest efforts of Cord Meyer's International Organizations Division in Latin America. ORIT's founding was a brainstorm of George Meany's favorite anti-Communist activists in the AFL/CIO.

Keeping an eye on ORIT required the same kind of delicate balancing of the personal interests of important people in activities in which CIA invested funds but was unable to control because of the influence of the non-CIA elements, such as the Asia Foundation. Neither Jack nor I had any role in running the show, we simply reported things we heard back to Washington via our separate channels. Jack tried to write as little as possible about ORIT or anything else. He told me he learned not to in the very first month of his first assignment, as labor attaché in Nicaragua.

"I wrote this report about Communist activity in one of the labor unions and sent it to the State Department classified top secret," he told me. "The next week a high functionary from George Meany's office came down to Nicaragua to see me. He had a copy of the report in his hand and he demanded to know why I had called one of the guys in the report a Communist. That taught me not only who was running the State Department's labor attachés' division but never to classify a report top secret. Now when I do send in anything, I never classify it at all. Then Meany's boys don't think it's important enough to read, let alone have their penetrations of the State Department steal copies for them."

Jack had studied in Mexico as a young man and married a girl from Guadalajara. Because of his warm personality, excellent Spanish, and his and his wife's roots in Mexico, he had contacts with a greater variety of interesting Mexicans than anyone else in the embassy. One morning he asked me to his office, saying he had a special favor to ask. Jack explained that he knew a woman in Cuernavaca, an American who had become a Mexican citizen thanks to a special act of President López Mateos rewarding her work as a public health nurse with the Indians of Oaxaca, and she needed help.

"She went to Spain during the Civil War as a nurse for the Abraham Lincoln Brigade, and she refused to answer some questions during the McCarthy era, so she's been blacklisted and can't get a visa. She wants to go to New York and see her grandchildren," Jack said. "She's asked me if I can get her case reviewed. In fact she said, 'Isn't there somebody intelligent up there in Mexico City in the embassy intelligence services whom I could talk to?' I immediately thought of you."

"Thanks, Jack. When did you last kiss the stone? What's her name, and I'll check into it."

"Lini de Vries. If you can help her I'll say even nicer things about you. I think you'll find her a very interesting person to know, in any case."

When I tried to find out whether our files contained information on Lini de Vries I ran into Stan's stone wall. Her index card was marked "MHCHAOS" and led to one of his special safes, which I couldn't open.

"My God," Stan exclaimed, when I went to him with my problem. "Lini de Vries is one of the ACGM leaders. She's mixed up in CI-DOC, the wild place in Cuernavaca which that crazy radical priest Ivan Illich founded a couple of years ago. It's supposed to be some kind of school and it's crawling with all the long-haired bead wearers who come down to Mexico. You're right in the middle of a hell of a serious matter. Let's go see the chief of station."

The three of us discussed the matter at some length and I was given an MHCHAOS briefing and permission to read Lini's file. We agreed to talk things over again after that and decide whether I should go to see her or not.

Lini's file consisted of five folders, each one filled to capacity. Win Scott, who retired as chief of station, Mexico City, at the same time I arrived, loved keeping records. He was chief of station, Mexico City, for fourteen years, a feat for serving in one post which surpassed even Bob Jantzen's Singapore and Bangkok stints. By June, 1969, more station space was taken up by files than by people. Win's fancy for storing every scrap of information was one reason Lini de Vries's file was so full. The other reason was that the information had been collected jointly with the FBI. J. Edgar Hoover insisted that all FBI memoranda be written on especially heavy bond paper, thicker than the paper used by any other agency of the U.S. government. Any file containing FBI memos quickly became fuller

403

than any file which didn't. Also, only the FBI surpassed Win Scott's zeal for collecting trivia.

The first thing I learned was the initials ACGM stood for "American Communist Group in Mexico." This was a group which, as I read the file, seemed to be extremely sinister and an object of great and continuing interest to the FBI. The Bureau had been following the moves of these people ever since they had come to Mexico. In all cases this had been twenty years or more ago. The file of everyone identified as "ACGM" was filled with telephone tap transcripts of all their calls, surveillance reports, and informant accounts.

The curious thing to me was that none of this information contained any indication that these people acted as a group, except, now and then, they did talk to one another on the telephone. These calls, however, were social. The surveillance reports were the boring collection of minutiae they always are. The informant accounts contained no facts, only suppositions and hearsay. The one thing that seemed to make the ACGM a "group" in the FBI's mind was that all had fled the United States during the McCarthy era. Several were members of the Hollywood Ten—the screen writers who had been convicted of contempt of Congress in the 1940s for refusing to say whether they were Communists, one had been an AFL/CIO organizer in the 1930s, when some people considered such activity subversive, one wasn't even an American. He was the British writer Cedric Belfrage, who had edited the *National Guardian* and campaigned for Henry Wallace. Lini de Vries and Frederica Martins were two nurses who had served the anti-Fascist forces in Spain. They were people with a past the Bureau considered suspect, but there seemed to be no indication they were doing anything subversive now. And most of them were at least sixty years old.

There was one thing in Lini de Vries's file that classified her as a ACGM "leader" and made her the object of so much attention, however. She had been identified by Elizabeth Bentley, the repentant ex-Communist star witness of all the investigative committees of the 1940s and 1950s, as the girl who had recruited her into the American Communist Party. Bentley had not only told the investigators this, she had written up the story of the recruitment in her book. When Lini de Vries was questioned about this, she had confirmed it. She refused to provide the FBI information on other people she had known in her Party days before World War II and

404

said she was no longer a Party member. In December, 1949, she took her three-year-old daughter and fled to Mexico.

According to informant reports, she had been teaching Communism to students at the University of Veracruz and the University of Morelos since coming to Mexico. Her specialty appeared to be helping American students in Mexico find housing and become accustomed to the country. She had also worked among the remote Indian villages in Oaxaca as a nurse. One report said she actually had spent her time in Oaxaca organizing the Indians into Communist cells. She taught a course on Mexican history at CIDOC and was in charge of the student housing program. An FBI informant in Cuernavaca reported she "has a store in her house which helps her maintain her links with the Indians in Oaxaca as she sells their wares. Her home is also a boarding house which provides her the opportunity to hold meetings there with her boarders and others under apparently innocent conditions." I could certainly see why Stan had her file in the MHCHAOS project.

The chief of station, Stan, and I talked the case over again. I suggested that I look into the background of CIDOC carefully before going any further. Perhaps I would find some way to talk to her about CIDOC to get an initial impression of her before we decided to risk identifying me to her in the way Jack O'Grady wanted. I knew Win Scott had been curious about Illich and his school and had even met CIDOC's founder. Win knew everybody worth knowing in Mexico. I called him up and asked him to lunch.

Win Scott, to me, always had an air of importance about him. I don't mean he was pretentious. It was that he seemed to be a man who was closely connected with many important matters—what an earlier age would have called a man of affairs. He seemed always to know just whom to call to arrange neatly, precisely, and profitably any business you might have. When he retired he established an office as an insurance actuary, putting his long-neglected background as a PhD in mathematics to work. But he did much more. His ventures seemed to lead off everywhere. I wasn't surprised, therefore, when I saw him coming up the stairs to the second level of Carlos Anderson's restaurant, where I was waiting, bringing a tall blond young man with him. Win always liked to eat at Anderson's, which was just across Reforma from his office. Anderson's is also the place where Mexicans and members of the international

405

colony who are doing things, Win's kind of people, eat, and the menu is excellent.

"Joe," Win said when he reached the table, "this is Edward Finch Cox. His father is an important client of mine in New York. I thought he would have something to tell you you'd be interested in. Edward has just spent the summer at CIDOC."

Another perfect Win Scott move, I thought. I had told him I wanted to discuss CIDOC so he produced this surprise for me. Edward Finch Cox was no long-haired bead wearer. He was a model of an old-line Eastern Establishment young man—quiet, self-assured, intelligent, and articulate. He sipped a Dubonnet while Win and I drank two martinis. There was the generation gap in that regard but in none of the ways that concerned the MHCHAOS program.

His impressions of CIDOC and Ivan Illich were extremely enlightening, especially for someone who had been reading FBI and MHCHAOS files. He told me that he was enrolled in the new double-track graduate program at Harvard. Upon completing five years' work, he would receive both a law degree and a master's in business administration from the Harvard Business School. He liked to spend his summers in a more interesting way, he explained. He had spent the summer of 1969 working for Ralph Nader and this past summer, 1970, he spent at CIDOC.

"CIDOC," he said, "is something everyone is talking about on all the campuses in the United States, these days. I just had to try it."

He had found it interesting, but not the exciting experience working for Ralph Nader had been.

"It really has no definite form," he said about CIDOC. "Of course, that's part of Illich's doctrine in his attack against the schooling models in our society. Illich wants to have encounters. Centro Intercultural de Documentación means collecting the results of these encounters. Actually, CIDOC is a very talky place, with Ivan doing most of the talking."

"Would you say it's a center of New Left ideas, where protest groups get inspiration?" I asked.

"Hardly," he replied. "CIDOC is an eighteenth-century salon where people toy with the notions and ideas that are fashionable today, just as they did with those that were fashionable then."

"Did you meet Lini de Vries?"

"I certainly did. She's a charming and interesting woman. I

wasn't too pleased with the housing she arranged for me, but I enjoyed sitting around her pool and talking with her. All the students do."

Cox had shaken the images of CIDOC, Illich, and Lini de Vries the MHCHAOS files had given me. He obviously was an astute young man. He also was obviously not planning to take part in the destruction of our society. The fact that he didn't find the people with new ideas and different life-styles in Cuernavaca threatening seemed to be something we should keep in mind in making our judgments. I decided I definitely had to meet this woman around whose pool the CIDOC students liked to sit and talk. The picture of a grubby Communist boarding-house keeper with a little store in her parlor that the FBI's informants presented clearly had no relation to reality.

When I related the story of my lunch back at the station, I had another surprise. I evidently had spent too much time in the file room and not enough reading the newspapers from home. "My, my," the chief of station remarked. "Edward Cox is the guy who's been dating Patricia Nixon."

Stan was still skeptical, although there was one thing about the situation which appealed to him—the tinge of classic counterespionage control. "Well, if she'll swear to play ball with us, I guess it's okay. If she plays ball, we'll give her the visa. If not, she'll be on the blacklist for the rest of her life," was his comment.

I told Jack O'Grady to telephone his friend and tell her I would be down in Cuernavaca the following weekend to talk to her. Jeanne and Andy and I drove down on Saturday morning and checked into our favorite inn, Posada Arcadia. Julie wouldn't go along because she had been there. It was a pretty dull place for a high school senior, but we liked it because it was practically in the center of town and had a magnificent garden. Andy enjoyed the pool. The Americans who ran the place took good care of us. He had been an Asia Foundation representative in India and was now retired. Somehow his past added a touch of nostalgia to the Posada Arcadia for me. Julie thought it was an old people's nursing home. It is true we were among the few people who stayed there who were under eighty years old. The proprietors once told us, according to legend, the curious series of rooms stretching down the hill on which the hotel was built had been constructed by Cortes for his mistresses. "Looks as if they're still here," Jeanne muttered.

407

For this particular occasion another advantage of the Posada Arcadia was that it was just two blocks from Lini de Vries's home.

Lini de Vries's place I found to be one of the large, charming houses Cuernavaca is noted for. Just forty-seven miles from Mexico City, three thousand feet lower than the capital's sometimes taxing altitude of 7,600 feet, Cuernavaca for centuries has been a favorite place for Mexicans to relax. Whether or not he kept his mistresses in the Posada Arcadia, Cortes was the pioneer weekender in Cuernavaca. He built a palace there. Others of the Spanish elite followed their leader and the affluent have built fine homes there ever since. Lini had managed to acquire an older one with a beautiful acre of garden, swimming pool, and huge first-floor reception area with open archways leading to the garden on two sides. Diego Rivera had painted the beginnings of a mural on one wall of the dining room. Upstairs, where she did indeed rent rooms to guests, was equally charming. The roomer who was enjoying her home the day I met her was not some Communist conspirator, as the FBI informants tried to hint when they wrote about her "boarding house." He was Victor Urquidi, director of Mexico's finest graduate school, Colegio de México, and an internationally famous economist. She did have a store too, in a room off her entrance hall. It was not stocked with junk to sell at Communist Party rallies but filled with extremely interesting rugs, shawls, and other woven goods—the finest I had seen in Mexico—original designs I discovered that her Indian friends in the mountains of Oaxaca made especially for her.

If the distortion in the political activities of Lini de Vries is as bad as the distortion of the description of her house, I thought to myself as I waited for her servant to get Lini, a serious slander had been made.

I found Lini a vigorous, forceful woman, a bundle of energy, and a chain-smoker with an attractive twinkle in her direct gaze.

"I'm only talking to you because I trust Jack O'Grady," she said. "I have been treated shamefully for more than twenty years and I want something done about it. I know terrible things have been said about me. They are not true. I want my file reevaluated. I want to get the true story of what I have done since I came to Mexico on the record. Here are some letters I'd like you to read and I'll tell you anything I can about myself the letters don't."

"I'm from CIA. I'll be glad to read the letters and I'm most anxious to hear your story. I'll also be glad to tell you anything you

408

want to know about CIA and about me. I think you may have a lot of wrong ideas about us, too."

The letters were testimonials from the widow of the former American ambassador to Uruguay, who was now her neighbor; from Laura Nader, the anthropologist; Ralph Nader, her well-known brother; from Senator Jacob Javits; and from a half-dozen others. They told an impressive story—the story of Lini's heroic work in the mountains where she taught the Indians basic hygiene, how to deliver their babies with some cleanliness, and how to fight syphilis—a disease that raged among them.

I told her I found the letters impressive. I then talked to her about CIA and about myself, emphasizing that CIA fought Communism on a worldwide basis and sometimes used the Communists' own tactics against them, but that we also did things such as supporting projects to teach peasants how to help themselves improve their lives (the Binamira project of Gabe Kaplan's minus the names). About myself, I explained how I had evolved politically from a small-town Republican bigot into someone with more political sensitivity. She relaxed considerably.

I said I had met a young man, named Edward Finch Cox, who had been at CIDOC and who had paid her compliments.

"Oh my, yes, Ed Cox was one of the gang around the pool this summer," she said. "He came to see me with a letter of introduction from Ralph Nader. I saw he was a rich boy from New York and fixed him up to live with one of the wealthiest and best Mexican families in Cuernavaca. I'm afraid that wasn't what he wanted. You know, I also understand he wants to get engaged to Patricia Nixon, only his family objects."

We looked at each other and began to laugh. "It's time for the classic remark," I said, "and I'll say it before you do. Nixons are all right in their place, but would you want a son of yours to marry one?"

Lini and I talked for three hours. She had been born Lini Führ of Dutch immigrant parents in Paterson, New Jersey. As a child she went to work in the silk mills and at thirteen was on the picket line. When not being brutalized at work she was being brutalized by her mother at home. Her mother locked her in the dirt cellar for punishment. Lini sometimes was confined for hours, shivering with terror for fear of the rats. In her late twenties she managed to scrape together enough money to enroll at Columbia to study nursing.

409

The depression was relentless and her life a struggle of part-time work and part-time study. She joined the Communist Party. "Because I needed a home," Lini said. "You can see how badly I needed one.

"I also needed the opportunity to do something. I believe in action. I am an eternal do-gooder and so much needed to be done in the 1930s. That's how I met this young Vassar graduate. She was a social worker and I was a nurse. Elizabeth Bentley was very much like a lot of these kids from upper-middle-class homes today. She had a terrible guilt complex because she was a rich girl in the midst of so much misery. I didn't recruit her. She recruited herself. She begged to join the Party. She said she was a descendant of American revolutionary ancestors. 'All good Americans are revolutionaries, aren't they?' was the way she put it. I told the Party I had doubts about her background. I didn't think she was sincere. They called me a 'proletarian snob,'" Lini laughed.

She had barely gotten home from Spain when she was permanently disillusioned with Communism. "Like a lot of other people, I realized that it wasn't just capitalist propaganda. When Stalin made his pact with Hitler, I knew he was an evil man, and his social system was perverse."

In the 1940s she found the attitude of the FBI frighteningly similar to Stalin's. "They refused to believe me because I refused to give them names of people they could question and harass as they were harassing me. I simply had to leave. I didn't think I was rejecting the United States. I thought the United States was rejecting me."

Her life in Mexico was a model of her action creed. She taught Indians, Mexicans, and Americans. She taught this last group how to understand the first two. Gingerly, I told her the concerns of MHCHAOS—explaining that it was not dissent or protest in themselves that bothered me, but her Party experience certainly could help her understand that possibly the Vietnam War protest was neither innocent nor spontaneous. I asked if she would tell me whether she suspected any links between Cubans or Soviets and CIDOC students.

"If you mean I must be a CIA collaborator in order to get a visa, I can't accept such terms. I can tell you I don't believe there are any Soviet or Cuban links with CIDOC students. I say that honestly and

410

with a clear conscience. But I'm not going to spy on students for you. You've heard my story. How could I?"

While listening to Lini I had been thinking what her story meant in terms of MHCHAOS. If we started now building dossiers on student protestors, these records would make Lini's file look small in time and they would probably be just as false. The students would change their views but we would never change the files.

"You've been trying to tell me CIA does positive things too. From what you've said about your barrio worker project in the Philippines, I believe you. If you ever have any positive ideas about Mexico I'd love to hear them. I'll be glad to give you my opinions whether they'll help or not," Lini continued.

"You see, forgetting all their silly talk and obscenities, helping people is really what concerns the students today. More than ever before, it seems. I love that. It's wonderful, and I try to steer them away from protest to doing things, positive things.

"I share your concern that possibly they could be manipulated. I loathe the destructiveness that some of them have embraced—drugs, bombs, that sort of thing. But we must try to change even the destructive ones, because, I believe, there's even hope for them.

"I'm not ashamed of anything I've ever done—not even of once having been a member of the Communist Party. It was the way to do something positive, I thought. I found out I was wrong. I am a humanist and I discovered the Communist system is not. I still want to help people make this a better world. I always will. I hope I can help the kids find out how they can do this too. Forget the visa."

I told her I would not forget it.

There was no question in my mind Lini was right. MHCHAOS was wrong. Lini had rejected Stalinism only to become for twenty years a victim of police-state tactics. The United States government simply should not go that far in copying the enemy in order to cope with him. We might have, at times, a paranoid president, but we must not have a police state. I returned to the embassy and made certain Lini got her visa.

When I called to tell her the good news, she said, "I knew from the first you're not a cop."

"I'm not, and I never was."

22

Let's Recruit the Tass Man's Dentist

From the terrace of the little weekend house Jeanne and I have built in the village of Tequisquiapan, about a hundred miles north of Mexico City, I can look across a field to the place CIA hid Raya Kiselnikova when she defected from the Soviet Embassy. Recruiting a Soviet intelligence officer was the number one objective of our station when I was a member of it. The closest we got was Raya's defection. Raya was a secretary in the Soviet Trade Mission whose members were all KGB. In 1969, forty-nine of the fifty-eight people in the Soviet Embassy in Mexico City were intelligence personnel. We couldn't recruit one. Raya defected for very personal reasons.

MHCHAOS was also a top priority but even that program was not as important for the Mexico City station as the pursuit of Soviet intelligence people. Perhaps one reason the Clandestine Services in my day got into so much trouble was that we had too many top priorities. The concept of priority loses its meaning when a number are lumped together and all are listed as "Priority A Objectives." Of

413

course, it is convenient when you fail to achieve one of these objectives to be able to say you're busy on another.

In any case, trying to make a Soviet intelligence officer into a CIA agent is the highest-priority objective of the Clandestine Services. No matter how many sophisticated satellites we put over the skies of the Soviet Union, without an agent who moves in the highest circles of the Kremlin we will never know when the Soviet leaders may press the button on their little black box. Where a Soviet intelligence contingent as large as the one in their embassy in Mexico City exists, the CIA station automatically must put attempting to recruit a Soviet above any other activity.

If we failed to recruit any Soviet for the vital task of finding out the intentions of the Soviet leaders while I was a member of the Mexico City station I don't think it was because we were incompetent. I think it's an almost impossible task. The KGB, the clandestine Soviet security service, functions inside the Soviet Union and abroad as the organization which makes the Soviet police state work. The Soviet Union does not divide the essential job of protecting national security, and the KGB is the responsible agency. The KGB makes possible control of speech, travel, work, education, even personal relationships, in Russia. Abroad it is the principal apparatus of Soviet espionage. There is one other organization in the espionage business in the Soviet Embassy, the GRU. The GRU is the intelligence division of the Soviet General Staff and engages primarily in collecting strategic, tactical, and technical military intelligence. Because of its role in spying on Soviet citizens, the KGB is the senior service. GRU officers are subject to KGB scrutiny if their actions are suspicious. No congressional committees investigate the Soviet intelligence services. The KGB does all the investigating that is done in the Soviet Union. It is an elite organization. Even President Nixon's White House palace guard did not enjoy the elitist positions Soviet KGB officers do.

They are as self-assured and as content with their lot in life as might be expected. They are well paid. They have good housing in a country where families still have to share apartments. They are chosen from the top graduates of Soviet universities and have the best education which the Soviet Union has to offer. As the Soviet Union has become more sophisticated, so have they. Gone are the baggy pants, the short box-cut jackets of the 1950s. They speak fluent English and they speak fluently the language of the country

414

where they are stationed. They know how to appreciate to the hilt the culture and comforts of these foreign countries where they serve. In Mexico they collect pre-Colombian art, buy paintings and artisan products, and visit the country's fabulous variety of interesting vacation spots. They go to Cuernavaca, Cuautla, Valle del Bravo, Puerto Vallarta, Cancun, and Acapulco as often as any Americans.

We like to think the pleasures of the Western World, the freedom to travel as we please, and the other freedoms of our society, which are unknown in their country, might tempt them to want to stay and, therefore, we have a good chance to recruit them. We like to imagine KGB wives would get fed up with their role as charwomen in Soviet embassies. KGB notions of security are so strict they will not permit Soviet ambassadors to hire a local char force. KGB wives have to scrub the embassy floors and clean the offices.

We forget they enjoy both the wonderful new life-style abroad and enough exciting things to do to make the wives endure their unpleasant task, and at home they have the satisfaction of privileged positions and status symbols. Even if they were to find our world better physically or politically what we want them to do would require that they forego their newfound happiness in foreign countries and return to the Soviet Union to lead nerve-wracking double lives as CIA agents. We want a man in the Kremlin not in New York.

We aren't quite as naïve as the above may sound in the methods we use when we try to recruit a Soviet, but I'm afraid we don't reflect enough on what we expect a KGB or GRU officer to give up in order to work for us.

In Mexico City we tapped the Soviet Embassy's telephones, watched who went in and out from across the street, bugged the apartments of the Soviets we were interested in, hired an army of access agents—people who come into normal and frequent contact with the Soviets, such as shopkeepers, travel agents, sports club personnel, even attractive women who catch their eye—and we made a point of meeting them ourselves. Everyone in the station carried in his wallet a list of license numbers of all Soviet cars, in case one of their cars showed up in some odd place. We had pictures of the Soviets on our office walls so we could memorize their faces. All these efforts were directed to finding the key that would turn them into our agents or even just tempt them. Raya Kiselnikova, on her own, found a boyfriend and decided she liked the boutiques and discotheques in the Pink Zone enough to walk out of the embassy, but nothing we tried could move the target we selected as our most likely candidate, Edward Saratov, a KGB specialist in operating against Americans who was in Mexico under cover as a representative of the Tass News Agency.

For the first time in my career, in Mexico City, I became involved in the business of trying to recruit a Soviet. I worked on Valeri Nicolaenko, a young KGB officer who had the cover rank of first secretary at the Soviet Embassy and whose covert responsibilities we did not know.

Working on the Soviets was a complete change from my past operational experience. Much had changed in the Clandestine Services by the early 1970s. Des Fitzgerald dropped dead on the tennis court of his country home in Virginia in July, 1967. By that time he had been promoted from CWH to DDP and directed all CIA's covert operations. Every moment of the cold war, every job he held, every assignment he ordered undertaken was a great adventure to Des. The greatest adventure his successor, Thomas Karamassines, could imagine was staying out of trouble. In this he was a reflection of the man who chose him for the job—Richard Helms. Helms had skillfully managed to keep out of the Bay of Pigs operation although he was Richard Bissell's deputy at the time. Rather than being swept away when Bissell was forced to leave, he replaced Bissell as DDP. Helms became the first career Clandestine Services officer to be Director of Central Intelligence.

Ironically, Helms and Karamassines, masters of caution, were the men who led CIA into its worst misadventures and the men who had to face congressional committees to answer for MHCHAOS and talk about the $10 million they spent trying to prevent the man the Chileans elected, Salvadore Allende, from becoming president of Chile.

The explanation is simple. They were cautious bureaucrats to whom holding onto their high positions was the most important goal in life. When the President ordered them to do something illegal or impossible, as they testified to Congress regarding MHCHAOS, in the first instance, and the plan to stage a coup in Chile, in the second, they did what the President wanted. They kept their doubts to themselves.

Caution was the byword of Soviet recruitment operations. Such

416

operations, in Mexico and everywhere, were corporate station efforts. Each officer worked on part of the puzzle, which, when completed, was supposed to show the image of a Soviet recruitment candidate. Most of the effort was dedicated to compiling more and more information on the person chosen as a likely recruitment prospect. More and more access agents were constantly recruited for the same purpose. Hours were spent talking over the access agents' opinions of the Soviets who came into their store or with whom they played tennis. In Mexico City we had four women who worked all day long comparing and checking tapes and reports from access agents with tapes of telephone and bedroom conversations of the KGB officers we were pursuing. I have said that I think it is a terribly difficult job and I can't find fault with thoroughness. I also think, however, these activities were often a substitute for boldness and imagination which had gone out of style in the Clandestine Services by the time I got to Mexico. The effort spent on access agents and collating vast amounts of trivia on Soviet intelligence officers kept many people busy and out of trouble. If we couldn't recruit the Tass man, we could recruit the Tass man's dentist. This was almost entirely safe, whereas approaching a Soviet with the proposal he go back to Russia to penetrate the Kremlin for us risked refusal and retaliation.

We were so busy analyzing hundreds of pages of this kind of data on Edward Saratov's personal habits, we had no idea Raya Kiselnikova was about to defect. If we had, we would have tried to contact her and convince her to stay in her job in exchange for a good salary and future rewards we would hold in escrow. Raya was only a KGB secretary but so are many successful spies. Secretaries, even Soviet ones, usually know more than their bosses about what is really going on in the office.

One night in February, 1970, we received a tip that Raya Kiselnikova had walked into a police station asking for political asylum. Mexico's policy toward granting an alien this privilege assured approval of her request. The Mexican authorities were happy to turn her over to us and forget about what happened to her. Raya was spirited off to Tequisguiapan, where we were certain the KGB security officer, charged with seeing that things like Raya's walkout didn't happen, would never think of looking for her while we planned what to do next.

She was scared and didn't want to talk. She just wanted to stay in

Mexico and never go back to Russia. She wanted a job. Since she spoke four languages fluently, was an excellent secretary, and a pretty young woman, finding her a job wasn't too difficult.

"Get packed, you and I are going to Acapulco," I surprised Jeanne pleasantly by announcing when I came home from work one night two weeks after Raya's defection. We had gotten Raya a job in a plush Acapulco hotel as a secretary in the public relations office. Now the problem was how to get her to talk. I had contact with an American writer living in Acapulco. Taking Jeanne along as cover for a brief "vacation," I was going to Acapulco to see if he could interview her on the pretext he wanted to write her story— splitting with her the profits from sale of the article to a big U.S. magazine. This would test her reaction to cooperating with an American and how much she would tell. If results were favorable, we would then send in a trained CIA interrogator and get as much information as we could from her.

Our plan worked. Raya was soon telling her story to a CIA officer. She was thirty years old and had been a widow for several years. Her husband, a young Soviet physicist, had died of radiation. This caused an immediate sensation. Specialists flew in from Washington to try to pinpoint the cause and make sense out of it. She was also able to tell them about a nuclear experiment station we had hitherto known little about.

After that, however, her information and insights dropped to our customary level of personal information and gossip about KGB people in the embassy. We found out some new information about who disliked whom, some covert love affairs that were going on, and the general state of morale. One important thing we did identify was the location and layout of the Referentura—the KGB equivalent of a CIA station.

The principal use we were able to make of Raya's information was to make it public in order to embarrass and harass the KGB officers in Mexico. In the intelligence trade this is called "burning." The KGB officer we decided to burn with the hottest fire was Oleg Nechiporenko. Nechiporenko had arrived in Mexico City in 1961 and, hence, had been there nine years by the time Raya defected. We decided to pay special attention to him because he had been a recruitment target for all these years and a hopeless one. Since we couldn't recruit him, we took advantage of Raya's defection to give wide publicity to the fact he was the KGB security officer and, with

418

the help of Raya's press conference, we invented the story that he had been a major instigator of the Mexico City student riots of 1968, which culminated in a shoot-out in which a number of protesters were killed.

Nechiporenko was an extremely able operator. He evidently had some Spanish blood, possibly one parent was a Spanish Communist—one of the thousands who fled to Russia after the Spanish Civil War. His Latin looks, fluent Spanish, and sharp wits enabled him to move around Mexico with greater ease than any of his colleagues. Once he had even gotten into the U.S. Embassy posing as a visa applicant and was not discovered for several hours. How much he learned about the way the embassy offices were arranged and what other information he gleaned, we didn't know. So he was someone we were particularly happy to harass.

As a result of our identifying him as a dangerous KGB officer and someone who had intervened in Mexican affairs, when the Mexican government uncovered a small band of guerrillas and found they had gone via Russia for training in North Korea, Mexican authorities blamed him for this even worse intervention in their country's political concerns and threw him out of Mexico. Getting KGB officers publicly identified as such, and wherever possible, declared *persona non grata* was something we tried to do whenever we failed to recruit them.

The trouble with "burning" is that two can play the same game. CIA officers are the number one recruitment target for the KGB. Their aim is essentially the same as ours, to be able to obtain thereby otherwise unobtainable information. Despite the way spy stories tell it, this is not very often a violent game. We want a live KGB officer in the Kremlin and they want a live CIA officer in Langley, Virginia. Publicly identifying each other is about as violent as things usually get. This results in benching an able player from the opposite team. Burned intelligence operators have to cool off for a long time at home before being able to go back to work abroad. If you are not a KGB or CIA officer you probably can't appreciate or even understand the warm glow of satisfaction reading the other fellow's name in print can bring, or the cold anguish felt when you read your own.

In the mid-60s, the East German satellite Soviet service had a book published in German and English called *Who's Who in CIA*. It was a masterpiece of burning. CIA then assisted John Barron with

material for his book *KGB, The Secret Work of Soviet Secret Agents.*
Barron's book contains an appendix of fifty-one pages listing KGB
and GRU officers. He also used our story about Nechiporenko
among the many examples he gave of Soviet spying. I am certain
Barron's book and Philip Agee's are related. When Agee contacted
the Cubans, it is small wonder the abused Soviet intelligence service
through their Cuban surrogates returned the compliment by having Agee write a book naming as many CIA officers as he could remember. Agee's book has two appendices: one of twenty-six pages,
listing CIA officers, and another of six pages, naming organizations
used by CIA.

I was never named in any book or newspaper article or radio or
TV newscast. I was proud of that and I was a bit disturbed about
getting involved in working on the Russians in Mexico City. As
soon as I met my first Soviet intelligence officer, I knew he would be
able to recognize I was CIA. Again, despite the imagination of writers of spy novels, the techniques of professionals in "developing a
contact," as it is called, are basically few. As Paul Linebarger pointed out to us in his seminar, our profession is the same as the con
man's. A teenager may be taken in by his first pornographic book
describing a large number of positions for sexual intercourse, but
the practitioners of the oldest profession know they are only
changes on a few simple ones. Spy fiction devotees may think there
is a huge bag of tricks available to good agents; practitioners of the
second oldest profession know it isn't true.

The man who replaced Nechiporenko as our number one candidate for possible recruitment was a splendid operator, but his
manner of doing business was to concentrate on two elementary
tactics—copying his American victims' habits, and sex. Edward
Saratov was a tall, good-looking man in his early thirties. Although he was the Tass representative in Mexico City, people
who met him usually thought he was a recent American university graduate. He was.

Saratov had gone to Yale. During the thaw in the cold war in the
late fifties, known as the "spirit of Camp David" after Eisenhower
and Khrushchev met there, he had done graduate work at Yale in
political science. Although not as true blue and Yale all the way
through as Jack Armstrong, Saratov was a reasonable facsimile of a
well-bred, well-educated young American. His accent was American, he liked a good dry martini, and he had a large collection of a

variety of American jazz. His specialty, of course, was recruiting Americans.

Before coming to Mexico City, Saratov had cut a swath through Washington. The FBI was too embarrassed to give us all the details, but he successfully seduced several of their secretaries. The careful work of our collators of reports from Soviet defectors had enabled us to identify him, but he moved from Washington to Mexico City without being caught.

In Mexico City he exploited his friendly American manner at the Foreign Correspondents Club. He became vice-president and by virtue of this office was able to expand his contacts still further in both the international colony and within the Mexican government. He aspired to become president of the club. In that position he would be able to open still more doors by directing a broad program of club activities focused on any groups or individuals he wished to develop through the flattery of invitations to be guest speakers at the club and so forth.

Win Scott, in the tradition of cold warrior activities I had been raised on in the Clandestine Services, ran an election operation in the Foreign Correspondents Club in order to thwart Saratov's presidential ambition. We didn't subsidize this club, as we had the one in Manila in Magsaysay days, but enough members were in arrears in their bar bills, as is true of all such clubs, so that Win was able to defeat the Tass man. The objective of recruiting Saratov was not served by this tactic. By the time I got to Mexico, however, all the appropriate tactics were in use. Saratov was under surveillance, his home telephone was tapped, his apartment bugged, and he was surrounded by access agents.

We even had an access agent concentrating on Saratov's favorite operational approach—the one he had employed so successfully against the FBI. An attractive American woman, divorced from a Mexican, had agreed to serve in this capacity. Someone as devoted to the cause of meaningful cryptonyms as the person who chose MHCHAOS had selected hers. "LI" was the digraph indicating Mexico. Her cryptonym was LIBOX.

Saratov's charm, interesting background, bright mind, and good looks were not all he had going for him in his pursuit of women. One day a tape from a conversation in his apartment revealed something else. His wife was talking to another Soviet embassy wife who had dropped in for a visit. Saratov was taking a nap. He liked

421

to sleep in the raw. His wife took her friend into the bedroom and with genuine awe in her voice said, "Look at that. Did you ever see one that size? And he's completely relaxed."

Some sexologists claim that penis size is a masculine fantasy imposed on feminine sexuality. Neither Mrs. Saratov nor LIBOX thought so. Her case officer tried to treat the details of her work delicately, but he told me more than once when he came back from meeting her that LIBOX purred all through their meeting when she had met Saratov the night before.

The affair did not produce what we wanted, which was something specific in the way of a lead, some desire, some weakness, some interest of Saratov's on which we might build a recruitment pitch. Then we learned he was being transferred to Chile. Allende had been chosen president by the Chilean congress and we couldn't imagine what Saratov was going to do in a country with a Communist president who was committed to reducing, if not entirely removing, American interests from the country. Washington became excited and decided a recruitment pitch must be made before he left Mexico. The decision was based on the belief that this would be the last time for a while any CIA officer would have a chance and on the hope that if recruited before he left for Chile, he would be an invaluable source on what was transpiring there.

Headquarters sent one of its cockiest young officers to do the job. He had already decided how he was going to do the recruitment even though he had only read the headquarters file on the case and lacked a lot of information on his target. His plan was to make what is known as a cold approach, which means going up to the Soviet, telling him you are a CIA officer who can offer him a sizable sum of money, and hoping the shock will give you a clue as to how to proceed. Sometimes a cold approach works. I had made one to Roberto Noble. But I never heard of one working on a Soviet. This self-confident young man was sure it would. He considered himself as good-looking as Saratov and possessed of as many talents. I had no idea whether or not this was true in one important respect, but I felt that, even generally speaking, he was no match for the Soviet.

Because of my past experience, I had been working on the Foreign Correspondents Club. My years of dealing with press people were considered sufficient credentials for this. I had obtained diplomatic membership in the club, which had a very loose membership policy since the club management hoped thereby to find some people who would pay their bills. Our eager recruiter had decided he would meet Saratov there and sought my advice as to the best time to try.

I thought this was a bad idea. The club was used sparingly except for a few habitués who gathered there in the afternoons to try to impress each other with tales of imaginary scoops they were on the track of. I never had met Saratov there. I told our recruiter that I thought this was a poor place to try a recruitment. The club consisted of three small connecting rooms on the ground floor at the back of the Hilton Hotel. Although it was nearly empty most of the time, there were no quiet corners in which you could escape being noticed by the few persons who might be there. If they didn't try to butt in on a conversation between Saratov and a stranger, they surely would inhibit his paying attention to the pitch.

He ignored my advice and had the surveillance team follow Saratov. Stationing himself in the lobby of the Hilton, he had one surveillant in sight to signal him when Saratov approached the club. One evening, he found his man. As soon as our recruiter entered the club he discovered my description of the place was accurate. He walked up to Saratov and said he had an extremely important message to deliver if Saratov would please follow him into the hotel lobby.

Saratov blinked but accepted the invitation. He listened to our man blurt out his pitch. Then he grabbed the young recruiter by the collar and told him he was crazy. Saratov advised him never to try anything so stupid again and stomped out of the hotel.

Shortly thereafter our Tass man left for Santiago. We had no idea what his assignment there was going to be, but all those in the station who had served in South America knew he would enjoy his stay. Chilean women are famous all over the southern hemisphere for their love bites during orgasm.

The approach to the Soviet officers we used which I liked best was to meet them personally, exploiting our diplomatic cover. In Mexico City, as in many other places, there are diplomatic associations for those officers below the rank of ambassador. They are supposed to provide informal opportunities to exchange off-the-record remarks at luncheons and other social and relaxing affairs the association may arrange.

In Mexico City the association is known as AMCOSAD, the Spanish acronym for Association of Ministers, Counselors, Secretaries

423

and Attachés. AMCOSAD was an organization which the foreign service officers in our embassy shunned. They had as much contact with other diplomats at receptions and cocktail parties as they could stomach. We CIA officers were too low in diplomatic rank in too large an embassy to be invited to such affairs very often and had no other way of meeting our KGB friends who were serving under diplomatic cover. Almost the entire American contingent at an AMCOSAD lunch was CIA. The same was true of the Soviets. Of course, in their case it could hardly be otherwise since there were almost no other officers except the KGB and GRU on the Soviet Embassy's staff. The same thing held for the Cubans. Their entire AMCOSAD group was DGI, the Cuban service. When the Chinese Communists came to town in 1972, they joined us.

AMCOSAD luncheons at the Hotel Reforma once a month, and later at the plush Camino Real, were interesting affairs. We and the Russians spent them getting to know each other. We had a lot of the kind of friendly conversations intelligence operators and con men have when sizing up the mark. This disgusted the Cubans, who were under strict orders from Castro not even to speak to us. The Russians didn't like the Cubans to talk to the Chinese. I greatly enjoyed speaking to the Chinese, as, naturally, did the officer headquarters sent to work on the Chinese target when their embassy opened in Mexico City.

The Chinese Communist minister counselor of embassy and I became good friends because we had chanced to meet at a cocktail party opening the Argentine Embassy's new cultural and information office. I think it was the first event Li Shan-yi attended in Mexico City. I introduced myself as soon as I saw him. We conversed via his interpreter. The interpreter and I spoke Spanish and English (when I forced him to). Li spoke only Chinese. I was amazed to discover how shy and uncertain he was. I was told that the Chinese lived in greater isolation than any other nation, but I was amazed to find he really needed help to cope with Western life.

Li would show up at AMCOSAD lunches with one interpreter and sometimes two. We always sat together when he did and he would ask me such questions as how to deal with "these Mexican women who come to the embassy asking for money for the Red Cross." I told him our embassy wives helped the Mexican women with the annual fund-raising and suggested he should be sure to make a good-sized contribution in the name of his great country.

When I suggested I come by the embassy to see him, he demurred. "We don't have diplomatic relations yet," he said through his interpreter. I learned after my retirement that the AMCOSAD board threw Li out of the organization. He would pay only one membership, for himself, and never even offered to leave a tip for the free lunches his interpreters ate. I had always treated Li more diplomatically even though our countries' relations didn't conform to protocol.

The most ridiculous moment in the exploitation of AMCOSAD as a meeting place for Soviet KGB and GRU staff and CIA officers was the special tour of the annual home show in the spring of 1973. This event was sponsored by a group of Mexican businessmen as a promotional activity. They always tried to represent the show as a kind of official activity and to further this cover for their money-making scheme for selling their appliances, furniture, and a great assortment of other goods, they invited AMCOSAD for a noon drink and tour of the National Auditorium. Representatives of other countries either had already seen the show, or they didn't care to, but AMCOSAD affairs were business meetings for us and the Soviets. Except for the dapper Argentine minister, who was president, the only AMCOSAD members and families who showed up were one GRU, four KGB, and five CIA staffers with wives and children in tow. The senior KGB officer had a son Andy's age and the two boys hit it off well. We looked at each other and laughed. I think we were both amused to see how well the next generation was carrying on our work.

I met Valeri Nicolaenko at an AMCOSAD lunch. He was a slightly built, studious-looking young man of thirty-two. Two things about him were interesting. He held the rank of first secretary, an unusually high position for a man his age, and he seemed to keep apart from the other KGB officers. The first time we met we sat at a table with the first secretary of the Israeli Embassy and the counselor of embassy of Egypt. The four of us had a fine time together making a big joke of how we were showing everyone it was possible for Americans and Russians to break bread with their rival client states. I was impressed with Valeri's friendly, easy manner and thought I should follow up this contact.

Our station files contained little information on Nicolaenko. Defector reports had identified him as a bright young KGB officer. He was married, had a young child, and was on his first tour in Latin

America. His father was manager of an automobile factory, and Valeri was a graduate with honors from the University of Moscow. He was, in other words, a typical KGB officer of the type being sent abroad in the 1970s—a polished product of the Soviet ruling class.

Much serious study had been given to trying to decide general criteria for selecting which Soviet officers we should work on. Nicolaenko fit into several important categories. He was young, hence, possibly had a questioning attitude toward the establishment in his country. This was a characteristic of people of his generation all over the world and there was solid evidence that the phenomenon existed in Russia. We knew that Andrei Sakharov was not alone. Nicolaenko's background and the fact he held such a high cover rank indicated he was a young man with a promising future ahead of him in his organization—exactly the kind of person we'd like to latch onto now and stay with as he rose to a top KGB post.

Two theories existed as to the best type of CIA officer to go after young KGB staffers. An American of the same age, attuned to the nuances of the generation that was challenging the current world order, seemed the most likely candidate. At the same time, our psychologists thought that a father figure, sympathetic and understanding, might be just as effective. Valeri was almost twenty years my junior and only seven years older than my older daughter. I seemed qualified for the second role.

I sought him out at the next AMCOSAD lunch and we had a long talk about the need for new attitudes and approaches to relationships between our two countries. He seemed to be quite open for a Russian, not as suspicious and devious as most of his colleagues. Russians are noted for their "clandestine mentality" among CIA officers. They seem to seek a roundabout and covert way of doing things when such an approach isn't necessary. It has been said, with some exaggeration but a great deal of truth, that when a Russian wants to find out a simple piece of information, he thinks of some covert way of getting it. It has been claimed that the Russians have tried to recruit an agent in the U.S. Meteorological Service in order to get weather information, but talking with Nicolaenko was like talking with one of our own younger officers.

We had a number of pleasant lunches. AMCOSAD tried to arrange at least one big trip each year to visit some interesting part of Mexico. In 1972 we went to Yucatan. I spent a lot of time with Valeri as we explored Chichén Itzá and swam off Isla Mujeres. I

426

decided to invite him to a private lunch. I didn't expect to recruit him but I wanted to see how he would react to this rather obvious maneuver. I invited him to lunch at the University Club. The University Club is Mexico City's equivalent of the Union League or Metropolitan Club. The American Chamber of Commerce of Mexico gathers for lunch there once a month to talk about free enterprise. It was a good place for the KGB officer to see the solid face of capitalist society. He readily accepted my invitation.

I tried to make the theme of our three-hour lunch the importance of avoiding stereotypes in our concepts of our two countries. The University Club seemed to me to afford the ideal contrast to what I was saying. It gave me something tangible to make fun of to show I was an iconoclast. I wanted to draw out something similar from him. He agreed, as usual, with my suggestions that both the United States and the Soviet Union would profit by closer cooperation in facing the great universal problems of pollution, food supply, and population explosion. We talked about the troubled younger generation. He enjoyed exchanging ideas about the causes of dissent in the United States and Europe. Then I brought up Sakharov and Russian dissent.

Valeri said, "Although I agree with you about the need to be more flexible in our relationship and that our two countries should sit down together and talk over a lot of foreign policy problems we have, Sakharov's idea that our two societies should modify themselves and each grow to be more like the other is nonsense. He's a disturbed man, mentally disturbed. We have no dissent in the Soviet Union such as you have, because we have firm beliefs. They can't be changed. Ideologically we will always oppose you."

He had drawn the line. He wanted me to understand I could never recruit him. We could have these friendly conversations, probing each other's weaknesses while pretending we were having a highly civilized chat, but he wanted me to know that the KGB and the CIA are locked in a continuing conflict.

I suddenly felt old and tired. I said to myself, this is a young man's business. It's time I examined my illusions. One thing I knew was no illusion. This young man was telling me politely he was my mortal enemy.

Illusions, of course, are an unavoidable part of life, and they change, which can be confusing. The image of the world I had in my mind in the 1950s was as clear-cut as the gray flannel suit, my

427

school uniform at Harvard, which I continued to wear in Washington. When our war babies grew up most of them refused to wear proper clothes or think proper thoughts. For the last decade we have all been living in a mixed-up world. The illusions that the Soviet Union directs a world Communist movement so powerful that any means are justified in combating it and that the United States has the right to shape other societies so that we feel safe have been happily abandoned. I hope the illusions that the Soviet Union is just a nation like all the rest and that its security service is not devoted to destroying us do not replace them for too long.

23
"A Policeman's Lot Is Not a Happy One"

Although I was happy to agree with Lini De Vries's comment that I was no policeman, the cold war cliché about the United States being the policeman of the free world lingers in my mind, and Gilbert and Sullivan's refrain keeps running through my head. When I decided to quit in June, 1973, I was relieved, but not happy. I was disillusioned, but not in any simple way. Some of my disillusion stemmed from my appraisal of my career in CIA and some from my appraisal of American society.

I had spent the best years of my life in pursuits my father and grandfather would have considered the profession of depraved or desperate men. They believed fervently that gentlemen must fight fairly. They would have considered my career without honor and deserving no reward. When I thought of the medal I couldn't mount on my wall, I had to agree. In a larger sense, however, I totally rejected this judgment.

The errors of the ways of a clandestine operator are not difficult to discern. I have pointed out the most grievous ones in the course

429

of my story. We sometimes reported only the intelligence that supported our case for actions we thought should be taken, as we did in Indonesia in 1957 and 1958. We lied to ambassadors who tried to thwart our plans and even maneuvered their reassignment when they persisted in opposing us. Living lies and inventing self-serving excuses for failures, and, worse still, believing them, eroded the character of CIA officers from the lowest to the highest.

Arrogance and career opportunism compounded the evil. As I have said, I suffered from these shortcomings myself when I thought I could remake Philippine politics, and I am convinced these same traits among key officers in the Cuban task force sealed the doom of the Bay of Pigs operation. We all became accustomed to begging questions and could make statements such as William Colby's answer to Oriana Fallaci when she asked him about Chile in the interview which appeared in the March 13, 1976, issue of *The New Republic*.

Colby insisted, "CIA had no part in overthrowing Allende in 1973. Read my denial in the Senate report when I say 'with the exception of six weeks in 1970. . . .'"

"Sure," Oriana Fallaci interrupted, "when Nixon called Richard Helms and ordered him to organize a coup to overthrow Allende who had just won the elections."

"It only lasted six weeks. . . . And we did not succeed. . . . We had no part later."

"Really? Tell me about the financing of the strikes that ruined Allende's government, Mr. Colby. Tell me about the intervention through ITT."

"Well, we gave a little bit of money, yes. A tiny amount that, I remember, was about $10,000. We gave it to other people. I mean we gave it to a group who passed it to another. . . ."

We all were able to convince ourselves, at one time or another, that this kind of statement was entirely frank.

None of these flaws, however, are related to the larger sense in which I believe a CIA career and CIA operations should be considered. Narrow minds, mean spirits, and self-deception are no monopoly of CIA officers. More important, they are not the reason the CIA has so often, especially for the past several years, found itself neck deep in bitter accusations.

I quit, it is true, because I could no longer find satisfaction working in the elephantine bureaucracy which had grown up within the

430

Agency, an entangling alliance of the men who most abundantly possessed these flaws, who feared initiative and feared still more to speak their minds and make known their objections to the legally and morally questionable demands Presidents Kennedy, Johnson, and Nixon made upon us. But the change which had come upon the society CIA sought to serve oppressed me more. This change was the reason CIA's role was so continually called into question.

My story has covered a generation of American life, more than enough time for great changes to occur. No one needs me to say such changes have taken place in unprecedented kind and number. Alvin Toffler wrote a 417-page book to tell us that we suffer from a new nervous disorder he called Future Shock. I have been writing about events which transpired in world politics. They unfolded under the same relentless impetus that has transformed the world.

In 1950 most people did not think the cold war was a figment of Harry Truman's imagination or his desire to show off at Potsdam in 1945, or an American invention, as revisionist historians today would have us believe. The Soviet Union, under the leadership of Josef Stalin, embarked on a systematic strategy of expansion; to build a ring of protective satellite states on its European borders, then to expand Soviet control over the Middle East, beginning with Iran, and to overwhelm the Asian continent, beginning with China. I have explained how I came to be convinced of this during the spring and summer of 1951. The United States was the only power left after World War II to oppose this expansion effectively and permit peoples in the wake of the Soviet advance to have an option, an alternate future. I was proud and happy when I found myself part of the great enterprise of explaining my country's purposes abroad and confounding her enemies. The CIA I joined was a most exciting organization. Although our operations were secret, I was certain most Americans would agree with my appraisal that they were necessary for our nation's safety. Both the Agency and the country changed as the years went by. The majority of Americans in the 1970s were tired of the effort required to be guardians of the free world and when CIA's operations were revealed most people were ashamed.

I was sad to see the changes that came over the Clandestine Services, to see the "skilled administrator" rise to power. Others I know felt the same way. No one put it better than Harry Rositzke,

431

one of the Agency's ablest officers, in the January, 1975, issue of *Foreign Affairs* in an article entitled "American Secret Operations—A Perspective."

"The lethargy and timidity normal to a civil service bureaucracy," Rositzke wrote, "enact a particularly heavy cost in an intelligence service where taking chances based on personal judgment is its main business."*

Actions and attitudes which in themselves are sound are all too often confused. To distort the main business of an intelligence officer—that is, to take chances based on personal judgment—leads to the arrogance and opportunism I have described. A distorted estimate of the implacable determination of a highly dedicated foe, the Soviet KGB, led to the illusion of an enemy who should be fought by any means, however immoral. Distortion of the need for secret diplomacy and secret counterintelligence in the interests of national security led to the near breakdown of American constitutional government. As Mr. Colby put it in his interview with Ms. Fallaci, "Until a year ago, the President could call the head of CIA and say to him, 'Do that and don't tell anybody.'" Distorted disappointment with losing the Vietnam War seems to me to be leading to a loss of national will.

I have recounted how we failed to accomplish anything when the World Assembly of Youth met in Singapore because of stupid bureaucratic wrangling. I could have told many similar tales but they would have been as dull and disappointing to read about as they were to live through. We did many things as foolish as spending taxpayers' money to stop the Tass man from being elected president of the Overseas Press Club in Mexico, when frustration distorted our reasoning because of the failure of our efforts against the KGB. Nothing demonstrates more clearly how our constitutional system became distorted during the cold war than headquarters' reaction to the publication of *The Invisible Government*, by David Wise and Thomas B. Ross, which was the first full-scale exposé of CIA's covert activities. All stations were deluged with dispatches giving instructions how to handle the matter. There were phony book reviews, written by the Propaganda Guidance Section which I had headed during the Bay of Pigs era in 1960 and 1961. I was in

*Harry Rositzke, "American Secret Operations—A Perspective," *Foreign Affairs*, (January, 1975), p. 347.

Argentina when the reviews arrived, but I could recognize the writing as something Henry, my old Covert Action Propaganda Support Branch boss, had inspired.

When *The Invisible Government* appeared in the spring of 1964, the Agency considered the mention of the Special Group the information most vital to protect among all the revelations Wise and Ross made. We were told every effort should be made to counter the book's impact in this regard, either by avoiding the subject or by countering with the line taken in the book reviews Henry's propagandists concocted. This was because revelation of the existence of the Special Group showed that the President of the United States approved all our secret political warfare against countries everywhere in the world. The line the book reviews took to explain such presidential authority contained a view of the President's office which would have forced James Madison to rewrite the *Federalist Papers*. None of the founding fathers would have recognized either the Congress or the President the fake book review described.

"Our democracy is a representative democracy and not a debating society," the review asserted. It went on to explain this paraphrase of Hitler's criticism of the German *Reichstag* with this reasoning.

The electoral process submits political representatives to a process of re-examination only periodically. During the periods of tenure these representatives are presumably free to operate according to their best judgement subject only to possible impeachment or censure within the government for improper actions. Unless they themselves are willing to do so, the representatives are not subject to the constant sounding out of their opinions or viewpoints of [sic] their constituents. By the same token, the President of the United States is subjected to an electoral re-assessment every four years and at that time the people pass the only judgement that a democracy can pass upon his past performance and his promise of the future. *Once he is installed in the presidency, he has in his hand (and should have in his hand) the instruments necessary for the performance of his functions according to his interpretation of those functions and of his oath of office.* [Italics mine.]

433

The Rockefeller Report and the Church and Pike committees' reports have enabled the American people to understand just how far they were taken down the road toward the thoroughly unrepresentative democracy outlined above. In the process of correcting old mistakes, however, we must be careful not to make new ones.

The congressional committees which investigated CIA have asserted splendidly their constitutional role of checking the President. They have reined in the President's secret intelligence and action service, which, as Colby said, took all sorts of illegal and doubtful actions in the President's name and didn't tell anybody. Congress has halted CIA's drift toward Gestapo status, which I'm certain was never intended, but which came too close to reality. In the process, however, Congress nearly destroyed the Agency.

Freedom is as difficult to keep as it is precious to have. In the unsettled, dangerous world of the last half of the twentieth century, a nation without an effective secret intelligence service cannot be certain its freedom will endure.

In our anguish after Vietnam and Watergate, I fear we have lost sight of our national purpose.

I recall one evening about five years ago I was arguing about the Vietnam War with my daughter Ruthven and her husband Phil. "If we surrender in Vietnam, we'll no longer be the leading world power," I cried.

"But, Daddy," Ruthven pleaded, "maybe we don't want to be the leading world power."

I do not want to put too heavy a burden on my daughter's words, but I think she spoke for most young Americans and perhaps a majority of her countrymen and women.

At this point I must mention again and without apology that I believed in the American Century. I have concluded that the American Century lasted only twenty-five years. It began in April, 1950, when Harry Truman signed NSC 68 and the Clandestine Services became a vital part of the resources that document called for to help America protect the free world. It ended in April, 1975, when we withdrew our support and the weak, corrupt, and ineffective client state we had propped up in Saigon since 1954 collapsed almost before we could get out of town.

We may not be living in the American Century but we are living in a disordered, turbulent, and hazardous world. The view of the world now prevailing in the United States is that we should be much less involved everywhere, but this view does not prevail in the Soviet Union. The Soviets and their Cuban allies showed in Angola their determination to intervene wherever they can gain an advantage. The Soviets will continue to try to extend their influence in every vulnerable area in the world. The majority of officers in the Soviet Embassy in Mexico City are still GRU and KGB personnel. The United States may not need cold warriors but it must have a professional intelligence service. The point need not be belabored. If you don't believe me, take a KGB man to lunch.

This professional service should be much smaller than the one in which I served. Its operations must be supervised by some method other than a review by three old men as President Ford proposed when he sent Congress his ideas for reorganizing the intelligence community. One thing I hope a reader of this book has recognized is that covert operators and con men are professionally related. I hope you will, therefore, agree with me that any intelligence service which cannot fool three old men, however distinguished, can't conduct any operations worth the taxpayer's dollar. A more effective supervisory mechanism, responsible to both the President and the Congress, is essential unless we agree with the CIA propaganda shop's 1964 version of presidential authority.

Much of the work of such a service would be to conduct effective liaison with the intelligence services of friendly countries, for which activity one or two officers in an embassy should suffice. Such officers would not suffice, however, for handling secret negotiations with threatened democratic political parties and leaders who must have access to our support when such support has been determined to be vital to United States' interests. Nor could such liaison officers work efficiently enough in trying to penetrate the Kremlin, something we had better do if we are going to survive.

This new service must consist of well-trained and capable people. This alone, however, is not enough to earn the right to be called professional. In spite of the few dunces I have enjoyed talking about in this book, most of the officers of the Clandestine Services were capable and well-trained and some were even brilliant. Our intelligence officers must be more professionally covered, supported, and protected in the future than they were in the past. Before I left CIA, we had come a long way from giving everybody the name of Viola Pitts as a credit reference, but we had not come far enough. Although I have pointed to the treachery of Philip Agee

435

and his friends, they alone do not bear full responsibility for the death of Richard Welch.

I have shown how simple it is to discover who are CIA officers under embassy cover—by reading the State Department Register and picking out the officers designated Foreign Service Reserve, by obtaining an embassy telephone book, or talking to some local embassy employees and asking them who occupy the "special offices" which they cannot fail to spot. I have also shown that enemy intelligence services have had this information for a long time. It is so easy to acquire because of CIA's inadequate cover arrangements that I'm sure the assignment of compiling such data must be given to the greenest Soviet, Chinese, Czech, or other intelligence recruit on his first day in the office.

When I swam with Valeri Nicolaenko and his little girl among the thousands of small bright fish off Isla Mujeres, I thought, she will grow up in the next dozen years and will not tell her father she feels the Soviet Union shouldn't be the leading world power. I just hoped the matter of who dominates the world is then not so obvious that the question will never arise in anyone's mind. A strong, responsible American intelligence service will help ensure the subject is still debatable and may somehow have enough impact that Nicolaenko's daughter can tell off her father as young Americans could do in the 1970s. To my mind, this would be a happier world for the young Russian girl and for all of us.

Index

437

338, 339, 341, 342
Bay of Pigs operation, 12, 15, 86, 105, 319, 324, 326, 327–29, 331–36, 340–48, 416, 430; effect of, on CIA, 327, 346–48, 349, 350, 354; failure of, reasons for, 328–29, 332–33, 345–46, 347
Belfrage, Cedric, 404
"Bender, Frank," 341, 345. *See also* Droller, Gerry
Bentley, Elizabeth, 32, 40, 404, 410
Betancourt, Romulo, 350, 351, 352, 353, 354, 361, 381
Big Con, The (Maurer), 94
Binamira, Ramon, 266–67, 268–69, 271, 272–74, 295–96, 304, 409
Bissell, Richard, 319, 324, 325, 326, 328–29, 346–47, 348, 354, 416
"Bi-Weekly Propaganda Guidances," 333–34, 335
Black propaganda operations, 88–89, 90–98, 104, 146, 169, 234, 383, 398–99, 400
Blackstock, Paul, 327
Bohlen, Charles, 282–84, 285, 298, 310
Bolivia, 385
Boylan, Bob, 141, 142, 149, 153, 154–55, 157, 335
Bridges, Styles, 232
British Guiana, 357
British Information Office, 140
British intelligence services, 140, 145–46, 147–49, 158, 159–60, 161–62, 164–68, 173–74, 175, 178, 180, 182, 193–94, 195, 197, 199–200, 201, 203, 234, 236, 397
Brownell, Herbert, Jr., 281
Budenz, Louis, 32
Buenos Aires, University of, 375, 377, 378–79, 384
Buenos Aires *El Clarín*, 389
Bugging, 129, 245, 294–95
Burke, Patrick, 158, 159–60
Burma, 75, 76, 77–78, 99, 115, 147, 252, 368
Burnham, Forbes, 357
Buwono, Hamengku, 219–20, 244

Caldwell, Bill, 337
Cambodia, 169
Campbell, Mike, 139–40, 150–51, 158, 181, 184–92, 304
Camp Peary, Virginia, 121

Canada, 175, 339
Cañas Abril, Pedro, 344
Cao Dai, 80
Carr, E. H., 42
Case officers, 124, 128, 129, 132–33, 136–38, 313; deep cover, 232–33, 362
Casey, Hugh, 259
Castro, Fidel, 13, 15–16, 86, 105, 323, 324, 325, 328, 331, 332, 333, 337, 338, 339, 342, 343, 345, 346, 347, 352, 363, 367, 372, 385; CIA assassination attempts, 367, 384– 85
Castro, Raul, 338, 340
Castro Sanchez, Eduardo, 390–92
Catherwood, Cummins, 259
Catherwood Foundation, 258–59
Catholics, in Vietnam, 80–81, 179
Central Intelligence Agency (*see also* under CIA), 429–36; administration of, 225–26, 228–29, 241–42, 354, 356, 435; assassination policy, 81, 105, 137, 243–44, 384–85, 400; books on, 327–28, 432–33; cover businesses, 116–20, 251–52, 338; covers, 103, 116, 118–19, 120, 232–33, 256–59, 362, 435–36; covert functions, 66, 67–70, 325; cryptonyms, 395–96; Eisenhower and, 101–2; Kennedys and, 326–27, 349–51; operations training, 115, 116–38; overt functions, 66–67; police training programs, 220–21; political action operations, 210–11, 228–29, 241–42; promotions and job assignments, 64–65, 206, 209, 210–11, 240–41, 354; psychiatric studies, 379–80; station offices, 155–56; structure of, 66–68, 73–74, 115–16, 162–63; task forces, 241, 242; terminology, 123–24; and U.S. citizens, 395–97, 399, 400–11; and U.S. missions abroad, 115–56, 229–30, 284–85; U.S. passports, use of false, 251–52
Chamberlain, William Henry, 38
Chambers, Whittaker, 36
Chen Ping, 181, 182, 184, 188, 189, 190, 191
Chiang Kai-shek, 35, 37, 77, 78, 83, 84, 114, 199, 284
Chile, 229, 337, 350, 380, 381, 385, 416, 422, 430
China, Communist, 35, 36–37, 51, 55,

438

441

443

165–66, 207, 236
Min Yuen, 183
Miró Cardona, José, 345
Moore-McCormack Lines, 377
Mt. Pinatabo (airplane), 249–50, 251
Movimiento Revolucionario del Pueblo (MRP), 343, 345
Muñoz Marín, Luis, 350
Murdock, Kenneth, 40
Murphy, Charles, 327
Mutual Security Agency, 179
Mutuc, Amelito "Mel," 305, 306, 309, 311, 313

Nader, Laura, 409
Nader, Ralph, 406, 409
Nahdat'ul Ulama (NU) party of Indonesia, 214, 215
Nanyang Sin Pao, 169, 180
Nanyang University, Singapore, 199, 200–1
Nasser, Gamal Abdul, 211, 245
Nasution, Abdul Haris, 228
Nation, The, 345
National Agrarian Reform Institute of Cuba, 344, 383
National Executive Committee of the Progressive Citizens of America, 40
National Guardian, 404
Nationalist Party of the Philippines, 250, 254, 279, 290, 291–93, 298–99, 301, 303, 306, 312, 315, 317, 320; and Grand Alliance, 314
National Movement for Free Elections (NAMFREL) of the Philippines, 108, 112, 113, 252–53, 266, 268, 269, 271, 278, 305
National Security Council (NSC), 66, 81, 330, 334, 397–98; 40 Committee, 229; orders overthrow of Castro, 331, 335–36; Special Group, 217, 229, 233, 238, 240, 241, 325, 354, 433; 303 Committee, 229, 355, 356. *See also* under NSC
Natsir, Mohammad, 214
Nazis, 34–35, 126–27
Nechiporenko, Oleg, 418–19
Nehru, Jawaharlal, 113, 175
New Frontier, 327
New Left, 406
New Republic, The, 430
New York *Herald Tribune,* 30
New York State Council of the Arts, Sciences and Professions Committee, 40
New York *Times,* 30, 33, 39–40, 112–13, 345
Ngo Dinh Diem, 101, 105, 178, 179–80, 198–99, 202, 210, 211, 252, 279, 310
Ngo Dinh Nhu, 180, 198–99
Ngo Dinh Nhu, Madame, 180
Nicaragua, 402
Nicolaenko, Valeri, 416, 425–27, 436
Nixon, Patricia, 407, 409
Nixon, Richard M., 15, 87, 312–13, 385, 388, 401, 414, 430, 431; and Bay of Pigs, 325
Noble, Roberto, 389–90, 422
North, Bob, 97
North Asia Command, 104
North Atlantic Treaty Organization Council (NATO), 30
North Korea, 77, 83, 129, 378
North Vietnam, 176, 178, 179, 399
Noticias Gráficas, 376
NSC Directive 303, 355
NSC 68, 66, 68, 434
Nunez Jiminez, Antonio, 344
Nu U, 75, 147

O'Dwyer, William, 28
Office of Strategic Services (OSS), 37, 41, 57, 67, 78, 97, 163, 207, 208, 241, 326, 330
O'Grady, Jack, 401–3, 405, 407, 408
Ongania, Juan Carlos, 364, 365, 373, 374, 376, 380, 390, 392
Operational climate, 132
Operation Brotherhood, 179–80, 252
Operations Coordination Board (OCB), 334
Organization of American States (OAS), 381, 382, 383, 384, 385
Organization Man, The (Whyte), 61
Osmeña, Sergio, 250, 251, 267, 291
Osmeña, Sergio "Serging," Jr., 250, 251, 291, 302–3, 305, 306, 307, 310–12, 314, 316, 317, 356

PACD (presidential assistant for community development) of the Philippines, 253, 267, 268, 271–74, 290–91, 295–96
Padilla, Ambrosio, 291, 300–2, 303, 305, 306, 307, 311, 312, 315, 317
Padilla, Antonio Rubio, 341–42
Pajo, Juan, 293, 294, 314

444

Sampson, Richard, 14
Samuel Adams School of Social Studies, 40, 41
San Juan, Frisco "Johnny," 291, 315, 316
Saratov, Edward, 416, 417, 420–22, 423
Sastroamidjojo, Al, 213, 228
Saypol, Irving, 28–29, 36
Schlesinger, Arthur, 327, 341, 342–43, 344, 349, 350
Scott, Win, 403, 405–6, 421
Seabury, Samuel, 258
SEA Supply Company, 75, 77–78, 102
Sécretaría de Informacion del Estado (SIDE) of Venezuela, 360, 361, 362, 363, 368–77, 378, 379, 381, 383–84, 386, 392; Accion Psicologica, 370–71, 374, 376, 378, 384; Departamento de la Guerra Revolucionaria, 370, 377, 379
Seven Days in May (Knebel), 399
Shackley, Ted, 11, 12, 13, 14
Shapley, Harlow, 39
Simbolon, Maludin, 228, 232, 246
Singapore, 145–47, 148, 152–53, 155, 156–57, 158, 161–72, 180, 193–98, 199–204, 206–8, 222; 1957 elections, 235–36, 237
Six Crises (Nixon), 325
Sjafruddin, Prawironegara, 246
Smith, Andy, 362, 392, 407
Smith, Jeanne, 24, 26, 28, 33, 50, 67, 70, 71, 140, 144, 145, 151, 153–54, 158, 245, 257, 278, 308–9, 310, 329, 362, 392, 395, 407, 418
Smith, Joseph "Big Joe," 241, 356
Smith, Joseph Burkholder: born, 19; named twice, 20; childhood, 20–22; at Harvard, 23–24, 25; in Army training program at Yale, 24–25; teaches at Dickinson, 25–26, 28, 29, 41, 43, 50, 68–69; studies for PhD, 27–28; formulates ideas on cold war, 30–43; seeks intelligence work, 43–44; applies for CIA job, 46–56; hired, 56, 59; processed, 60–65; first briefing, 65–70; on Plans Staff of Far East Division (FE/1 Plans), 67–74; studies Southeast Asia, 74–84; attends psychological warfare seminar, 86–96; first "black operation," 96–98; attends operations training course, 115, 116, 120–38, 148; transferred to FE/4,

115–20; as Singapore OPC chief, 120, 139–80, 193–202; his instructions, 145, 146–49, 152–53; plants Vietnam propaganda, 169–70, 172–80; travels in Malaya, 181–82, 184–92; and Singapore politics, 193–98, 199–202, 206–8, 235–36, 237; returns to U.S., 206; as Malaya desk chief, 207–9; as deputy branch chief of FE/5, 209, 226; reads into Indonesian situation, 209– 21; and Sumatran colonels' revolt, 225–39, 241–48, 251; and forged Sukarno blue film, 239–40, 248; in Philippines, 245, 251, 255–56, 259–323; his cover, 256–58, 259; terminates provincial press project, 268–71; assesses community development project, 271–74; and Recto group, 274–82, 285–87; and 1959 elections, 289–93, 296–321; and Grand Alliance, 313–18; Grand Alliance defeated, 318–20, 328, 344, 354; returns to U.S., 320–21, 323; as chief of Propaganda Guidance Section, 324, 329–30, 333–35; writes propaganda guidances on Cuba, 323–25, 329, 331, 333–36, 337–39, 342–44, 345, 346–48; and Kennedy staff, 323, 325–36; on Bay of Pigs failure, 328–29; briefed on Latin America, 331–33; writes cable on Cuban brigade loss, 346–48; transferred to Western Hemisphere Division, 351–52; assigned to Venezuela, 352–53, 354–57; and British Guiana project, 357–58; loses Venezuela job, 358–60; in Argentina, 360–93; his pseudonym, 359; arranges deep cover, 362; advises SIDE on propaganda, 368–73, 374; learns about coups, 373–77; as University of Buenos Aires contact, 377–79, 384; refused approval of election operations, 380–81; and Venezuelan arms cache, 381–85; gathers intelligence on Argentine politics, 386–93; refused approval for attempt to avert Ongania coup, 390–93; returns to U.S., 393; teaches covert action seminar, 268; teaches Vietnam black operations seminar, 398–400; in Mexico City, 395, 400–28; learns of spying on U.S. citizens, 395–411; and Soviet intelligence officers, 413–25;

447